RUNNING ON EMPTY

A NOVEL LOOK AT EDUCATION

———

RICK STEIN

Create Space
An Amazon Company
North Charleston, SC

Cover design: Michael Zabrocki

Running on Empty

ISBN: 0615637965

ISBN-13: 9780615637969

Library of Congress Control Number: 2012922797

Rick Stein, Fort Myers, FL

This book is dedicated to everyone involved in public education.
It takes the efforts of all to create the right conditions for learning.

ACKNOWLEDGEMENTS

Along the way, there have been so many students and colleagues who helped shape my perspectives and thoughts about schools and what happens in them. The list would be too long to thank everyone. But there are a couple of mentors who made a big difference for me. Thank you Bev Stibaner; I could not have made it through my first year of teaching without your support. Then there's Davis Parker; I owe him a great deal for his professional guidance and friendship throughout my career.

I also want to thank my friends who kept saying "Go for it, do it." All of us need the encouragement of others; it was special to have it while I was writing this book.

I also want to thank Paul, John, Jean, Peter, Fred, Marilyn, and my best friend Fran who read all or a part of my manuscript at various stages. Their suggestions and feedback really helped me on this journey.

However, the biggest thank you goes to my wife Pat. She challenged my ideas, commented often on the characters and kept me grounded. Her patience and guidance made this endeavor possible.

INTRODUCTION

The first drafts of this novel were actually a non-fiction management book. However, I felt that genre did not afford the freedom to fully represent the demanding work asked of educators.

It is my hope you will enjoy Andrea and Bea's characters. It is important for a new teacher to have the support and guidance of an experienced veteran. Bea provides it for Andrea. At the same time, mentors can also be learners. Andrea has a lot to share with Bea as they work together.

Schools are demanding places to run. Building Principal, Dorothy Washington, is an experienced leader. She fights every day for her school and the needs of the children it serves. Too often, the demands placed upon school principals are underestimated or simply misunderstood. Dorothy provides the opportunity to put into the context of the daily life of a school some of the issues a principal must constantly address or prioritize.

District office work, especially the political and practical challenges faced by a school superintendent, is a different breed of cat. The job has high turn-over. District-wide goals frequently end up not accomplished or become so chopped up they are unrecognizable in the end. John Handler is a superintendent who tries to make real changes.

Over the course of one school year these and other important characters will interact. Through their work, and personal lives, the story will unfold. While many things are shared, more is left unsaid than said. That's the nature of most things in life. But let's get started on the journey beginning with Andrea and School #3.

CONTENTS

CONTENTS

CITY SCHOOLS
TABLE OF ORGANIZATION

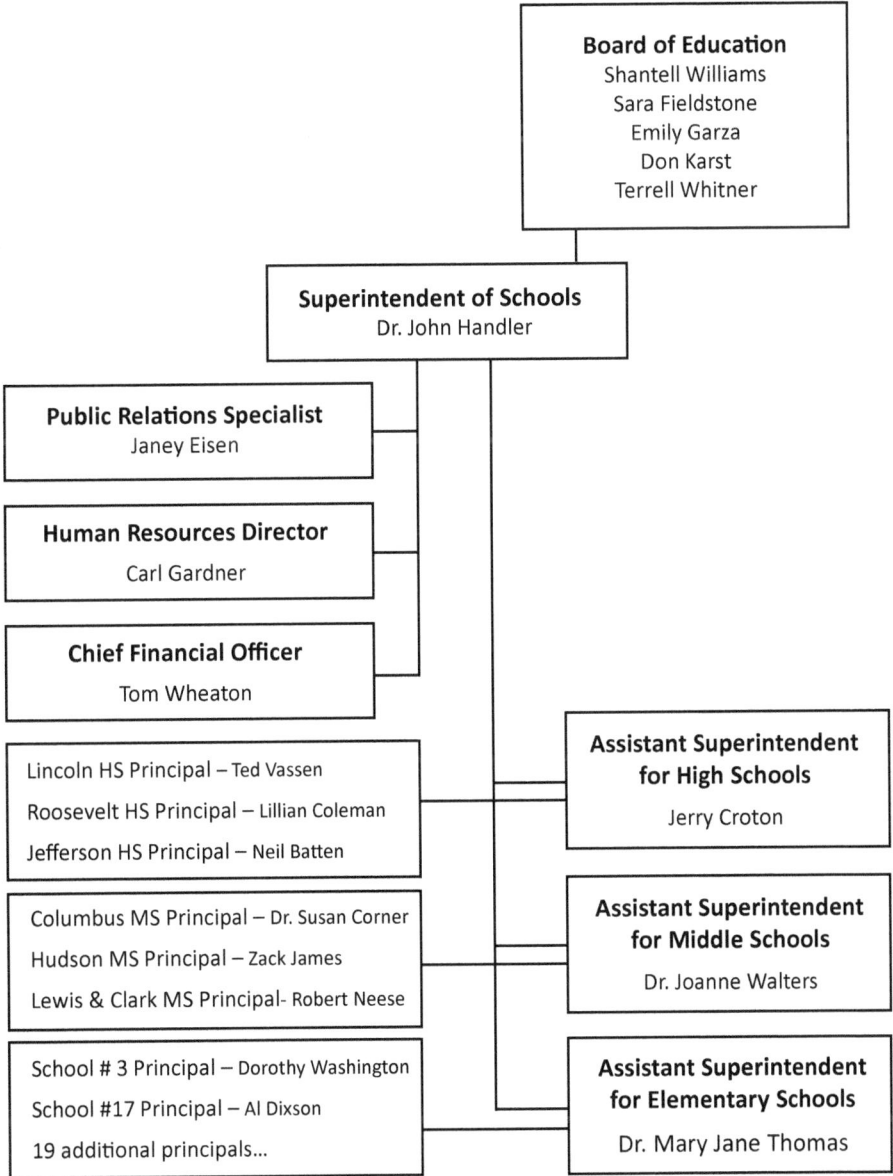

Board of Education
Shantell Williams
Sara Fieldstone
Emily Garza
Don Karst
Terrell Whitner

Superintendent of Schools
Dr. John Handler

Public Relations Specialist
Janey Eisen

Human Resources Director
Carl Gardner

Chief Financial Officer
Tom Wheaton

Lincoln HS Principal – Ted Vassen
Roosevelt HS Principal – Lillian Coleman
Jefferson HS Principal – Neil Batten

Assistant Superintendent for High Schools
Jerry Croton

Columbus MS Principal – Dr. Susan Corner
Hudson MS Principal – Zack James
Lewis & Clark MS Principal- Robert Neese

Assistant Superintendent for Middle Schools
Dr. Joanne Walters

School # 3 Principal – Dorothy Washington
School #17 Principal – Al Dixson
19 additional principals...

Assistant Superintendent for Elementary Schools
Dr. Mary Jane Thomas

FIRST SEMESTER

"Right Now"

Try, will our table turn?
Lay your hands there light, and yearn
Till the yearning slips
Thro' the finger-tips
In a fire which a few discern,
And a very few feel burn,
And the rest, they may live and learn!

Robert Browning

CHAPTER 1

SCHOOL 3

She was thinking about the street where she grew up with the neatly trimmed lawns and 'Leave it to Beaver' homes as she cautiously drove down the road leading to School #3. Andrea noticed most lawns here were really weed beds and the shrubs along the foundations were often overgrown or dead. Many of the old homes had front porches cluttered with an assortment of items including broken furniture, old newspapers and garbage cans brimming with junk. Now and then there was a home neatly kept, like a tiny island in a river of neglect.

The trees lining the street were old and shaded the area like table umbrellas on this warm mid-August day. A breeze had picked up, gently swaying the trees while old papers and plastic bags went tumbling along the curb and out into the street. Andrea did her best to dodge what she could as she approached her new school. A funny way to think about it since the school was truly 'new' in 1912 when it opened.

Andrea drove her cobalt blue Honda Civic into the parking lot. With the help of her dad, she traded in "Buddy," her weary Volkswagen Jetta, on her first new car. Buddy had been her loyal traveling companion, seeing her through not only her later college years but also the last two years of work as a bank teller. While she was excited to have the new car, a sign of progress connected to her first teaching job, she missed Buddy and wondered if he'd be better suited to travel the city streets she was about to frequent.

A rusty chain-linked fence surrounded the lot on three sides. The lot had many patched areas and no lines marking where to park. Andrea found a spot near the fence figuring it was as good a place as any to leave her shiny new ride.

She moved briskly across the parking lot to the front door of School #3. As a high school and college cross country runner she could move comfortably at a fast pace which seemed natural and not hurried. She'd noticed the teenage boys sitting on a porch across the street laughing and drinking Red Bull. In this foreign land she could feel their staring eyes following her. But at that moment Andrea was focused on the school's front door and the anticipation growing with each step.

The two front doors of the school were old and weather beaten. The wood needed paint and the base of each door was blackened by time. Both doors had small windows lined with wire mesh making it almost impossible to see anything inside. As she grabbed the heavy brass handle and pulled, she expected the door to open, but it held like the bank vault door where she had worked. She noticed two or three other cars in the lot and was told the school would be open, so this surprise added new tension.

Stepping back she was unsure what to do. A boy from across the street yelled, "Ring the fuckin' bell!" She smiled at him but she didn't see a door bell button alongside either door.

The boy was now strolling towards her, while those still sitting on the porch yelled, "Open her door James." She trembled and felt the hair on the back of her neck rise as he boldly stepped into her space. She didn't know what was going to happen, but James simply pushed the button which was mounted on the top of the rusted wrought iron railing.

A crackling voice rose from a speaker mounted above the doors sounding like one at a McDonald's drive through. She heard a reassuring, "May I help you?" She yelled in a voice unexpectedly shrill, "I'm Andrea Bauer, the new fourth grade teacher." She wanted to add, "Now open the damn door," as James loomed over her. She heard the voice again, "When you hear the buzzer pull the door open, but be sure it latches behind you when you come in." At that moment, James smiled, and began his saunter back across the street. Her introduction to the neighborhood had begun.

Stepping across the threshold, Andrea entered the school with relief and expectation. She heard the door close behind her but she still gave it a strong tug to be sure it was latched. This fortress in a hostile land was unlike the rambling one story elementary school she attended. That school was named after John F. Kennedy.

The corridor floor of School #3 was covered with dark green and black tile. Its walls were painted a lighter green with a narrow yellow stripe serving as a chair-rail. Overall, the paint and floor combination gave the hall a dark and dingy appearance. She immediately noticed a strong smell which was a mixture of paste, crayons, musty basement and floor wax. It was a smell she'd come to actually enjoy each time she entered the school. The halls were filled with desks. It was obvious summer cleaning was going on in earnest, although nobody was in her line of sight.

She saw the black and white sign above a nearby door stating, 'Main Office.' When she walked in she faced a tall counter. In fact it was so high she wondered how the person sitting behind it would notice a child who came in on an errand.

The office had an air of organized chaos. The teacher mailboxes were filled with papers and the counter was stacked with incoming school supplies. Behind all of this sat Janet McGee. She was a middle-aged woman wearing a pair of tight jeans on her overweight body. Janet's outfit included an unflattering bright orange blouse. But, what Andrea noticed most was Janet's smile and warm greeting. It was reassuring and welcoming at the same time.

Andrea judged Janet to be only a few years younger than her mom, a suburban high school teacher, who reminded her a school secretary could be a great help or a huge pain in the ass. Andrea sensed she was lucky. Janet stood up saying, "I bet before we do any of the show and tell stuff, you'd like to visit your classroom."

Andrea laughingly said, "How did you know?"

Janet smiled warmly, handing her the key to Room 204, "It's up the stairs which are down the hall to your left. Once upstairs your room is the first one on the right. It's a warm summer day and the room is going to be hot so you may want to open the windows. Be sure to close them when you leave or your first introduction to Fred may be unpleasant."

Andrea wanted to run out of the office and race up the stairs. Instead, she kept her composure assuring Janet she'd close the windows and be back for some orientation. "Take your time," Janet said as she knew it was a special moment for a first year teacher. Through her 19 years as a school secretary she had met many 'newbies' as she called them. She quickly sensed Andrea's energy and looked forward to showing her the ropes.

Andrea went down the hall at a fast pace not noticing Fred standing nearby smiling and enjoying the energy and enthusiasm of the new recruit. She hit the stairs at nearly a run as her excitement overcame any last effort at decorum. The stairs creaked with every step she took. It's hard to imagine how many feet had trod those steps over the years. The wear marks sculpted into every tread were clear reminders even the toughest oak had its limits.

Reaching the upstairs hallway, she noticed the old tile was buffed to a shine and no desks were lining the walls. The custodial crew was obviously working its way down from the second floor. Their work to prepare for the coming school year was largely finished here. She turned the key in the door with the old brass number 204 on it. She didn't know exactly what to expect, but the fulfillment of her life-long dream to be a teacher began on the other side. Swinging the door open she was smacked by the heat. While it had been a pleasant 80 degrees with a nice breeze outside, her room was stifling. Nonetheless, she stood in the doorway with tears of joy streaming down her cheeks.

The room had a wood floor with desks already neatly lined up in rows. The desks, with chrome legs and composite yellow tops, looked out of place in a room with oak trim and slate blackboards. Those blackboards were at both ends of the classroom. The one stretching across the front was composed of two large pieces of black slate. One piece had a jagged crack working its way from the top right side down to a mid-way point. It reminded Andrea of the eastern border of Massachusetts. The wooden chalk trays were clean, but showed their years of wear.

Before looking any further, Andrea scooted across the room to open some windows. She noticed they were composed of massive, wood-framed sashes. Two brass handles, turned mostly black through time, were attached to the bottom of each sash. She tried to lift the window; it wouldn't budge. Assuming it was stuck, she moved on to the next and again struggled to open the window. Then she met Fred hearing "Good morning" in a voice both smooth and deep. She jumped, startled by the unexpected greeting. "I am sorry Miss ah…"

"Bauer" she replied, "Andrea Bauer."

"Hi, I am Fred. Most of the kids call me Mr. Fred. I'm the school's custodian."

"Nice to meet you," Andrea replied.

"I knew you'd have trouble with the windows. Two years ago Ma'am told me to screw shut every second floor window facing the street because kids were throwing stuff out onto the sidewalk down there. Ya know somebody could get hurt."

"You mean there's no way to open a window in this room," Andrea asked in a voice as pleading as any Fred had heard over the summer.

"Let me show ya how it works. See the long pole with the hook on the end over there?" Andrea spied the pole in the far corner. It looked like a boat hook actually and she wondered what it could be.

"Yes," she replied.

"I'll show you how to use it." Fred moved to the first window Andrea tried to open. In one easy motion Fred placed the hook end of the pole in a brass hole in the middle of the top sash and pulled. The window moved down smoothly and cooler air entered the room. "You can do the next one." Fred really wondered if she could. This new teacher probably was no taller than 5'4" with a slight frame.

Andrea sensed Fred was looking at her and she was a bit uncomfortable stretching to open the next window. She realized it took a little practice to get the hook soundly in the hole to move the sash down. She pulled hard and the sash came crashing down on its stops. Fred laughed, "You'll get the hang of it Miss Bauer. It is Miss isn't it?"

"Yup," Andrea said still looking at the window.

"The tougher job is closin' 'em. If you need help let me know before you leave. Every window in this room has to be closed or we'll both answer to Ma'am," Fred announced as he strolled towards the door.

"Who is Ma'am?" Andrea called out.

Fred turned and said, "She's the boss."

Andrea knew he meant Dorothy Washington, the long time principal of School #3. Taking a deep breath, Andrea started to inspect her classroom. She counted the desks, reaching thirty before stopping.

She noticed the built-in wood coat racks along the wall common with the hallway. It was apparent the racks hadn't been attended to in any real way for years. The label, 'Functional', came to mind as Andrea looked at them. She noticed a small bulletin-board next to the room's door and two larger bulletin boards at the ends of the front and back blackboards. The walls were painted a light grey, not offensive but certainly drab. A white faced clock hung over her door with a small American flag mounted next to it. On the wall above the front blackboard she saw an old projection screen nearly retracted in its metal case with a dangling string she'd have trouble reaching. Her desk was green metal, with drawers on one side and a center drawer with most of the paint worn off from use. It was locked and she did not have the key, something to ask Janet about she thought.

Being computer savvy, Andrea looked for any sign of an internet connection but she did not see one. She hoped the building would at least have Wi-Fi points. She noticed only two plugs in the room. One was at the front; the other at the back. Seeing this, she doubted computers would be available in the classroom. She had hoped to use her ample 'PowerPoint' and internet skills when presenting her lessons to the class. Andrea noticed the old books on the shelves running along the window wall. They were social studies textbooks. She opened a shopworn one, noticing its copyright date was 1989. Andrea conceded the room and its contents were as old and tired as some of the junk cars she'd passed on the street coming to this school. Coupled with the lack of school supplies in the room, she was worried. This was far different from the classrooms she'd attended or been assigned to for student teaching. Andrea took a deep breath and trusted she and the children would make it comfortable and welcoming in no time.

Andrea sat at her shopworn desk. After lingering a bit she got up and using the window pole pushed the windows closed. 'Great,' she thought, I can do this without any help. It was her first victory.

Andrea returned to the office to see Janet for her starting orientation. After visiting her room she had several questions. In the office two women were busy chatting with Janet. When Andrea entered the conversation halted. She felt like the newcomer interrupting those in the know. Janet smiled and introduced Andrea to Peggy Linn, a first grade teacher who appeared to be in her mid-thirties and Sue Jones, who looked to be about 50. Andrea learned Sue was the building's physical education teacher, something she never would have guessed as Sue was clearly overweight and, from the smell on her clothing, a smoker.

Sue spoke first after the intros were made, "What will you be teaching?"

Andrea said, "Fourth grade. I am so lucky; it's the grade I really wanted to teach."

Sue smiled and said, "Lucky you, you get all the state tests."

"Don't worry too much about it now," said Peggy, "It's a terrific grade to teach. Lots of good content and the kids really get into it." Before anymore could be said, the ladies were out the office door, continuing their animated conversation.

"I hope I didn't interrupt anything."

"No," Janet said, "We were just catching up on all the summer news. Actually, it is time I did something productive. They think I have time for nothing but conversation."

"Would it help if I came back later?"

"You are one of the reasons I'm here, dear. Let me fill you in and answer your questions."

Andrea asked, "Do you have a class list?"

"Sure, but I have to tell you it was made in June and now it's August 12th. It will have changed some." Andrea looked puzzled. Janet caught the look and said, "The kids move from place to place a lot. They may be with mom, a grandparent or a guardian. These things change all the time. Downtown they call it our 'Mobility Factor' and we have a big one." Andrea thought Janet would go to her computer to print out the latest list. Instead she opened a file drawer and pulled out a listing with "Teacher to be determined" written at the top. "I'll make you a copy of this. Right now you have twenty-eight kids, eleven girls and seventeen boys." Knowing the kids and looking at the list, Janet could see the staff did Andrea few favors. In fact, lots of kids who had serious needs were on her class list. The old guard had put together a challenging group for *Teacher TBD*.

Andrea took the list, excited to have the names of the children who would be the first students she would teach. "This will help me get my room ready, thanks."

Janet told her, "I'll put any changes to the list in your mailbox." Walking over to the mailbox area she pointed out Andrea's slot. "I'll put your name on it as soon as Ma'am gives me the green-light."

"Does everybody call Mrs. Washington Ma'am?"

"Most everyone does. It's easy for the kids and Ma'am thinks it helps them with their manners."

"When will I be able to meet her?"

"She's downtown at staff meetings all week. She won't be back here until next Monday, unless those folks think they can take more of her time away from here." It was clear Janet felt the downtown district office staff was more of a burden than a help.

Janet told her the school housed more than four hundred children from kindergarten through fifth grade. The oldest staff member was Ma'am who was sixty-two and had been the principal for twenty-seven years.

Janet asked, "Did you get your letter from downtown for your new hire orientation?"

Andrea nodded.

"You will be meeting Kelly Slocum, one of the downtown 'Fashion mavens'. Don't wear jeans when you go to the orientation next week. Choose a tasteful outfit with thoughtful jewelry. Also be sure to use make-up carefully and have your nails done."

Andrea thought this was a bit over the top, but Janet explained Kelly Slocum, who ran the district's elementary training office, made conscious decisions out of the gate about the potential of new staff members based solely on how they were dressed. She said Kelly was renowned for her own dress. Many thought she never wore the same outfit twice and she spent more time clothes shopping than working. Andrea would learn over time Janet was right about all of her suggestions, but one thing more she'd learn on her own, Kelly knew her stuff.

Janet told her only three men were in the building. Fred, the custodian, was thirty-eight, married with three children. Tom Dowling was the only male classroom teacher. He'd taught fifth grade at the school for twenty-four years. Janet said the kids really liked him and he was a terrific story teller. "Watch out for him! He plays jokes on the staff, especially you newbies." The third man in the building was Dave Clifton, the music teacher. Janet did not say much about him. Andrea noticed when Janet had little to say about a staff member it was likely she didn't care for them much.

One of her two fourth grade team members was Bea Johnson, the only person of color on the school's teaching staff. Bea had been teaching at the school for nineteen years. Janet told Andrea Bea had a decisive way of doing things, and she was one of the few staff members who lived inside the school's boundaries. She often told the staff what was happening on the streets and many children, even those not in the fourth grade, confided in her. "Be careful when you meet her though," Janet said. "She's got a powerful hug!"

The other teammate was Pam Kilborn. Janet didn't have much to say about her, other than she had been teaching in the building for five years. Andrea asked, "Who was the third member of the fourth grade team last year? Did she transfer?" She silently wondered, 'Why was this position open when jobs were so hard to come by?' Janet's eyes welled up and she caught her breath. Andrea learned the third member of the team for most of last year was Riley Thompson. Janet told her Riley died at the age of 49 after a brief but intense struggle with cancer. It was evident the grief from her death was strong and Andrea didn't press Janet for more details.

As Andrea left the building for the day her head was filled. Not only had Janet shared the routines, she also chatted about the staff and the school in general. School #3 served an impoverished neighborhood where virtually every youngster had a government supported free breakfast and lunch. Andrea was surprised to learn about the breakfast program as this was not something she had experienced at her school growing up, nor at the suburban school where she completed her student teaching. In the months ahead she would learn a lot more about the effects of poverty on children and families.

Andrea's self-reflection on the first visit to School #3 ended at her car. There stood James, the teenage boy who helped her at the door about three hours ago. "Miss Bauer," he said.

Andrea wondered how he knew her name; then remembered she'd shouted it into the speaker to get in the school. She turned to face this tall boy with his plaid boxers well revealed for the world to see. He stood right in her personal space. Looking up she smiled and let this be the opening for whatever came next.

"Miss Bauer you be teachin' fourth grade, right?"

Andrea was nodding yes, and before she could say anything more James jumped on this affirmation. "You gonna have my brother, Michael. Miss Bauer, watch out for him. He's smart and I don't want anything bad for him." James grinned as he swaggered back across the street. All this was being observed by the other boys on the porch, who were laughing and arm punched him as he landed on the ragged lawn chair positioned at the top of the steps. Much surely happened this morning, but none of it dampened her enthusiasm for the profession she had chosen.

CHAPTER 2

DOROTHY & DOWNTOWN

Dorothy Washington, a well respected school administrator, was the second most senior elementary principal among a group of twenty-one. The newest was starting her first year on the job. Dorothy knew how to advocate for her school, but downtown staffers thought she often ignored directives. On the first of a multi-day session of administrative meetings, she came to the district office early to meet with Carl Gardner, the human resource director.

Dorothy felt Carl was one exception to the downtown bureaucrats. She and Carl were usually on the same page. However, today she was fuming and felt he had not considered her school's needs. Getting out of her silver Lexus, she strode across the parking lot with a head of steam strong enough to move a freight train. She had on a purple dress accenting her dour mood. She yanked open the front door of the downtown office building ready to do battle with those on the third floor.

The central administrative office was built in the mid-sixties and critics of the structure said it added nothing notable to the architecture of the center city. It was located near city hall which was either an advantage or curse depending on whatever the current relationship was with the mayor. At this point, most of the downtown district office staff wished they were further away from city hall as Mayor Jane Hueset was an unrelenting critic of the school system. She felt the district wasted money and was top heavy with overpaid administrative staff. She used the lack of student success on state tests as raw meat she would throw to a hungry press when venting about the high cost of the broken public education system in her city.

The front entryway at the district office opened into a drab institutional foyer with a security guard stationed at a counter blocking any further entrance to the inner building. The guard had to press a button releasing the lock on a glass door which allowed visitors to enter the inner building and the elevator nearby. The door and glass wall structure were added after 9/11. Its aluminum and glass construction did not reach the foyer ceiling. While it was functional, it only emphasized the unwelcoming nature of the entrance.

Normally you were asked to sign in, show your badge if you were an employee, or a form of ID if you were not, before being allowed to enter. Today Dorothy never broke stride as she passed the checkpoint. "Not today George," she said. At 73 years of age, George knew enough not to stop her.

He grinned instead and said, "Have a nice day," as he pushed the door release button.

Dorothy yelled back over her shoulder, "We'll see!" A few moments later she was pacing by the elevator repeatedly striking the "Up" button.

The third floor, called the "Tower" by those in the field, was the power floor where the superintendent's office was located. Dr. John Handler was starting his second year at the helm, but Dorothy wasn't planning to speak with him yet about her concern. She was headed for Carl's office. The staff supporting both the HR and Superintendent's needs covered most of the open floor space looking like a rabbit warren of cubicles. Also on the floor were offices for each of the five school board members, the Board Clerk and Board President's secretary, as well as the Public Communications office. Two large conference rooms and several smaller ones used for various meetings were also on this floor.

Striding off the elevator, Dorothy moved with an air of distain to the HR receptionist's desk. She announced she was there to meet with Carl. "Hello Mrs. Washington," said Emily, the office's pleasant 26 year old receptionist. They didn't call her Ma'am downtown, although they all knew it was common practice within her school. Previous superintendent's made it clear they were not going to yield any power or special status to her when she entered the building. Staff had been firmly reminded she was always to be called Mrs. Washington. Dorothy knew this and was inwardly pleased each time she thought of it, knowing this type of political game was an acknowledgement of her real influence in a particularly downtrodden part of the city. But this morning she growled, "I hope he's ready and doesn't make me wait!"

Carl was an experienced player. He'd previously served as the district's contract negotiator and now led the process as a part of his overall responsibilities. He worked in the district for seventeen years, putting his law degree from Syracuse to good use. He'd served six different superintendents and knew how to survive regardless of who was at the top.

Carl was not looking forward to this meeting with Dorothy as he knew she was furious about his recent placement of Andrea Bauer at her school. Dorothy wanted an experienced teacher to replace Riley Thompson. He now waited with trepidation holding the blistering email from Dorothy letting him know she was more than unhappy with his placement decision. But before he could see her he had to deal with the PR office head, Janey Eisen, who was pacing at the door.

"Carl, I need a statement from you right now!"

He knew this had to be about the bus drivers' union as their contract with the district had expired last June. A new agreement was stalled. But it wasn't over money issues; driver safety was the stumbling point. The union wanted an aide on each bus to help them with student control. They had a point given the rising number of discipline incidents on school buses; however, no funds were accessible to cover such a large increase in the transportation staff.

"The drivers called a press conference. They claim our buses are unsafe and the district is turning a deaf ear to the problem. You were at the Board meeting last night and you know they are blaming you!"

Carl knew, as the administrator responsible for negotiations, he was an easy target, especially since the union's current strategy was to drive a wedge between the district's bargaining team and the Board.

"Janey, you'll have to say our buses are safe and we are working to develop additional procedures and steps to keep them that way."

"Carl, they'll ask me what those are."

"Say it's a negotiations matter and we are not bargaining through the press. I don't know what else to say at this point."

"It won't be enough. I got a call from Jane Hodges this morning. She told me the PTA executive committee has called a special meeting to discuss it."

Carl didn't like to pass things off, but knowing the gravity of this and the public comments made at last night's Board meeting by numerous drivers, he was sure Dr. Handler would want to be involved in any public statement. "I think you should tell Dr. Handler about the PTA call and develop a draft statement for him to review."

Janey saw Dorothy Washington scowling and knew Carl had a tough day ahead. What she had from him was the best she was going to get. "Thanks Carl, can we talk later about this? I may need your help on the negotiations rules and what we can say to the public."

"Sure" Carl said, "But it will have to be late afternoon as I'm booked solid today." Nonetheless, Janey had to prepare a draft statement and get to the superintendent before he went to the administrators' meeting.

Dorothy stepped into Carl's well appointed office. It had a wood conference table where six could sit comfortably. On the wall his Juris Doctor degree and the fancy court certificate admitting him to the bar were displayed proudly. Pictures of his wife and three daughters were nicely arranged on a credenza sitting under a window looking out on the parking lot. Carl lived in a well to do suburb. His girls attended what many felt was the best public school system in the county.

His desk was a busy one with numerous folders piled less than neatly on it. It was hectic two weeks before school started. He really couldn't afford the time to meet with Dorothy; however, he knew putting her off would only send her to the superintendent to air her concerns. If she did, it would only take up more of his time in the end.

As she was escorted into Carl's office, Dorothy declined an offered cup of coffee. Carl asked for a cup knowing it would be brought to him by his secretary. It would provide a helpful interruption for him to gather his thoughts as he knew when Dorothy was upset like this things could become difficult.

Once they were seated Dorothy fired her opening salvo. "How could you assign another rookie to my school? You know how tough it was to lose Riley. She was an anchor, one of my best teachers. You guys here think you know better than those of us working in the real-world with the children!" Carl listened knowing Dorothy wasn't finished. "Carl, I asked you to transfer Joe Donalty to my school. He was an excellent staff member when he taught at #3 four years ago, I wanted him back. I also have only one male classroom teacher. #19 School has four."

Carl felt this was an opening. He'd approached Joe who said he absolutely did not want to work at #3 again, despite his respect for Ma'am. Carl pleaded with him to go, but Joe stood his ground. School #19, where he currently taught, had a much lower poverty rate, and the school was one of three new ones built in the city over the last eight years. Joe said he felt less pressure on test scores and the work environment was not as intense. Despite Carl's repeated efforts, Joe made it clear he was not interested in a transfer.

Carl did not share with Dorothy the number of times he'd spoken to Joe. What he said he hoped would bring closure to this issue, "Dorothy, the union contract recognizes seniority status in transfers. Joe's seniority gives him the right to decline an involuntary transfer." However, this simply opened the door for an additional realm of comment.

"Damn it Carl, how could you have agreed to such useless contract language!? We need to be able to assign teachers where they are needed most!" He reminded Dorothy this concession was a trade-off for the union's agreement to make a 3% contribution to their health insurance premium cost.

"All right, so we can't transfer him. Why did you give me another rookie?"

Carl knew city hall had been putting great pressure on the district to cut costs. One of the budget controlling efforts the district office staff made was to strictly limit hiring experienced (expensive) candidates for teaching positions. They did this by giving him a salary budget per hire of $38,000. Since the starting salary of a new teacher was $34,500 he had an inadequate budget to pay for experience or advanced degrees.

At the elementary school level the district had over six hundred applicants for seventeen teaching positions. As a result, he felt little pressure to pay for experience; any budget funds available were being saved to lure experienced math and science teachers at the secondary level. "Dorothy, you know how tight the new hire salary budget is and how many qualified applicants we have for elementary teaching positions." His answer only made Dorothy more upset. Carl could see it in her face as her eyes were turning to steel as she glared at him. Her stare was renowned around the district and nobody wanted to be victimized by it; even Carl felt its sting.

"You mean my school doesn't deserve an experienced teacher, but the high school does!"

"Look Dorothy, I assigned a great candidate to your school. Andrea Bauer is one of the few elementary teachers we hired who has a Master's Degree. The reading degree should be a big asset. I think she is a winner if you give her a chance."

"I don't have any choice do I?" Dorothy responded, "You know I'll break my back giving her a chance, but you did me no favors. I'm not forgetting it any time soon, Carl!"

Carl thought this was unfair and his anger welled. Not only was Andrea Bauer an excellent candidate, he had been very supportive of Dorothy. He'd arranged substitutes for many of the School #3 staff to attend Riley's funeral. He'd personally gone to the building several times to be sure grief counselors were on hand for the staff and children.

Dorothy sensed she'd gone a bridge too far with Carl. Even so, she debated whether or not she'd carry this further by asking to see Dr. Handler.

Carl said, "I hope this disagreement stays here since you know all I have done for your school." He really hoped Dorothy would cease her venting as her clout could not be under-estimated.

Before Carl could say anything more, Dorothy was on her feet. "I have to get to today's important meeting you folks have scheduled for all of us principals just before school starts when we have nothing else to do!" Dorothy turned on her heels and left. She really didn't know what she was going to do at this point, but it was evident Carl was not going to change his mind on the hiring and placement of Andrea Bauer at her school.

Carl took a deep breath and started back to his desk from the conference table where they had been sitting. His secretary, Elaine came in and handed him his coffee.

"I'm sorry this took longer than expected; the pot was empty when I got there." She added, hoping to reset the tense atmosphere, "But it really looks like you need something stronger. Why don't you take a minute before you start the candidate meetings." Carl had eleven half-hour salary and benefit meetings with new employees. They were scheduled back-to-back, as he worked long hours to fill as many teaching vacancies as he could before the school year started.

"Thanks," he said. "Give me ten minutes and then let's go to work."

CHAPTER 3

THE MEETING

John was tired, it had been a long Board meeting the night before. He, along with everyone present, endured countless comments from bus drivers who were upset by the lack of progress in contract negotiations. They claimed district buses were unsafe and the human resource director, Carl Gardner, and many principals turned a deaf ear to their concerns. They demanded Dr. Handler get personally involved. The media had a boatload of comments and reactions to share with the public as a result of the fireworks at the meeting.

John thought the concerns were overstated and he was angry the union was making such a public issue over it. Of course the mayor said the superintendent needed to listen to the drivers' concerns, and along with the Board of Education, take steps to curb the rising violence in the school system. He was determined to call the mayor and give her a piece of his mind. He was sick of her making news cycles at the district's expense. But he had important tasks to complete before he'd make the call.

He was looking out his office window onto the busy street below. He thought about his conversation with Board President, Shantell Williams and the need for her help in keeping Board members out of the media after a night where they had gone on and on about the driver negotiations. They believed many of the concerns were valid. One Board member, Sara Fieldstone, really let loose during the executive (private) session. She demanded Carl Gardner be fired before school started.

Her outbursts led to a serious exchange regarding the superintendent's role and the Board's related to hiring and firing any staff. It had been a tough night all around.

As he looked away from the window he saw Janey Eisen, standing at his door with a draft statement about bus safety. He knew she was going to ask him to go on camera as well given the pounding they had taken at last night's Board meeting. The union press conference this morning would only make matters worse. "Good morning Janey," John said in as pleasant a voice as he could muster. "Do you have something for me to read?"

"Dr. Handler you know I do."

John took a minute to review the statement. It included what she and Carl had previously discussed. "I'd like you to add the district has a daily responsibility to assure students are safe when traveling on its buses. The administration will not ignore any incident taking place. Over the next six months we will be installing cameras and a GPS system on every school bus to document what happens."

"I didn't know we were going to do that!" Janey exclaimed.

It was a decision he'd made and quietly shared with the Board in a confidential memo. To their credit, they'd kept a lid on it even through last night's meeting. John told the Board members he wanted to wait until the appropriate time to bring it out in the open. After last night's session he'd decided now was the time.

"Does Carl know?" Janey asked. While they had discussed how and when they might put it out in the open, John had not had any time to alert Carl he was going to do it through a press release today. John felt it would catch the union off guard and force them to answer questions from the media regarding it.

"Yes he does, but would you let him know the plan is to release it now? He'll understand the strategy."

Both John and Carl had a suspicion the union wouldn't like the GPS and camera system as the whereabouts of every bus could be tracked in real-time and the cameras would record not only student behaviors, but the driver's actions as well. Knowing they could not hire an aide for every bus, the cameras and GPS were a good alternative.

Janey asked if he'd go on camera. John ultimately decided not to. He'd let the statement speak for itself and see how the union leadership responded. He was playing a game of poker and raising the stakes.

Once Janey left, John's focus turned to the administrative meeting about to take place. He'd spent a great deal of time over the past several months thinking about how he could move the district forward. It would not be an easy task. He was the third superintendent in four years; the first of the trio having served for three years, his successor, an interim superintendent, served for one year. 'Would this group follow his lead?' It was tough to be sure. They had grown callused and found ways to survive on their own. Each school had become an independent fiefdom.

The statistics for change were compelling. The drop-out rate at the three high schools ranged from a high of sixty-two percent at Jefferson to a low of forty-eight percent at Lincoln. Roosevelt was sitting at fifty-six percent. The rates had risen noticeably since the onset of the "No Child Left Behind" legislation. Middle school and elementary level state test results were no better. Failing schools were his challenge from stem to stern.

The data revealed poverty rates throughout the city's schools were staggering. Many elementary schools had more than ninety-five percent of their students receiving free and reduced lunch based on the incomes of their households. The effects of long-term poverty had taken a toll, especially on the children.

While those statistics were well known, and often referenced by the staff and press as reasons for failure, John was going to pay special attention to some different data this morning. He'd learned 78% of the teaching staff did not live in the city. Those who did live in the city were often young staff members without children. They generally lived on the trendy north side, far from the impoverished neighborhoods marking general city life.

The stats were no better at the district office level. John was divorced and his former wife and daughter lived nearly 600 miles away outside of St. Louis in a beautiful suburb. Since becoming superintendent, he had taken residence in a condo building inside the city limits, but he too was safely ensconced in secure setting. The only other district office administrator living in the city was Joanne Walters, the Assistant Superintendent for Middle Level Education. She had no children attending a city school.

The data for principals and assistant principals indicated only one in six lived inside the city limits. The civil service workforce of aides, food service workers, secretaries, bus drivers and cleaners ran counter to this, with three out of four living inside the city's boundaries. Many also had children attending the schools John now led.

This lack of connection to the neighborhoods was troubling. John felt the inability of the leadership team and teaching staff to be connected to the life and pulse of the city seriously affected their perspectives and undercut any consistent ability to recognize the deeper needs of the students they served. It also sent a resounding message to city residents that educators at all levels did not want their children attending the schools where they worked.

Today he would announce to the leadership team his intent to ask the Board to adopt a new hiring policy. The policy would require eighty percent of all new hires in the teaching and administrative ranks must already be, or become within one year, city residents. Carl Gardner told him he could expect strong push back from the teaching and administrative unions over this. He predicted there'd be legal and contract claims forthcoming almost immediately. John accepted this knowing the months ahead would be demanding ones over this issue. But the need for more connection to city life could no longer be ignored.

However, it was only the opening step in a larger plan for change. Many city schools had been neglected and most required major repairs. Some, knowing their age and condition, should be demolished. John learned the hard way how common it was for electrical and heating systems to fail. He'd closed seven schools last year for several days at a time to make emergency repairs. Asbestos abatement surfaced whenever repairs were needed. John was going to ask a study team of architects to develop an overall "Assessment of Building Conditions" to present to the Board. He could hear the mayor's reaction now, "No new taxes, we're broke!"

John respected the Gates Foundation findings stating successful schools incorporated a new 3 R's. Those were *Rigor, Relevance* and *Relationship*. Two of those 3 R's had been largely ignored in the city district. That needed to change! The relevance of what was taught needed to be linked more directly to a student's life and, most importantly, relationships with students had to be developed on more than a formal classroom level. John believed if you were 'known' you could then be taught. Too many students were not known on a more personal level by those working in the system.

From his perspective he also had another significant leadership challenge. Board members were used to having their way and often overstepped their roles. It was their habit to delve deeply into day-to-day operational decisions rather than staying above the fray at a policy level. This was understandable given the high turnover in the superintendent's position and the system's over dependence on the Board for leadership and information. But it had to stop. Too many spoons were in the broth. The result was confusion and a serious lack of trust decisions would hold.

He was going to have to take risks if he was going to get out front and be the CEO. He felt he'd paid his dues going slow the first year. He'd set limits when they were needed and built relationships with key players. Now it was time to see whether or not he could move forward with a clear agenda for change.

In preparation for moving ahead, he discussed the agenda he was about to present to the administrators in a previous two-day summer retreat with his Board. He had, after lengthy conversation, secured their unanimous support for this change agenda.

The room was filled with nearly all of the administrative team: twenty-seven principals: three high school, three middle school and twenty-one at the elementary level. Also present were the twenty-one assistant principals serving at the middle school or high school level. This was coupled with eighteen district office administrators in attendance. Everyone except Carl Gardner was there. He had a jam packed agenda, leading John to excuse Carl from the meeting. Counting himself, sixty-seven full-time administrators filled the downstairs meeting room. It was a formidable group of experienced players who were ready for a meet and greet session with the superintendent and Board president before moving on to a mundane but necessary agenda of school opening tasks.

As he was getting ready to enter the room John thought about one part of a recent discussion with Board President Shantell Williams. She planned to welcome the group as had been her practice over the past several years. He strongly discouraged this, as he wanted to reinforce his belief the team worked for him and he in turn worked for and was accountable solely to the Board. This had not gone over especially well, but she acquiesced. This was a small but necessary step to reestablish the superintendent as the educational leader of the district; something his employment contract stated, largely forgotten by the Board members.

"Well," he said to himself as he crossed the hall into the room, "Here we go!" As John entered he talked with several people, most of whom he'd come to respect. He could address each person by name, something the previous two superintendents made little effort to do.

He noticed Dorothy Washington was mingling with a group of elementary principals and Mary Jane Thomas, the Assistant Superintendent for Elementary Instruction. They were having an animated conversation about a local sports figure in the headlines for a DWI arrest.

John walked up and greeted the group, then looking at Dorothy said, "Good morning Ma'am." It had been many years since anyone called her Ma'am in this building. Dorothy was so taken back by this greeting she lightly choked on the coffee she was sipping and could only cough a good morning greeting back. Several nearby raised their eyebrows as the superintendent changed a long standing behavior with his greeting.

John moved on to talk with others in the room including Lincoln High School's principal, Ted Vassen. Ted was a traditionalist and a veteran of the district having served for sixteen years as Lincoln's principal. Ted was also the administrative union president. John knew he and Ted would have lots more to talk about in the months ahead. Ted told him he was pissed at the drivers. John did not want to get dragged into the conversation again. It was one he'd had enough of the night before. As a result, he headed for the front of the room.

John's PowerPoint slides were ready. A boring projection of the district's logo was on the large built-in screen at the front of the room. It was the first slide in a seemingly endless supply of such presentations. Nobody sensed anything different was about to happen. Standing in the front of the room, he removed his sport coat and rolled up the sleeves of his white shirt. He'd chosen white so any sweat marks would less noticeable.

As the team settled, he felt a pang of doubt. 'Was he really sure he wanted to go down the road represented on the slides?' He could still say the usual things and be on his way. Another year of hard work and assorted crisis would come and go and little else would change. It had worked for nearly 100 years …nobody really expected anything substantially different to take place. But it wasn't in him to let things slide another year. Time was too important an asset to waste.

He reminded himself he had a scheduled meeting with the Teachers' Association President, Cliff Greer at 1:00. While it was clear they saw many things differently, they both worked hard to not surprise the other. Their lines of communication were open and candid.

John planned to meet with Cliff and share with him his goals for the coming year. He anticipated Cliff's support would be a mixed bag. Some items he'd likely agree with even if he didn't openly support them. Others he knew they'd have equally strong differences of opinion and the opposition could become loud and very public.

John planned to ask Cliff to keep their conversation confidential until opening day. They both knew candid lines of communication required a basic level of respect and trust on both their parts. After the opening day announcements, Cliff would be free to comment or not in whatever fashion the union chose.

Back to the present moment, John pinned a wireless mike onto his yellow and blue striped tie. He took a deep breath knowing the status quo wouldn't serve this generation of students or the ones to follow. The world was very different and it was time schools changed to address today's realities. He pushed the clicker and two words in bold letters appeared on his first slide: **RIGHT NOW!** Everyone sensed this was not going to be a business as usual morning with the superintendent.

CHAPTER 4

COLLEAGUES

Andrea had been to her classroom every weekday in late August, with the exception of the two day new hire orientation. She was looking forward to the start of school. Her room was slowly transforming from something drab and institutional into a purposeful learning area. Each child's name had been neatly printed off her personal laptop and ink jet printer and placed on the top left corner of the desks. The printer she'd left on her desk and the laptop she transported back and forth from home. She did not fully trust her locked classroom door.

While working to get her room ready, Andrea met a number of the teachers who were busy doing the same thing. She really liked Colleen Sheehan, a third grade teacher, who dropped by with a mug of coffee in hand. Colleen looked at her class list and desk arrangement. She knew most of the children having taught some of them the year before, or through listening to her colleagues in the faculty room.

Colleen told Andrea not to sit Laticia Stevens and Awilda Rivera near each other. Their older sisters fought over a boy, leaving bad blood between them. The girls often mimicked the trash talk of their older sisters and things could easily erupt into a fight. Andrea wondered why the girls were placed in the same room. But she would learn in the weeks ahead, the neighborhood's always changing dynamics played out in every room. A well worn path leading to violence and conflict was easily found on the streets and they often had to contend with its results at School #3.

On what Andrea thought was a more typical level, Colleen told her Daryl Owens and Jackson Wayne lived next to each other and they were like brothers.

"They should not sit next to each other Andrea or they'll never stop talking and horsing around. We thought about separating them, but there's been so much tragedy in their families we felt keeping them together was the best thing to do."

"You better tell me what happened," Andrea said.

"It's not one thing; it's really a lot of bad things. Let's sit down and I'll tell you," Colleen said as she pulled out a chair from behind a student desk near the front of the room. There they were, two teachers on a mid-August day sitting on hard chairs in a fourth grade classroom decorated purposefully with a vocabulary word wall, pictures of colonial America which they'd soon study and colorful math symbols in what would be a math learning center in the corner of Andrea's room. They were about to discuss two childhoods far removed from either of their life experiences.

Colleen explained Daryl's mom was a cocaine addicted prostitute. She was currently in jail, arrested for assaulting an undercover police officer. Nobody knew who Daryl's dad was. He had two older brothers, one of whom was in jail and the other had disappeared into the streets. He was being raised by his maternal grandmother who was only 43 years old; she did her best to keep him clothed and attending school.

Andrea learned Jackson's dad was shot by a drug dealer. He was left to die on the street with multiple gunshot wounds for doing nothing but being in the wrong place and mistaken for a rival gang member. His mom was now struggling to hold on, working a late night shift at Wal-Mart. Jackson and his younger sister were left, on their own, to get up and dressed for school each day. It was the best their mom could do for them under the circumstances.

"Oh my God," Andrea was crying as Colleen told her the stories of other children who would be walking into her classroom in just over a week. The impact of poverty, drugs and violence had taken a devastating toll. Andrea wondered if what she heard was even descriptive of America. The life stories and experiences Colleen shared seemed more like something from a third-world nation. Yet, it was all taking place less than 17 miles from where she grew up. How different life's circumstances were over such a short distance.

After giving her a big hug, Colleen handed Andrea a Kleenex from the box sitting on her desk. Andrea brought in the box after she learned the school supplies did not include it as an item.

"I know how difficult it is to hear this. Many of us have a similar reaction. We do the best we can for these kids. Many of them don't even make it from kindergarten through fifth grade here. They move from school to school because their families can't pay the rent or a new boyfriend enters the picture. You'll get used to it."

Andrea doubted she'd ever get used to it. 'How could life be so heartless to the innocent?'

She and Colleen agreed they'd meet in the faculty room for lunch in a few hours. Both had numerous things they wanted to accomplish in their classrooms.

Andrea knew Ma'am was in this week and she wanted to meet her. She decided to walk down to the main office and see if Ma'am had a moment to talk. As Andrea left her room, huffing up the stairs with a shopping bag full of stuff came Bea Johnson. Andrea had not met her yet either.

"Oh aren't you just a sweet little thing," Bea said as she set down her bag. Her arms were open and Andrea remembered Janet's warning about the power of Bea's hugs. Those big arms wrapped around her with reassuring warmth. Andrea knew in an instant this woman was special. "You follow me honey, I want to know all about you!" Bea picked up her bag and opened the door to her classroom across the hall. "I hear you are all full of excitement. They tell me downstairs you've been working on your room every day for the last two weeks. Child, you are gonna put us all to shame if you work like that!"

Andrea knew she was kidding as a lot of the staff had been working hard on their rooms, preparing for another school year. Nobody got paid for this time or many of the supplies they brought in. It was the fate of elementary classroom teachers no matter where they worked.

Andrea shared she had just finished a conversation with Colleen about the background on several of the children in her classroom. Bea's face wrinkled as she folded her arms in front of her. She took a deep breath and said, "These children have boatloads of pain, but the river of love we have for 'em keeps their boats movin'. You a part of the river now and you'll do just fine once the children learn how much you care. Come on, you tell me about yourself, Bea needs to know about you! A girl as pretty as you, you got a boyfriend out there?"

"Yes," Andrea smiled as she said his name, "Jason. He is an insurance salesman. We went to college together, but he graduated two years before me."

"So this is a serious thing; you live with that man?"

'Wow! How she cuts to the chase,' Andrea thought. 'I've got to get in front of this before she has my whole life story in five minutes.' "Yes I do. Now tell me something about yourself."

Bea smiled. She liked how Andrea had turned the conversation; she had some backbone. Maybe she could survive here with some help.

"Well I'm forty-six years old, been a teacher for half those years. My husband left me, said I was too smart for my own good! Ha, I think it was too hard for him to have me makin' more money than he did at the garage. The good 'ole boys there made fun and it became more than he could handle."

"Please tell me about Riley, Bea."

"What do you want to know Andrea?"

"Anything you'd feel comfortable sharing is fine with me?"

"Well, girl, she was a terrific friend and great teacher. She had the gift ya know."

"Gift?" asked Andrea.

"She could teach with her eyes closed. I mean she knew what kids needed and she was so good with the tough ones. She could see right through 'em and knew how to reach 'em. Riley also listened to everyone; she made you feel like you was the only person in the room. She was loved by everyone, especially Ma'am. When she died, Ma'am was grievin'; it was one of the few times anyone saw her cry at school."

"I can't fill those shoes!" Andrea nearly shouted. A sense of overwhelming concern was flowing over her.

"Of course you can't! You walk in your own shoes. If Riley were here she'd be the first to tell you that. She's also cheering for you from heaven. Believe me girl."

"I haven't met Ma'am yet. What is she like?"

"Oh praise be, where do I start? The woman has been the heart and soul of this school for so long nobody can remember when she wasn't. She'll be in your corner; she backs teachers and doesn't let anybody push 'em around. But, she expects a lot of us. She says her kids need the best and she wants to make sure they get it. She'll like you girl, but she's not an easy one to know, so give it time."

Bea was one of the few in the school who knew Ma'am wanted Joe Donalty to replace Riley. Knowing it didn't happen was a blow and Andrea might have a challenging time proving to Ma'am she was the right one to take Riley's place. She wasn't going to share what she knew with Andrea as she suspected it would be too much for a new person to bear and anyway she had to respect Ma'am's confidence.

Andrea said she was headed to the office to introduce herself to Ma'am when she met Bea.

"Come on Andrea, I'll go with you and we'll say hi together." Which Andrea appreciated, as she was a bit afraid to meet Ma'am given what she'd already learned about her.

Bea walked into the main office ahead of Andrea and Janet called out to her. Hearing Bea's voice in the outer office Ma'am yelled, "Get in here Bea I have a bone to pick with you!" Her voice seemed to rattle the walls and it scared Andrea.

Bea knew otherwise and said, "I'm comin' but I'm bringin' a friend with me." Bea gave Andrea a wave and she cautiously followed her into Ma'am's office.

Ma'am was sitting at a big, time-worn wooden desk. Her chair was a high backed black leather one and Ma'am filled nearly every inch of it. Peering over the top of her half-moon glasses she said, "Who you got there?"

"This is Andrea Bauer! " Bea exclaimed.

Ma'am rose from her chair, reached across the desk and simply stated, "Welcome to School #3 Miss Bauer."

'Oh my,' Bea said to herself, 'This one is going to be tougher than I thought.'

"Pleased to meet you Mrs. Washington," Andrea wasn't sure it was right to call her Ma'am at this first meeting.

Dorothy sat back down and ignoring Andrea said, "When you have time Bea come back and see me."

Janet had been standing near the door and knew Ma'am was surprisingly cool to the new recruit. It wasn't her style and she wondered what was up. But she put on smile and said to them in a voice Ma'am was sure to hear, "She's got a pile of work after getting back from the downtown meetings and our principal is a bit grumpy."

Hearing this, Ma'am got up from behind her desk and stepped into the outer office. "What do you mean grumpy!" She yelled in a thunderous voice. "You haven't seen grumpy, but be careful or you will!" But in a much more pleasant voice she said, "Miss Bauer I hear you've been working hard in your classroom. Mind if I stop up later to take a peek?"

Bea smiled, 'Ah better,' she thought, 'There's hope.'

Andrea beamed and couldn't help herself, "Yes Ma'am."

Janet looked at Andrea giving her a wink.

Andrea was feeling good as she headed back to her classroom. Bea lingered in the office wanting a few moments with Ma'am. She stepped back into the inner office closing the door behind her. Bea spoke first. "What was that about? I'm glad Janet reminded you your manners needed some fixin'. The girl's a sweet one; she's gonna need all our help if she's makin' it here. Shame on you, you grumpy old woman!"

"I know" said Ma'am, "I'll make it up to her when I visit her room."

"You better, I like this one. I'm thinkin' Riley picked her even if you didn't."

"Okay, okay!"

"I wanted to tell you about the downtown meeting."

"Oh no," said Bea, "Another waste of time eh?"

"No, it was not."

Bea sat down, as Ma'am never said positive things about a downtown meeting. "What went on?"

"Where do I start? This guy has an agenda Bea. It's going to be a different year. He shared with us his vision statement for the district."

Bea raised an eyebrow at this.

"No it's one sentence. He said he wanted a statement which captured everyone's work, one understood on Main Street and in an aisle at Wal-Mart."

"Well what is this wonder statement? You've got me on the edge of my seat!"

Ma'am knew Bea was having a good time with this. But she was excited. "His vision is, 'Each day we will create the right conditions for learning.' He means it and he says it starts 'Right Now'. He's asked me to serve on an elementary instruction committee. We've been charged with rethinking elementary instruction. He told me I can pick two of the people who will serve on it."

"What else did he tell you all to do?"

"Bea, he told us to be creative, we need to seek new solutions to our problems. He's also forming similar committees at the middle and high school levels."

"You believe him?"

"Bea, for some reason I do. I think this man's serious about changing things. It's going to be different this time I am sure."

"How do you know that?"

"Well let me tell you some other things he said. 80% of all new hires from now on have to live in the city."

"You aren't serious are you?" Bea felt the staff didn't know enough about what happened on the streets. She was alarmed by the cultural knowledge gaps, even amongst the best teachers and administrators, "Wow, the man's got my attention now!"

"Oh there's a lot more, but let's start with you serving on the elementary instruction committee."

"Really, you know I'd love that. I've got some different notions about elementary teachin'." Bea left a short time later, knowing the coming school year might be a different one from what she expected.

CHAPTER 5

GETTING READY

Andrea had all the teacher's editions in hand. She was disappointed to see the reading series was an old one. She had been trained in the latest reading instructional strategies, which were greatly assisted by a ready supply of children's literature of varying difficulty. Andrea knew 'leveled books' were not found under the roof of School #3. She also visited the school's library hoping to find a rich assortment of books and materials she could use to supplement her classroom texts. This was especially important with the outdated science and social studies textbooks for her class.

Andrea was surprised by the dated materials in her own classroom, but she was appalled by the state of the school's library. The books and materials on hand were worn out. Like her classroom, the resources available were often old and of little use as supplements for the texts she had in her room. Since her room did not have internet access or computer resources she knew she was at a huge disadvantage as compared to her suburban counterparts.

Andrea wondered how this could be, 'How could a city school system with such impoverished children have so little to offer?' She assumed there would be a plethora of resources available. What she discovered was something far different. It was heartbreaking.

As the months went by, Andrea would learn a lot of money went towards the special education staffing and the related support services for high need students. The ravaging effects of poverty strained everything within the system and they could not address all the learning demands coming from every school. It formed a vicious cycle which further disadvantaged the most needy children.

Andrea knew she needed to develop her own materials and resources. The effort would not be supplemented by any district budget; the cost would be out of her pocket. She talked to her mom about this. Brainstorming the problem, they decided to ask the student service club at her mom's suburban high school if they would be willing to do a book drive for Andrea's classroom. The high school students could collect money and books to provide materials from a prioritized literature list Andrea would prepare. Her mom thought the service club at the school would sink their teeth into the effort. Andrea was encouraged, hoping her mom was right.

On top of all of this, Andrea was coming face-to-face with another reality. The first day of school was one week away and she had to decide what to do on the first day of class. She had no experience related to this, and she was growing more anxious.

The school day was six and a half hours long. She had to plan for more than five hours time with the children. This was excluding her lunch break and a time when her class was at music, art or gym. It was looming as a much more daunting task than she could have imagined. It wasn't just the first day, but every day she had to have good plans in place. 'How did people do it?'

She asked Bea and Colleen for suggestions on what to do. They both shared their plans with her. Andrea borrowed liberally from both of them, yet she knew she had to find her own voice in the classroom as well. It would have to begin on the first day of instruction.

Andrea found herself working day and night on her plans. Her relationship with Jason was suffering because he felt she was not attentive. He thought things between them would go on largely as usual. He'd quickly learned the preparation to teach a class of children each day was demanding. Andrea was stressed and tired. He felt she was spending way too many hours on work already and school hadn't even begun.

Labor Day weekend flew by and Tuesday morning Andrea was awake bright and early. It was the first official day of school, although today was a faculty only day. Andrea was excited to meet the rest of her colleagues and attend her first faculty meeting. She also was anxious to talk with Bea and others again about what they planned to do on the first day of school. 'How should you get started with a group of children?' Many friends who were teachers told her to be tough out of the gate and only loosen up after the kids had gotten into routines. 'Did that make sense?' she wondered.

The job was more challenging than she'd expected. But she was still excited and couldn't wait to get to school. What a big bag of emotions she was holding. Every time she opened it a different feeling popped out. One moment she was confident and excited, the next she felt truly overwhelmed. 'Would it always be like this?'

Riding a rollercoaster of emotions all the way to work, Andrea pulled into the parking lot. She noticed many of staff members were already there. Nearly leaping out of her car, Andrea hustled along the sidewalk to the school's front door. Today the door was open and she could walk right in. Fred would lock it once the staff assembled for their meeting with Ma'am in the school's cafeteria.

Inside, Andrea noticed teachers already walking to the cafeteria and realized she had not met a number of them. She got polite smiles and nods from folks; it was clear they assumed she must be the new staff member replacing Riley. However, they did not introduce themselves.

After dropping some things off in her classroom Andrea saw Colleen in the hallway. She grabbed Andrea's arm and said, "Hi Andrea, follow me." She was relieved since she didn't know how a faculty meeting worked. Colleen must have sensed this saying, "Nothing to worry about. These things always go the same way. Ma'am will introduce you at some point and she'll remind us about fire drills and all the administrative stuff we need to keep track of. You can sit next to me. There are no assigned seats for this."

Andrea and Colleen walked into the cafeteria with its old wood floor which creaked and moaned, as if it were resigning itself to another year of abuse. A lot of the staff members were chatting; in fact the room had echoes of laughter and heart-felt hellos bouncing off its walls. Like all school cafeterias, when lots of people talked, the room became noisy. School #3's was no exception.

Andrea followed Colleen to the coffee pot getting a cup of coffee and Danish. She learned Ma'am supplied these for the first meeting.

Then different grade level teams took turns providing snacks and buying a can of coffee for the monthly faculty meetings. Andrea also learned after today's opening meeting the union contract allowed only one regular faculty meeting per month and it could not last more than 45 minutes. It also had to start within 10 minutes after the last bus left the loop.

Once everyone was seated Ma'am welcomed them and then introduced Andrea as the school's newest teacher. She told them Andrea had a Masters Degree in reading. "If you want to find out about the latest reading strategies you can ask her about them," Ma'am stated with a smile.

Bea then stood up saying, "She is a nice girl with a boyfriend named Jason. He is a lucky boy. Her room looks great too; this girl is ready!" Andrea blushed, but the staff got the message. It was time to move on and give the new teacher a chance to make her way out from under Riley's shadow.

Ma'am then got down to business. "Dr. Handler has developed a new vision statement I really like. Every principal has been asked to share it today." The playful groans were audible. Ma'am asked, "How many of you can quote the old one?" Nobody volunteered. "To be truthful I am not even sure we had a vision statement. So, I guess it's time we had one we might all remember; it's one sentence and you'll be seeing it in lots of places. The statement is *Each day we will create the right conditions for learning.*'

The staff was quiet, Ma'am paused to let the silence linger. "Think about it, what employee doesn't play a part in making that vision a reality?" I know we all strive to do it here at School #3, now we have a simple way to share it with everyone. I also bet you will remember it since there'll be a test on it at the next faculty meeting." Everyone laughed, but they had to agree it was a vision statement which made sense and challenged everyone to work hard. However, Andrea had her first bit of quiet cynicism. She wondered how someone could declare this as a vision, and yet have so many aspects of the program out of date. Maybe that's why it was just a vision. She hoped it wasn't a pipe-dream.

The next thing shared got a whole different reaction. "The superintendent has asked us to drop the school number as our name. He feels it is too impersonal and institutional a reference. We have to give him three suggested names for our school in rank order by December 1 of this year. He said the school could not be named after anyone who is still living; so you can't name it after me!" This drew a lot of laughter. "He also said the process must involve the community and students in some fashion."

This was an unexpected request which had resounding support. Ma'am used it as a moment to reinforce the new vision statement, "This is an example of what he feels is an effort 'Right Now' to provide the right conditions for learning. If you are interested in serving on the Name Selection Committee let me know. I want three teacher reps and I will be asking three community members and three paraprofessional staff to serve as well. I'd also like one student from each fourth and fifth grade to serve as non-voting members. We will meet after school every Tuesday."

Sue Jones, wearing her union hat, raised her hand. Ma'am knew what was coming. "Is this a paid committee?" Sue asked.

"No it's not; it's strictly a voluntary effort." Sue was the school's union rep and Ma'am knew this question and her answer would be reported back to union president Cliff Greer.

"There are two other committees I want to announce. The first one, which I will be serving on, is the Elementary Program Committee. We will be reporting our recommendations to the superintendent and Board of Education in early February. I have asked Bea Johnson to serve on this committee as well." Some murmurs from the staff were heard over this as they all knew Bea and Ma'am were tight. "I also can nominate one other member. If anybody is interested let me know by the end of next week.

The last is a District-wide committee chaired by the superintendent." This raised some eyebrows as the superintendent had never in anyone's memory chaired a specific committee. "The committee will develop a 'Quality School Summary.' This will backstop our new vision statement. The superintendent believes the definition for quality is centered solely on our results on state tests. While our efforts for student success on those tests won't diminish, he wants the descriptors of quality to encompass much more than that."

The looks on staff members faces formed a picture she wished she could capture. It had been a long time since such an ambitious agenda had been put forward. It was clear they simply did not know what to make of it.

Ma'am gave Sue a sideways shot saying, "By the way Sue, the other two committees are extra comp ones. Dr. Handler has asked three of the principals to appoint two members each to the Elementary Program Committee and the union to select six reps."

Ma'am then dropped the bombshell. The principals had a video they were asked to play for the staff. In the video Dr. Handler shared with the staff the statistics on staff residency in the city. He expressed his serious concern about the gap in cultural knowledge that resulted. He noted the new 3 R's he was endorsing as the backbone for instructional change.

As a result of the stats he announced his plan to ask the Board to change its hiring policy, noting eighty percent of all new hires must reside in the city within one year of being hired. He made it clear all current employees, even those just hired, would not be affected by this policy.

The staff's reaction was mixed. Sue Jones said loud enough for all to hear, "We'll see what our union has to say about this!" Ma'am let it pass, hoping her colleagues in other buildings, if they got a similar response, would do the same. It was a controversial decision and in other forums it would be debated. A faculty meeting though should not be one of them.

Ma'am unfolded a new banner. "This will fly throughout the year whenever the American flag is at the top of our pole out front." On the flag were the two words 'RIGHT NOW' in white capital letters on a navy background. Ma'am explained this was a reminder every moment was important and changes needed to happen *Right Now*. "The banner will fly on every flag pole in front of every district building." The staff was quiet at this point and Ma'am sensed it was a place for a break saying, "Let's take a stretch and start again in 10 minutes and then we'll start on our regular agenda."

As soon as she said this Sue Jones was on her feet headed for the door with her cell phone in hand. Ma'am had no doubt in her mind who she was calling.

CHAPTER 6

OFF TO THE RACES

ndrea knew she was as ready as she could be for school to start. Standing in the doorway, planning to greet her students, she felt a surge of anticipation unlike anything she had experienced before. The first footsteps were hitting the stair treads and soon her career would really begin. 'Who would be the first student to step into her teaching life?' Around the corner came Daryl Owens and Jackson Wayne racing to the doorway. Their back packs, provided by the United Way at several city locations, were bouncing from side-to-side on their backs. This morning Andrea didn't have the heart to tell them not to run.

Bea seeing this said, "Daryl and Jackson, you boys know you're not supposed to run. You take a minute and slow yourselves down before goin' any further."

Bea, looking at Andrea, mouthed, "Routines."

Andrea greeted every student as they came to her door. She reached out to them shaking hands or accepting hugs. Wherever the first moment led was fine with her. She told each student to find their name card inside the pockets on the front bulletin board and match it with the name card pocket taped to their desk. It was a morning routine helping her to take attendance quickly.

There were the usual rituals students of all ages in classrooms across America experienced. The Pledge of Allegiance was said, and Andrea established a routine for using the bathroom down the hall.

After these traditional routines were addressed, Andrea did something different. She was using her laptop connected to a basic video projector her folks gave her as a birthday present. Andrea had scanned in pictures of her students using the school picture pasted in their record folder. She left a digital camera with Janet and asked her to take a picture of any new student when they registered.

Doing her morning walk, Ma'am noticed Andrea had a student picture projected and Laticia Stevens proudly proclaimed, "Me and Grams went to Wal-Mart. She got me new shoes." Laticia loved her new bright pink sneakers. The children giggled as Laticia swayed up a row of desks showing them off like a fashion model on a runway.

As Laticia spoke Andrea caught her words, typing them next to Laticia's picture. As she did this, the children saw it projected. The stories the children told were captured one at a time.

The final picture was Andrea's. It was her fourth grade picture. It revealed a little girl with pigtails held in place by yellow bows. The students laughed when they saw it. It was a moment though where laughter was binding the children to their new teacher.

Ma'am stayed to listen to the children's stories. She knew Andrea had created not only a powerful relationship building moment, but a wonderful language experience using each child's own words and memories. Ma'am left the room, reflecting on her visit to Carl Gardner's office. Bea had said this new teacher may be a special one and Ma'am was beginning to wonder if she could be right.

It would be Andrea's routine to begin each day with a 20 minute session where children could share their experiences. She would capture them on her laptop and the kids would see their comments on the screen. The narratives would become part of a classroom journal.

The first morning flew by and before she knew it the children were off to lunch and Andrea headed to the faculty room. The room had old wooden tables and chairs. The coffee pot seemed to be always half full and the smell of burned coffee filled the air. Behind the coffee pot was a timeworn pegboard wall, painted lime green. Hanging from hooks on the peg wall were staff members' coffee cups. They composed an assortment fit for a white elephant sale. The room had one window, with drapes in place since the late 90's. The only concession to a more updated appeal was the plain green and blue tight-weaved carpet covering the floor. Despite this, the old wood floor underneath still creaked as staff members moved about the room.

Andrea headed to the frig next to the coffee pot. She opened the door and saw it was filled with bags and an assortment of beverages fit for a grocery store aisle. It took Andrea a minute to find her yogurt and juice.

The half dozen staff members in the room were all enjoying their break from a very busy morning. They were already sharing their experiences with the children.

Pam Kilborn, one of her fourth grade colleagues, was in the room. She was sitting with Amy Fontaine a fifth grade teacher whose class went to lunch ahead of the fourth grades.

"How did it go this morning?" Pam asked before Andrea was even sitting.

"It was a great morning!"

"Spoken like a first year teacher," Amy piped in.

Amy turned back to Pam, finishing their conversation before heading back to pick up her kids. "You were right, this group is gonna be a real tough one. That Dwayne! How did you do it? I'm tired already!"

"Good luck, I paid my dues with him last year, it's your turn now."

Andrea was surprised by this conversation. She was anxious to share her morning experiences, and witness the excitement of others. Instead, she was learning two of her colleagues clearly didn't have her enthusiasm.

Andrea wondered why Bea hadn't come into the room, asking Pam where she was.

"Oh Bea eats with her kids the first week; she thinks it helps get them settled. She's got more courage than I do! Let the aides take care of them. I need a break."

Andrea wanted to get up and go back to the cafeteria, but she was committed and wished Bea told her about the routine.

The afternoon, like the morning, flew by. The children had phys ed on Monday, Wednesday and Friday. Since this was Wednesday, her kids had a 30 minute PE class, giving her a chance to do some chores and stop by the main office to check her mailbox.

Entering the office, Janet saw her and smiled. "Ma'am told me she stopped by your class this morning. I can tell when she's impressed. She liked your warm-up with the kids."

Andrea felt good hearing this. She was standing at her mailbox and noticed a hand written note card inside. She opened it. It read, "Nice job this morning Andrea." It was signed by Ma'am. Andrea knew she would always treasure the note.

Bea stopped in for a minute after school, "How'd ya do?"

Beaming, Andrea shared some of her experiences. Bea reminded her the novelty of the first day at school would quickly pass and she needed to keep the children busy with something before the morning bell rang or they'd find their own distractions.

"What about breakfast?" Andrea asked.

"They'll pick it up in the cafeteria starting tomorrow and then eat in the room. You have to be sure the kids have something else to do."

"What do you do?"

"I have a riddle of the day. Here, let me give you mine for the next week if you want to use 'em."

Andrea welcomed this, thanking Bea for the suggestion and help.

Andrea also liked to use music and she decided tomorrow she'd have a piece by Holtz playing as the kids entered the room. She also knew Bea's morning riddle would fit right into the routine.

It was nearly 5:00 before Andrea headed for the parking lot. She prepared some worksheets for the math corner. She also re-read the morning stories and thought about what she'd share with her students tomorrow.

Andrea loaded her brief case with the teacher's edition for reading and some writing papers to correct. She would start some small group work in language arts and she knew the planning for this needed some adjustment after meeting the children. It would be a long night of 'homework.'

CHAPTER 7

THE STREET

The phone rang by their warm bed a little after 5:30 AM. Jason was the first to respond, although they were both startled by the ring as they didn't get up until 6:00. They had been in a last stretch of dreamy comfortable sleep with their bodies spooned together.

Straining to find his voice Jason answered hoarsely, "Hello."

"This is Dorothy Washington, can I talk to Andrea please." Jason quickly handed the phone to Andrea, who was now sitting straight up in bed, mouthing, "Ma'am."

Finding her voice Andrea got out, "Good morning." It was the third week of school and things had been going well. Andrea wondered what was causing Ma'am to call at this hour.

"Andrea I am sorry to call you this early, but a shooting on Clyde Street took place last night. Dedra Sherman's 15 year old brother was killed."

Dedra Sherman was one of Andrea's students, a quiet girl whose morning comments often referenced her older brother Johnny. Dedra was going to be devastated.

"Oh my God! I will get to school as soon as I can," Andrea exclaimed.

Jason was now looking at Andrea with eyes as wide as coffee cup saucers. He couldn't imagine what the hell was happening.

Ma'am told her the crisis team was meeting at 7:00AM in the faculty room. She had more calls to make and she'd see her at school.

Andrea was now on her feet moving quickly. "Jason, the older brother of one of my students was shot and killed last night. We're meeting at 7:00 to plan what we'll do to support the children."

"What a hell-hole part of the world you are working in!"

"Jason, I don't have time for this, I've got to go as fast as I can."

Andrea pulled into the parking lot at 6:45. She felt a bit disheveled, but ready to do what was necessary to support the children and her colleagues. It was going to be a rough day.

The response team included Nancy Drake who was the Director of Elementary Special Services, Hanna Strassman the school social worker, Jane Plantania the school nurse, Jim Dayton a district-wide school resource officer, Janey Eisen and Ma'am. Also attending the meeting was Bea Johnson, given her knowledge of the kids and neighborhood.

Jim Dayton started the meeting describing the events. "Here's what we can tell you at this point. Johnny Sherman, the victim, was 15 years old. He and Denton Jones, a 14 year old, had a $100 buck bet on the Monday night football game between the Cowboys and the Eagles. Johnny lost the bet and Denton came to claim his winnings. When Johnny didn't pay up, Denton pulled a gun and shot him three times in the gut."

Tears rolled down Hanna and Jane's faces. Both boys had attended School #3. Denton was the youngest in his family. He had two older brothers, both of whom were serving time for a robbery of a convenience store. Johnny was a great kid with a crowd pleasing personality. This was going to be a nightmare day, not only for the kids, but for many staff members at the school.

Officer Dayton continued, "Look this was a rough one. Johnny didn't die quickly. He was gut shot and he bled hard; not only from the wounds but through his mouth and nose. He died there on the street before help could get there. As he died his body twitched and his bowels let go. This was one hell of a scene. It was witnessed by kids and adults who came out to help or see what was happening. I know this is a real tough description, but I think you gotta know what went down. Johnny's little sister Dedra saw it all."

Andrea, couldn't hold back her tears. "Oh God!" she said.

Bea sitting next to her, put her big arms around her, "Get it out now girl, cause we got lots to do today."

"We did arrest Denton Jones at his home about 10:00 PM last night. This whole thing happened around 8:30."

The meeting moved forward with each team member contributing their ideas. It was agreed if Dedra came to school Ma'am would talk with her before she would go on to Andrea's classroom, if at all that day.

Janey Eisen confirmed no press would be allowed in the building and they would do all they could to keep them away from the children. This usually wasn't a problem, but Janey would stay until after the first bell and return at the end of the day when school dismissed.

Nancy Drake would make arrangements for the crisis response team of social workers and psychologists from around the district to be present throughout the day. The team was well trained for this intervention, and as everyone knew, too often had experience responding to shootings across all ages. Nancy also noted a major response team was headed to Roosevelt High this morning where both boys attended school.

Ma'am knew Janey Eisen would be needed there a lot more than at her school this morning. "We can handle things here Janey. Why don't you head over to Roosevelt to help Lillian. She's a principal who is going to have a bigger problem than us."

"Are you sure?"

"Oh yeah, this isn't the first time we've been down this road. You will be much more help to Lillian and Doc Handler over there."

Roosevelt High was only two miles away and Janey knew she could be there before the school day began at 8:00.

While this was far from the first time Ma'am dealt with violence affecting the children of her school she was exhausted by it. It had become a never ending cycle of blood and tragedy. Its latest victims were two young boys she knew well. Despite all their efforts to work with these two boys, and the hundreds like them who passed through School #3, it was apparent the street claimed too many victims. She truly wondered if it would ever cease.

Andrea was standing in the faculty room, even though the meeting ended. She stared blankly out the window. It was a grey day, fitting under the circumstances. Bea had her arm around her shoulder. Andrea was shaken by the events and Bea was taking a moment as well to contain her own feelings. Both boys had been in her classroom, although not together in the same grade. No words needed to be said. They both made peace with the things that would follow.

However, Bea and Andrea talked about the morning routine. Andrea asked, "Do we go on as usual Bea?"

"There's security in the routines Andrea. The kids need to know we care about 'em and we need to let 'em get their feelins' out. But we gotta keep things goin' too. We have to see how they come through the door and use our best judgment on what to do and say. Remember Andrea, these kids have seen this before. They've lost cousins, parents, friends, and siblings to violence. This isn't a new event; it's just the next chapter in the street's story. You gotta remember this is life as they know it child."

"But Bea it's an awful story! I guess I never knew it was this bad. I haven't lost anyone in my family to violence. How can this be happening? How do we stop it?"

"It isn't easy to stop somethin' that's got so much power. It'll take more than me and you, but today we're on the front lines and maybe we can help one or two of our kids avoid somethin' bad like this in the future."

Andrea felt no way to win against such terrible odds, especially when poverty was always dealing a losing hand to those who lived in this neighborhood.

Andrea's morning routine included playing some type of music. Over the weeks she'd played nearly every genre. 'What should she chose today?' She thought of several different things to play and then decided a simple classical piece would likely be best.

Michael Makin was the first child to speak during morning share time.

"Me and Daunte were ridin' our bikes; we saw the whole thing."

"Who is Daunte?" Andrea asked.

"He's a friend of mine who lives across the street. He is in Mrs. Lovell's class."

Andrea knew this meant Daunte was in second grade. Damn, a seven and a nine year old witnessed the shooting and death of a fifteen year old on a street two blocks from school. 'How could the world these kids lived in get worse!'

"Yeah, we saw Denton and Johnny arguing. They was hot. Then Denton, he pulls a gun and bam, bam bam shoots Johnny. Johnny falls down holdin' his self. We knew he was dyin' right there."

Jadira piped in. "His mama, she came runnin' out of the house. She was holdin' Johnny rockin' and wailin'. She says, 'Don't die, don't die!' Blood was all over her too."

Others in Andrea's class told how they'd witnessed shootings on the street. The sharing took nearly an hour. Andrea felt she needed to go with it, even though this was much longer than the usual 20 minutes they spent each morning. When it was done Andrea was shaken to the core by what these little children saw and could easily share. She was glad Dedra was not in her classroom this morning. She wondered if she had come to school at all. She was also trying to think about how she could help her when she returned.

Nothing in her training prepared her for this.

CHAPTER 8

PATIENCE

John Handler was sitting with Jerry Croton, the Assistant Superintendent for High School Instruction. Jerry was becoming a good friend and confidant for John. It was nearly 5:00 in the afternoon and they were talking about recent events.

"Man Jerry, the unions are killing me over the residency thing. I thought they'd come out of the gate tough, but after the initial bullshit died down I thought we'd be able to get somewhere on it. I met one-on-one with Cliff Greer yesterday. He told me the teachers would oppose this proposed policy change with every means open to them. That they would go to the state legislature to get a bill put in place banning such a thing. With their political action committee they could pull it off. But then he says they'd consider a monetary incentive to encourage teachers to live in the city. Everything comes down to money and contract. It never stops! I am really tired and fed up with having to negotiate everything."

"John you can't be surprised. Like you said, you expected them to oppose it. Union leaders always look for ways to have their members benefit from any change we make. It's always about more bucks or more rights. Maybe the incentive is the way to go to get things started. How much did he propose?"

"I didn't ask him. I really don't want to go down that road. Then there's their newsletter! You see it?"

"Yes, I got a copy today …love the headline, 'Not Now!' You gotta fight on your hands John; no doubt about it."

"Can you believe it? How can we change anything in this damn entitlement environment? Some days I think why am I trying! Then the shooting last night of Johnny Sherman, he was only15 years old. It's been an awful day over at Roosevelt."

"I know, I've talked with Lillian. She's a high school principal who's earned her keep today! She's anxious how this is playing out with the gangs. There's been lots of talk that Denton shot the Sherman kid as part of a gang initiation thing. They had three bad fights today. One was in the girls' lavatory and two different ones happened in the cafeteria. Each was about what went down between those two boys. It's going to take some real time and effort to get everyone settled down over there."

"You know Jerry it seems at every turn we're dealing with things which can get out of hand and eat you alive. On top of the shooting and union stuff, the city is broke and the state has a looming budget crisis so money is going to get tight real quick. But you can bet they'll still be asking us why the scores aren't up. I'd like to tell them why. We're fighting a war with more fronts than any war in history. We can talk about street violence, poverty, cultural identity and diversity issues, drugs, politics, unions and money to name some off the top of my head. Oh, and how could I have forgotten the Board! Those five people have been driving me nuts with their emails and calls all day long today. Jerry, the poverty in the city is generations deep. I wish we had better strategies and approaches to break the cycle. Instead, we find ourselves in the midst of a self perpetuating culture."

"Man you have had a rough day! I haven't ever seen you this discouraged. You remember the saying, How do you eat an elephant?"

"I know, one bite at a time! It's hard to know how to take a bite since the size and bad temper of this damn elephant makes him almost impossible to approach on any level. I have to start the Quality School Committee tomorrow and the teacher's union is still asking its members to boycott it because of the residency thing. I'm not sure anybody will show up and I'll end up talking to myself. But I'll be darned if I'll cancel it. The train is leaving the station even if it's empty."

"John you are being tested. In fact the whole team is. The agenda you've put on the table is a good one. But we've got to give the seeds time to grow before we can harvest the crop."

"Aren't you full of pearls of wisdom," John said laughing for the first time.

"John, be patient."

"Jerry, I'm going to be patiently impatient; we have to move forward right now for the sake of this generation of kids. We cannot fail them. Too much is at stake."

Janey Eisen appeared at the door. "I thought you might be here." Janey looked tired and stressed. "John I hate to tell you this but the mayor's office just called. They want to know if you'll join the mayor in a press conference tomorrow morning to address the growing street violence."

"Oh sure Janey, I'll run right over there and go on camera with the mayor so she can pass the blame on to the schools like she always does."

Janey sighed heavily. "John, I know the mayor's got an agenda on this; they always have one over there. But we may be able to open some doors a bit if you stand next to her on this one."

John paused, thinking about what Janey had to say. He was tired and upset, not the best time to be thinking about political strategies with the mayor's office. But Janey needed to let them know if he would do it. "Janey, I am sure the mayor's office will begin with a prepared statement. Ask for it to be sent over. I want to know what they have in mind before I step into the lion's den. You can tell them I am willing to do it, but I won't let her scapegoat the schools on this. Let the team over there know if she says we've got to do more, then I will begin my statement by pointing out the mayor cut five police resource officers."

"Dr. Handler are you sure you want me to get into all that?" She went formal on John hoping to get him to think about his threatening posture. In Janey's mind this wasn't the time to be throwing down any gauntlets.

"Okay Janey, use your judgment on it. I'm tired and I know she's using us to deflect blame. In fact, I can't remember the last time she's asked me to stand with her at a press conference. She's usually the one who will push aside anyone in the room to get in front of a camera. No matter what, I want to see any statement before the press conference begins and tell them they owe us one. It will communicate we know what they're trying to do."

"That's fair, I'll let them know you will be there at 10:00 tomorrow morning. The press conference starts at 10:15 and I don't want you and the mayor getting into a fight before a press conference on decreasing violence." They all laughed and Janey turned on her heels and headed down the hall to call the mayor's office.

John turned back to Jerry after Janey was gone, "You know everyone out there thinks a superintendent's job is to be an educational leader. Given all the politics and fires lit by others I don't have enough time to fill that bill. All I can do is try to keep things off your back so you folks can focus on instruction and those damn test scores. There's a good bottle of wine waiting for me at home; I'm ready to sample it."

Jerry watched the superintendent leave his office. He knew John was a good man and a strong leader. He also knew the burdens of the job were weighing heavy on him right now. Jerry decided to talk to his colleagues tomorrow to be sure everyone took some time to tell John he was on the right track and doing a good job.

CHAPTER 9

THE JOURNAL

Three weeks passed since the shooting of Johnny Sherman. Ma'am asked Andrea if she would prepare a sampling from her morning classroom journal. Ma'am saw something special in this effort and she was giving serious thought about how she could use it herself and possibly with the staff. She knew she'd have to be cautious about how it was shared with other teachers. Her experience over the years taught her when you touted the work of a staff member it could easily backfire. Why that happened was hard to fathom, but the faculty room could serve up harsh criticism making a good practice a hard meal for others to swallow.

Andrea was thrilled to share some parts of the journal with Ma'am. Having so many entries made it hard to choose which ones to give her. With seven weeks of school under their belt the children had grown comfortable with this morning routine. They looked forward to telling about what happened in their lives. They also looked forward to Andrea's own stories too.

After careful thought, Andrea decided to share six journal entries. Once she picked the entries she sat down to write Ma'am a short cover note to accompany them.

Dear Mrs. Washington:
I have chosen six entries which different children have shared in class.
They are part of a much larger journal. We have used these entries in

many ways. We've created classroom theme books as well as personal journals for the students. The kids read them and sometimes add words and pictures to them as part of their writing experiences.

I am very proud of their stories. They have come from all corners of their lives. The kids have spoken of pain and joy. No matter what the story, I know they have spoken from the heart. I hope the six entries I picked are a good example of what they've shared. I have not edited them and they don't capture all that has been said, as many times I stopped writing and started talking with the kids.

September 20ᵗʰ – Carmen Mena
Jim and me stayed at my house last night. His mom had to work all night at Wal-Mart so he stayed with us. We watched videos and talked a lot. We ate all the pretzels. Grams let us stay up cause we didn't have school on Saturday. It was fun. I hope Jim's mom has to work at Wal-Mart all night again.

September 20ᵗʰ – Anthony Padilla
Mom and me went to the jail to see my brother. His name is Alexis. He's there because he robbed the Seven Eleven with a gun. The jail smelled bad and my brother was wearin' a brown suit. He looked funny. My mom couldn't stop crying. I cried too. We gonna be goin' there for a long time. My brother be in there until he is 26. He told mom to keep me outta' there.

September 29ᵗʰ – Laticia Stevens
Last night an SUV slammed into a house on my street. The cops came but the guy drivin' it ran away. People know who done it, but he's in the Bloods and nobody sayin' anything on account of that. The house really got hit.

October 5ᵗʰ – Michael Malkin
My brother James, he joinin' MA. James says that being in MA will be good for us. James got some big friends, they always sit by our porch watchin' out for things.

October 7th – Durrell Frazier
I was in my bed last night and a rat bit me. It was a big rat too! I tried to hit 'em, but he still bit me hard.

October 13th – Dedra Sherman
My mom has a picture of my brother, he's lyin' in his casket dead. She hold it every night prayin' to Jesus for him. Sometimes I pray too cause we know Jesus, he take care of him now.

Shortly after turning in the journal entries Andrea was excited to learn the students at Trimbell High School, where her mom worked, collected nearly $600 for the purchase of books for her classroom. She was anxious to get real-life stores and other reading materials for her students.

Her mom was proud of Andrea's work. She shared many of the things happening at School #3 with her high school colleagues. Her mom was learning how difficult and challenging it was to work at an inner city school. She also wasn't surprised to see how dedicated her daughter was to her class and all she was doing to try to address their needs.

It was this constant demand for her time which led to Andrea's increasingly strained relationship with Jason. He could not accept the overwhelming amount of hours it was taking for Andrea to be prepared to teach. It seemed to him all she ever thought about was the kids in her class.

Like so many outside the teaching profession, Jason assumed a vacation filled calendar and the early end to the school day made for an easy work life. The reality was far different from what he'd expected.

Andrea was upset by Jason's lack understanding. She thought she and Jason were a couple and they'd build a life together. She knew since school started she'd been preoccupied with work and her kids. The planning for teaching took way more time than she'd expected and she often came home too exhausted to be a good partner at home or in the bedroom. She accepted her part in what was taking place. But why couldn't he see she needed time to settle into a new job?

CHAPTER 10

COMMITTEE WORK

It was a busy seven weeks for Ma'am. She was working with the committee to prepare a list of possible names for School #3. The kids suggested Michael Jackson and Dr. Martin Luther King Jr. as potential names. Several presidents had been mentioned by community and staff members. Also on the list was a local hero from World War II, Daniel Thompson. Strong support for him was expressed.

At the last meeting Sylvia Davis, a special education teacher aide suggested Rosa Parks. Many on the committee were surprised no one thought of her before. It had unanimous support from the group and was their first choice as the namesake for the school. They also decided Daniel Thompson should be on the list. Ma'am hoped the committee could decide on a third name and send the list downtown by early November. Ma'am wanted to get the list in early so she'd have plenty of time to press Dr. Handler to give them their first choice. She felt it was the perfect fit for their school.

Ma'am, Bea Johnson and kindergarten teacher Myrna Gaylord served on the district-wide Elementary Program Committee. Here the progress was crawling along at a snail's pace. While the majority of the committee was understandably focused on what changes they should recommend to improve test scores, a smaller group led by Ma'am saw it differently.

Everyone acknowledged the elementary state test results were dismal. More than half the elementary schools in the city were defined by these scores as failing schools. School #3 was one of them. Every school felt the pressure to get the scores up. Administrators working downtown blamed the principals and teachers for the poor results. Each year they developed new strategies for the staff to implement and staff training programs rolled out like cars off an assembly line. The strategies rarely changed things, only creating busy work for all involved.

Ma'am reluctantly went along with a lot of the training and support programs offered or mandated. It was evident some made a small difference, sharpening skills and improving professional practices. Everyone at School #3 could (now) look at data and understand its application in their classroom. In fact she had a data team at the school meeting once a month to share ideas and suggestions related to what could be mined from the scores and applied in classroom. Kelly Slocum was especially helpful in this effort. She worked with Ma'am and the data team at School#3. These efforts made a small difference overall, and in some cases, with particular children a dramatic difference. But the scores were still terrible with only a small percentage of the children demonstrating fourth grade reading proficiency.

At the last meeting of the district-wide committee Bea's frustration with the data driven conversation reached the boiling point. Ma'am had seen it coming over the past several meetings where Bea sulked and did not actively participate in the conversation. She understood Bea's passion for change, but her behavior on the committee had been far from stellar.

Ma'am was reflecting on this when she saw Bea was going to speak. An explosion was coming. Ma'am had seen the look on Bea before and this was not going to be pretty.

Bea rose to her feet and in a thundering voice with her eyes nearly bulging from her face roared, "I can't keep it in any more! You folks all think doin' more of what we've been doin' and spendin' all kinds of time lookin' at numbers will fix it. It's never gonna be the answer! We gotta start over and all you want to do is make scores better."

Bea grabbed her purse and coat leaving her committee work folder on the table and stormed out of the meeting. It was quite a scene. Mary Jane Thomas, the Elementary Assistant Superintendent for Instruction who chaired the meeting was angry. This was a meeting people were going to talk about for days to come. Ma'am knew Bea would not give in and the committee would likely not listen to her given the outburst.

Ma'am and the other reps, including Myrna Gaylord knew Bea's statement, "We gotta start over," was not said lightly. She joined the committee with this hope in mind and it was increasingly apparent it was not the agenda.

Following the committee disaster, Ma'am called Mary Jane the next day. Mary Jane was hot from the moment she picked up the phone. "Bea is argumentative, she sits there meeting after meeting with a damned scowl on her face and her arms crossed. She's a blocker and a bully!"

Ma'am thought, 'This is going to be like climbing Mt. Everest. Mary Jane is never going to forgive her and Bea won't apologize for her strongly held beliefs.' Ma'am asked Mary Jane where she saw things going from here. She wondered if she was truly receptive to other voices for change.

Mary Jane said, "I think we have to look at improved training. We have to have a consistent curriculum. Too many schools are going their own way and not following what's prescribed, including yours! We need to ask for a new reading and math program, our materials are old. I also think we should press for class size to be lowered."

Ma'am asked Mary Jane if she saw any links between the program committee and the architectural review of schools underway. "What do you mean? Sure we've got to build new schools. But I'm talking about what goes on under the roof whether we get new schools or not!"

Ma'am ended the conversation saying she'd talk with Bea about her behavior, but she was discouraged by Mary Jane's narrow take on things. She felt Dr. Handler was asking for more and the door was open to new ideas. She couldn't let this opportunity slip by.

Ma'am knew Bea was right but she was going to have to risk their friendship because her committee behaviors were out of line. If she continued to behave badly any chance the committee could be persuaded to move in a different direction was hopeless.

Sitting at a desk littered with papers and messages, Ma'am noticed Andrea's journal entries at the top of her in-basket. She picked up the stapled papers with Andrea's note at the beginning. Ma'am read and re-read each of the entries. They revealed what she already knew. However, there was poignancy about them which rang as clear as a church bell on a quiet Sunday morning.

Ma'am thought, 'I know people understand life is hard for children and families in the tough neighborhoods of the inner city. But somehow we continue to think we can be successful with the majority of these children if we just try harder. Yet, I see how hard my staff works. I know I can't ask any more of them. I see the long hours they work and the devotion they have to the kids. Why isn't it enough? Something else is wrong that makes us keep missing the mark.'

Ma'am talked with Bea at the end of the school day. After they shared the day's events, Ma'am got to the point. "Bea you behaved in an obnoxious manner at the committee meeting. You've got Mary Jane so upset, I can't reason with her. I tried to calm her down but she was having none of it. We can't influence these folks if you keep insulting them for their thinking."

Bea's eyes flamed with passion again. "You bet my anger is takin' over! I don't know how you can sit there. You are acting like an administrator and just playin' along with downtown."

It was Ma'am's turn now. Her looks could be formidable and one was framed on her face now as she spoke to Bea. "How dare you play the administrator card on me! That's a bullshit label and you know it. Name calling isn't going to get us anywhere, honey. Nobody's listening to you because your anger is taking over. I agree with the points you are making, but I can't side with you when you behave so poorly."

It was a moment. These two women had been friends for a long time. Would this conversation end their friendship? Neither of them knew the answer. Not knowing what to do, Bea left without saying another word.

Ma'am sat holding her head. It seemed no matter which way she turned she was going to hit a wall. As she was in this tailspin of negative thoughts Myrna walked in, knocking lightly on the door as she did.

"Ma'am, I have some thoughts to share about the meeting." Ma'am looked up with tired eyes, not knowing what to say. She motioned for her to sit.

"I think Bea's right. We aren't going to change the committee's thinking no matter what we do. But maybe we could form our own program group here. What if we thought things through and proposed some type of pilot program? We've got nothing to lose in trying."

Here was this quiet kindergarten teacher sitting in her office. In fact, Ma'am was surprised when Myrna volunteered for the committee. She was the last person she'd have thought would want to do this work. Not because she wasn't smart, but because she was so reserved outside of the classroom.

Myrna wasn't finished, knowing she had Ma'am's undivided attention. "You know Dr. Handler is right about staff living in the city. I'd move in, but I wouldn't live in this area. It's too rough for me. His idea is only half right; if he gets people back in the city, they aren't going to live where they are really needed."

"Why are you sharing all this with me?"

"Because I know how much you care. But I think things need to be done that aren't being talked about. I've done a lot of thinking and reading about this. Because I'm quiet doesn't mean I don't have some things to say."

"Well," Ma'am said, "I am sure listening now." Their conversation went on for over an hour. Ma'am ended the conversation with a whole new perspective on the quiet kindergarten teacher at the end of the hall. She was much more revisionist in her thinking than anyone could have imagined.

CHAPTER 11

THE CONVERSATION

It was Saturday of Columbus Day weekend. Andrea and Jason agreed to meet at a diner near their apartment. The diner had old grey and red vinyl booths and the Formica topped tables were used so much the fake wood grain finish was worn to dull black in many places. But somehow it had a quaint feel. The smells from the grill when Sammy cooked breakfast were a sensory feast drawing everyone in.

Andrea got there first and sat at an empty booth near the door. She wanted to be able to leave quickly if needed. Her emotions were on a hair trigger. She didn't want to make a scene in a place where everyone knew them as regulars.

Betty Jane came to the table, "You want the usual? I see your sweet man is coming in. I'll get his order before he sits down." Betty Jane did not know about their pending separation and this meeting was to sort out what to do about the apartment and their things. It was just as well she didn't know at this point. Betty Jane was a gossip and the news would be shared with all the restaurant's regulars.

Jason sat down in the booth looking at Andrea across the table trying to get some nonverbal sign from her. Nothing was forthcoming but a far from encouraging look. Despite this he felt he needed to say something. "How are you?"

"I'm fine," Andrea answered more coolly than she meant to. She dreaded this moment and really didn't know what to do or say. She knew too many emotions were lurking near the surface and they'd trump reason if she let them get the upper hand.

They knew each other very well and she could sense Jason was just as tense. Betty Jane came by giving them their juice and coffee. Her timing was perfect as it took the edge out of the, 'What should we say now,' moment.

Jason held his coffee cup in a tight grip. He decided to break their silence. "Andrea, I will really miss you. I've thought a lot about what I want to say to you so let me say it before you talk."

"Okay Jason, I'm all ears." 'Damn!' she thought, 'Why did I say that with such an edge?'

Jason frowned, reacting physically to her sarcastic rebuke. But he pressed on as he'd thought too long and hard to not say what was on his mind. "Andrea, I love you." She started to say something and Jason looked at her, "You agreed to let me finish." He was right and she took a deep breath giving him the cue to go on.

"Andrea, I am afraid for you. Since you started teaching at School #3 you've had your car broken into, the side of it has been keyed twice and you've got a gang member across the street telling you to take care of his brother. I keep wondering what will happen if that street punk wakes up one day and decides you're not doing right by his little brother. I have to admit I've let these fears push us apart. I know how much School #3 means to you. I was not prepared for how much work you have to do. I really have to compete for your attention. I can't remember the last time we talked about something other than school. I want to be with you, but I can't say I'm not going to worry about you every time you drive into the hood to go to work. I also need to have some times together where school isn't always at the center."

Andrea held her breath for a moment collecting her thoughts. The future of their relationship was now squarely positioned on her response. She hadn't expected this kind of sensitivity from him, given their experiences over the past several weeks. She needed a minute to think. She smiled at Jason and took a long swallow of coffee.

"Jason, I love you too," she said in a voice halting with emotion. "But you have to accept how important my work is and how much these kids need help. The neighborhood around School #3 is tough. I understand your fears and have them too sometimes. But they aren't as strong now because I know there are so many good people who live there. They are just trying to get by. I've seen it; you haven't. If we are going to make it, you have to see things differently. I can't have you afraid every time I leave the house and I can't stand you calling it the hood."

Jason started to speak but Andrea had more to say. She took another sip of coffee as Betty Jane delivered breakfast. She could tell the two of them were in a deep conversation so she smiled and left them to themselves this morning. "Jason, I've wanted to teach my whole life. I'm doing what I love and my work is so important to these kids. I can't let them down."

"What are you telling me? You love me but your work is more important. That's what I am hearing right now."

"Jason, I need time to think. I do love you and I can't think of anyone else I'd rather be with. But the last two months have been tough for both of us. I know I'm not giving you the answer you want today. But this is too important to think everything will be okay because we've had this one talk."

"So, what is it you are saying?"

"I want to move my important stuff back to my parent's house for now. I need some space to think this through. You stay at the apartment and let's see how things go for a bit. I'll come next weekend and we can be together. I do love you Jason. You have to give me some space so I can make sure I can give you what you need."

CHAPTER 12

MAKING A DEAL

One of the struggles John faced as a superintendent was trying to decide when to let his staff hold the reins and when he needed to take them. It was a delicate balance of using the power of his office versus trusting the staff to accomplish things without him getting in the middle. The bus driver negotiations were the most recent example of the struggle. John stayed on the sidelines, but little progress had been made at the bargaining table. Making matters worse, several serious incidents had taken place on school buses since the start of the school year. Each incident was cannon fodder for the union. They used each as an example for why more adult supervision was needed.

Like many districts, the majority of the incidents were happening at the middle school level. The early adolescent age was a time where bullying and self-assertion seemed to rise to the surface on the bus rides to and from school; the rides home were especially challenging for drivers. Knowing this, John would ask staff members to imagine teaching a class of almost sixty kids, a task in itself, but then having to do it with your back turned to the class and your attention focused on other critical details. Most everyone agreed they would not accept the challenge, let alone day after day like the drivers.

John had a report sitting on his desk summarizing all the serious incidents to date on school buses. They were mostly fights or serious acts of bullying or insubordination. The majority of the incidents took place at two middle schools, Hudson and Lewis & Clark. The data also revealed the number of serious incidents was down compared to the same period last year. It was evident some drivers really did have their hands full. At the same time, the vast majority of school bus runs went off without a major hitch; however, the union's strategy of making every incident an event was taking its toll. Minor incidents usually handled by the drivers were now filed as incident reports for the administration to address. Every major incident was documented in a union press release. These were becoming a PR nightmare. John couldn't go anywhere without someone in the community asking him, 'What is going on on those buses?' His Board was also pressing him to do something as their constituencies throughout the city were calling them seeking answers. He had to bring this to an end soon. It was undercutting everything else they were trying to do and consuming huge amounts of time people didn't have.

At his weekly meeting with the Board President, Shantell Williams told John in no uncertain terms the Board was losing confidence in his leadership on this issue. She was concerned and let John know he had to do something. He knew he could not convince her otherwise.

Not wanting to undercut Carl and the district's bargaining team, but needing to make a move, John called Larry Betton, the drivers' union president, asking if he'd meet him for an early morning breakfast.

The next day John got to the diner first and had time to order a cup of coffee before Larry joined him. The two men didn't have much history together, and with the history of the past nearly eight weeks neither had too much trust in the other.

Since John asked for the meeting he had the burden to start the conversation. He felt he might as well get right to the point. "Larry did you know we've had fewer serious incidents on our buses this year than during the same period last year?"

"Dr. Handler, am I supposed to feel good about that? I really don't need to listen to this!"

"Yes you do need to hear it! Because if we're going to find a solution, you need to acknowledge we cannot afford to put aides on every bus. Most buses are safe and with the cameras you know things will get better when we get into he said she said situations."

Larry was no fool. He heard the superintendent say he couldn't afford to put an aide on 'every' bus. So he'd just opened a window. To date there'd been no movement for any support on any bus. "My drivers are worried about the cameras. They think they're going to be used against them. They don't trust Tom Foley who you hired as the transportation manager. Tom is a hard-ass who doesn't listen."

John did not want to get sidetracked on this issue; especially when he had no solid information about driver morale or their take on the new manager. "Look Larry, I know the teams are meeting tomorrow. I want to let you know the district team will be putting our best offer out there."

"So it's going to be a take it or leave it one. Is that it?"

"Damn it Larry, stop twisting my words! The aide issue is a tough one for us. With benefits the part time aides will cost us nearly $20,000 a year per position. We have 120 buses on the road each day. If we put an aide on each bus it's a $2.4 million add to our annual budget. You know we can't afford it. So don't lecture me on this when you guys haven't moved a bit on your position that an aide must be added on every bus. It's never going to happen!"

"Dr. Handler your buses are unsafe. Why should we move on this when you guys keep saying it isn't a big problem?"

"Well, you guys keep running to the press as a bargaining pressure tactic; don't tell me you don't. What would you do if you were in my shoes? I am not going to say our buses are unsafe. It's not true. Are there challenges? Sure. Do we have some runs where support would be useful? You bet. But I'm not bargaining in the press. If we're going to make progress on this issue, it's not going to happen on the six o'clock news."

Their breakfast arrived. John had a muffin and got a refill on his coffee. Larry had scrambled eggs and toast along with his coffee.

"Look John, since you guys don't have any money, let me buy breakfast." This statement broke the tension between the two men. The roosters in the barnyard had done their prancing.

John indicated over breakfast his team would be willing to fund a small number of aides which could be assigned as trouble shooters on problem buses. The union could have a voice in where they were placed. Larry admitted an aide on every bus was not realistic. He said he'd work with his team to keep the number they wanted reasonable. John could only hope they held a similar definition of reasonable.

Returning back downtown, John dropped by Carl's office to to let him know about the breakfast meeting.

"How did it go?" Carl asked once John was seated.

"We'll see. We did talk about the aide issue, but neither of us put any specific numbers on the table. I leave it to you to bargain out. In any event Carl, I've worked with the business office on this and Tom Wheaton says we can't do more than 24 max. I don't want to tell you how to play it, but any number less than that will sure help when it gets to budget season in a few more months. Carl, do all you can to settle this thing. I'm losing the Board on this. They're starting to really believe our buses are unsafe."

"John, I'll talk with Larry tomorrow in caucus. He's a good negotiator. I think putting the aides on the table along with your face-to-face this morning may get the job done. Now what about residency and the teachers? They're never going to let up on their opposition."

"Carl, what do you suggest?"

"John, ask Cliff to form a joint study committee with all the unions. We can study the issue for several months and then report back. You'll both save face and you can move on. Is this really your top priority?"

"It's one of them! Damn it Carl, too many of our teachers and administrators don't live in the city."

"You know John I don't live here and quite honestly I don't want to either."

John started to get angry and Carl could tell he was walking on thin ice with his comment. "John, I got a call from Dorothy Washington this morning. She said while your residency idea was good, it would still miss the target."

"How so?"

She reminded me the residency requirement doesn't mean staff members have to live on Warsaw, Clyde and other similar streets. Everyone will want to live on the north side."

"Carl, why didn't she call me?"

"John, even with Ma'am you are the superintendent. She was a good soldier passing the message downtown, but she left it to me to decide whether or not to share it. I really think she's got a point. If I had to live in the city there are certain streets I'd never live on in a million years with my family."

"Let me think on it. If I go down that road would you be willing to chair the study team?"

"Sure, as long as you are willing to accept the idea is not going to happen the way you'd like it to."

John left Carl's office thinking about the observation Dorothy shared. When he got back to his office he was going to give her a call to hear her thoughts firsthand.

CHAPTER 13

UNEXPECTED EVENT

M a'am was sitting at her desk. She had 16 bus behavior referrals to address. Since the drivers were without a new contract, their union instructed them to fill out referrals for even the most minor incidents. The paper work related to each referral had to be completed promptly and then forwarded downtown for statistical purposes. Each principal felt the impact of this work action. Ma'am also knew, under the state's violence reporting process, the referrals would inflate her incident numbers making the school's violence status look bad. She knew when the press got those figures from across the district next fall, it would be the headline for a story on rising violence.

Ma'am also had three parent phone calls to return and several notes from staff members on various issues or problems. As her computer was revving up she saw the alert stating she had 49 new emails. Along with all the paper issues, she was scheduled to do two teacher observations.

With 26 teachers in the building and the teacher's contract requiring two formal observations per teacher, a goal setting meeting and an end of year evaluation, Ma'am had a full plate. She figured this year, counting the 2 mandated observations per teacher and the 2 post observation conferences following her 45 minute classroom visits, along with the fall goal setting meetings and the final evaluation conference, she had one hundred fifty-six personal meetings that had to take place. Considering the length of the school year she had to keep up a pace of at least one formal staff meeting or visit a day. This did not take into account the time it took to write up each observation, document a teacher's goals and write a final evaluation. It was extremely difficult for any principal to get the work done, let alone find the time for any creative or spontaneous leadership activities. But oh yes, they were the ones first in the accountability line when those test scores didn't hit the mark!

As Ma'am was going through all the paper on her desk, Janet walked into her office, "Dr. Handler's on the phone for you."

"Thanks Janet, please close my door will you." Janet gave Ma'am a quick wink and closed her door.

"Good morning Dr. Handler," Ma'am said in a pleasant but business-like voice. She wondered why he was calling. It was not a regular occurrence for the superintendent to call.

"Good morning Ma'am. I'm calling to follow up on your conversation with Carl on the proposed city residency policy."

Dorothy took a deep breath, unsure where this conversation was going to head, knowing John's commitment to making needed changes in where the staff lived.

"John we were talking about the policy and one of my teachers pointed out the places where staff really need to live, like the neighborhood School #3 serves, aren't the places people will chose. So, I shared with Carl the proposed policy is only half right. I think the residency idea is on the mark, but until we get staff members living on many different streets throughout the city, it won't have much impact here."

John understood the point Ma'am was making but he was still undecided about what he should do. "What do you think we should do now that I've put a stake in the ground on this policy goal?"

"That's a tough one. My observation is you've got your neck stuck out there pretty far and in the end it's not going to get you what you want. I think your committee on defining quality is much more important. The teachers will help you on that, but the faculty room chatter is they are not buying the residency piece and they won't help on the other stuff until it's addressed."

John thanked Ma'am for her candor, appreciating the honest feedback.

From her perspective, Ma'am respected this guy. She knew she'd given him critical feedback running counter to what he wanted to do, yet he was thoughtfully considering it. It had been a long while since folks downtown sought, much less listened to, feedback from the field.

Janet saw the light go off on Ma'am's phone. She quickly came into her office. "Ma'am we have six kids in the nurse's office with diarrhea and throwing up. It's a mess over there and it's only 9:45."

"Oh boy, a stomach virus! This is going to go through here like a freight train on the main line. Janet call downtown and let them know what's going on. Also give School #5 and School #17 a call and see if this has started at their places. I'm headed to the nurse's office."

By lunch time the number of children who were ill doubled. The faculty room was buzzing as teachers and staff came in for lunch. The veterans had seen this several times before and could anticipate what they were in for.

Amy Fontaine, a sixth grade teacher who was in her third year at the school said, "Well who goes down first? Ya know it's only a matter of time!" The faculty knew they worked inside a germ factory and with their close contact with the kids a significant number of them would be affected despite their best efforts to avoid it.

Janet had her hands full. A number of parents had been called to come in and get their child. But several had not returned calls. She was looking up emergency contact numbers trying to reach a responsible adult.

Ma'am came back to the office looking worn. Her hair was no longer in a neat bun and her pressed suit was stained. Janet could easily surmise why.

Ma'am asked Janet if she'd reached the other schools.

"Yup, nothing at School #5 but #17 sounds a lot like us!"

"Okay, let's call our three best substitutes teachers right now and ask them to come in tomorrow. If we don't do it now the sub pool will be empty once this virus starts hitting the staff in other schools."

"I'll get on it," Janet said holding a phone in her hand. Oh, what a day this was turning into.

As she was making a call Mrs. James came in to pick up her son. Ma'am greeted her and went with her to the nurse's office to get him. She was glad one less sick student would need attention.

It was clearly going to be rough for several days. Ma'am suspected with the level of her exposure she could soon be on the sick list herself. Her thoughts about scheduled observations and what to do about her recent argument with Bea would simply have to be put on hold.

CHAPTER 14

THE WALL

The stomach virus ravaged School #3. More than half the staff was hit over the next week. This was combined with nearly two of every five students coming down with the virus. Janet and Ma'am had it at the same time. That brought the office to a halt.

The 'survivors' as the staff called those working on any given day had a motto, 'Fall forward'. They worked with few breaks, covering other classes, doing stints in the main office and orienting any new substitute willing to come in once the news of the virus got out.

Sue Jones, despite all her union whining, was a real trooper. She helped cover classes by doing double PE sessions in the gym. Given the shorthanded status, this was a real godsend everyone appreciated.

Andrea was one of the lucky ones who did not get the virus, but both Bea and Pam did. With both of them gone, Andrea found herself the fourth grade leader. She gave substitutes plans and brought some of the more difficult students into her room from Pam's and Bea's classes.

When the virus passed, and things started to return to normal, Andrea got her first new student. Her name was Antonia Juarez, who spoke almost no English. Registration paperwork indicated her mom and dad were migrant farm workers and her father had recently been jailed for an assault. Mom moved with her four children to live with a sister. Antonia was 'age placed' in Andrea's classroom. Nobody had any real sense of this child's schooling or abilities.

The good news was several of Andrea's students spoke Spanish. Andrea did not, although she'd recently purchased software to learn the language enough to be more helpful to the many Hispanic students and families School #3 served.

Antonia's needs necessitated a referral which had already been made to the Committee on Special Education (CSE). In the meantime Sue Dabeck, a special education teacher in the school who spoke Spanish, would work with Antonia along with a large number of other language deprived students at the school. This would mean Antonia would be pulled out of Andrea's classroom about 30 minutes each day. Andrea would have to work with her the rest of the day as best she could.

Antonia was far from the only child in Andrea's classroom who had significant learning or emotional needs. Recently Dedra had been added to the list of children needing support. Since her brother's death she had become withdrawn and often cried. She was a little girl with a full blown depression. Andrea was worried about her. Despite numerous efforts to reach Dedra, she had been unable to unlock the door that would let her in to help.

Along with these two girls Andrea had thirteen other children with Individual Education Plans (IEP's) approved by the CSE. As a result, she coordinated a three ring circus of pull-outs and support services coming into her classroom. At times, three different adults were in her room and she was somehow supposed to keep all of them up to date. This was accomplished without any email or scheduled coordination time. She and her colleagues often met after school, but it was a rare time when everyone was truly on the same page. The system could not handle the load and the necessary coordination time to deliver what was on paper. The good intentions of special ed services was one thing, the reality of delivery was quite another.

Andrea doubted if the support would make any significant learning difference for the children. She often talked with Colleen about this. 'How did she manage so many people and children coming and going from the classroom?'

Colleen had a full time aide in her room for a youngster with severe emotional needs. Colleen and her aide, Rita, often shared the coordination load. Rita would not only follow little Jerome Johnson throughout the day, but in quiet moments she'd help Colleen pass along information to other special education and speech teachers who were working with the kids. Andrea didn't have extra help.

With the addition of Antonia, and Dedra's high emotional needs, Andrea was feeling overwhelmed. The seven reading groups she'd established demanded a great deal of planning. She had children reading at barely the first grade level at one end, and Michael Malkin and some others who were above grade level. Most children were falling between second and third grade levels in their reading scores and needed a great deal of support if they were ever going to improve their reading ability to 'at grade level' achievement.

Despite all of her training, Andrea never thought she'd see such disparity and varied levels of need in one classroom setting. When she mixed in the emotional issues of several students, and now a non-English speaking new addition, she went home exhausted. For the first time since she was a young girl, Andrea questioned whether or not she was cut out to be a teacher.

Bea could see the stress on Andrea's face. She did not have an enthusiastic bounce to her step and she was much less animated in her conversations. She knew Andrea and Jason were going through a difficult time. At first Bea surmised this was the root cause of Andrea's distress. However, as time passed Bea knew she had seen this before with new teachers. Andrea was hitting the wall.

Despite all the college courses and student teaching experiences, nothing truly prepares a person for the job of teaching until you experience it with your own students. There's a loneliness to teaching. It's you and the children. There's the responsibility for teaching and managing them throughout a week. Many new teachers, when hitting the wall, become disheartened and leave the profession. Bea did not want it to happen to Andrea.

It was a Tuesday afternoon and the day had been a particularly difficult one. The weather was gloomy and Halloween had been celebrated yesterday; a holiday that challenged the patience and resources of every parent and teacher. Today there were many kids with less sleep and more sugar than normal. It was a day the staff was glad to see come to an end.

Walking into Andrea's room, Bea saw her sitting at her desk staring blankly out the window. Andrea looked like she had been drawn through a knothole. She was trying to catch her breath and let a tough day go.

"Girl, you look like you need some TLC. You got any dinner plans?" Andrea looked up and smiled at Bea.

"No nothing on the docket for me tonight, except correcting papers."

"Well then you are comin' home with me and we'll have some dinner. I've got a pot roast I'd love to share with you."

Andrea didn't need to be asked twice. Not only was she tired, she was lonely too. She wondered how Bea did it day after day, year after year.

"Okay Bea. What time are you headed out? "

"Why don't you take another half hour, correct those papers, then follow me home. We can relax and have a good woman talk before eatin' the pot roast. You look like you need some soul liftin' girl."

"Deal," Andrea said with the first enthusiasm she'd felt all day. Bea was pleased by this and would soon be at Andrea's classroom door to collect her.

Andrea followed Bea's car, a green Ford Crown Vic, a big and street tired vehicle; not neglected, just well used. Andrea knew Bea lived only a few blocks away, and she wondered what her home would be like. Turning the corner onto Bea's street, Andrea saw all the familiar trappings of an impoverished city neighborhood, litter and neglect, along with a group of young men loitering on the corner by their black BMW. The group looked at her and Andrea felt a tinge of fear as she drove by.

Among the group was MA gang leader Jermain Woodsen. He ogled Andrea and thought to himself, 'Oh yeah, what a fine lookin' woman.'

Bea's big old white house with a front porch looked like most every other house. However, Andrea noticed right away Bea's home was one of those oasis places. It was cared for, with a well-tended yard. Even though it was too cool to sit on the front porch most nights, two green wooden rocking chairs were neatly set there along with an attractive small wrought iron table. It was clear Bea used her porch, as the floor's paint revealed a well worn path from the steps and front door to these chairs.

Bea's front door had a heavy bolt lock which was a concession to the neighborhood's character. She also noted the prominent ADT sign indicating a security system. Once inside the front vestibule, Bea quickly disarmed the system and unlocked a second inside front door.

As Andrea passed through the second door the delicious aroma of a pot roast filled her senses. Bea had placed it in a crock pot where it simmered throughout the day. Bea's living room was not what Andrea expected. A beautiful oriental rug sat upon a highly polished hardwood floor with an over-stuffed couch positioned to one side of the room. Two cozy side chairs were placed near a well-used gas fireplace. Perched on the mantle above the fireplace were several pictures of Bea's two children. Andrea heard Bea speak often about her daughter Jasmin, who was a senior majoring in political science at Duke. However, Andrea didn't ever recall her talking about the young man in the pictures on the mantle.

Andrea walked directly to one picture. It was a man in sailor garb. She asked Bea to tell her about him.

"He's my boy, Andrea."

Bea left it right there, walking away swiftly. "Girl come join me in the kitchen. I'm havin' a beer. I suppose you'd like some wine?"

Andrea laughed. "Bea, this girl likes Bud. Do you have any?"

"Matter a fact I do! Let's crack 'em open and start talkin'. I've got some things I want to share with you."

Andrea's eyes were still scanning Bea's home. Her kitchen was small. The new cupboards were white, and the kitchen had green granite countertops. The floor was highly polished oak hardwood like the living room. The hardwood was also relatively new, having been done, Andrea surmised, when the kitchen was remodeled. A table would not fit in the small kitchen, but the counter over a lower set of cupboards by the stainless steel sink, had an overhang accommodating two wood stools.

Bea opened a can of salsa and fresh bag of Tostitos. With beers in hand, the two headed back to the living room. Because it had been chilly, Bea hit the switch and the gas fireplace came on with a strong flame. "Love that," Bea said. "I sit here at night and read by the fire. No logs to light, it's livin' I tell ya."

Andrea looked up at the pictures on the mantle again. Bea knew she was wondering about her boy's picture. "His name is Ford. We named him that because his dad loves workin' on Fords. He is servin' in the

Navy on an attack submarine somewhere in the Atlantic. It scares the hell outta me."

Andrea sensed Bea was not going to share any more. "I don't see a TV Bea, but I know you watch shows because you always talk about Glee."

"I've got a 60" flat screen Andrea. It's mounted to the wall in my bedroom. I like it better up there than down here. I have a nice sittin' chair in my bedroom and a fireplace up there too. It's my space and I can watch things in real comfortable clothes, or no clothes." Bea laughed as she caught Andrea's incredulous look.

"I like things my way in my house. I keep it real clean, and without a man under my feet, I can do things just the way I like to."

As they sipped their beers Bea asked Andrea how she was feeling. Andrea didn't expect it to happen, but the tears started flowing. "Bea, I feel so overwhelmed. The kids have so many needs and I feel like I am failing them. I can't keep up. I go home exhausted and I'm planning and working day and night. I don't think I can keep this up much longer. I am not sure I am cut out for this. How do you do it?"

"First thing is you gotta have some balance. You're so wrapped up in the work you don't know if you're comin' or goin'. Nobody can keep that up. It's askin' way too much of yourself."

"But Bea, you do as much as I do and you aren't feeling like me. You have something I'm missing I think. I see everybody else keeping their act together. Why can't I?"

"Well we're havin' a good pity party here! Girl teachin' isn't easy work, the kids have lots of troubles that's for sure. I know the weight of it can be mighty heavy. You feelin' the weight now. I see how hard you workin'. You tryin' to do something every day for every child. As much as that's what they need, you can't bring that much. Nobody can."

Andrea was sobbing and Bea could see she was letting her frustrations out. She was pleased Andrea was, and felt it was important to see the conversation through before they had supper.

"You listen close to Bea now, girl. I am tellin' ya, ya can't do everthin' for the children. You can't be their savior, you're their teacher and that's where you gettin' confused. You are plannin' and worryin' too much. You can't take care of the children if you aren't takin' better care of yourself. You are a good teacher, I see it every day. Believe me I know good from bad teachin'. You gotta get some balance."

"How do I do that Bea?"

"There's not one way. Each of us has to think it through and choose. I've watched you, and listened to the teachers who come in your room. Everybody sees how much you do for each child. You've got too many groups goin' for one thing. How many readin' groups do you have each day?"

"I have seven groups."

"That's what I mean. You're tryin' to make sure it's just right. You have to average things out. I have three groups. Each week I ask myself who is strugglin' the most. I pick two or three and those are the ones that get some extra attention the next week. How many times you tryin' to meet with the other teachers workin' in your room?"

"I try to talk to at least one or two every day. I come in early or stay late to do it. I often skip lunch or my breaks if I can meet with them."

"Girl, again you're tryin' to be perfect. You have to make sure to take time for yourself. Those other teachers know what you are doin' and they know what they're doin'. You've gotta trust 'em more and let 'em figure things out. I meet once a week with each of 'em. I know it would be great to see 'em more often, but I can't do it. Are you willin' to let me help you on this?"

"Oh my God yes," Andrea said.

"Okay then you and I are gonna have dinner at my house every Thursday night for a while. We are gonna talk about plans and the children and you are gonna do what I suggest, no arguments. We will get you straightened out. You got talent. You gotta flow it out better. Now let's have supper and tell me what's goin' on with your man."

CHAPTER 15

SURPRISES

Board President Shantell Williams arrived early and was sitting in her office, awaiting Dr. Handler's arrival. She'd left word with his assistant Ann, she wanted to see him as soon possible.

John arrived at about 8:30, he'd stopped to talk with Columbus Middle School principal Susan Cornish about a sexual harassment complaint filed against one of her vice principals. The complaint was made by a respected classroom teacher. Susan talked with the teacher and wanted John's advice on how to proceed. It was going to be a tough issue given the serious nature of the complaint.

John expected to have a meeting with Joanne Walters, the Middle Level Assistant Superintendent for Instruction and Carl Gardner. Together they'd discuss the problem and develop the process steps to be followed regarding the harassment complaint. It was something which couldn't sit long.

As John walked up to Shantell's office door he heard her say, "Starting late today Dr. Handler." It was a comment, not a question. John was annoyed by her demeanor and judgmental nature. Things had been tense between them ever since he asked her not to speak with the administrators at their summer workshop.

John decided not to explain what he'd been doing as he did not want anything out on the complaint from his end until he was prepared for all the questions and comments to follow. Anyway, it was obvious his Board president had something on her mind and he was in a hurry to hear it and move on with his day.

"John, the Board and I have been talking. We're really concerned about the progress of the bus drivers' negotiations. We think we should send a representative to the table at this point."

John took a deep breath, deciding what he'd address first. Since the Board's independent behaviors were his consistent concern, he decided to begin the conversation there. "How is it you and the Board members have been talking and I'm not in the loop Shantell?"

"Now John, don't go getting defensive on this like you always do!"

"I am not being defensive. You all are out of line talking about district business without me being in the loop. We've talked about this over and over. You have to stop the behavior or I am going to start looking elsewhere for work!" Wow, that came out of his mouth without much immediate thought. He'd never taken the conversation there before.

"John, you are always telling us to keep out of things which aren't our business. We were elected to oversee things and make sure the district is running right."

"No Shantell you were not! A superintendent has that job and you have the right to fire me in accord with my contract terms if you are unhappy with how I am doing it. Board members have a distorted view of your roles. Your job is to set policy, act on my hiring and firing recommendations, determine an overall budget and conduct business meetings on a regular basis in accord with state regulations. The interference behaviors have to stop. It undercuts me and sends the wrong message to everyone."

"John, you don't understand how tough it is to be in our shoes. You think we're all supposed to follow wherever you lead. It is not going to happen! We have our own minds on things and you need to do what we think is right."

"No Shantell, it's you who has it wrong. If you are going to hold me accountable for things around here, then it's my call on how things are run. It's what you hire me to do. We have to get this settled; I can't keep fighting you all on this. If you believe what you are saying then I need to start a job search again because I can't make changes looking over my shoulder all the time to see where the Board is. I want a closed session with the Board as soon as it can be scheduled. By the way, I was going to send everyone an email today to tell you the bus drivers' contract was settled last night. We compromised on the aides and will have 17 added to the workforce as bus trouble shooters. Carl did a great job on this and the union is satisfied with the agreement. I've said this before and I will say it again, you have to trust my staff and I know what we're doing. If you don't, we can all talk about it at the closed session. If you do trust what I am doing, this behavior has to stop."

Shantell gave John a long hard stare. "You really want me to call the meeting Dr. Handler?"

"Yes I do, the sooner the better."

John had not planned on this confrontation; it just came his way and he didn't feel he could avoid it. The showdown was brewing with his Board. He knew they had to realize how easily he could get side-tracked by inappropriate Board behaviors.

Ann Stanley caught John on his way back into his office. "Is everything okay?" Ann knew most everything that happened; John rarely kept a secret from her and it wasn't going to start now. She was a real pro who worked as the lead person in the superintendent's office for almost 15 years.

"Ann, it's the same old thing; who's in charge here?"

"I thought so." She paused a moment then said, "Both Carl and Joanne have called, are you ready for them?"

"Yes."

"I'll call and tell them to come down. Should I clear your calendar for a few hours?"

"Yes, tell Janey we'll have to talk later about the joint press release on the bus driver settlement. See if she's free for a working lunch here. If she is, order us some subs and we'll get the statement we need sorted out then."

A short time later both Joanne and Carl were in his office. John had to bring them up to speed on the call he'd received from principal, Susan Corner and what he'd learned from her in his face-to-face at Columbus Middle this morning.

"Well we've got a serious problem on our hands. After school yesterday sixth grade teacher Ron Post went to Susan Corner's office to tell her he had been sexually harassed by Janice Mills."

Joanne, with an incredulous look on her face, exclaimed, "You aren't serious are you? I've known Janice for years; this isn't something that makes any sense."

"Well this is one for the books," Carl stated. "I've handled a number of harassment complaints before, but a male teacher saying he's the victim of sexual harassment is a new one. What's Susan's take on it?"

"She doesn't know what to think. Two respected staff members she trusts are at odds here. She told me Ron said he was in Janice's office talking about a parent conference coming up. According to Ron, Janice said she thought a prostitute would be attracted to him. She also told him she was attracted to him."

"Oh shit," said Joanne. "This can't be happening."

"What did Ron say happened then?"

"He said he ended the meeting as quick as he could and came to the principal right away with his complaint."

Carl spoke up, "I suppose nobody else saw or heard this right?"

"The door to Janice's office was closed, so no, but her secretary, Linda St. James, was in the outer office."

Ann quietly knocked on the office door and entered. "Cliff Greer is on the phone Dr. Handler, do you want me to take a message or do you want to talk with him?"

"Thanks Ann, I'll take the call."

Joanne and Carl started to get up but John said, "No stay here. I bet he's calling about the same thing we're talking about. Bad news travels fast."

John picked up his phone, "Good morning Cliff."

"Good morning Dr. Handler, I suspect you know I'm calling about Ron Post. I heard you stopped by Columbus this morning."

"Yes I did. I stopped to talk with Sue Corner who called me last night. Joanne and Carl are with me in the office and we're coming up to speed on the situation."

"Ron called me last night too. He's pretty upset. This one could really blow the lid off at Columbus."

John asked, "Well, what's your take?"

"Of course I believe Ron. I assume you'll need to talk with him. I want to be sure a union rep is with him when you do though."

"Let's take this a step at a time Cliff. I'll have Carl call you when we have a plan on how to proceed." John turned back to his two colleagues and said, "Okay folks, let's figure out how we want to attack this one."

John had hoped he'd have some time to think about the Quality School Committee meeting later that afternoon. Since he and Cliff agreed to form a study committee on residency there had been some progress on what the committee members thought defined a quality school. John was encouraged by the recent conversations, but orchestrating the meeting required careful thought and today, given the number of events stepping up to claim his time, he was no longer in charge of his calendar. He'd be forced to wing it more than he wanted to do.

CHAPTER 16

A NEW APPROACH

Ma'am called and asked for an appointment to see Mary Jane Thomas. She was trying to think about how to approach her with an idea she had about the Elementary Program Committee. She knew it was going to be a touch and go option. She had no idea whether Mary Jane would buy into it, but she had to give it a try. Today Ma'am was a much more humble person approaching district office on a school item than the last time she was here to see Carl Gardner.

She stopped to say hello to George at the front check-in desk. She asked if he had any new pictures of his grandchildren. He didn't, but nonetheless they talked about their grandkids. Ma'am had seven at this point and was proud of each one.

All the instruction offices were on the second floor. Ma'am headed there slowly, thinking and re-thinking how she'd approach Mary Jane. This was not going to be easy. Mary Jane could be defensive and slow to see another's point of view. She was a stickler for detail and protocol, making her difficult to work for. In fact, Mary Jane had gone through more secretaries than anybody else in the district. Her perfectionist traits and lack of sensitivity drove them all away at the first opportunity. It was into this lion's den she was about to tread. But Ma'am saw no other choice at this point.

Mary Jane was ready and waiting for Ma'am when she arrived. Ma'am stepped into Mary Jane's office noticing absolutely nothing was out of place. Her retentive nature was evident for all to see. Not one thing was on her desk including her computer area which was as neat as a pin. Her office included a nicely framed picture of her husband along with one of her two teenage boys. Ma'am wondered what it must be like to live in the Thomas family home.

But her mental speculation ended quickly when Mary Jane abruptly asked, "How can I be of help to you?" There was no good morning or how are things going? Mary Jane cut through it all getting right to the point.

Ma'am taking a minute to settle said, "I've been thinking about the committee. I know Bea has been difficult. I've spoken to her about her behavior, but I don't see it changing much, knowing her passion for the topic."

"Well she should resign from the committee then."

Mary Jane reacted as Ma'am hoped. A door wasn't open, but maybe a window was.

"I totally understand how you feel. I have a thought on how a resignation could turn into a win-win for both you and Bea."

"I could care less about a win for her! But you obviously have something in mind."

"I'd like to chair a sub-committee with your blessing. Knowing where things are headed, I am wondering if the subcommittee could propose a pilot involving only School #3. We serve the poorest area in the city. Perhaps a different approach would make sense."

"It sounds like a charter school to me. Why should we do a pilot somewhere? I think putting another group in place with a free rein to do what it wants will confuse things. I don't think I can support it."

Ma'am knew Mary Jane's first reactions could easily become her last. "We'd report our findings and recommendations to you. You could attend any meeting you want; if you get too uncomfortable we'd stop. Bea would no longer disrupt your meetings but Myrna and I would still be regulars at the main committee sessions where you could count on our support."

Mary Jane leaned back in her comfortable office chair. She gave Ma'am a long look. It was clear she was pondering this proposal. Not having Bea disrupting her meetings was almost worth it in itself. "Let me talk with Dr. Handler about your proposal. If he's comfortable with the subcommittee idea, we can try it. But, I reserve my right to stop you at any time."

Ma'am knew, if the subcommittee got underway, it would be hard politically for Mary Jane to stop it. She'd accomplished all she could hope for at this meeting. "Okay, let me know as soon as you can what John thinks." Ma'am used the superintendent's first name as a reminder to Mary Jane she wasn't the only one who could approach him with this proposal.

"I'll call you in the next couple of days and let you know where things stand. Thanks for dropping by Dorothy." Just like that Ma'am was dismissed. She'd had as good a morning here as possible and she knew it was time to get out of Dodge quickly.

Ma'am thought about how she'd approach Bea. Since their last conversation the two hadn't spoken much. The tension needed to be broken and Ma'am felt the subcommittee would be right down Bea's alley. But limits were still going to have to be set with her or Ma'am would find herself in the same place Mary Jane had. Bea was not easy to handle and her beliefs were strong on this topic. Bea would have to be more flexible because it wasn't all going to move her way.

Ma'am asked to see Bea at the end of the day. She decided to temper the meeting by also inviting Myrna. The three met after school. Ma'am began by saying, "I met with Mary Jane this morning. I proposed a subcommittee to develop a pilot concept effecting only this school. After some talking, she has agreed to take the proposal to Dr. Handler. I am pretty confident he'll support it."

Myrna was first to speak. "It will give us the freedom to develop something here and not be ground down by all the others who want to head in a different direction."

While Ma'am was not surprised by Myrna's comment, having heard similar from her before, Bea was. "Myrna, you have been so quiet, I didn't know where you stood."

"Well now you do Bea! I think we've got to try something outside the box, but it's also got to be something others could pull off as well if it works."

Ma'am added, "Bea are you in for the whole 10 rounds on this one? I can't have you getting upset when things don't go the way you see them."

This was a direct conversation with Myrna present. Ma'am was taking a risk on many levels saying it now. But the three of them were going to be hauling the freight and had to have a team agreement on things.

Bea gave Ma'am a long look. This was the boss talking to her, not her close friend. Bea understood this, nodded her head and said, "I'll do my part. We've got a chance here and I won't do anythin' to wreck it. But I've also got to be able to express my mind."

"You can, but no pouting or shout-outs. We have to be on the same page in the end or the downtown politics will chew us up and spit us out. It's going to take all our skills and then some to try anything different. Mary Jane isn't going down easy and you've really ticked her off."

"I agree. Now, how do we get started?"

"We have to develop a subcommittee of volunteers. No extra comp will be paid for serving on it. I don't want Sue Jones spouting off because of that, so before we announce it at large to the staff for volunteers, I want some key players already hooked up. You two think tonight about who we should approach, not only here but in the larger community. We're going to need some horsepower to get any change. Let's talk tomorrow morning before school and see if we can get going on this fast."

They both nodded their agreement with Ma'am's assessment.

"Bea, can you stay an extra minute?" Myrna understood this as her cue for a diplomatic retreat and she took it gracefully. Once Myrna left and the door was closed Ma'am had a few more things to say. "Bea, I can't have you misbehaving. I meant what I said. You pull any crap with me on this I will forget we were ever friends."

Ma'am had never been this directive with her. "I promise you I will behave on this one."

"You can speak your mind Bea, but you have to listen to others and compromise like we talked about with Myrna. I took some heavy artillery from Mary Jane on your behavior. I agreed you would be off the large committee. Myrna and I will be going to those meetings without you; no debate on it. You are off the group."

Bea swallowed hard at the loss of face in leaving. But a larger more important goal was perched in front of them and Ma'am had maneuvered well to keep the ball in their court. Bea understood the play that had been made nodding her acceptance.

Ma'am smiled, "Okay, tell me what else has been going on."

"I've been working with Andrea Bauer. She's hit the wall and I am worried about her."

"Really? You know as much as people think a principal has time to mentor a new teacher it's a rare day when we can do it with all the other responsibilities on our plate."

"I'm glad to do it, the girl's got great potential. I really like her, Dorothy."

"She's lucky to have you. Keep me posted on how I can help. Now get outta' here."

Bea smiled and left knowing things were moving ahead and she and Ma'am were getting back on track.

CHAPTER 17

ASSAULT & BATTERY

Andrea's mentoring by Bea was paying dividends. She'd spent three Thursdays at Bea's home eating dinner and talking about teaching. Andrea learned to rescale her expectations. Ma'am arranged a substitute for Bea to spend a day in Andrea's class and one for Andrea to spend a day in Bea's room. Tonight they shared their observations and both learned from the exchange. In fact, Andrea was proud to have shared some ideas on leveled books. It had been an eye opening experience for Bea. She saw with the right materials the strategy could lead to better student success.

Andrea was headed home from Bea's knowing she'd stop at school for a minute to pick up a few things in her classroom. She knew the school was open and a scout troop meeting was taking place. Fred left the side door to the gym unlocked for them. Since the troop met in the gym, the door could easily be watched until they all left.

It was about 7:40 when Andrea pulled into the dark parking lot. She had stepped out of her car when a black BMW skidded right next it. The first guy out of the car jumped up onto the hood of Andrea's Honda and ran across it, jumping down to block entry back into her car. The other two began circling like hungry wolves getting ready to leap on their prey.

They began to sexually taunt her using their fists with a thumb projected as substitutes for their male anatomy. Andrea stood in the dark corner of the parking lot, her body shaking and sweating from every pore. She had nowhere to go. The only thought she had was to yell something in the hope someone would hear and come running or call for help. In a voice cracking with terror she screamed, "What do you want?"

One of the thugs whispered in her ear, "You know what we want, pretty girl like you." Andrea was holding back her tears and in a voice now trembling with fear pleaded with them, "Let me go please." Andrea's mind began putting the pieces together. These were the guys who watched her turn onto Bea's street when she went there for dinner. They were on all sides of her now, so close she could feel them rubbing against her. Their faces were only inches away. One of them was breathing in her ear, another was looking directly in her face, but saying nothing. The third was moving his hands across her body and she could feel him pressing against her. Andrea believed she was about to be gang raped. "Survive," she told herself, "Just survive!"

Andrea couldn't believe her eyes as Bea's big Crown Vic came hurtling into the school parking lot. She slammed on her brakes screeching to a stop at an angle twenty feet from the BMW. She stepped out, but made no move towards the three young men. "Germain, you and the boys get your sorry asses in the car and leave right now! You understand what I'm sayin'? I've called the cops; they'll be here right quick."

"We just talkin' to this pretty teacher."

"You go sweet talk your mama!"

"Shut up you old bitch! You get outta here before we come over there and sweet talk you!"

Bea, moved away from her car taking some steps towards the punks. Bea knew they had guns and things could go a number of ways. The only advantage she had was she knew each of them. Two she had taught and they knew when Bea was totally serious. "You boys get your asses movin' right now!"

Germain was not ready to leave. He pulled his gun from the big pocket in the front of his sweatshirt. Holding it out straight-armed, twisted gangster style, he looked Bea in the eye. "You bitch," he said. In the next instant he pulled the trigger, bam, bam, bam!

Andrea dropped to the ground screaming, "Oh God, Bea!"

The first two shots struck Bea's car; the third hit Bea knocking her backwards.

Germain turned on Andrea, he held the gun inches from her face. Rage was in his eyes and Andrea thought she was surely going to die in the next instant.

In the background sirens began to wail and the three assailants knew the cops were coming. "Germain, come on. We gotta get out of here now!"

Germain saw Bea was hit, but sensed his shot was not fatal. He decided killing two women was not the thing to do. "Neither of these bitches is worth anything. Let's go," he said.

Once they were gone, Andrea picked herself up from the ground and ran to where Bea was lying. Bea looked up, "I'm okay girl. They hit me in my shoulder." Andrea was sobbing and her body was soaked from a sweat formed by terror. She cradled Bea in her arms as the police cars came rushing into the parking lot. Bea closed her eyes succumbing to the shock and pain of her wound.

Soon the parking lot was ablaze with flashing lights. Police radios could be heard blaring out commands and inquiries. The parking lot also held the boy-scout troop that had been in the gym. The boys saw Bea on a gurney knowing she was hurt and Andrea huddled near Bea with a blanket around her shoulders. The police were talking in earnest with Andrea. At first they wondered if Andrea shot Bea. But they could tell by what was happening this was far from the case.

Andrea gave the police a description of the car, the three men and the fact one was called Germain. She told them two others were former students of Bea's. With this information they knew arrests would likely be made soon.

Andrea went with Bea to the hospital to be checked out. The medics asked her who they should contact and Andrea told them her parents. They assured her they'd also tell her parents she was okay.

The police notified Ma'am about what had occurred. Because this was a serious event which happened on school grounds, Ma'am immediately called John Handler inform him. Knowing the press carefully monitored the police radio, the cops knew this was going to be a major media event. They had to get control of the crime scene and take statements from the boy-scout leader and the boys to determine if they had seen anything. It was going to be a busy night in the School #3 parking lot.

Ma'am immediately headed to General Hospital to see how Bea and Andrea were doing. Upon arriving, she learned Bea was in surgery for a gunshot wound that did not appear life threatening.

Ma'am found Andrea in an emergency room cubicle. Andrea was sitting on a bed holding her hands to her head, crying softly. Her clothes were covered with Bea's blood. Ma'am came to her side. Sitting next to her, she held Andrea's hand offering her comfort and support. Ma'am wasn't there long when Andrea's parents came rushing into the cubicle. It was an emotional reunion. Andrea gave up any pretense of composure, sobbing heavily in her mother's arms. It was ten minutes before things settled down. Andrea then shared the experience from start to finish with her mom, dad and Ma'am.

Andrea's dad felt helpless but growled, "If I get my hands on those sons a bitches,"

"Shush Craig!" her mom scolded. "We don't need any more violence than what's already happened."

Ma'am excused herself, knowing Andrea was now in good hands. Before leaving Ma'am told Andrea's mom she'd call tomorrow; both women agreed Andrea would not be expected at work on Friday.

Ma'am left the emergency room, only to be greeted by a phalanx of cameras and microphones. Ma'am looked at them firmly stating, "I do not have much more to report than what you may already know. Fourth Grade teacher Bea Johnson was shot in the School #3 parking lot. She's in surgery as we speak. Andrea Bauer is also a fourth grade teacher at School #3. She's been through an ordeal, but has suffered no physical harm."

A reporter shouted out, "Was she raped?"

Looking truly upset by the brazen question, Ma'am glared at the reporter and said, "No."

She then moved to the quiet security of her car. Ma'am knew this was only the beginning of a long string of events which would take place. She had to update John Handler. She also had to notify the school's crisis team knowing they would need to meet in the morning. Ma'am decided the building phone tree should be activated notifying all the staff of an emergency faculty meeting before school started tomorrow.

Ma'am met with the crisis team at 6:45 AM. They discussed the things they needed to do. It was agreed Ma'am would send a letter home explaining the incident. The letter was to assure parents they were taking steps to ensure their children's safety. The letter would also encourage parents to listen to their children's comments about the event and to contact the school if any support was needed. The team discussed how they would help the staff. This was an incident that would upset them. Janey Eisen was present, and this time Ma'am welcomed her support and coordination of any contact with the press.

Ma'am knew the staff had to be told the full story of what had transpired and Bea's current condition. Her surgery had been successful, but her shoulder may need a second operation at some point since the bone damage caused by the bullet was significant.

The staff met in the library. John Handler decided to be present at the meeting, but he wanted Ma'am to speak to the staff before he said anything himself.

Ma'am, began by summarizing the confrontation. A number of people had tears and visible emotional reactions to what occurred. It was agreed the staff social committee would send fruit baskets to both Bea and Andrea. They also would circulate a card later in the day for Bea, who would likely be in the hospital for several days.

John told the staff how sorry he was about this violence. He reaffirmed his support as they worked through their emotions and concerns surrounding the incident. "We are one school family, and though you are running on empty I am confident you'll do your best to help the children."

Friday proved to be a demanding day. The press were camped out on the street in front of School #3. This created excitement and anxiousness amongst the children. It was a challenge to keep the reporters at bay, but Janey Eisen did her job effectively, informing them of the school's plan to send a letter home to parents and how everyone was doing overall. They'd all have a copy of the letter going home to parents before the end of the school day.

John Handler came out and spoke with the media. He decried the violence and asked the community to support the school as they struggled with the injury to a brave teacher and the trauma experienced by another. Janey was pleased with his statement and visit; she thought it meant a great deal to everyone he was there with them.

CHAPTER 18

ROLES & RESPONSIBILITIES

On Saturday morning John was at the office getting ready for the special meeting with his Board. It would be a private session to discuss his working relationship with them. Either he'd leave with an understanding or he'd have to seriously consider initiating another job search. He hoped the Board had a willingness to consider new options and structures for instructional delivery. Without Board support the road would be almost impossible to travel.

Before he could get down to the planned agenda, he knew he'd have to spend some time updating the Board on the status of the School #3 shooting incident. The youths involved had been arrested. The news media had their mug shots on the front page of the morning paper, they were also on line and on the TV news. All three previously attended School #3 adding to the drama of this story.

John began the meeting giving his summary of what happened. They all felt Bea was a hero and the district would need to recognize this at a future meeting. They discussed security and lamented the growing level of violence in the city, wondering when would it cease.

Once the air was cleared and questions were answered, the Board's five members moved on to the second agenda item. On the role of the superintendent, John had a good idea where two of them stood. Both Shantell Williams and Sara Fieldstone believed they should have a say in most decisions and John should be seeking their views before acting.

Don Karst owned several successful dry cleaning stores in the city. While fiscally conservative, he rarely second guessed John's actions. Emily Garza was a teacher in the suburbs. She liked John and supported him but was easily moved by whatever way the wind was currently blowing. The last member was Terrell Whitner. He was John's best supporter. A black minister in the city, he had deep roots and powerful political connections. He wanted change to take place and believed John had the skills to do it.

The Board rarely worked as a team, each having pet areas of interest. Overall, the only thing predicable with this Board was its unpredictability. This was especially true when the chips were down. John had been warned about this as an applicant. "Dysfunctional" was the word headhunters often used to describe this Board to prospective candidates.

He wondered how much progress could be made towards understanding and accepting his and their related, but different roles. It was clearly John's task to get them on the same page.

It was Shantell who spoke first. "Dr. Handler originally asked me to call this meeting to talk about his authority. He actually threatened to quit when I told him we wanted to have one of us involved at the table with the bus drivers' negotiations."

John took a deep breath, bit his tongue and decided to let Shantell continue without interruption.

"He's made it clear to me," she said, "he does not want our advice on how things should be run around here. He wants us to follow him and keep our mouths shut. I told him I couldn't agree, and he demanded this meeting."

Sara Fieldstone decided it was her turn to speak. "I feel the same way as Shantell. Dr. Handler wants to be a dictator. The man isn't listening to us. I think Carl Gardner should be fired and he won't even discuss it with me. This isn't the way we should be doing things around here. If the superintendent wants to look for another job let him."

John noticed Sara could not look at him when saying this and she often referred to him as if he wasn't even in the room. In its own way this was indicative of their behavior and the way they treated the last two superintendents. He felt it was time to enter the fray.

"Sara, I'm right here. If you want me to begin a job search then let's start the conversation by referring to each other in the first person. Quite frankly, I am willing to begin a job search if that's what this Board wants; however, it is not my desire."

Terrell Whitner looked at his fellow Board members and said, "I for one would like to hear John's take on things and I don't want anybody speaking until he's finished."

Shantell looked at her Board colleagues seeing non-verbal assent for Terrell's suggestion. He was a force to be reckoned with and Shantell was in no position to take him on.

John took a moment, stood up and moved a wheeled whiteboard to the head of the table. "I do not want to be a dictator; there's a role for all of you to play and it's critically important. But you have roles and functions so confused we are going to constantly be at each other if we don't get them defined and accepted. That's why I wanted this meeting. I don't have the energy to fight with you and at the same time take on a significant agenda for change. In fact any agenda for change will fail if you don't support me and the necessary steps to improve student learning."

Playing a teacher's role, he moved to the whiteboard and said, "Let's start by listing some of the key things you are responsible for. First on the list is employing a superintendent. It is a decision belonging solely to the Board. You also have a large book of Policies you have adopted. They guide my behaviors and everyone else's within this district. It is your responsibility to establish and set those Policies. Sure there's often input regarding them, but you have the bottom-line authority to accept, reject or modify them. You have the responsibility to establish an overall budget. Right now our budget is almost six hundred million dollars. You have a responsibility to conduct audits and to monitor expenditures. You also have the basic responsibility to hire and fire people."

Sara interrupted, "Then we can fire Carl, I knew it!" Sara was shushed by the other Board members and she slouched back in her chair.

"Now let's look at my role as the chief school officer. I have the right to organize the leadership staff in a manner I feel is most effective. You gave me that right in my employment contract. I also have the right to recommend the employment or discharge of employees. I cannot do either without your support, but you also cannot act independent of my recommendation. On employment issues we are bound together, mutually dependent on the other to act. On the budget, I have the responsibility to legally and efficiently deploy the resources. While you have clear oversight responsibilities, I have the authority to make day-to-day spending decisions. I also have the right to make operational decisions up to limits you've set in Policy. I can't and won't stop to ask your permission to make them; it's what you pay me to do. Also, and this is key, as hard as it is for you to accept, the staff works for me, not you. I don't appreciate the around-me communications you have with the staff. Those communications confuse things, sending mixed messages. You must discipline yourselves to minimize your emails and personal conversations related to administrative actions or seeking peoples' feedback on those actions."

When he finished, John had two lists, one summarizing what the superintendent does and the other what the Board has authority to do in relation to the district's business.

A long moment of silence occurred as everyone looked at the whiteboard deep in their own thoughts about it. It was Emily Garza who broke the silence. "John, limiting our staff conversation the way you describe feels like a gag order. I am really uncomfortable with that."

"Me too," Shantell spouted.

"Let's look at it from a different perspective. Suppose a teacher tells you that the Roosevelt attendance policy isn't working. Most of you would want to hear more about it. 'Why isn't it working?' you'd ask. The staff member will be happy to tell you why and to seek your opinion or help to fix it. Instead of going down that road, I'd ask you to redirect the comment back by asking, 'Have you talked with the principal about your concerns?' Look, I realize you are out there and people want to share things and you want to listen. But, I want you to be aware how much your comments get used. People have agendas and they want to let everyone know when a Board member doesn't agree with the administration. If you don't agree, or you've heard something call me. I especially don't want you calling the principal to check up on an issue. That's my job not yours. When you call them, they get confused about who is in charge and to whom they report. It's simple; they report to me and my staff not you."

This was a tough message, one that many Boards fail to comprehend. John let it rest before continuing.

"I need your constant public support. Behind these doors, you can challenge my judgment, and ask questions about specific individuals. I am accountable to you as a Board to answer them. Here's an example. We are working diligently on a quality school definition. Ultimately, I will recommend the definition as a Policy statement. You will then say yes or no as is your right. You can also at that point say yes, but we want this added, deleted or restated. That's your job. Some of you have asked me why you can't serve on this committee. I have not asked you to serve because I don't want your Board role co-opted by committee service."

Sara Fieldstone, looking at John asked, "What about Carl? I don't think he's doing a good job."

"Well Sara, in here you can say that and I need to hear your concerns. But all the same, as I've said, Carl works for me. He is a part of my staff and I feel he's doing a great job. I can give you a list of reasons why I think so. Maybe that will change your opinion; maybe it won't. As the chief negotiator, he has a bull's-eye printed on his chest. You will hear negative comments about him in the heat of collective bargaining. However, if I keep him on against the Board's wishes, that's something you hold me accountable for not him."

"So John, you are saying that you are accountable to us for the poor work of your staff?" It was Don Karst who asked this.

"In essence yes, I recommended them for hire and I evaluate their work. If a pattern of staff errors and poor work is occurring then it's a leadership issue I must address. If I don't do that to your satisfaction, that is something we need to talk about as a part of my job performance."

The discussion went back and forth on various issues for almost two hours without stopping. They all needed a stretch and a break in the tension. After fifteen minutes they returned to summarize where things stood.

Sitting back at the table, it was Terrell Whitner who spoke first. "You know I am a strong supporter of John's. We've been through a lot over the past several years. We have not had a good fit with the past two superintendents and we blamed it on them. Now we're grumbling again about fit. It's time we held up a mirror and talked about whether we're the problem." Terrell, pointing at John continued, "I trust this man. I think he's on the right track and we've got to let him do the work. How do the rest of you feel about it?"

Emily Garza spoke saying she was with Terrell; she had no appetite for looking for another superintendent. Don Karst reinforced her view.

That left Sara and Shantell. Sara said, "You know John, I don't like Carl, I think he's arrogant and difficult with people. But other than our strong disagreement about him, I can support what the others are saying."

Shantell was no fool. She saw the political momentum of this conversation and was too fond of her president's role to jeopardize it by being out of step with the other four members. But she had a serious point to make before she let the conversation end.

"John, I did not appreciate you threatening to resign. If we are to trust you, then we need to know you'll stay with us and not jump onto a new district when things here get tough. I want a guarantee you'll finish your contract."

Everyone was now looking at John feeling Shantell did have a point.

"I'm willing to consider something. Let me make a proposal to you by the end of the month." Head nods around the table acknowledged consent.

Then Shantell spoke again, "John you should leave here knowing we do trust you and we will support you. However, maybe I am a minority of one, but I still think you want too much control. So I want more sessions like this where we can clear the air and keep things moving forward."

John knew it was a beginning but he'd still have a great deal of work to do to keep his Board informed yet flying at 30,000 feet rather than micro-managing at ground level. He also knew because they said they understood things today, tomorrow would bring new perspectives and concerns. Old habits would die slow and hard with this group. Not for the first time, he seriously questioned whether or not this Board could hold up under the stress of a serious change agenda.

CHAPTER 19

THE DECISION

Andrea was shaken to the core when she returned from the hospital on Thursday night. She knew a call to Jason was necessary, even though it was almost midnight. When she reached him he was distant and aloof, having already heard about the shooting and the fact Andrea was a victim on the 11:00 news.

Andrea tried to tell him about her experience, but Jason was too hurt to give her his full attention. Speaking through his emotions he said, "I am so relieved you are alright, but I can't believe you didn't call me right away! I feel left out of your life and I am not sure what to say or think. The one thing I can tell you is I am not surprised. I kept telling you it was too dangerous there. Now maybe you'll believe me!"

Andrea told Jason she was alright and she had a lot on her mind. They'd talk more when things settled down.

Andrea's mom was holding a late night cup of coffee in a shaky hand while she looked at her grown daughter sitting there. She wasn't sure what to say. She surmised Andrea was moving away from Jason, despite her strong feelings for him and wondered if Jason might be another victim of the night's horrible events.

Andrea's dad walked out to the driveway when the police brought Andrea's car to their home. With the outside light on he saw the dents and scratches on the hood of her Honda. They were clear evidence of the altercation which happened only a few short hours ago. He looked at the car knowing it was only three months old. However, the car's condition suggested it was much older. His whole body tensed as he clenched his fists, anger and frustration competing for his attention.

When they got home Andrea shared with them she was on the verge of giving up. Her mom gave her a tender hug and said, "Let's get some sleep and see where things are in the morning."

Andrea crawled into her childhood bed with the terror of the experience replaying in her thoughts. However, the bed did its part by cradling her in its warmth and security as she finally drifted to sleep.

The next morning Ma'am called Andrea. She said Bea was doing much better after surgery and likely would go home sometime next week.

Ma'am asked her how she was doing. Andrea, choked down her tears and told Ma'am she wasn't sure how she felt. Ma'am asked if she could pick her up for lunch on Saturday. Andrea was pleasantly surprised by the offer.

Just before noon on Saturday Andrea was a comfortable passenger in Ma'am's silver Lexus. While in that quiet setting Ma'am asked Andrea how she was doing. "I am having a real hard time," Andrea said as tears welled in her eyes.

"I'd be surprised if you weren't. You know we all are worried about you. It was a horrible experience for anyone to go through."

"I am feeling responsible for Bea being shot. If I hadn't stopped at school this wouldn't have happened!"

Ma'am consoled her, "You can't take on such a burden. You had every right to stop by school. It should be safe for you to do that. The fact it wasn't isn't your fault."

"But it isn't safe at night. I should have known better. People keep telling me it's too dangerous for me to work at School #3. My boyfriend thinks I should quit."

"Well nobody can tell you what to do. You are a grown woman and you have to make up your own mind."

They pulled into a nearby restaurant where a booth beckoned. Once they were seated with their order placed, Ma'am spoke with Andrea about teaching and her work at School #3. "Andrea, there are some things I need to share with you. I hope they will help you as you make up your mind on what to do. When you were first assigned to my school, I told Carl Gardner I didn't want you, I wanted somebody with experience to replace Riley." Andrea gave Ma'am an incredulous look thinking, 'How was this going to make her want to stay?'

"It wasn't long after you arrived Bea started telling me you have a gift for teaching. I have witnessed it myself as I've watched you work with the children. Bea told me about your planning struggles and I know she's mentoring you. She's never done that with anyone before. She believes you were guided to us by Riley. She's a lot more religious than me, but I can tell you now, how wrong I was to want someone other than you to take Riley's place. School #3 is better because you bring yourself through its front door."

Andrea was comforted by Ma'am's comments and sincerity. It felt good to know she'd earned her respect. But she was still struggling with the fresh memory of that terrifying experience. "Ma'am, I don't know. I was stupid to go back at night the way I did. I know that now. But when I pull into the parking lot I'm afraid I will relive what happened there."

"I know, it was an awful experience. But you have a gift for teaching Andrea, and forgive me if I'm selfish, but I want you to continue to share it at School #3."

Andrea told Ma'am on the way back to her parents' home she had given her a great deal to think about. Andrea said she'd call Ma'am tomorrow with her decision. Ma'am offered a substitute to cover her class for a few more days if she needed more time. Andrea thanked her and assured her she'd let her know.

Ma'am left it at that. She'd given it her all and knew she'd have to respect whatever decision Andrea made. In fact, she wasn't sure what she would do if she found herself in the same circumstances at Andrea's young age. But as she left the driveway, she said a silent prayer to Riley hoping she'd find a way to intercede.

Ma'am's Saturday work wasn't finished when she left Andrea behind in the driveway. She went to the hospital to see Bea. True to form when she arrived at the hospital Bea was more concerned about Andrea than herself.

"I know you met with Andrea. How is she doin'?"

"She's really shaken and is struggling about whether or not to return."

Bea looked at her intently, "She'll come 'round, she loves her kids."

"I hope you're right. Carl plans to offer her an immediate transfer to another school if she wants it. There's an opening at School #18 because of a child care leave. It's a third grade."

"I'm tellin' ya Dorothy, Andrea will come back. She's strong. Like I said, she loves her kids, no transfer is gonna win out."

"Okay, okay, now let's talk about you. How are you feeling?"

"The doctors say I'm a tough one. They say I can go home on Monday if I keep getting better and don't get an infection in this shoulder of mine. But they tell me I can't go back to work for a while. We'll see about that!"

"Well let's take it one day at a time Bea. Your job right now is to get better, then get back to work. In that order, you hear me?"

"Yes, I do hear ya. But I'd like to drop by school the end of next week to see my kids and friends. Will that be okay?"

"Yes, as long as your doctors say it is."

Bea and Ma'am talked for about an hour. When Bea's eyes started to droop, Ma'am knew it was time to leave and let her recovery continue with the aid of some well-deserved sleep.

Carl Gardner called on Saturday afternoon after Ma'am met with Andrea. He told her if she wanted a transfer from School #3 it could be arranged in light of what went down. He told her School #18 had an opening in third grade. Andrea expressed her appreciation for the call and the opportunity to be transferred. She told him she'd think about all he said.

Throughout the weekend teachers called Andrea. Their outpouring of sympathy and support was terrific and it made a deep impression on her. School #3 was a family, and she was clearly a valued member.

In the end Andrea knew she was bonded to the children in her class. It was through her work with the children she could ultimately get past the event. She called Ma'am on Sunday to tell her about her decision. Ma'am was delighted, telling her if she needed anything, they'd be there to provide support.

As Andrea reflected on what had occurred, she knew Monday was going to be a trying day. She hoped she was up to it.

CHAPTER 20

JOINING FORCES

On the Monday after the School #3 shooting John had a great deal on his plate. He wanted to write a thoughtful summary of his Saturday meeting with the Board. He felt something in writing would be helpful as a reference. He was looking at the whiteboard and gathering his thoughts. His assistant, Ann Stanley, knew it had been a rough weekend and her boss had gone the extra mile on many levels. But there she was having to tell him the mayor was on the phone hoping to talk with him.

John smiled at Ann as she closed his office door. He picked up the phone and wished Jane Hueset a good morning.

"John, I know how busy you must be, but I am hoping you could make some time for me to drop by today. I'd like to talk with you about the violence we're experiencing, not just this most recent shooting, but all that's taking place in our city."

There was something different in Jane's voice. John sensed her frustration and fatigue, and he understood it. "How about 1:00 o'clock?"

John stepped out of his office after completing the conversation to tell Ann the mayor would be coming at 1:00 o'clock. "That's a first," she said.

"Yes, she sounds as troubled as we are about all the violence taking place. Maybe out of these terrible events there's a chance we can finally get on the same page. I'm encouraged by her call and the fact she is coming over here. We'll see."

His morning passed quickly and before he knew it the mayor was sitting in one of the comfortable chairs in his office.

Janey Eisen had seen the mayor come in and asked Ann, "What's up?"

"They're talking. The mayor asked if she could drop by."

Janey smiled for the first time in several days as she headed back to her office.

"John, I feel like we are losing the battle more days than we are winning. The chief wants me to hire more police officers. He says he needs more boots on the ground. We can't afford much more and I'm not sure they are getting at the root cause of the violence anyway."

"I understand Jane. You know we finished a similar conversation with our bus drivers about needing more help. Like you, I know we can't afford to do much more. I feel like we are just addressing the overt side of this problem, not getting down to the causes for it."

"John, what do you see as the cause?"

"Jane, I think generational poverty is the most basic issue. But we've failed on many fronts. I am reminded of an old quote from Daniel Webster who said, *'The intelligence of the people is the security of the nation.'* We have not successfully addressed it in the city. Our families have a history of poor education and poor jobs which results in crime and distress. We have to figure out a way to break the cycle of poverty. Until we do, I believe we'll only be treating the most outward symptoms of the problem. Too often the most visible symptoms are rooted in violence."

"I don't disagree with you about the effects of poverty. But John, our social services budget is wheeling out of control. How much more can we do to stop what's happening?"

"Jane, I think we've got to stop thinking short-term and start thinking long-term. We have to figure out how to get a toehold on this problem. I think we have to start small and carefully build out from there."

"Do you have something specific in mind?"

"Yes and no. I am leading an entitlement culture with lots of momentum to maintain the status quo. It's steeped in tradition and grade structures. It is hemmed in by regulations and labor contracts. As a result, nothing happens easily or quickly. I think these issues have become the excuse for public education not to change. It's led to the charter school movement as an alternative. But charter schools aren't the solution. I think public schools can change, but it will take a lot of political will and practical thinking to do it. However, I do have an evolving strategy to get the ball rolling which I am trying to implement, one step at a time. I'm not naïve and am not sure if it will work. But standing still is no longer a viable option. That's why *right now* we have to get moving."

"Are you willing to share it with me? I am open to it. It's time we started working together. I have to admit I have been difficult to work with at times."

"Oh really," John was smiling as he said it. Somehow he felt a real opportunity for a breakthrough in their relationship was possible and it was up to him to take a risk. He decided to fall forward as he often encouraged others to do.

"Okay if you'll put up with a small example from me to make a point I'll tell you what I have in mind."

"What's the example?"

"Jane you are a skilled politician. You wouldn't be mayor of this city if you weren't. You have a deep understanding of civic issues and the democratic process. You also have a college degree from a prestigious institution, so this should be easy for you. I have three questions I'd like to ask you in the privacy of this office. Are you game?"

Jane wasn't sure where this was going, but she saw the grin on John's face and trusted it would not be too painful to play along. "Sure," she said.

"Okay here's the three questions:"

1. *What was the main reason the Articles of Confederation were replaced as the basis for US Government?*
2. *What was the major problem facing American farmers in the 1920's?*
3. *In which case did the United States Supreme Court rule that segregated public facilities were constitutional?*

Jane looked at him with a blank stare and asked, "Do you know the answers?"

John smiled, "Only because I have the answer key. But our kids are supposed to answer questions like these in order to get a high school diploma. I am not saying testing is a bad thing, but how many of us remember this stuff after we graduate. We push them like racehorses around the track to get better scores on tests. Getting a diploma and moving on in life rides on knowing the answers to questions like those.

When we add the other required exams for graduation, it is a daunting task for a lot of our kids. Of course we are all rated on whether we're passing or failing schools based on those results.

I have been working with teachers, administrators and some community folks on developing a wider definition of quality. We have four major themes identified in our outline of quality. Those themes are: *Student Success, Learning Environment, Educational Programs* and *School Culture.* Under these headings we are defining what attributes are connected with each theme. If we can get acceptance of the broader definition then maybe we can re-examine whether or not test scores should play such a dominate role in getting a diploma."

"Are you saying you want to make it easier to get a diploma?"

"No, I am saying we have to be receptive to multiple definitions for student success. We have focused on what kids' can memorize for tests, but we've lost sight of how knowledge is applied and what students can create with their minds and hands. I am not comfortable with defining student success based solely upon an American history trivia exam even you and I can no longer pass.

Once we have a better definition we can ask schools to start thinking about new ways to meet the broader statement of quality. Then I hope new answers will begin to surface. Creating the right conditions for learning will take on different forms depending on the age, interests and unique abilities of our students."

"That's interesting John, but pardon me for saying it sounds like a lot of educational gibberish and not much for getting at the issues we were talking about."

"I know, but I need to get people, including you, accepting our success is dependent on more than good test scores. I can't do that if I don't have something sound to offer as a better definition of overall quality. If we stay focused just on test scores then high school graduation rates are not going to change much and the poverty cycle will not be broken."

"I'm still not sure where you are going John. I came here worried about violence and what we can do to decrease it. I can't see how this will do anything in that regard."

"Okay, I hear you. Let me try a different approach. Jane, we have long-term poverty straining all of our resources and defeating many of our best efforts to make a difference. I think we need to start over with our systems and strategies. This is particularly true with our youngest students. Too often they are far behind before they even enter school. We see it in neglect, poor medical care, lead paint issues; the list is a long one. I am trying to create an environment where people think outside the box; something very hard for those of us in the schools to do. I am hoping a quality discussion might be the entry point."

"Okay John, suppose I sign on to that effort. What are we going to do in the meantime?"

"Jane, I know you must have something in mind yourself or you wouldn't be here. How do we work together on this?"

"I'd like to form a joint task force on violence. I would ask you and some others from the school, including Cliff Greer, to join with us. I want key civic leaders and people from both parties. This cannot be seen as a political maneuver."

"I would certainly support it by my participation. I also think we should get some social services experts involved as well. But I've got to tell you, like your feelings on the quality school effort, I am not sure it's going to bring much real change unless we get down to ground-level issues and new models for delivery of all services, including schooling."

"John I think it's time this community saw us united in a broad effort. I am willing to publicly support your initiatives if you'll join me in mine."

"That's pretty open-ended for both of us isn't it?" John said. "We haven't really had a trusting relationship on much and now we'd be jumping into the deep end of the pool holding hands."

"I know, the water could be quite cold John. We'd have to establish improved lines of communication with people seeing our support for that. We'd need to communicate regularly and openly so we can sort out issues and be on the same page. I am willing to do it. This violence and our lack of success, from the streets to the schools has to change."

"I am glad to hear you say that Jane. Neither of us is naïve about this and we're both going to be taking some serious risks in depending on each other in a different way. But I am willing to give it a go."

"Speaking of 'Right Now' are you willing to make it our theme collectively and start flying the pennant from city hall?"

Jane thought for a moment. It was the first of many thresholds they'd have to cross on each other's behaviors. She looked at him smiling, "Yup, if we can announce it in a joint press conference. We could also confirm our partnership to prevent violence."

"You got it. When do we hold the conference?" John asked.

"Let's tell them we want to go on-the-record together at noon tomorrow."

After the mayor left, John knew a real breakthrough in their relationship occurred. Maybe they could do something together to change things in the long-term.

CHAPTER 21

Q & A

Carl Gardner had to undertake the active investigation of the sexual harassment complaint filed by Ron Post. He also was trying to wrap up the final contract language with the bus drivers so the document could be ratified and signed by both the superintendent and union president. As with any negotiation, the devil is in the details. After the concepts were agreed to at the bargaining table, it could prove difficult to put them in print.

Carl knew vice principal, Janice Mills reasonably well, and respected her. She'd earned an excellent reputation as a VP at Columbus Middle School. She had good follow through, a sound work ethic and was trusted by her principal Susan Corner. It was surprising to him she'd be caught up in a complaint like this. But there it was, and he had to keep an open mind on things.

Carl asked Janice to come downtown on Tuesday morning. He felt it would draw less attention to Janice than if he went to her office for the interview he now had to conduct. Janice understood his logic and was grateful for his discretion.

After they were seated at the conference table, Carl confirmed she had chosen to come without any representation from her union or from outside counsel. He advised her he would be taping the interview and all of their conversation would be on-the-record. Janice was a bit surprised by the formality Carl was demonstrating but knew this was a serious matter requiring careful documentation.

Carl began by asking Janice if she was aware of Ron's complaint. Janice said, "Yes." He then asked Janice to tell him about the meeting between Ron and her.

"Ron came to my office to talk about a parent conference we were going to do together. The mother was a difficult one. Ron felt she would be resistant and defensive. Because of this, he'd wanted me to be with him. I knew the boy was a real problem. He'd often been absent or late from school and was sullen in his behaviors. Ron suspected mom was a prostitute. Given this, we talked about who'd take the lead regarding its impact on her son. I told Ron he was the classroom teacher and I felt he had the best knowledge of her son Jeremy's behaviors. I did kid him saying knowing mom's interests, she might find him attractive. In hindsight it may not have been a good thing to say, but I was kidding. We talked about the timing for the conference and agreed we'd try to schedule it for after school. Anyway, we talked briefly about my role, I would remind mom of our responsibility to assure Jeremy was in school and we'd be referring his absences to the school district's attendance officer. We hoped this might push mom to get out of bed and make sure Jeremy got on the bus in the morning. I also was going to ask mom for her support in referring Jeremy for a psych exam. This could help us understand what appeared to be his depression and sullen behaviors. That was it. Ron left; the next thing I knew Susan was telling me Ron had marched to her office to say I'd sexually harassed him."

"Did you see any changes in Ron's demeanor or did he make any comments to you indicating he might be uncomfortable with what you said?"

"No, he didn't say anything. I was sitting at my desk and he was in the chair on the other side. He didn't get up or do anything that made me feel like he was offended."

"Was your office door closed while you were talking?"

"Yes, it was a sensitive issue and I didn't want anyone who might come into the office to overhear what we were discussing."

"So your secretary didn't witness any of this?"

"No, Linda was in the outer office. Like I said, my door was closed. Carl, can I ask you a question? Susan told me Ron filed a sexual harassment complaint with her but she hasn't told me what he claims I did. Will you tell me?"

"I have not spoken directly to Ron yet so I don't know the specific points of his complaint. Until I do, I would rather not characterize it. You do have a right to know the specifics. After I meet with him this afternoon, I will share them with you. Can you come in again tomorrow morning?"

Janice was disappointed with Carl's sidestepping, but she knew him well enough to know nothing more was going to be forthcoming from him today. "I guess that's the way it will go then. I'll have to keep guessing what I supposedly did for another day. This whole thing is distressing."

"I know Janice. You are going to have to trust the process and wait for the details. I have to make a report of findings to Dr. Handler. I hope to complete my report this week, so you will hear soon."

"Not soon enough Carl, this is awful!"

Carl noticed Janice's trembling hands and near loss of composure as she spoke those words. He knew he had to draw this whole mess to a close for everyone's sake. He felt Janice had been forthright, but her story was different than the one the Columbus principal shared with the superintendent.

Carl had a lunch meeting with Joanne Walters, the Middle School level's Assistant Superintendent for Instruction. She was interested to hear Carl's take on the sexual harassment complaint. She also wanted to talk with Carl about the rumors running through district office.

They went to their usual spot down the street; a busy diner, noisy with mid-day business conversations. Sitting in a corner booth, Joanne began. "Carl, what do you hear about the superintendent leaving?"

"What are you talking about Joanne? I haven't heard anything."

"Carl, where have you been? The whole office is buzzing. John had an unscheduled special meeting with the Board on Saturday. Then the mayor came over to the office on Monday afternoon; she's never done that Carl. People think John has an offer somewhere else and even the mayor is asking him to stay on."

"Look, Joanne, you know how rumors go. I haven't seen any indication John's an applicant anywhere."

"Carl, we've all talked about how discouraged he's been. He's taken some real shots on his agenda and people think he's throwing in the towel."

"Joanne, has anyone spoken to John about this? You know he's a straight shooter. If he's got something going on with his career here, I really think he'd share it. Besides, I don't see him as somebody who easily folds his tent and leaves."

"I don't know Carl. Maybe you are right and it is just a rumor. I sure hope that's the case!" After their lunch was served, Joanne asked Carl where things stood on his investigation of the Post complaint. "I hoped to do the interviews with Janice and Ron yesterday, but then the School #3 shooting and all the follow-up work on it filled the day. Believe it or not, because it happened at school, a workers' compensation component is a part of this. We spent considerable time sorting things out. Bea has a serious shoulder injury and there's an open question on our comp liability. Anyway, I did interview Janice this morning and I thought she was very forthcoming. I have a meeting scheduled after school today with Ron Post and Cliff Greer. I will need to hear his side of the story before I can make any sense of this. Have you heard anything on it?"

"No, it's been pretty quiet over at Columbus. That's to everyone's credit. Ron hasn't said anything to anyone from what Susan has told me. Of course Janice is upset. She's embarrassed over this whole thing."

"I talked with Cliff in my office last week when this surfaced. While he is worried about it getting out and what it could do, he assured me he would keep the matter confidential at this time. I trust him. He won't say or do anything until we've made a judgment. I'm confident of that."

"Well, I think you need to get to a judgment as quickly as you can Carl. Susan is really stressed out and she tells me Janice is holding on by a thread."

Carl listened to this and it reminded him of his need to meet with Susan to see what may have been disclosed since they had talked on the phone about the initial complaint.

As they walked back to the office, Joanne said she was going to tell John about all the rumors circulating. She was really worried they might be true.

Carl looked at his watch and knew his day was far from over. He thought he'd place a call to Susan when he got back to his office. When he tried to reach Susan, her secretary shared with him she was doing a teacher observation. Following that, she had a suspension hearing and two parent meetings. She was not going to be free until well after 4:00. Carl set up a phone appointment for the next morning. He thought it might work out better anyway as he'd have had his meeting with Ron Post.

When 4:00 came, Ron and Cliff were waiting to meet with him. Cliff agreed he would be a silent observer during the conversation. Once they were seated Carl took out his tape recorder and advised Ron the interview would be on the record and the tape recording would be a part of the record. Cliff, although he promised to remain silent, asked Carl, "Did you tape Ms. Mills' interview?"

Carl frowned, but quickly answered, "Yes."

"Ron, I would like you to tell me in your own words what happened."

"I went to Ms. Mills' office to discuss a parent conference. I have a boy in my class I think may be neglected and he is often absent or late for school. His mom has not taken my calls and seems to be resistant to any school contacts. I wanted Ms. Mills' help on what I thought would be a tough conversation with a difficult parent."

"Go on, tell me about your conversation with Ms. Mills."

"I was getting to it. I wanted you to know why I was meeting with Ms. Mills, but I suppose you already know that."

Carl sensed the defensiveness, but he let it pass keeping an open posture to Ron and letting him know he was there to hear his story.

"I was talking with Ms. Mills about the mother. I think she's a prostitute and it's a major reason why things at home are such a mess. Then she says to me, well you'd better have me there, she may come on to you. You know you are a handsome guy and most women around here are attracted to you."

"Did you say anything to her when she said that?" Carl asked.

"Not really, I tried to laugh it off. It really caught me off guard."

"What happened next?"

"Well she looked at me, kinda funny and then she said, 'You know Ron I think you are a handsome man too.' That made me really uncomfortable. Man, I know she's single, but I'd never had a cougar come after me. I didn't know what to do. So I finished as quick as I could and got out of there! Then I went to Dr. Corner and told her what happened."

"Ron, why didn't you tell Ms. Mills she was making you uncomfortable?"

"I should have, but I was so surprised I just wanted to leave. She's my boss so I didn't expect her to come on to me the way she did."

"Is there anything else you want to say, or anything you want to ask me?"

"Yes, Mr. Gardner what happens now? I mean I am real uncomfortable and I have to work there. We talk to our VP a lot and I am afraid to be alone in an office with her."

"The next step for me in this process is to interview Dr. Corner and Linda St. James. Then I will make a report to Dr. Handler. He has to make a judgment based on my recommendation. I expect to make my report to Dr. Handler by this Friday. In the meantime, if you have any issues needing administrative attention take them to Dr. Corner and she'll handle them."

Cliff asked if he could talk with Carl after he had a few minutes alone with Ron. Carl agreed as he was interested in Cliff's take on this.

When Cliff returned he said to Carl, "This is a tough one isn't it?"

"Yes they both told me believable stories. In fact there's a fair amount of overlap between them, but some real differences too. Nobody but the two of them were there so I am at a loss right now on where the real truth is on what happened."

"Well Carl, Ron is pretty shook up over this. You are going to have to do something to settle the waters."

"Cliff, do you have any suggestions?"

"Not at this point, Carl. Let's talk Thursday about it after you've had a chance to finish your interviews. Between now and then I'll talk with Ron and see what he thinks should happen."

"Okay, let's leave it there for now. I appreciate your help on this. I don't know what to think about it with what I have now."

CHAPTER 22

ARCHITECTS & ANGST

John Handler along with Tom Wheaton, the chief financial officer and the district's three assistant superintendents were poised to meet with members of the firm hired to do a comprehensive assessment of the condition of all district facilities. Bud Peck, the head of buildings and grounds also was asked to attend the meeting. This morning they were going to discuss the preliminary architectural and engineering report.

The lead architect on the assessment project was Sara Vaughn. Sara was a talented architect and an able presenter. She had an understanding of school buildings and their needs. She worked for a top flight firm and led their public facilities division. Accompanying her to the meeting was another architect and an engineer who guided the work of the mechanical (plumbing and electric) assessment group.

After some casual conversation Sara got down to business. She provided a PowerPoint summary highlighting the major aspects of the assessment. Her presentation began with the words, "Creating the right conditions for learning." Moving into the substance, Sara told those assembled the first area was a category labeled, "Reconstruction." The school buildings included in this aspect of the summary were judged to be in need of replacement, not repair. Sara said, "These schools are beyond even extensive repairs. We see major faults in their structural integrity as well as mechanical problems beyond a repair or replacement stage. The elementary schools on this list are #'s 3, 7 8 and 11. Also on the list is Jefferson High School. Based upon our review of the square footage of each school and the most recent bids for similar structures across this region of the state we'd estimate the construction of a new elementary school would likely cost $17 million. The high school's replacement cost would exceed $100 million." Not only did these figures take the oxygen out of the room; but, everyone was surprised by the number of schools on the rebuild list.

John asked, "Why do you think replacement is the best option? Can you give us a little more detail?"

Jack Ellington, the mechanical engineer took on John's question.

While Jack was a knowledgeable engineer, he came across as pompous. He had a deep voice and a slow, condescending delivery style. "Well Dr. Handler, let's start with the heating systems. They are ancient in these schools. The boilers are in terrible shape and need to be replaced. Steam heats these schools. When heat is called for valves need to open to release the steam to the area needing it. These valves are pneumatically controlled. They often stick or just fail. New valve systems are electric, they can be set room-by-room and can be computer controlled. So bottom line we've got a complete heating system replacement. Complicating replacement, nearly every current pipe is wrapped in asbestos. Next, the electrical panels and circuit breakers are so old we can't get any replacement parts for them. We've got so many systems cobbled together it's simply a disaster waiting to happen. If we get a major breakdown, you would have to close the affected school for several months to get repairs completed. Dr. Handler, if I go on to the general plumbing status in these buildings we'll be talking all morning. The pipes in many places are galvanized and…"

"Okay Jack, I've got the picture. These building are just this side of falling down right?"

"Dr. Handler, mechanically speaking, they already have!"

Sara, trying to recapture everyone's attention, summarized the serious structural problems with the buildings noting windows, doors, and roof replacement issues. "At some point you cross the line. It's like a car with two hundred fifty thousand miles on it. Things wear out and you do a cost/benefit analysis of what's needed and it becomes easier to rebuild."

"Okay," the financial guy, Tom Wheaton spoke up, "Doing the math here we've got an estimated one hundred eighty-two million total for the proposed reconstruction of five schools. Right?"

Sara nodded in agreement with the number adding, "I'd feel better if we rounded it up to two hundred million though."

John noted, "If we gave the go ahead today, it would be almost four years from now when they'd come on line by my estimate. Will these schools make it that long?"

Sara looked at him and said, "Candidly John, I don't think you'll go long without some major mechanical failures. So you may be forced into a circumstance where you have to make an expensive repair to a school you plan to tear down."

The next aspect of the assessment was the electrical and plumbing work needed at the nineteen elementary schools not listed in the replacement category. All three middle schools were included in this part of the preliminary findings along with the two remaining high schools.

The costs included upgrading electrical wiring and circuit panels and bringing fire alarm systems up to code. Creating a functioning data transmission backbone in each building for technology access was also part of the electrical summary.

Each school's boiler and air handling system had been assessed. A substantial number of boilers were either terribly inefficient or running on their last legs. Heating system pneumatic controls were often failing and needed to be replaced. Before making these repairs, an extensive asbestos abatement project would need to be undertaken. Nearly every building had floor tile and carpet replacement needs. Many had major window replacement issues as well.

The total cost in this category was absolutely staggering. It was estimated at six hundred fifty million. The team broke it down into sub categories labeled: immediate and strongly recommended. The "immediate" category totaled four hundred seventy-five million.

John announced the need for a ten minute break. His head was spinning. The scope of repairs and the costs were almost beyond comprehension. The hardest part, as he listened to the presentation, was he didn't think the assessments or the cost estimates were wrong. The full scope of problems had been laid out in detail, and the sweeping nature of the range of issues was hard to digest in one sitting.

Sara caught John for a moment before they all sat back down to continue the presentation. "Dr. Handler, I know the numbers are huge and the problems you are facing related to the condition of the district's facilities are not of your making. But I must tell you, I have worked in a lot of school systems and the overall condition of your schools is among the worst I've seen. You have a good buildings and grounds team. Frankly, I am amazed by what they've been able to do to keep your schools open. But even they have their limits on creative problem solving. You will have to make some tough decisions or the crisis state you now have is going to mature into a complete breakdown at some of your sites."

John looked at Sara, he really didn't know what to say at first. But then he said with more frustration than he intended to reveal, "I'd like you to walk a mile in these shoes. Not only do I have crumbling facilities, I have no real technology plan, outdated textbooks and labor costs we cannot sustain. We are fighting a war here against illiteracy and poverty. If the US Army went into battle with as poor resources and equipment as we have, they'd likely suffer catastrophic losses. It's not just about the condition of the facilities Sara, that would be bad enough, but I have a crisis looming on so many different fronts I am not sure what to do first. Let's finish your report. I really don't have a clue on how we can manage this level of neglect and decay without significant help!"

Sara was getting an education. Her team focused solely on the physical structures, but the district's staff faced more than just fixing or replacing buildings.

It seemed almost anti-climatic but next came roofs. The team learned the roof area over all the schools could be measured in acres. Unfortunately the acreage was in a sorry state. Seven schools, including Hudson and Columbus Middle Schools needed complete roof replacements. Since they were beyond their useful lifespan, leaks and water damage issues were significant problems. In addition to these immediate full replacements, five more roofs were judged to be in need of substantial repair. The estimated costs for roof replacements and repairs totaled twenty-three million. When looking out over the next ten years the costs on roof repairs more than doubled.

John knew they weren't finished yet. "Sara, what other terrific news do you have for us?"

"Dr. Handler we have driveway and parking lot repairs and a whole host of odds and ends. Your high school outdoor stadiums need some serious attention. The bleachers are old and in many cases broken. I must also mention your bus garage facility needs a new fuel island and new bus lifts. Also your district office building has some structural cracking that should be addressed."

The team spent another hour covering all these additional issues. When the presentation was finished John and his team were looking at a total bill crossing the billion dollar finish line.

Nobody really knew what to say. The costs were simply mind blowing. Sara and her team knew they'd overwhelmed the group with their summary of needed repairs. However, they were asked to do a comprehensive study and they shared their best professional advice.

After Sara and her team left, the conversation amongst the leadership team was a sight to behold. They were so surprised by the sweeping nature of the problem they spoke sporadically about it. Nobody knew where to start.

The high school level's assistant superintendent, Jerry Croton, was usually an optimist, but today even he was taken aback. "My God John, I am thinking about the logistics of all of this. Their assessment didn't take into account how we'd coordinate all of this, and make sure we continue our instructional program. We can't do this without a lot of help. The costs on logistics weren't even mentioned, but they'll be huge."

"I know Jerry. We can't ignore the report can we? But without a tremendous influx of money not much can be done. Let's sit on this report for a few days and then come back together to start talking about the next steps. In the meantime I am going to have to share this information sooner or later with our Board and the mayor. Right now, I don't want this leaked. We need some think time before we let this genie out of the bottle."

A discouraged team left to attend to the day's problems and calls.

CHAPTER 23

ANDREA'S RETURN

ndrea's start back to work was helped by some quiet planning. Ma'am talked with Colleen Sheehan knowing she and Andrea were friends. She asked if Colleen would wait in the parking lot on Monday morning, believing this would be a rough spot for Andrea to overcome alone. They agreed when Andrea pulled in Colleen would step out of her car, as if she had just arrived and they could walk into school together. Colleen was willing to do this and waited patiently on Monday morning for Andrea to arrive at work. As planned, she stepped from her car when Andrea pulled in.

For her part, Andrea drove to work looking forward to getting back in her classroom. However, when she turned into the school parking lot her hands were sweating and she was becoming the victim of an active anxiety attack. What really helped more than anything was seeing Colleen step from her car, waving to Andrea. She was more than relieved to see her friend standing there.

As Andrea stepped from her car Colleen gave her a big hug. "It's great to see you. Are you okay?"

"I was good until I turned my car into the lot. Then it all started rushing back. It's great to see you. But we don't usually arrive at the same time, so how long have you been waiting for me?"

Colleen would not lie to her friend, "I have only been here about ten minutes. Boy you get here early!"

"I always like getting here before it gets busy. I have some quiet time to prepare for the day." Andrea noticed a lot of cars in the lot and asked, "Is there a meeting?"

"No, I don't think so. It was pretty crazy here Friday, with the press, so maybe people want to get a fresh start on the week."

Andrea and Colleen walked into school arm-in-arm this morning. When they turned the corner on the main hallway, the entire School #3 staff was there. They applauded Andrea. The hugs and greetings over the next five minutes were plentiful. People agreed not to make this a party so everyone quickly dispersed and went to their rooms. Nonetheless, a clear message had been shared with Andrea showing their support and care for her. This truly was her school family and she knew how much she loved being with them and the children they all served.

Andrea had been thinking about the children. She was especially concerned about Dedra Sherman. She had not been able to reach her since the death of her brother. This vibrant little girl had become withdrawn and depressed. Andrea, given her experience on Thursday night, had a whole new perspective on how witnessing violence could deeply affect you. She resolved to find a way to reach this troubled girl.

She also spent some time that morning talking to Sue Drabeck, the special education teacher working with several of Andrea's students. Sue was in Andrea's class on Friday and she shared with her how concerned the children were about her. Andrea knew she'd have to be careful how she talked with them about last week.

When the bell rang the students' feet were quickly pounding up the stairs. When they saw their teacher they came running, Andrea made no effort to stop them, even though she could still hear Bea's voice saying, "Routines Andrea, they are important child." The hugs this morning were heartfelt and plentiful. Andrea could feel the love of her students flowing over her like a waterfall. Its healing power was remarkable.

During journal time Jadira Hoptry was the first to share. She said her mom had a new boyfriend and he was scary. Jadira said he kept looking at her and she didn't like it. Andrea knew she and Hanna Strassman, the school social worker, would need to talk about Jadira and a possible referral to the Department of Social Services.

Darryl Owens shared his grandmother had a new job and he had to take care of himself now on the weekends when she was working. Andrea knew grandma had all she could do to make ends meet. Daryl's mom was in jail for assaulting a police officer and it was likely her day in court would lead to a continued stay in jail since she had a history of prostitution arrests and drug possession charges. Andrea decided to give grandma a call and see what was happening. Andrea had spoken with her several times. They were working together, hoping Daryl would be the one child whose life could be better than his mom's and older brothers.

When it was Andrea's turn to share she decided she had to tell them something about what happened to her last Thursday night. She began by saying, "I was headed back to school after having dinner with Mrs. Johnson. I decided to stop by school for a minute to pick up your stories so I could read them. I love reading your stories." The children giggled at this comment as Andrea hoped they would. She continued, "When I was in the parking lot three young men in a black BMW scared me."

Michael Makin, whose older brother James was in the same street gang, interrupted Andrea saying, "My brother says they wanted to do ya." The children were street wise so this comment did not shock or surprise anyone. However, it did catch Andrea off guard.

"Michael, I don't know what they wanted to do, but I was sure scared. Remember, we don't interrupt someone when they are sharing. We wait until after a person has finished to ask a question, or say something." Andrea paused to gather her thoughts. Then she told them Mrs. Johnson saw what was happening and came to tell the boys to stop. That's when she got shot. "I've talked with Mrs. Johnson and she's coming home from the hospital soon. She's going to be okay and will be back in school when she's feeling better."

It was Dedra who spoke first to Andrea. "Miss Bauer, I know you scared, I hate boys with guns! I am glad you are ok." Andrea felt a tear forming she could not stop from rolling down her cheek. It formed not only because of what happened, but also because Dedra chose to share something.

Laticia Stevens got up from her desk and hugged Andrea, "It's ok to cry Miss Bauer." Andrea got hugs from several children who came up from their desks. It was an intimate classroom moment Andrea would never forget. Healing took many forms and these children were a major part of her recovery.

At 10:15 Sue Drabeck came into Andrea's class for 45 minutes. This happened every day during the language arts block. Sue worked with one of the reading groups for 20 minutes then worked one-on-one with different children. Since working with Bea, and reducing her reading groups to three, it had been much easier for Sue and Andrea to plan.

It was 10:30 when Ma'am stopped by. She was pleased to see Andrea busy with a group of children. She was unaware her principal was there. Sue looked up, saw Ma'am and gave her a thumbs up. Ma'am smiled and quietly left the room.

At lunch time, Andrea stopped by the main office to check her mailbox. It was filled with notes from the staff. She knew she'd need to take time to read them after school. Janet came from her desk, stepping over to give Andrea a warm, motherly hug. She told her the good news of Bea's release from the hospital.

After stopping in the office, Andrea walked into Hanna Strassman's small workspace. Hanna was there and Andrea shared Jadira Hoptry's revelation about her mom's new boyfriend. Before making any calls, Hanna agreed to talk with Jadira by the end of the day. She planned to get her right after their physical education class. Hanna was in and out of every classroom so the children would hardly notice her asking Jadira to come with her.

Each day after lunch Andrea taught either a science or social studies lesson. Today it was social studies. One part of the state test in social studies required students to read a document and then answer questions. This in state speak was called *Document Based Questions* or DBQ's. Knowing the widely varied reading levels of the students, Andrea made up different documents on the same subject. This would not be the case on the state test however.

The children hated doing the DBQ's. If disciplinary issues happened with the students it was in the afternoon when they surfaced. Today it was James Tharp who had a meltdown. He struggled with reading, having a short attention span. He shouted out, "I won't do it!" He pushed his desk over in a tantrum. Andrea had to physically restrain James as he began throwing things.

When James had a major meltdown, the children all knew it would take a real effort for their teacher to get him back in control. Andrea quickly recognized she was going to need help. Anthony Padilla was the errand person today. She asked him to go to the office and tell Mrs. McGee James was upset.

Over the past three years, James would often tantrum when he reached his frustration level. The staff previously teamed on him so whenever a report on him came up to the office everyone knew it was a call for immediate help. From experience the staff knew the school nurse, Jane Plantania, had the best chance to calm him down. Whenever possible she'd respond to a teacher's need for support.

Within two minutes Jane Plantania was in the room. She helped Andrea coax James to the door and convinced him to take a walk with her.

With James' low frustration level, Andrea knew they were going to have to develop special strategies when he took the state tests. The reading levels of those tests were well beyond his ability. He was certain to have a meltdown when asked to "do his best" on them.

While the students went to physical education class, Andrea stopped by the nurse's office to see if Jane had any comments or advice. "It was a rough one today Andrea. He really does get angry. He told me the questions were too hard. You know he has already repeated first grade, his reading level is barely past that despite all our efforts. The lead poisoning he experienced as a baby is going to have life-long effects. We need to team on him again. I think it may be time for a more specialized placement. Andrea agreed teaming on James made real sense, although she wasn't sure what the best strategy was to support him going forward. She hoped others on the team could help.

On the break, Andrea called Bea's home where Bea's daughter, Jasmin answered. Andrea didn't know she'd come home from Duke to be with her mother. Once Andrea identified herself Jasmin said, "My mom has been asking about you. How are you doing?"

"I'm fine. It's your mom I am worried about. How is she?"

Jasmin answered, "Mom is really sore, she needs help getting dressed and doing personal things. I have to go back to Duke on Wednesday, so we're trying to figure out how to get her some help."

Andrea had an idea and asked if she could stop by for a visit after work.

Jasmin replied, "My mom would love that."

Andrea looked forward to seeing Bea and meeting Jasmin. Doing something unusual, Andrea left shortly after the children did. She needed to talk to the woman who was such an important part of her life.

Soon, Andrea pulled up in front of Bea's home. The late afternoon sun was setting, the air was chilly on this November day. Getting out of her car, Andrea could instantly see her breath. She stopped in the driveway to wipe her glasses with her scarf as they fogged over. As she did, she noticed the two bullet holes in Bea's Crown Vic. Seeing them sent a different kind of chill through Andrea's body.

As she approached the porch the front door swung open and Jasmin warmly greeted Andrea. "My mom said you were a sweet little thing. I can see what she means." Andrea smiled, noting Jasmin was almost the exact same size as she was. They hugged; it was the first embrace in what would become for both a treasured life-long friendship.

"Well let's get inside, it's really cold out here!" Jasmin remarked as she led Andrea into the warm house. Bea was stationed beside the fireplace. The instant Andrea saw Bea she experienced a sense of joy knowing her friend was okay. However, she could plainly see Bea was weak and tired.

Andrea looked forward to this moment and moved quickly towards her friend. As she did Bea said, "No hugs girl, my shoulder can't do it. Just sit yourself down and tell me about things."

Before sitting down, Andrea reached out and took Bea's hand. In a voice barely above a whisper Andrea said, "Thank you."

Jasmin was touched by the moment; she saw the powerful connection between her mom and Andrea. She decided they needed some time to talk. "I'm going to make my mom some coffee. Would you like a cup, Andrea?"

"I'd love one Jasmin, thanks."

Looking at the tired woman sitting across from her, Andrea asked, "How are you really doing?"

"I am doin' ok, but the doctors are sayin' my shoulder is not gonna be the same for a long time, if ever. The bullet did mess things up in there."

"Oh, I am so sorry Bea."

"What are you sorry about? You didn't shoot me! That was Germain's doin'."

"If I hadn't gone back to school, then none of this would have happened."

"Girl, it wasn't the smartest thing you've ever done. But you can't go blamin' yourself for me getting shot. We never know what's gonna happen to us, do we? I coulda just called the police and left it there. It was me who followed you to school after I saw those boys crusin' close behind you. It's neither of our faults. You have to promise me you will stop blamin' yourself for something you didn't do. You hear me on this!"

"I do, but it's easier said than done."

"Oh, you want to feel sorry for yourself some more? We both got to move on girl. We can't let those boys win. The shootin' is done and we both gonna be ok. Now tell me about school and the kids."

"Not so fast, Bea," Andrea said. "You have some immediate care needs until your shoulder gets better. Jasmin has to get back to Duke this week. How are you going to get by when she leaves?"

"I'm a big girl Andrea. I'll be able to take care of myself."

"So that's your plan?"

"I can get some in-home help since my health care plan pays for it. I can get by."

Waiting for the coffee to brew, Jasmin stood in the doorway listening to this exchange. She sensed Andrea had something in mind, and wanted to hear it, adding her support if it made sense. Her mom could be terribly stubborn and this was one of those times for her own good when she couldn't get away with it.

"I have an idea," Andrea said. "It can help both of us. What if I moved in for a few weeks? You could help me with some full-time mentoring, and I could assist by helping you in the morning before I leave for school and at night when I get home. It's a win-win."

"Whoa, what are you saying? You want to live with me here in this house. I'm not sure that's a good idea."

Jasmin stepped into the room. She was standing behind Andrea's chair by the fire. "Mom, stop being so hard-headed! I think Andrea has a great idea. I know I'd feel better if she was helping you out."

"I think you girls are plannin' things behind my back," Bea said with a smile.

"No, we just agree about what you need," Andrea affirmed.

"Well I guess I'm out numbered. But what about that boyfriend of yours; does he have any say in this?"

"No he doesn't."

Jasmin noted, "You can use my room. It's near mom's and a lot of my stuff is at Duke so there'd be room for your clothes in my closet and dresser. I can rearrange some things to make it easier for you. I also have a desk in the room. My mom made me study up there 'cause she said I wouldn't get distracted. So you could use it as a quiet space too if you want."

Andrea smiled, "That sounds perfect."

Jasmin exclaimed, "Come on I'll take you upstairs so you can see the room."

"Not so fast there girls, I want this one to tell me what happened at school today."

Both girls smiled knowing Bea was still in charge and had some things to hear and say before anything else took place.

Andrea sat in the comfortable chair beside the fire. Over the next hour the two women shared not only what was happening in school, but they relived what happened to both of them. While this went on, Jasmin served coffee and began making supper. She knew the three of them would be enjoying each other's company throughout dinner.

CHAPTER 24

SPINNING PLATES

John Handler had been busy addressing a number of different problems. He felt like the guy in the circus act who kept a number of plates spinning each on its own tall stick. To prevent a plate from falling all he could do was run from stick to stick giving each one a quick twist. Right now John was attending to needs on the Quality School Committee. He also had to prepare a summary report for the Board which would become a public announcement of preliminary construction and repair estimates for the district's schools and facilities. Also on the immediate list was attending to Carl Gardner's report on Ron Post's sexual harassment complaint. That was the first spinning plate he would address and hopefully put to rest.

John entered Carl's office with the report findings in his hand. "This one looks like there's going to be no clear resolution."

"John, I know. It's a 'he said, she said' thing with no witnesses."

"Carl, what is Susan's take on all of this as the building principal?"

"She is in the same place I am. Flip a coin; both are honest and respected staff members. She doesn't know what to make of it."

"Like you I think Janice was a little too flippant with her remarks to Ron about the prostitute mother. I don't think it was harassment, but she could be more cautious about her comments. I agree with you, some follow up training for her on harassment would be a good idea. I also think a carefully worded counseling memo from you on this would be appropriate. While I expect, given the history and her work performance, this won't surface again. If it does, I want something on-the-record."

"You know she won't like that. We will likely get some push-back from the administrator's union. "

"I know. Once they finish barking I don't think they'll feel a real need to bite. I believe we'll be okay."

"Now Carl, what do you recommend we do with Ron?

"I think Susan Corner and I will need to get Janice and Ron together. Up to this point they appear to have had a good working relationship. I think Janice should apologize to Ron for the statement she admits. It is my hope Ron will graciously accept. But who knows, he may well leave the meeting feeling we were too supportive of Janice."

"Carl, I owe Cliff Greer a call. Let me give him some background regarding our findings and plan. He's a pragmatist and will know we've done all we can. He'll be the key person to guide Ron on this and keep the meeting from getting out-of-hand."

"Okay John. When should I schedule a meeting with Janice to tell her what we are doing?"

"I know she is anxious to hear what's going on. Ted Vassen, called me on her behalf. So let's put this on a fast track to the finish line."

"I'll get it done this week and update you if anything goes off track."

John knew there'd be lingering feelings on this and come spring he'd have a one-on-one with Janice to see if she'd like a transfer if the dust hadn't settled. He also knew she'd be irked with him for not taking a stronger stand of support for her story. He could do nothing to prevent it. It was a lose/lose situation with both Ron and Janice. He'd take some heat as a result.

John moved on to Shantell Williams' office to tell her about the construction and repair cost summary. The architects and engineers would be coming to a public meeting to present their assessment. Sara Vaughn would lead the presentation. John wanted to spend some time with Sara in preparation, as once the report was out in the open there would be a lot of press and political backlash. The process started this morning by getting the Board president updated on the findings. It would not be an easy meeting, especially since the relationship between them was strained.

John's assistant, Ann Stanley scheduled a 10:00 meeting with Shantell and John was running nearly 15 minutes late. He lightly knocked on Shantell's door, apologizing for his tardiness. Closing the door behind him, he sat down to tell Shantell the difficult news and the surprising cost to address all needing to be done.

* * * * *

John wasn't the only one who had to deal with spinning plates syndrome. Ma'am had her hands full with all the day-to-day tasks associated with running a school. On top of that she had been busy recruiting people to serve on the ad-hoc committee to propose a new vision for elementary education within the School #3's attendance area.

She recruited Reverend James, a respected minister and community activist. He and Ma'am did not always see things through the same lens, but he was a strong advocate with lots of political clout which could prove to be beneficial down the road.

Myrna Gaylord recruited Linda Morgano, a highly regarded second grade teacher. Linda worked in the building the last seven years. She was innovative and thoughtful. Myrna was pleased she volunteered. Sue Jones also volunteered, even though no compensation for service was offered. Cliff Greer heard about the committee from Mary Jane Thomas. He decided the union needed a representative so they'd remain in the loop on whatever was being proposed.

Other members of the committee included Betty Jackson, a classroom aide and the parent of two children attending School #3. In addition to these members Bea convinced two others to join in the effort. One was a neighbor, Laticia Baxter. Laticia had three children, the oldest was seven. The other was Thomas Coleman who had grown up in the neighborhood. Tom was a captain in the fire department. While he didn't live in the community anymore, he knew the streets and people well from his youth and through his work.

Ma'am was pleased with the committee's makeup, and was looking forward to the first meeting of the group the next day. She wondered though, could this group really develop a new vision for elementary schooling in this neighborhood? It was a tall order.

Along with this new effort, another had drawn to a close. The school naming group concluded its work and had a prioritized list of three possible names. Ma'am sent John Handler an email stating they had concluded the process and asked how he wanted to proceed. John replied he'd drop by later to talk with Ma'am about the next step. Ma'am was a cheerleader for their first choice. Hopefully it would be the one Dr. Handler supported.

At 12:30 John pulled into the parking lot of School #3. He stepped from his SUV and took in the surrounding area. As many times as John drove through the city, some areas still deeply affected him. This was one of them. It was more than the poorly maintained houses and an old school building capturing his attention. It was the cumulative effect of passing through the last four blocks. The street corners were framed by old and abandoned store fronts. The few active businesses and stores had their windows covered by heavy iron grates. Poverty was king here; his rule enforced by violence, neglect, drugs, prostitution and hopelessness.

John was very proud of his staff. He knew they were waging an often solo battle against poverty's overwhelming forces. School #3 was clearly on the front line of the battle. How they achieved any success with so little in assistance and support was truly astounding. Despite all those saying schools like this one were failing these children, he truly believed otherwise.

Like every visitor, John stood at the front door and rang the bell. Once the door opening routine with Janet McGee was completed he was inside. The architect's report caused him to look more carefully at this school. He did see the ravages of time, both inside and out. This school was like his aged mother in a nursing home. She tried to maintain her dignity while her body was falling apart. It was much the same here.

Janet alerted Ma'am Dr. Handler was coming through the front door. She stood in the outer office when he stepped in from the hallway. "Good afternoon, Dr. Handler," she greeted him enthusiastically. Ma'am was thrilled he decided to visit. This was so different from her experiences with previous superintendents who always seemed to stay downtown. "I've got the coffee on, would you like a cup?"

"Ma'am, you bet I would."

With the welcoming done, they sat down in Ma'am's office with coffee in hand. Once settled, Ma'am told John their first choice, by a country mile, was 'Rosa Parks.'

"Ma'am, I think she is a terrific choice. Give me some background on the committee's thinking."

"John you know her history. She was a black woman with tremendous courage and a clear conviction about right and wrong. In this school community, those admirable traits are ones we want our children to model. We need heroes here and she clearly is the genuine article."

"Here's what I'd like to do, if you are comfortable with it. I have some tough issues coming up at our next Board meeting. One involves your school."

That got Ma'am's uneasy attention. "John, it sounds like you've got some bad news to share today. What's going on?"

"I am not sure it is really bad news. We met with the architects and engineers and they have advised us School #3 should be torn down since its overall condition is so poor. In its place we'd be building a new elementary school. However, when this is put on the plate with all the other building repairs and reconstruction, the cost is overwhelming. When we get to the Board meeting, those figures are going to make headlines for days."

Ma'am rocked back in her chair. "I am not sure how to think about it John. This school has so much history. Generations of children have walked its halls. But maybe something new would be the spark this neighborhood needs to start getting back on its feet. How does the school naming process fit into things?"

"I am thinking you could present to the Board your request for School #3 to be renamed, *Rosa Parks Elementary School.*" It will get the ball rolling on the overall naming process. It also will give the press something else to write about. I don't mind a small handhold on the side of the steep cliff we'll be on when the news gets out about the scope and cost of repairs and reconstruction to our facilities."

"John, can I ask how much that is?"

"You can but I have to keep the number confidential until after the Board has the details. But it is a huge number. I also need you to keep this school's status confidential until it is made public."

"John, what about the naming proposal? Should that remain on the QT?"

"I'd ask you to keep it quiet until after the Board package goes out on Friday. Hopefully, they'll give you the green-light on this and then you can plan a dedication ceremony. I'd like you to be prepared for a ceremony shortly after the New Year. Can you do that?"

"Absolutely, I know the staff and kids will be thrilled with the timing. It will be a special moment."

John was pleased by this and was getting ready to leave when Ma'am decided to press her second agenda. "John, with your support we are forming an ad-hoc committee to propose elementary program changes linked to our children's needs. I think this will lead to a conflict with Mary Jane. I know she's my boss and I respect her role. But I have to tell you I think the main committee is looking to polish an apple that is far beyond ripe."

John sat quietly for a long moment. Ma'am really wondered whether she'd gone too far. "Ma'am, I don't know what you and the group may propose, so it is way too early for me to take any position on it. What I can tell you is I support your search, but I can make no promises on where I will stand when you have something to propose. I expect you to keep Mary Jane up to speed. If you two cross swords I will have to make a judgment." Locking eyes with Ma'am he said as directly as possible, "Try not to get into that position if you can avoid it. I'd rather not be forced to choose between you and Mary Jane if there's a showdown."

"I understand John. But I am not sure in the end it can be avoided. We see things differently. But I promise to try as hard as I can to keep the waters calm."

"That's all I can ask. Do me a favor though? Keep me posted on what you are doing."

Ma'am smiled, "I'll be sure to keep you in the loop. Trust me on that."

CHAPTER 25

THE ARGUMENT

Andrea planned to settle in with Bea over the weekend. She felt she'd be with Bea for maybe two or three weeks and then she'd head back to the apartment. With all that happened over the past week she was thinking about Jason and their need to spend some time together.

Andrea thought he had a right to be hurt that she didn't call him when she was taken to the hospital. She was fearful he'd be so angry over what happened he'd want her to quit working at School #3. She was far from ready for that to happen. But she also wasn't being respectful of Jason's feelings. She felt she had to apologize.

After having dinner with Bea and Jasmin on Wednesday, Andrea decided to go to the apartment in the hope Jason would be there. Jason wasn't a neat-nick, and over the past several weeks of staying at the apartment by himself, the signs of neglect were readily apparent as Andrea entered. But she hadn't come to clean-up; she stopped to see Jason and tell him she'd be taking care of Bea for a few weeks.

When she came in, she could hear Jason on the phone with a client. He often made calls after normal work hours to talk to people about their insurance needs. Jason was a hard worker and he was slowly but steadily building a good client book.

When he saw her enter, he smiled and quickly completed the call. "Wow! I didn't expect to see you," he said. " I'd have cleaned up a bit if I knew you were coming."

Andrea smiled, "Jason, it looks like we have a cleaning day in our future. I want to apologize for not calling you when those creeps tried to hurt me and shot Bea. It was wrong. You had a right to be upset with me. I was afraid you'd tell me to quit working at School #3."

"Well that's putting it all on the table isn't it? We haven't talked much since last Thursday. You did hurt my feelings Andrea and I am not sure what to think about it. I thought our relationship was stronger than I guess it is."

"I don't know where to begin, Jason. I really love the kids in my classroom. They need so much. I know now I was naïve about some of the dangers. I'm not anymore, believe me! But the kids I'm teaching live in that terrible area 24/7. It's awful Jason! There's so much poverty and neglect. I can't ignore their needs, I just can't." Tears were running and Andrea was surprised by the depth of her emotion as she shared her feelings about teaching at School #3.

"I know how devoted you are to your work. I've had plenty of time to think lately. I understand I must respect your decision. But I am really worried about your safety. I can't lie to you. You know children everywhere need good teachers. It would be a lot better if you were working someplace else. However, I don't have much say I guess."

"I feel the city is where I am needed most. I will do most anything for you Jason, but I can't give up my work there. It's too important."

They were sitting on opposite ends of the couch. It was a standoff moment. Neither Jason nor Andrea could build a bridge over their strongly held views on the place where she worked.

Andrea looked at Jason and said, "I think we are going to have to agree to disagree on this. You promised me you'd try harder to see things my way."

"Andrea, the promise was made before they threatened to rape you in the school parking lot and shot Bea. Look at it from where I'm sitting. I don't want to lose you, and I know I have no choice but to accept your decision, but I am never going to like it."

"I do understand your feelings, Jason. I know you are worried about my safety. I promise I will not go to the school at night and be much wiser about what I do. But I have something else I need to share with you."

"What now, Andrea? What other decisions have you made we haven't talked about?"

Andrea knew he was right. She was making too many decisions without his input for the relationship to survive. The fact was she'd made the decision to take care of Bea and she had to see it through. She could only hope Jason would see this too was very important for her. "Jason, I have offered to stay at Bea's home for the next few weeks to help her as she recovers from the shooting."

"What!" Jason was off the couch and on his feet. "You mean you are now going to live in that damn neighborhood. What are you thinking? You told me you weren't naïve. Andrea, I think you've lost your mind!"

"Jason, Bea saved my life. She needs help and I'm going to do it. I know I will be safe in her house. It will only be for a few weeks and then we can start to get our lives back on track."

"So again, I've got no say in how things go. Andrea, I don't know what to think about all of this. I feel like I am losing you and I'm helpless to do anything about it."

"Jason, you are not losing me. I went through something awful and need to heal. Bea is a real part of my healing."

"Oh, and I'm not! How is this supposed to make me feel better about us? I'm not part of your healing process, but some woman from the slums is!"

"Jason, stop talking like that! I am the one who had the terrible experience not you! I'm the one who needs to heal from it and I'm asking for some space."

"It's all about you isn't it! I went through that horrible thing too. Don't underestimate my need to recover. But I have to go through my feelings alone. I don't get to share with you, hold you, cry with you and heal together with you. I don't know what to say. You are going to do what works for you and I'll have to make the best of it, I guess."

Andrea knew Jason loved her. She could feel the pain in his words. She wasn't emotionally equipped to provide much support. How terrible that night had been for both of them. She could see it now. She knew he had needs and she wasn't meeting them. They both had a lot to think about.

"Jason, I know I haven't been there for you. I know over the next few weeks I won't be here much either because of Bea's needs. Please be patient with me. We can work this out if we are both patient."

"I don't have much choice do I? Just be patient Jason and things will be better. Well forgive me if I'm not so sure."

Andrea didn't know what else to say. She came for a few things and went to get them. They hugged as she left the apartment. Both wondered what would happen next. Only the passage of time would tell them.

CHAPTER 26

GETTING STARTED

Ma'am had not seen Bea since she returned home and was looking forward to catching up on things and driving her to the meeting. When Bea answered the door, Ma'am could tell by her demeanor she was still uncomfortable. Once settled in Bea's favorite chairs by the fireplace, Ma'am opened the conversation. "Girl, it's just us here. How are you really doing?"

Bea was not one who often cried. But her friend Dorothy, could see Bea's eyes moisten as she prepared to answer her question. "Dorothy, I'm having nightmares. I am not sleepin' well. I can still see those boys. I thought they'd kill me for sure once the shootin' started. I had a victim's assistance counselor from the police stop at the hospital. She told me if I needed any help she'd get me connected to support. I guess I might take her up on it."

Bea was one of the strongest women Dorothy knew. For her to recognize the possible need for some help was surprising. "That sounds like a good idea. What you went through was awful and being able to talk about it with somebody who can help is something I'd do if I were in your shoes."

Bea did not want to travel any further down this road, even with Dorothy. "Okay, enough of this. What's happenin' at school?" she asked.

"Well, not much since you were there last week."

"I know, but how are my kids doin'?"

"I talked to them after you were shot. They know you are okay. But I think your idea of coming in soon is a good one. That will settle them down some. It also will be good for the staff to see you. Maybe we could do a visit at the end of a day and have a little meet and greet after school."

"That makes sense to me; how about next week sometime? My shoulder is still sore and I get tired Dorothy. I think maybe Thursday of next week. I'll have seen the doctors again and I hope I have some strength back."

"Bea, are you feeling up to the committee meeting today?"

"No Dorothy. I still get tired."

Dorothy smiled, "But I don't want you staying away for long."

"You don't have to worry about that!" Bea laughed heavily now and it felt good. It reminded her she hadn't really laughed since the shooting."

"Let me tell you what I hope we can accomplish today. We've got a group that doesn't know everybody, so we'll do some warm-up activities to get everyone talking and sharing. I also need to tell them what we can and can't do."

"What's up?" Bea asked.

"We have the right to recommend things, but it doesn't mean it will be supported downtown."

"No surprise there, but I thought you said Dr. Handler was different."

"I trust him and I really think he will be there for us in the end. But we've got to be careful and not pick any fights with the rest of the folks downtown, especially Mary Jane."

"I've already picked a fight with her, so I guess he means you've got to be careful."

"Yes, we'll have to walk on eggshells with her. So I need to be clear with the group our process needs to be low key. We can't go poking any sticks in her beehive or we may be stung. I want to position Dr. Handler to support our ideas and not get them lost because we screwed up the process."

"I get what you're sayin' but how ya gonna do that?"

"Carefully, I guess. I want to tell the committee we need to keep a low profile and develop our ideas thoroughly before making any recommendations."

"But you're forgetting one thing."

"What?"

"Sue Jones is gonna hot wire everythin' back to the union. They're gonna know our moves before anybody and no tellin' what they'll do. They could easily use downtown to kill something."

"I know, but if it happens much Sue and I are going to have a real heart-to-heart."

"Yeah, but you'll lose. Her loyalty is to her union not to any fresh ideas which may change the way we do things."

"Bea, we have to live with it. I can't throw her off the committee. We will have to take things slow and careful as we can and hope we can get to the finish line." Dorothy was showing her frustration. Bea knew she'd said what she needed to about Sue Jones.

"Dorothy we really are skatin' on thin ice. You gotta watch our back downtown and with the union. We don't have much chance of gettin' any changes when we gotta run through such a defense!"

"Okay, you got the picture. So remember, if you get angry you swallow it in our meetings; you say it to me in private. We have to be real smart here if any change has even the slimmest chance."

"I understand. Trust me, Bea will behave like the best girl in the class."

They both laughed at this. Oh, how Bea enjoyed laughter again.

CHAPTER 27

TOO MUCH MONEY

John asked the mayor if she had time to see him for an hour. Jane looked at her busy calendar and opened up a spot late in the day. City hall was an old, but well kept building. The foyer opened four floors to a skylight. People could be seen scurrying through the foyer and in the corridors above. The mayor's office was on the top floor . It had a good view down Main Street. In its heyday, the view would have revealed busy stores and businesses. Shoppers and business people would have filled the wide slate sidewalks along both sides of the business district. Today, the perch offered a view of shuttered shops and a decaying Main Street. It was far from a unique problem for once prosperous city centers.

John enjoyed a good cup of coffee and Jane had one ready when he entered. The office was steeped in tradition. The mayor's desk dated back more than 100 years. It had been used by every mayor since 1894. The office had an old, but well maintained shinny oak floor. A large rug emblazoned with the city seal sat under a conference table surrounded by eight green leather chairs. The table, like the desk, had been a long-time fixture in the office. Bookshelves filled with historical documents and city code books lined one wall behind the conference table. Jane co-opted several shelves for family photos and various mementos. A signed picture of the President of the United States held a prominent place on the wall near the shelves. Overall, the office was one of quiet power and a reminder of times past when the city was rising in its strength and influence. How times had changed over the last 50 years.

Once they exchanged greetings and attended to their coffee, John told Jane he received a preliminary report from the architectural and engineering firm BTG. BTG was a highly respected firm and Jane was well aware of their expertise in assessing the condition and needs of public facilities.

"Well John, I suppose you didn't come over here to tell me the good news. I suspect you have some real issues on your hand. Am I right?"

"Jane, you couldn't be more right. I was shocked by the report. My whole team was. When I shared it with my Board president, she was trembling when I finished."

Trying to add a little humor, Jane quipped, "Well let me ask my staff to bring in some oxygen before we get started then."

"Probably not a bad idea Jane," John was laughing lightly as he responded.

"Well let me give you the bottom line and then I'll back up and share the details. The overall estimate is $1.2 billion dollars and $800 million is considered to be in the necessary or immediate category."

Jane was now sitting back in her large leather desk chair. "My God John, I expected a big number, but this one's really hard to comprehend."

"I feel exactly the same way Jane." For the next half-hour John provided the details. They talked about the various items and in the end it was apparent to Jane the scope of the problem was well documented and based upon sound assessments of the schools and other district facilities.

They then turned to the practical problems which would transpire once the report was made public at next week's school board meeting. "John, when the media gets these figures and the building studies, there are going to be a number of feature articles and reports. I think we can both see the headline. Beginning with the big figure in bold print."

"I know, Jane. It is going to be a huge problem. We will both be captured by it. I have asked Sara Vaughn, the lead architect, to brief any team you put together. It can happen before the Board meeting if that's helpful."

"I will take you up on it. I would like a chance for my team to be briefed."

"Jane, if you don't mind I'd like our CFO, Tom Wheaton and our Buildings and Grounds Director Bud Peck to sit in on the briefing. I suspect you folks may have some practical and financial questions they can answer."

"Okay. I plan to attend this meeting too. I would like one more person to be there as well."

"Okay, who else would you like?"

"I want you sitting next to me. My team needs to see we are on the same page. There's been a lot of back and forth politics between my folks and yours. This could easily be another opportunity for them to tangle. I think our both being there will keep them in line."

"I appreciate the invitation; I didn't want to presume it. I would look forward to being a part of the meeting."

"I'm not so sure I'd look forward to it John," Jane laughed.

"You're right. It's going to be tough sledding for all of us."

"John, politically there are some other folks we need to get to before the report goes public. We need to make our two state representatives aware of the findings and recommendations. We don't want them to read it in the newspaper. We're also going to need their help and support on what we do here. I'll call them. They won't want to sit in on our briefing personally. I suspect they'll want some distance. But they may send senior staff people to it to be briefed. Now let's come back to the numbers. I have no clue as to how the city can support this. You know as well as I do we're broke and we have our own repair needs, our streets are crumbling, sewer and water lines are quickly aging out, not to mention our own facility repair needs. Before this report, we were already in deep water with those issues. My staff has been struggling with how to address them, now this. They're going to run us all out on a rail if we raise taxes to cover it."

"I know, yet if we don't address it with some plan, we are going to have major failures at some point. It's a loser no matter how we cut it. The state's finances are in such terrible shape I am not sure we can count on a lot of additional support there. We'll get substantial building aid from them, but they will drag their feet on approvals. They don't have the money and they don't want to further erode their already downgraded bond status."

"Well you have to make the report public. All we can do is try to put a good spin on it. Can we say the next step is to develop a long-term plan to sequence the needs and work with others to help us with the funding burden?"

"It's a stretch to say long-term, given the needs. But out of the gate I think it is a reasonable position to take. Let's see if we can get Janey and your press guy working on statements we can have ready."

CHAPTER 28

TWO STEPS FORWARD AND ONE BACK

Andrea had a tough day. James Tharp had another meltdown and it took a lot to calm him. He tipped over furniture and shouted expletives that would have challenged even the saltiest sailor. In addition, Dedra had not spoken in two days. Andrea was convinced she was falling into a deeper depression.

Andrea also was at quarter end and facing the completion of report cards for the first time. It was a daunting task. Nearly every child was failing fourth grade material. However, most every child was working at or near capacity. 'How should she grade the children, on effort or standards accomplishment?' She was feeling frustrated with a reporting system which forced her to give many children failing grades. They would take the reports home and lord knows what would happen. 'Would she lose her children's trust?'

In addition, Andrea was struggling mightily on how to accommodate Antonia Juarez's language deficits. She had not learned much English and Andrea was certain she was lost most of the time. She was waiting for an overall assessment of her abilities. The district's Spanish speaking psychologists were on overload with referrals. It would likely be several weeks before Andrea had any solid data about her abilities and foundational knowledge.

When Andrea walked into Bea's she quickly realized no one was there. Then she remembered the elementary program committee was meeting for a second time. She knew Bea would be hungry after it was over so she started a stew in the crock pot. Andrea climbed the stairs to Jasmin's room. She set her work down on the desk and changed into blue jeans and a comfortable sweatshirt. She wanted to go for a run; but doing it alone at dusk would be dangerous. How sad it was that so many things she took for granted weren't possible here.

While she waited for Bea, she thought about the children and her need to grade their work. There was a comment section in each report card. The report card was a five part carbonless form. One copy for each quarter, and one copy for the child's permanent record at the end of the year. She started drafting on her computer what she wanted to say in the handwritten portion of the card. She reminded herself if she wrote small, she had room for about three sentences. Andrea wanted to make every word count for each child when she transferred the drafts to the actual report card.

Shortly after 6:00PM Ma'am delivered Bea. When she came through the door Andrea sensed her fatigue. This was Bea's first outing and it was evident a couple of hours was still a lot to ask of a body healing from a nasty wound.

"How was the meeting Bea?" Andrea asked pleasantly.

"It was a good one. We're all thinkin' about how to do a better job for the kids."

"Great! There's lots more we should be doing for sure."

"Give me an example, girl."

"For one thing our reading materials are old and our library collection is an embarrassment. We need updated books and leveled materials to capture the kids' interests. We've talked about this Bea and I've showed you some things. But believe me there's much more we could do." Andrea knew Bea understood her point. However, there was more to it than replacing outdated books and materials with new ones.

"Did any ideas get shared at the meeting you liked Bea?"

"Myrna talked about how far behind the children are when they get to kindergarten. She thinks we need to start school much earlier."

"Do you agree?"

"I do, but I don't think downtown will go for that. They're always talkin' about how little money they got."

Their conversation continued as Andrea got dinner on the table. She shared how much she was struggling with writing report cards. Bea told her she'd be lucky if she got a half dozen of the envelopes returned with parent signatures. She told Andrea many of the children 'lost' them on the way home. Report cards weren't important to many kids and families.

"You've got to be kidding!" Andrea exclaimed in response to Bea's observations. "It was a big day in my house. My mom had report card day on the family calendar."

"Look, most of these parents failed in school too. You gotta see it from their side. We got these nice folks in this big building down the street. They're workin' with their kids and they appreciate you are carin' for 'em. But in the end too many don't see school doin' much good for 'em or their kids. Like Ma'am says, it's the poverty cycle. It's tough to stop it. If you think a report card is the way to do it you got another thing comin', Andrea."

"What do you do about the grades? If I grade on standards then the kids' cards aren't going to be pretty. Most would fail to meet the grade 4 standards."

"I grade 'em on the quality of their work. In my comments I tell 'em it is below grade standards. It's worked for me and Ma'am is okay with it too. Ya know she will want to read your report cards before you send them home? I don't know how she does it. She even writes comments on some of 'em."

Andrea shared Dedra's behavior with Bea. "I am really worried about her. She isn't talking much with the kids. I've talked to the lunch aide and she says Dedra sits by herself and doesn't talk. We have a team meeting scheduled on her next week. But breaking through to her seems to be more and more difficult to do. She was such a delightful and active girl, now this."

"That girl saw something horrible. We both know how bad it can be. But her brother died and her mom, she's a mess. I hear that from folks at church. I want to talk with Reverend James. Let's see if we can do some things for both Dedra and her mom. I think we've got to work the whole thing."

Ma'am called a special faculty meeting for Monday after school. Because it exceeded the union contract's authorized meetings per month, it had to be a voluntary meeting and the notice announcing it had to clearly state it was. Ma'am complied with this requirement, and Janet placed the announcement in everyone's box on Friday morning. The contract also mandated at least one work day advance notice for any meeting, voluntary or not, unless it was an emergency. This meeting did not fall in the emergency category and had to be announced Friday morning before noon to meet the time frame requirement for notification.

The steps she had to take to get her staff together for an important announcement were frustrating. Ma'am often wondered if people in the outside world understood the boondoggle of contract and political hurtles needing to be jumped to get something done. It was a real challenge for principals, especially those new to the job.

At the meeting Ma'am planned to tell the staff about the presentation she'd be making to the Board of Education the next day on the naming of School #3. She was respecting the Board's need to have the information ahead of time, and she knew the Board would get their meeting packets on Friday afternoon. But she wanted the staff to know the naming process was moving forward on a fast track.

Ma'am was also reflecting on her the ad hoc Elementary Program Committee meeting the previous night. Ma'am was pleased Myrna wanted to talk with her afterschool on Friday as she was interested in her take on things.

Friday flew by. Unexpectedly, Ma'am had been called to a meeting downtown. At the meeting John summarized the preliminary facilities report for all the building principals and district office staff. Like every meeting so far on this topic, it took their breath away.

Following the meeting, several principals went to lunch to discuss what they'd heard. They could not imagine how the report and its findings could be ignored. Yet costs were so high! They did not envy John and the road ahead on this issue.

It was late when Ma'am drove back to school. She had to cancel a morning observation and she knew things would be backed up for days. When she came back in the office Janet looked up saying, "Another meeting downtown. Don't they know how busy you are?"

Ma'am smiled and asked, "What's on first?" After catching up a bit, Ma'am looked up and saw it was time for buses to be out front and school dismissal to begin. She put on her coat and headed outside to supervise and help students as they left for the day.

When she got back inside, Myrna was standing in the outer office looking forward to their planned chat about last night's program committee meeting.

Once settled in Ma'am's office, Ma'am asked Myrna what her take was on last night's meeting. "To be honest, I am worried about what downtown will do if we come up with something that feels more like a charter school than a part of the system. I am worried they'll shoot it down quickly if it does come across that way. But if we keep on doing what we've been doing nothing is going to change for the better."

Myrna was becoming more comfortable speaking her mind with Ma'am. "The traditional model won't work. How much more proof do we need? Many of the kids who come to kindergarten at School #3 are so disadvantaged. Too few have any letter recognition skills. Their understanding of basic concepts is even lacking. Over the years, I've had countless children who do not understand the difference between placing something *in* a box versus placing it *on* the box. Their basic vocabularies are weak and they have few experiences outside their immediate neighborhood. Ma'am, they are so far behind right from the start."

"I know Myrna. Our kids do have so much they have to catch up on. Their young lives are far from enriched or supported. But I am not sure how we break the cycle with some undefined new approach."

"Ma'am, you don't do it by starting at age five! We need these kids almost right after they are born. We really do have to think about educating them from the start of life. If we wait, they often have little chance at succeeding. We can't work hard with them for ten months and then turn them loose to be neglected all summer long. It doesn't make any sense."

"Whoa! What you are thinking hasn't got a chance to be supported. So why are you talking this way?"

"I need to speak my mind, and I know this has to be tempered by a whole lot of reality checking. But Ma'am, we have to wander a bit out in the prairie before we choose the place to settle. I am so afraid the traditions of how we do things around here will keep us from thinking differently."

"Myrna, I am quickly learning the quiet lady who teaches kindergarten has a lot to say. Why have you never shared this thinking before?"

"No real forum has existed for listening to anything different. Look, schools are filled with momentum and tradition. They are the toughest places to change. We've done the same thing for generations. We have this model with grades and structures supporting life in a different time. Where could I share different ideas with any hope for change? This is the first time there's been an open discussion. I believe you know something different needs to take place. I am speaking my mind now because before this I would have been tossing words and ideas into the wind."

"It will likely still be the case. But you do have important thoughts and I want to think a bit about how we put them on the table with the larger group. What else is spinning in your head?"

"I want to spend more time on the prairie thinking Ma'am. But trust me once it's settled in my head, I'll share it with you. What's your take on my ideas?"

"I think you are right about getting the kids younger. I don't know about the timing, but certainly before age five. I know downtown will struggle with how to pay for it. If we propose it in a plan we are going to have to think about how it's funded without costing more money than we are spending. I'm not sure how it can be accomplished, but it is a reality we must face. Let's keep talking and see what ideas other members of the committee have as well. If we trust the process, maybe we'll come up with something downtown will support."

"Okay, now what's the meeting about on Monday?"

Ma'am smiled, "Can you keep a secret?"

CHAPTER 29

KEEPING YOUR EYE ON THE BALL

The Board of Education meeting room was filled with the usual players. Heavier than normal press coverage surfaced due to the preliminary facilities review. Ma'am also had several staff members who decided to attend the meeting after learning the naming of School #3 would be on the agenda. They were excited to hear about the name being proposed and interested in what would happen when it reached the Board table.

While John was largely preoccupied with the preliminary facilities review, he was also pleased to have the name change for School #3 on the agenda. He wanted to be able to have a good example of how things could work for other schools involved in the process. It would be evidence the process could move forward to closure. In some cases, it would light a fire under schools where the grapevine was telling him little work had been done to date.

John strategically placed the name change as the first action item for the Board. Even so, the preliminary report on facilities would come earlier in the agenda as no formal Board action was required. John could only hope the press would hang around to the action item part of the agenda and pick up on the naming story of School #3. He really wanted some positive press, knowing the main story was going to be about the preliminary facilities report.

Sara Vaughn was a an excellent presenter. Her presentation at city hall last week sharpened her perspectives, helping her gain a better understanding of the thin ice on which she was skating. The mayor's team actively challenged her team's assessments. They wanted to know what other alternatives were considered. Was their timeline for repairs and construction too ambitious? Had they considered how difficult the funding process would be, and how long it might take? The questions and comments in the session went on for nearly two hours. Sara did not want a repeat performance tonight. With John's help she amended timelines, lengthening them where they could. She also planned to keep the summary general and the numbers stated in ranges to soften their impact. John and the mayor encouraged Sara to make the report seem more preliminary than it actually was at this point. They both wanted as much wiggle room as possible in the near term. It was her job not to overplay the hand.

Even with the preparation and hedging the report still shocked many who were in attendance. Sara reviewed the major aspects of the report. She talked about the need for timeline planning and breaking down the projects into prioritized lists. She did not provide the priority listing discussed earlier with the superintendent's team. John convinced her it would take Board members and the public over the falls. He also wanted more time to think about the priorities they were suggesting.

Sara's' summary report and PowerPoint slides were done in 20 minutes. However, Board member questions went on for another forty-five minutes before Shantell gaveled this portion of the meeting to a close. She reminded everyone this was only a report and none of the preliminary findings were moving forward as action items yet. John advised the Board the administration would prioritize the list of projects and make recommendations on next steps. John knew full well the emails and calls from Board members would begin pouring in over the next few days as they got questions from residents and the press.

When they finally got to new business items it was 8:45. Thankfully, most of the media was still in attendance in the hopes of being able to interview John and Board members when the meeting drew to a close.

Ma'am gave an overview of the process leading to the recommendation School #3 be renamed as, *Rosa Parks Elementary School.* She introduced her committee composed of parents, staff and students. Tonight, even the student members were present, a nice touch pleasing the five members of the Board. When Ma'am was finished, John spoke, reinforcing his belief a school name was important. He talked specifically about School #3 and how well this particular recommendation fit as the school's new name. Some School #3 staff members were both surprised and impressed by his knowledge of their school and his sound rationale for supporting the name change.

However, Board members were not going to be left on the sidelines. They had several questions about what other names were considered. They also asked John what the timeline for a rededication would be if they approved the change of the school's name. Shantell Williams, while supporting the name, wanted the Board to table action on it to give people in the community time to react to the proposal. John was surprised by this, as she had not shared the strategy with him during their preparation meeting. Other Board members nodded in agreement. Before much more was said, the action item was tabled for one month. John and Ma'am were complimented on their process. They wanted time to be sure widespread support existed for the name change.

This was not what John expected. The Board was inviting the larger community into the process. This could lead to numerous other suggestions and the Board could find itself on the hot seat before it was settled. 'Why didn't Shantell talk with him about this?' It was obvious she and other Board members were going out on their own again leaving him hanging. He was embarrassed and angry.

Ma'am took the action in stride; although she could see John was upset. She saw getting any real program changes by this group was going to be exceptionally difficult. It was good practice for the main event she hoped would come in the spring.

In fact, John had never been angrier with his Board and their actions. Shantell orchestrated another end run around him. He felt she was using the naming of School #3 as a chance to get even with him for his strong leadership style. By their action they'd invited community input on every naming process. No building principal was going to feel comfortable making a recommendation without a cycle of input and comment from the larger community.

John knew this action would give the building principals and their naming committees a lot more work to do. John and his team would have to spend a great deal of time coaching them on the process. With twenty-three schools to name over the next few months this process now turned from something exciting into a political staging nightmare. John thought to himself about how difficult it was to work with a Board when they did not communicate actions and needs until they played out at a meeting.

After the media session ended Board members were getting ready for the closed session. Once everyone was seated, John told them he was surprised by their decision to seek community input on the naming of School #3. He reminded the Board they agreed on the naming process and the committee input structure during their two-day summer retreat. "You can't surprise me at a meeting and then expect it's okay with me, it's not! I am tired and I'd appreciate it if we all called it a night."

Most of the members knew John was trying to step away from saying anything he'd regret. Nonetheless, Sara Fieldstone said, "I don't see what we did was wrong John. We want more process than what we'd agreed to last summer. We have a right to change our minds don't we?"

"Yes you do Sara; however, I didn't appreciate finding it out without any advance warning you all were thinking about going in a different direction. You continue to communicate with each other leaving me out of the loop. You don't see the implications of your actions in the larger context." For the next ten minutes John spoke without interruption. He laid out in detail how their decision to table the School #3 naming for more public input was, in his judgment, a huge mistake. He summarized the far-reaching impact of their actions. They had no idea how much work they put on everyone's shoulders. Political rain would (now) fall on them every time they discussed a school's proposed name.

When John finally came up for air, it was Terrell Whitner who spoke "John we didn't think you'd have a problem with public input. You've always been supportive of that."

"Terrell you are right you didn't think. The point I keep trying to make is when you talk around me you do not see the full impact of your actions. You are so used to doing it you don't even have a sense anymore of when you do it. Think about the facilities development process. We have huge issues and decisions to make in the months ahead. They will be far reaching and costly ones. If you continue your own private discussions and then spring them on me at a Board meeting, we will quickly lose control of the process. I'll be doing more damage control than strategic decision making. "

John took a deep breath; he knew his emotions were too close to overruling reason. "I don't know what else to say to help you see we must work together. When we are in our regular public meetings there can't be these surprises! Since you talk around me, you need to have a conversation about this and decide who you want leading this district, me or you."

Don Karst interrupted, "Wow, John! I don't know what to say here. We certainly aren't on the same page at this point."

"No we are not! I'm tired of this and I can't move forward with an improvement agenda if it continues. All I will be is a caretaker of the status quo." John asked them to reflect on what was said. They'd pick up the conversation again in two weeks at the next closed session. No one argued with his suggestion.

CHAPTER 30

ANOTHER DEATH

The next day John had some stops he wanted to make. He decided to drop by Columbus Middle School first thing and talk with Susan Corner about how the meeting went yesterday between Janice Mills and Ron Post. He had not had a chance to talk with Carl about it but thought he'd get a take on it from Susan. He asked Ann to call ahead to let Susan know he was stopping by. The buses for the middle school runs were on the road and he'd likely arrive just as school was getting started.

John was pulling into the parking lot at the middle school when his phone rang. The caller ID indicated it was Richard Young, the chief of police. It was not often he got a call from the chief. When he did it was always trouble. John answered the phone while sitting in the parking lot.

"Dr. Handler, I am going to get right to the point. We have a homicide at a Hudson Middle School bus stop. Two boys got into a fight at the stop and one pulled a knife and stabbed the other, killing him. We have not apprehended the accused as he fled from the scene, but we will shortly. Seven students were at the stop counting the two boys. It's on the police radios now and the press has already called our liaison officer. They will be at the crime scene in a few minutes."

"My God Chief! What about the other five students at the stop? Do you have them in protective custody? They are going to need counseling and support."

"Officers are interviewing them; we will contact their parents. If you are okay with it, I will ask the parents to pick up their children at Hudson once we've finished our initial interviews."

"What about the school bus? Was it at the stop when it happened?"

"No, and we waved them by without any comment."

"Has anyone contacted the school?"

"Yes, we have two officers there right now talking with the principal."

"Okay. Zack James is a good man. He and his staff are going to have their hands full. I will head there now. Can we talk once you feel you can spare the time?"

"My next call is to the mayor and I am sure you are going to need to talk about this as well."

"Do you know the age of the victim?"

"John the kids have told us he was in the eighth grade. The other boy who stabbed him was in seventh."

"Do you have any indication what brought this on?"

"The initial report is it stemmed from a lot of bullying of the seventh grade boy. It appears he lost it and stabbed the eighth grade boy who was taunting him."

"Chief, we'll be talking soon. This is awful! I can't get my head around it. For the second time this fall we've had one child killing another." When John arrived at Hudson Middle School he sat in his car a few minutes making phone calls. He asked his secretary, Ann Stanley to alert the district office crisis team. He told her he'd email the names of the students involved as soon as he had them. He wanted Ann to alert the elementary principal of the school the boys previously attended as there needed to be a support response there as well. Ann had two other tasks: tell Janey Eisen to head to Hudson then begin to draft an email informing Board members.

After listening to all of the requests Ann couldn't help but say, "It's a mess on some of these streets! Why do children kill each other like this? I don't understand what's happening."

"I wish I knew the answer Ann. If we did we could put a stop to this insanity. I will call you back shortly, once I've had a chance to talk with staff at Hudson. They are going to have a lot on their hands and we'll see what we can do to help."

John got out of his car and headed across the blustery bus loop. He felt the cold penetrate his suit coat as he rushed to get through the front door of Hudson. The school, built in the late sixties, was a two story building. The outside brick was brown rather than the usual red. The windows were aluminum with dark blue panels underneath. The school housed nearly 1200 students across grades six through eight. The main office was a bright one with large windows affording a view of the hallway. As John approached the door he could see inside the office. Staff members were meeting in clusters and he instantly saw how busy they were. At the same time others were hugging and consoling each other. It was a scene of action and grief happening simultaneously.

Stepping into the office, he walked quickly over to Zack James' secretary. Having dropped in many times, as well as talking on the phone, they knew each other reasonably well. "I'm sorry to have to be here this morning. This is a real tragedy Helen."

"I know Dr. Handler, but it is good to see you. We're all in shock over this. Mr. James is down in the guidance office right now talking with the counselors and other staff. He's trying to get things coordinated."

"Helen, do you know the names of the boys?"

"Yes, we know Tommy Hillen was the eighth grade boy who was killed. Dr. Handler, he was a good student." Helen's eyes filled with tears. But she composed herself and continued. "He came to us from School #17. He has an older sister at Jefferson High in the tenth grade. I don't know if she's been told yet what happened. The other boy is new this year. His name is Jerome Saxon. He's got a younger brother and sister at School #17. His brother is in fourth grade there and his sister is in fifth. Mr. James asked me to call both Jefferson and School #17 to tell them what happened this morning."

"Thanks. Can I use Zack's office for a minute to make some calls?"

"Sure thing, anything else you need me to do for you, let me know."

"Thanks Helen. I know you've got a lot to do. I'll be fine if I can have a private place to make a few necessary calls."

Zack James' office was filled with pictures, not only of his family, but also of middle school students doing all kinds of things. John respected his ability to build relationships with adults and especially with his students. He was a real hands-on guy, often in the thick of things. He knew most every youngster by name. The kids loved him and truly enjoyed being around him.

His desk was piled with papers. He knew from talking with Helen and others Zack was not one for organization or attending to details. Trade-offs in skills always happened since some principals were well organized and on top of things, while others were more in the halls and mixing it up, with the administrative details not always the first thing on their minds. Both styles were needed. A superintendent tried hard to surround each leadership style with staff members who could compliment it, hoping overall a good balance could be achieved.

John knew he had to call Ann and bring her up to speed on the new details. She'd already started a draft email to Board members alerting them to what transpired. She read it to John over the phone and he made some edits. They added the names of the two boys and some of their biographical details. He closed the email with an assurance he'd update them later in the day. Ann would proof the email one more time, copy Janey Eisen in on it and send it off to the Board. John finished saying, "Give me a call if there's anything you think I need to know. Please pass the student information on to Barbara Mason in pupil services. She'll be coordinating the district's crisis response team."

John made the next call to Shantell Williams. While she would get the email Ann would be sending on his behalf, he always made it a point to be sure most important messages were backed up with a personal call to the Board president. Shantell answered her cell phone on the second ring. John did not devote any time for a back and forth before entering the meat of the conversation. "Shantell, we've had another act of violence today. It involves two boys, a seventh and eighth grader at Hudson. The seventh grader stabbed to death the eighth grader. It all went down at their bus stop this morning." John went on to describe the events as he knew them.

"John this is tragic! Should I go to the school?"

John thought, 'She had no training and no authority, the last thing both he and the staff needed was the Board president roaming around.' "No. In fact, I am leaving shortly. I have to let Zack and his staff do their work. Our being here will only confuse communication lines and distract them. I have an email summary going out to all Board members and I'll update everyone again later today when we have more information. Right now there's not much more we can do. We have to let good folks do their jobs."

"Okay John. But I still think people would feel better seeing the Board president in their building."

"Shantell there will be a time for that. It's just not today. Be patient and we'll figure out how and when our support is needed."

"Alright," Shantell said in a wavering voice. He could tell she was digesting his answer. As the call ended he was not at all confident Shantell would stay away from Hudson. If she didn't, he was going to have another showdown with his Board president.

John talked briefly with Zack James. It was clear the district's crisis intervention team would be welcomed support as his staff had their hands full right now. John assured Zack he'd talk with the middle school level's pupil services director, Barbara Mason, as soon as he was back at the office. He also let him know Janey Eisen would be there shortly to interface with the media and to help in any public communication needs they had. They both agreed to talk later in the day, or sooner, if Zack needed any further support. While he was in the parking lot he decided to touch base with Jane Hueset. He and the mayor exchanged their private cell phone numbers and agreed they'd use them when an immediate communication was warranted. John felt this was one of those times.

Jane answered quickly. "I was about to call you; this is terrible John. The violence is never ending. We had a murder last night. It was drug related of course and now this, two young boys."

"I know Jane, the violence keeps happening. The kids and staff at Hudson are really shaken. Since the media will be all over this today, I want Janey Eisen to talk with your staff and see if together they can develop a coordinated statement. I will have to say something specifically as well, since it happened at a school bus stop and involved two of our kids. I am headed back to my office now. I'll email you a copy of my prepared statement once it is written."

"Okay John. Let's talk in a few hours. I am not sure there's much more we can do at this point. Let's see how the morning goes. It may help lead us to any next step comments or ideas."

John felt he'd made the initial round of calls required of him. He wanted to leave Hudson before the media vans arrived. Luckily, Janey pulled in and they briefly discussed the status of things. John then climbed into his SUV. As he left he noticed the first news van coming down the street.

CHAPTER 31

WHAT CAN WE DO?

Andrea completed her report cards and gave them to Janet McGee knowing Ma'am wanted to read them before being sent home. She hoped Ma'am would be pleased with her summaries and supportive of her grading strategy. Andrea followed Bea's advice and graded the students not on the accomplishment of standards but on the extent of effort to meet them. She also made clear comments on where each student's progress was in reference to the expected fourth grade standards. This was a compromise she hoped walked an appropriate line on progress reporting.

Andrea was looking forward to seeing Jason for dinner after work. They had not talked much since she'd been to the apartment and she hoped they'd make some plans for the weekend. Jason was already at the Italian restaurant when she arrived. They loved pasta and this was one of the better Italian restaurants in the city. Once both had a glass of wine in hand, they began sharing stories about what was happening at work. Jason made a good life insurance sale and he was excited about the commission he would receive. He talked about the attorney who bought the policy and how he'd met him playing racket ball.

Andrea spoke about the kids and how she had a tough time grading report cards. Jason listened attentively. It was a relaxing conversation and both were fully absorbed in each other's company.

Over dinner Andrea shared what was happening with Dedra and how she and Bea planned to take her shopping at Wal-Mart, hoping for a break-through. She asked Jason while they were having coffee if he'd like to come to dinner on Sunday at Bea's. Jason had not met Bea and Andrea was anxious for them to meet.

"Andrea, it's football Sunday and the Eagles are playing the Giants. It will be a great game. I invited some of the guys over to watch. You know me and football."

"I understand Jason, but I'd really like you to meet Bea." Andrea was disappointed Jason didn't offer to change his plans, but she decided not to express it. "How about some time next week; you can come over for dinner after work. I'll give you directions to Bea's house."

Jason promised to keep his calendar open and agreed to the dinner invitation. As they left the restaurant Andrea declined his invitation back to the apartment. She was more let down about Jason's decision to watch football than she let on. But when the opportunity arose to go back to the apartment and consummate an otherwise relaxing evening, she decided payback was in order. She saw the disappointment on Jason's face and thought to herself, 'How does it feel to be frustrated?'

On her drive back to Bea's Andrea thought about her actions. She was not pleased with herself for declining to go back to the apartment. She was really thinking about the ebb and flow of their relationship. 'Was she really committed to it?' She didn't have a clear answer right now.

Monday came around quickly with a morning team meeting on Dedra's needs. As she was driving to work, Andrea was thinking about what she wanted to share with her colleagues. She had come to appreciate the short drive from Bea's home to school. She was growing accustomed to the rhythms of the neighborhood; now stopping at the corner Seven-Eleven to get coffee on the way to school.

The way things worked in this part of the city was growing ever more familiar to Andrea. The past weekend she'd shopped with Bea at the local market. It was a different experience. The numerous social interactions between Bea and her neighbors were surprising. Previously, Andrea had an impression a culture of fear prevailed and people would move quickly to finish their grocery shopping. This was far from the reality. Of course it didn't hurt Bea was an outgoing women, whose recent assault was a reason for people to stop and talk. But there was more to it. Andrea liked the interactions and casual chat which flowed down the market's aisles.

However, the church experience was truly eye-opening. Andrea was a Catholic who dutifully went to mass. The mass had a routine and everyone sat in the pews and went through the robotic rituals with little effort or much enthusiasm. Once mass concluded a mad rush for the parking lot ensued with a resulting traffic jam.

At Bea's church, people met and greeted everyone. They introduced themselves to Andrea and genuinely wanted to know about her. Nobody felt a rush to get started. People talked their way into the church. Reverend James was an active participant in the pre-church habit of conversation. Once they started, the singing and praising of God was a full on faith happening filled with spontaneity. People responded 'Amen' numerous times as Reverend James gave his passionate sermon about the violence on the streets of the city. He talked specifically about the death of a young middle school boy at a school bus stop at the hands of a fellow student. Andrea was deeply moved by the depth of concern shared within the walls of this church. She also was impressed to hear a sermon related to what was happening in the neighborhood. This did not often happen in her suburban Catholic parish.

Andrea arrived at school, and was sitting at the morning team meeting which Ma'am chaired. The school's social worker, nurse, and several special education teachers were also regulars at each meeting. The purpose was to listen to a staff member's concerns and make decisions about how best to support a classroom teacher or address a child's needs with additional resources. This was not Andrea's first time at this type of meeting; she was used to what would take place.

Once Ma'am started the meeting she asked Andrea to share information and concerns about Dedra. Usually a teacher had about five to ten minutes as the team meeting took place about forty minutes before the first morning bell to start school. Often two cases were on each meeting's agenda, so time was precious.

Andrea began by sharing Dedra's behaviors since the death of her older brother. She noted how quiet and withdrawn she had become. She shared, briefly, some of her efforts to draw her out; for the most part with little success. Then she said, "I talked with Dedra's mom in the market on Saturday. She said Dedra was quiet at home too. Her mom is worried about this and does not know what to do. At church yesterday I talked with Reverend James about Dedra. He is going to talk with mom as well. He thinks mom's grief needs to be less evident for Dedra's sake. He's going to encourage her to do some things with Dedra and to celebrate life more."

Ma'am smiled as Andrea provided these insights. The staff rarely heard of these neighborhood contacts. Yet here was this young teacher making connections in the community for this little girl. Mom never attended a parent conference, yet one had happened in a grocery store aisle.

The group brainstormed different strategies Andrea could try. The team also decided some counseling support for the next few months would be a helpful addition. Coordinating sessions in Hanna Strassman's busy schedule as the school's social worker was going to be difficult. Andrea shared she and Bea were going to take Dedra shopping with them at Wal-Mart next Saturday. They hoped this might be another way to reach Dedra. Everyone was surprised by this, but strongly supported the strategy.

Ma'am was proud of Andrea and Bea's mentoring of her. Ma'am would have to call Bea later and share her observations about the connections Andrea was able to make by being part of the school neighborhood.

Ma'am had an elementary program committee meeting at 4:00 tonight. She was working out the final details of an agenda for the meeting. She planned to ask the group to brainstorm different arrangements for student organization. She was confident Myrna would put on the table the need to work with children at a much younger age than five. She wondered how the group would react to the idea. Ma'am thought with School #3 possibly scheduled to be torn down and replaced; perhaps they should talk about how to merge construction ideas closely with instruction needs and changes. 'What should a 21st century elementary school look like?' This would not be on the agenda tonight, but it was something growing in her thoughts.

Bea called to tell her she wanted to talk about the power of the neighborhood. 'How could they encourage more folks to participate in the schooling of their children? Was there a way to make the school more of a social hub for the neighborhood?' Bea was hoping Reverend James would have some suggestions since his church played a significant role in getting people together.

At the same time, they were all struggling with the failure rate of the children. The school's results were poor and the children were late out of the starting gate of life. Ma'am and her teachers talked again and again about the effects of poverty. Well meaning people kept saying like generations before, people of color had to pull themselves up by their bootstraps, 'America was the land of opportunity and with more self initiative they'd get closer to the American dream.' But the back of poverty was not easily broken by hard work. If so, more families would be successful among those served by School #3. As Ma'am was reflecting on the problem, John Lennon's, 'Imagine' was playing on her radio. She was trying hard to imagine success for her students despite all the odds stacked against them. 'Were they jousting with windmills? Could she and this small group develop something better?'

As she was reflecting on all these things, Janet came into her office to tell her Mary Jane Thomas was on the phone. 'Nuts,' Ma'am thought to herself. 'She never calls without something on her mind.'

"Hello Dr. Thomas, how are things downtown?"

"They're fine," she said in her no nonsense business voice. "I'm calling to alert you I plan on attending your committee meeting this afternoon. I'd like to stay in touch with what you are doing and I wanted to confirm 4:00 is the start time."

"We'll look forward to seeing you join us." This was a lie, but what else could Ma'am do or say? Her visit would complicate things, but she could not change the agenda at this point. They were going to have to go over the falls with Mary Jane sooner than she'd planned.

Right at 4:00 Mary Jane was standing in School #3's main office. Janet McGee directed her to the faculty room where the meeting was getting underway. Janet had little use for most downtown folks. Dr. Thomas was on her list as someone to avoid at all costs. She was glad she was on her way to the faculty room and her roaming judgmental eyes would be on someone else.

Mary Jane entered the room with a feeling she was entering enemy territory. She saw School #3 as a complete failure. She felt Ma'am was too defensive and the staff needed a great deal of additional training if things were going to improve. Bea and Dr. Thomas locked eyes for a brief moment and the animosity between them was hardly disguised. Ma'am alerted Bea Mary Jane would be coming securing a promise she would use every shred of self-control she could muster. Ma'am hoped she could do the same.

After Ma'am introduced Dr. Thomas to the group, Myrna talked about the needs of her students and how far behind developmentally they were when entering kindergarten. She expressed her view school needed to start much earlier than age five. No committee members disagreed with this perspective. Dr. Thomas could not hold back. "This is an elementary program study, not a preschool one!"

Ma'am was about to respond when Reverend James spoke up. "Dr. Thomas, do you disagree with the view children in this neighborhood are developmentally behind most children their age?"

"No I don't disagree with the point being made. We are charged to address the K-5 program, not to expand it. So I see this conversation as out of bounds."

"Really?" Reverend James continued. "Why are the needs of this population out of bounds for us to discuss? We are simply making observations here regarding needs. We have not proposed anything new yet on how to address those needs."

"Yes, but early childhood needs are beyond the scope of this committee."

It was Myrna who spoke up at this point. "Dr. Thomas, we all want the children who attend School #3 to succeed. The dramatic effects of poverty are most evident in this school. It serves the poorest and one of the most violent areas of the city. We can't cope with the level of need here by waiting for children to reach age five. I realize money is tight and our charge is to recommend improvements to K-5 program. But significant improvement rests on responding to the needs of the children we are asked to educate."

In a condescending tone, Mary Jane responded. "Myrna, I can assure you many other schools here and in other districts are doing much better than School #3 on student literacy success while not educating the children until they enter kindergarten. Blaming the first five years as a rationale for not meeting student needs in the succeeding years is an excuse."

It was Myrna's turn to speak her mind now. "You can't be serious! This staff works incredibly hard to address the needs of the children coming through our front door. The effects of poverty and neglect are huge here. I invite you to visit my kindergarten and see them for yourself."

Reverend James stepped in as well. "Dr. Thomas, you are missing the point of this team. We are trying our best to understand what we are up against before we address the school program. We don't know what a new beginning may look like yet. But we strongly believe we have to see what matters most before taking any improvement steps. Please don't pre-judge what we are trying to do here."

Mary Jane, feeling outnumbered in this setting, decided to retreat to silence. She folded her arms and closed down. Ma'am thought, 'She's behaving the same way as Bea did at her meeting.'

Ma'am was also pleased others on the committee took on the challenge. However, she knew Mary Jane would likely try to pull the plug on this group. Ma'am would have to work overtime to prevent it.

CHAPTER 32

FULL HANDS

John Handler had his hands full. The Hudson Middle School tragedy had filled his calendar the last few days. The press picked up on the bullying aspect of the story and this was a major issue for him. 'Was the district doing enough to curb bullying behaviors?' Numerous parents and students were on TV proclaiming they were victims of bullying in the city schools saying little support from the administration or teachers was provided when a victim reported it.

The active reporting of this problem now made it a center-stage issue his Board could not ignore. They were asked by the media and community members what the district was doing to respond to the, 'Rampant bullying problem'. Their emails and calls to John were filled with questions and concerns related to this problem. They were all under the spotlight and the heat was getting intense.

John talked several times with principal Zack James. The kids and staff at Hudson Middle School were grieving. Zack was exhausted and his team spent countless hours trying to respond to all the issues surfacing. Along with all the grief and counseling issues, Hudson was on the firing line for not addressing bullying behaviors effectively. A growing feeling of guilt surfaced amongst the staff. 'Had they really missed this? Should they have seen it coming?'

Shantell Williams visited the school twice, as John feared she might. She was sending her own email reports to the Board. On top of this she was speaking with the staff and asking them questions about the district's support for anti-bullying programs.

John was livid. She created some of the growing guilt by probing the bullying issue with teachers and administrators. Zack James felt he was losing the confidence of the Board and called John asking him what he should do. Shantell had absolutely no comprehension of the wake her boat was throwing.

John was meeting with Shantell this afternoon and was anticipating a stormy session. He could not condone her behavior. It simply had to stop. How to convince her of this was the challenge as nothing worked up to this point and he had little cause for optimism.

John spent some time considering what he wanted to say. He was trying to think about how he could help her see the road to hell was paved with good intentions.

Shantell expected another scolding from John. She couldn't understand why he didn't appreciate her help. She was convinced her compassion and visibility were assets to be drawn upon in this crisis. She also felt the Board appreciated her perspectives on what was taking place following the tragedy.

Shantell came to John's office as he'd requested. John decided to begin with a different point. Rather than reveal his anger over her visit, he decided to help her see some of the impact she hadn't noticed up to this point. John knew Shantell respected Zack James so he decided to begin the conversation there.

"We have the funeral tomorrow and it's going to be tough on everyone. We're doing many things to help support the staff and students. But we're not sure how things will unfold tomorrow. I think Zack James has been working like a dog on this. He's been tireless in his efforts since this took place. I wonder if you see it the same way?"

This was not the conversation Shantell expected and she was caught off guard. She did appreciate Zack's efforts and was quick to say so. "I think Zack has been terrific throughout this. He's been everywhere and the staff and kids adore him."

"So would it surprise you if I told you Zack called me worrying he had lost the Board's confidence?"

"What, are you kidding?"

"No I am not, far from it in fact. I had to assure him he did have the Board's confidence and he was doing all he could in a difficult situation."

"Why would he think that?" asked Shantell.

"Because you made two visits to his school, he thought you did not have confidence in his efforts. Your emails to the Board led to calls to him from Board members offering their help to reduce the bullying problems at Hudson. It all left him feeling like he wasn't doing enough."

"But I told him he was doing a terrific job! How could he possibly think any differently?"

"Shantell, you know I was there at the onset and then quickly let him and his staff work the problem. If I lingered he would have formed the same conclusion about my confidence in his judgment. I know you truly believe you are helping by being visible. Do you remember, I told you there was a time for that and it wasn't right now?"

"Yes I do, Dr. Handler, but I felt it wouldn't hurt to be visible."

"Despite what I said Shantell, you ignored my request. I have spent a lifetime learning how a school system works. It's my profession. I know your heart is in the right place. But it's not how things work. Your office comes through the door before your person does. We are always assumed to be in a judgmental state. It goes with the territory. I am not telling you to stay away as a power issue. I said then and say it now, I don't disagree with your logic, it's your timing. Tomorrow I'd strongly encourage you and other Board members to attend the funeral service. That is the time for us to show our support. There also will be a time when you can recognize Zack. A letter from the Board complimenting him and the staff will be much appreciated once the crisis and the high emotions have passed. You must begin to trust my actions and realize my requests are motivated by what is in the best interest of the district."

"Well John, I didn't know why you were so insistent about my staying away. It always seems you want the spotlight."

"Shantell, there are times when I can't avoid the spotlight. You pay me to stand in it and protect you and the system. Remember the list of roles and responsibilities we shared at the Saturday meeting? It is how you and the members help me lead the district. We are a team. You folks represent the owners, but I am the head coach and have to call the plays as I see them. You have to accept it. I am asking you to reflect on this conversation. I am not seeking the spotlight, but when it shines I need to be the one most often out front. I need you supporting me in the months ahead, because things aren't going to get any easier as we go along."

Shantell knew her superintendent's comments were heartfelt. He was candid and forthright. She wondered as she left his office what she was going to do in response to his repeated requests she and the Board dial it down.

John thought, 'I did all I could to explain my position. We'll have to see how it plays out.' Once Shantell left he met with Ann to prepare a communication for the Board. He also needed to have Ann set up a meeting with the mayor to talk about the Community Violence Committee. It was clear bullying behaviors would now be an agenda item. He wanted to be sure they were singing from the same sheet music.

The next morning promised to be a challenging one. A great deal of grief and pent up anger would be drifting across the ocean of emotions forthcoming around the funeral service for Tommy Hillen. Despite all the preparation, nothing could have prepared John for what would happen the next day.

CHAPTER 33

CONFLICT HAPPENS

Janet announced to Ma'am Mary Jane Thomas was on the phone. 'What a surprise,' Ma'am thought to herself. "Good morning Dr. Thomas."

"Good morning Mrs. Washington." Ma'am thought, 'Well we're both off to a formal start. It's her call; let's see where this goes.'

Mary Jane continued, "I was disappointed in your meeting last night."

"I know, everyone saw it. You behaved the way Bea did at your meeting." Ma'am wondered how she'd take the shot, but was glad it was delivered.

"I beg your pardon!"

'It wasn't going to go down easy was it?'

"What are you saying?"

"What I am saying is you folded your arms and closed down after being argumentative. After the meeting people talked about it. They were surprised by your behavior." Ma'am decided to take another shot, "Especially those members who never met you before."

"Dorothy."

'Good' Ma'am thought. 'At least she's not calling me Mrs. Washington anymore.'

"I am calling to tell you how surprised I was by the conversation at last night's meeting. Your people didn't have much data in front of them regarding your school. Your school, - Ma'am thought, 'It's my school whenever there's bad news and our school when it's good, typical downtown speak,' - "is one of the poorest performing in the city. It's flat out failing the kids and you are ignoring the data."

"Mary Jane, you couldn't be more wrong. We've worked with Kelly Slocum and the data queens," Ma'am thought she'd reference what the downtown data folks were called by the staff, "until our eyes have blurred. We know the data inside and out. It tells us we are failing. But it doesn't tell us why!"

"If you look at the data Dorothy, then you can do prescriptive teaching. It makes a real difference in student performance."

"Mary Jane, it certainly hasn't been the case in this district. We've only gotten marginally better despite ten years of data driven practices."

"That's what the K-5 Program study is for. We're looking for answers. I think we need new materials and better class sizes. I don't want us sidetracked with a whole new way of doing things. Your group isn't even remotely thinking along the same lines as the main team. I can't continue to support your work when you are so far afield!"

'Can I get to first base with this woman or am I going to strike out here at home plate?' Dorothy wondered. "Mary Jane, we don't know what we are going to propose. We are looking at lots of different things. The School #3 sub-committee hasn't made any decisions yet. We are brainstorming the problem and discussing all the different factors affecting the children we serve."

"But where will all the brainstorming and open-ended thinking lead?"

'Good, she's at least wrestling with the idea.' "I don't know at this point," Ma'am said. "What I do know is I have to allow the group to explore and think outside the box before we develop anything specific."

"Your kindergarten teacher, Myrna, she's not going to settle for anything less than a pre-school program Dorothy. How are we going to be able to fund that? Our charge was a K-5 improvement effort."

Ma'am thought, 'We're on first base. At least she's asking questions now and not saying no way.' "Let's say for the sake of this conversation our final recommendation does include some early childhood effort, like the Head Start program. I know we have to be able to fund it. The whole group knows we don't have new money on the table here so we won't be naïve about what can be done."

"Are you saying pre-school is on the table and will be in your report?"

"I am talking hypothetically to make a point. I realize money is tight. We can't go off half-cocked and think we can do whatever we propose. Please trust I won't let it happen."

"Well Dorothy I am not sure a hypothetical idea can be explored. I don't want to lose this opportunity to get new materials and put lower class size on the table."

"Lowering class size will cost a ton of money. I don't think one idea will overrule another. We won't get sidetracked because two committees are working. Perhaps what we develop will be a great compliment to what the main group does. We may end up with strength in numbers."

"I don't see it the same way. But if I pull the plug on your effort the blowback will reach Dr. Handler. At this point I need to share my concerns with him and see what he wants to do. I don't support you continuing. I expect to put a stop to it now."

"I understand. I am sure John will consider all the implications and make a decision in the best interest of the district." Dorothy was glad it was Mary Jane putting the issue on his desk. This question was all Mary Jane's doing. She'd invited herself to the meeting. She'd made a decision to shut things down and put the problem on John's shoulders. Dorothy decided to stay back in the eel grass and trust John would let her continue.

CHAPTER 34

THE FUNERAL

Zack James called John about 6:30PM on the night before Tommy Hillen's funeral. He and his staff heard many of the Hudson students were planning on skipping school to go to the funeral service. His instincts told him this could be a serious problem.

John asked, "Are you still at Hudson?"

"Yes, and so are my VP's. We felt we needed to call and alert you this was happening. With Facebook, Twiter and text messaging, it could grow fast overnight."

"I agree with you. I will call Chief Young. Let's see if he can meet us at your office in a half hour. I'll ask Joanne Walters to join us as well. We're going to need to get our heads around this or things could get out-of-hand."

John made the necessary calls while heading out the door. He knew the next 12 hours were going to be packed with crisis planning.

After working his way through traffic, John arrived at Hudson at about 7:00PM. Joanne came through the door shortly thereafter. The Chief said he'd make it by 7:30. He asked Roger Decker, a middle school resource officer, to join the group. Roger had a good rapport with the students and knew the early adolescent age level.

Before the Chief arrived, John and Joanne talked with the Hudson administrative team about what happened at school. Hudson VP Lou Pagano had checked some key Facebook pages and noticed kids were posting messages about skipping school and attending the funeral for Tommy.

Chief Young and Officer Decker arrived. The group spent a few minutes catching them up on the details. Once they were all on the same page, it was a consensus the students had to be taken seriously, requiring intervention planning.

"The church isn't real big," the Chief pointed out. "I think it can seat maybe 250 before the fire marshal will step in. Mr. James, how many students do you think may skip school and go to this funeral?"

"There's no telling! But if I had to guess, we may have as many as four or five hundred. Tommy was popular. Once the kids get something going, it's hard to predict the extent of it. I am worried; it might even be more than what I'm thinking. They'll be texting all night on this!"

"Does anybody know the weather forecast for tomorrow?" asked Officer Decker.

The seventh grade VP, Sara Drexel piped in, "It's not going to help us."

"Alright, let's assume we're going to have four hundred kids on the street by the church tomorrow. What options do we have to control the situation?" asked the Chief.

Zack chimed in, "We're going to have a lot to manage both here and there. The kids remaining at school are going to be restless, especially once they realize what's going on. Since the church is only five blocks from here, we may have more kids bolt during the morning."

"You are right." Joanne answered. "We are going to need more staff here tomorrow. We should get started now. Do you folks have a listing of subs who know building routines and have the respect of staff and kids?"

"No specific list, Joanne." Looking at his VP's, Zack continued, "You guys could put one together quick. Helen, is still here thank God. She can make personal calls to each sub you list asking them to come tomorrow." The three stepped out and went to work with Helen.

"Zack, I am not sure having extra subs on hand will be enough support," Joanne said.

"I wonder if we should plan on having key staff members at the funeral site. They would know kids by name and be able to help us keep order." Joanne's skills as a former middle school and elementary principal and now as the Middle School level's assistant superintendent were especially helpful as she talked directly to Zack about the multiple challenges to be addressed.

Chief Young spoke up. "I think having some staff at the funeral who know the kids and have their respect would be a real help. But, my officers must be in charge there. It is an area we will have the responsibility to control."

"The Chief's right, a few staff members at the site will be helpful, but controlling things at the church is their job." John wanted his folks to keep a tight grip on where their responsibilities rested. "Chief let us know what you need. We'll do our best to support you."

The planning process went on for another two hours before it ended. Helen reached fourteen of the seventeen subs on the make-shift list. Nine could make it to the school in the morning to help. Everyone agreed the first indication of the extent of the problem would come when they took attendance in the morning.

They agreed to meet at 7:00 AM, an hour before school started. John called the transportation manager, Tom Foley. The team agreed it would be helpful to have ten buses on standby near the church. They hoped the students would cooperate and go back to school after the funeral service was finished. They also agreed the police would send additional officers to Hudson at about 9:30. They would be there to assist VP's Sara Drexel and Leroy Becker who would be staying at school. Lou Pagano, the eighth grade VP and Zack James would be at the church. They also identified six other influential staff members to be near the church.

John felt they'd done all they could in preparation for the day. He was worried how things might go, but little else could be done. The behaviors of the students would dictate how things turned out.

The group gathered at 7:00AM the next morning. The plans they discussed were set. Everyone felt they needed to see how things unfolded. They got their first indication from Transportation Director, Tom Foley. He had been on the radio with his drivers as they were doing the bus pick-up run for Hudson. "John, my drivers are telling me their runs are very light. I hate to say this, but I think there's a big problem. I think you'll be lucky to have 700 kids at school this morning."

John told the team, "It looks like we are going to have a lot of kids absent today. Tom Foley's telling me the buses are coming in with less than half the normal number of kids."

"Damn it!" Zack said. "We are going to have our hands full here. Chief Young, I think you better prepare for an overwhelming number of kids at the funeral service."

Chief Young was already on his hand-held radio relaying the preliminary information to his command officers. He knew they were going to have a very busy morning.

Knowing with more certainty what was unfolding, Zack James made a suggestion. "Look, I know this is late in the game here; I've been thinking about how we get in front of this thing. I have an idea I want to share."

"We're all ears!" the Chief replied.

"What if we took the whole school there. It looks like we've got half or more going already. We could bus the rest. We could assemble the kids and most of the staff in the parking lot across the street from the church. We already have our AV guys setting up loudspeakers so the kids can hear the service. We'd have all of them in a contained space. Chief you'd have more of my staff to help with the control issues. We could keep all the kids in the parking lot and after the service is finished; we could bring buses down the street, load the kids on and take them back to school."

Silence held the moment as everyone thought about what Zack was suggesting. It was the Chief who asked, "John what do you think of the idea Mr. James has?"

"Wow, Zack. I'm thinking it has some merit, but can we pull it off is the question?"

"I've been thinking about it all night. We know the kids have deep feelings about Tommy Hillen's death. What if we follow their lead here? We can keep any kids here who for health reasons, or for lack of warm clothes shouldn't attend. Also, those who have strong feelings about not going could also stay here. We can run a video in the cafetorium for them and leave a VP and some staff to supervise. The street in front of the church isn't big, but Chief if you guys do all the traffic control, we could stage the buses in and out. We'll take attendance this morning and then again after the kids return. We'll know exactly who reported for school, who returned and who skipped all day. We can decide later how we want to handle that part of it."

John expressed his thoughts. "Maybe we could turn this into a real-life lesson on what happens when bullying and anger get the upper hand. I think it could co-opt the kids' efforts to skip school to attend the funeral. We will be on display for all the media outlets if something goes wrong." John was stating these reflections as he was beginning to internalize Zack's suggestion. As he did so, he was finding himself leaning more and more towards giving it the go ahead. "Chief, what do you think?"

"I could sure use the help down there. If we have more than five hundred kids, and only a few people who know them, we'll have our hands full. After the funeral is over those kids are going to be a roaming group. Anything could happen! I like containing them and getting them back on school buses after it's over. It's a real plus in my book."

"Okay, Zack you have our support for this. What do you need? "

"Guys, I need every minute to plan with my staff. If you don't mind, I can handle things here and update you in about an hour."

The Chief headed out the door. He and John talked in the hallway. "John, Zack knows how to think on his feet. I sure hope we can pull this off. I will have my folks get traffic control set up and we'll tape off the parking lot and nearby sidewalk as an assembly area for the school. I will also make sure the speakers are set, and update Reverend Pierce on what's going on. He's a good preacher; he'll love a bigger crowd. Call me and fill me in on the details. I've got lots of work to do on my end. My time will be better spent away from here with the troops."

"Okay," John said. "I'll call you with an update as soon as I have it." Janey Eisen was coming through the door with a harried look on her face. "Change in plans Janey, follow me!"

Zack James and his team did a terrific job over the next 45 minutes. They wrote a memo advising the staff of what was planned. They gave staff members the same option as the students. Those who did not want to attend the funeral service would be needed for supervisory duty for students who were staying behind to watch videos in the cafetorium.

The staff was advised students would be dismissed by loudspeaker from their second period classes. Students opting to stay would remain in the classroom and leave when a staff member came to get them. The secretarial staff was assigned to assume this escort duty.

The Chief and his officers were ready. They cordoned off a receiving area for the students across the street from the church and school resource officers were on both ends of the street to guide them to where they should assemble. Many students, arriving before their peers from school, were surprised by the organization. They were easily directed to the parking lot area. Once there, they were greeted by Hudson VP's Lou Pagano along with several staff members.

At 9:15 the dismissal to the buses began at Hudson. Most students and staff opted to go to the funeral; however, about 150 students stayed behind. They were supervised by the staff holding the fort in the cafetorium.

By 9:40 nearly one thousand students and one hundred staff were standing in the parking lot across the street from the church. The group was respectful and became nearly silent when the hearse carrying Tommy Hillins' body pulled up. The family was told about the school's plan; they were moved by it. No hats were allowed on while Tommy's body was lifted from the hearse and carried into the church. The mournful family was in plain sight, sending a powerful message of grief and loss to all who witnessed it.

Reverend Pierce's voice was deep and powerful. His message against violence and the loss of such a young life was well scripted. The cadence of Reverend Pierce's powerful voice echoed off nearby buildings. Not a student or staff member spoke, but tears and hugs were plentiful.

Most students knew the hymn at the end of the service; it was one they'd learned in sixth grade music class. Their added voices were so strong the people in the church could hear them over the choir inside. The students were saying 'good-bye' to Tommy, who only a few days before was sharing the halls of Hudson with them.

When the service concluded, Tommy's body was carried back to the waiting silver Cadillac hearse outside. The students removed their hats and stood silently. They could hear the voice of the undertaker as he instructed the pallbearers on how to guide Tommy's casket back into the hearse.

After the hearse and family left, all the students dutifully followed instructions of the teachers and police officers present. They boarded buses and went back to school. Throughout this whole process the media was not allowed to interview or speak to students or staff. However, Janey Eisen arranged for Zack James to meet with the media and respond to questions.

John and Mayor Hueset were also interviewed. They decried the violence and spoke of the lesson they hoped was learned by all the students who were there this morning. The reporters asked John why the whole school was allowed to attend. He shared they were moved by the outpouring of grief at Hudson. He credited Zack James for the decision and the subsequent support he received from everyone. The story was one of an outpouring of grief for the loss of this young boy's life.

CHAPTER 35

LIFE GOES ON

The coverage of Tommy Hillen's funeral made not only the local news, but also the national as well. Bea and Andrea watched the remarkable scene on the small TV in Bea's kitchen while getting supper ready. They talked about the tragic loss of a young life and the tremendous response.

Bea and Andrea were also talking about Jason. He'd come to dinner last night. It was clear Bea got a real kick out of having a man in the house. "Well Andrea, he's a handsome young man. You don't want him you let me know, maybe I can hook him up with my Jasmin."

"Bea, I don't know why I'm so confused about my feelings for him. One minute I think he's the one and the next I'm not sure where things are headed."

"I can't tell you what to think. But I can tell you you gotta have a life outside of teachin'. We talked about this Andrea. I still think you are spendin' a whole lot of time on your kids and not enough on yourself. If you spend more time on yourself, I think the answer will come. Right now I think you are conflicted 'cause you are tired and thinkin' school too much. You need some romance time girl, take a breath from all this! You're still adjustin' to your work and you had a bad thing happen. Give yourself some room, if it is meant to be it will be. If not, sure better to find out now."

"I know you are right," Andrea said. "But my need for answers seems overwhelming right now. I wish I knew how I felt. I hate this on-off feeling I have. It's not like me. But, hey let's talk about Dedra and our shopping trip to Wal-Mart tomorrow. She smiled when I told her we were excited about our chance to go shopping with her. But she still doesn't say much. I don't know Bea, it is so hard to reach her."

"All we can do is spend some time with that sweet little girl. We aren't gonna work miracles. You got to stop lookin' for one 'cause Dedra needs everyone's help. We all can hold her hand, but she's the one who has to take the steps back to herself. "

"You are right, yet I keep thinking things will start getting better right now."

"Give yourself time, like Dedra needs." Their talk drifted over many things and then it was time for her to get ready for her night with Jason. "Hey girl, you got something pretty to wear under those clothes?"

Andrea blushed, "Bea, you are embarrassing me!"

"No way, you gotta have some lovin' and romance in your life. You got to participate. You make love to Jason tonight and stop thinkin' about work!"

"Okay, okay!" Andrea was smiling as she said it. She knew Bea was right again.

It was a Friday night. Jason and Andrea were going out with friends and she was meeting him at the apartment at 8:30. Andrea needed to feel something powerful between them again and she hoped he'd feel the same way. Their plan was to meet several friends at a downtown comedy club around 9:00. Beyond that, they had no other commitments. She spent time getting ready. She did look terrific as she went out the door. Bea smiled thinking, 'Romance, the girl needs romance.'

When she arrived at the apartment Jason was ready. He was wearing his Dockers, a tee shirt and a nice crew neck blue sweater. Andrea couldn't help herself as she embraced him, kissed him and pressed her body to him. Jason responded the same way.

As they got in the car they were talking about the week ahead. "It's Thanksgiving and Jasmin will be home. Bea's physical therapy has really been helpful and she has more movement in her shoulder. I think it's time for me to come back to the apartment."

Jason smiled saying, "It's about time."

"I think so too Jason. When I get back I have some ideas about how we might be able to balance our time. But tonight let's just enjoy our friends."

On the drive back to Bea's home the next day Andrea realized she was pleasantly exhausted. She and Jason enjoyed a night with friends at the comedy club. When they returned to the apartment their passion for each other boiled over into a wonderful night of love making. Since the incident Andrea had been a reluctant partner. Jason was tender and caring and their time in bed was healing for both of them.

Over breakfast Andrea and Jason made plans to start again. With his help she'd move her things back into the apartment on Sunday. They agreed Wednesday night would be a night saved for the two of them. They called it their "date night." Andrea said she needed Sundays to plan for the coming week. She also needed time on Monday, Tuesday and Thursday nights. Jason accepted this knowing he'd schedule his after-hours insurance calls on those days. They both knew their relationship needed attention and hoped this would help them turn the corner on what had been a rocky experience over the past several months.

Bea was ready and waiting when Andrea stepped into the house. "Oh girl I see a glow in those tired eyes of yours. You were dancin' in the sheets!"

Andrea still blushed when Bea discussed this. Here was this woman who put it out there and expected Andrea to share things right back that seemed so intimate and private.

"We danced most of the night Bea. I was a love machine," she said laughing.

"I told ya you needed to get it on; now tell me, are ya movin' back in with him soon? You're not goin' home again are ya?"

"I am moving back to the apartment Sunday. Jason is going to help me get my things here and at my folks. We've got work to do on our relationship. One night of making love isn't going to fix it. But it was a good start!"

"You remember what we talked about. Your work isn't everything. You gotta make time in your life for yourself and Jason. You do your part, he does his; I'm thinkin' you'll do fine together. Now let's go get Dedra and have some fun doin' some shoppin'."

Off they went, this petite young white girl and the middle-aged black women who were more like sisters. Their friendship and ability to speak openly to each other blossomed during Andrea's stay.

Dedra was excited to see Andrea and when her teacher stepped out of the car she ran and gave her a hug. Andrea felt a tear welling as this was the most outward display of emotion Dedra had shown in a long time. While Dedra and Andrea talked about what they would do at Wal-Mart, Bea took a moment to talk with Dedra's mom. Always direct, Bea said to mom, "You got a beautiful little girl, you be sure you give her time. She don't need to see you cryin' everyday. You gotta help her get back to bein' a little girl. It'll do you both good." Bea got in the car with Andrea and Dedra and they began their shopping adventure.

Bea and Andrea agreed to let Dedra pick out a nice top. They also would pick out a book, Andrea insisted on it. After they finished their Wal-Mart shopping they planned to stop for lunch at a local diner and then go to the grocery store with Dedra if she wanted to tag along.

What a morning they shared with this little girl. Andrea held Dedra's hand as they walked through the parking lot. Dedra had never spent time with a teacher in this way. She was excited, even though she'd been to Wal-Mart countless times. Once inside, Bea told Dedra they were going to treat her to a new top. She gave Dedra $15.00 and said, "You gotta spend it wisely girl. You pick somethin' out for yourself, we aren't doin' it for ya." Bea then stood back up and winked at Andrea. This was part of their plan. They wanted Dedra to be an active participant and not just along for the ride.

Dedra surprised them. She said, "I really want to buy new pajamas. I ain't had any new ones in a long time and I need em."

Bea, who was taking charge of this part of the adventure said, "Well then that's what we need to buy. Can you find 'em in this store?"

Dedra took off running. Andrea was moved to tears as she saw this little girl, arms flailing as she ran down an aisle. The victories in life often came in fleeting moments. Andrea would hold the picture of Dedra running in Wal-Mart towards the pajamas in her mind for years to come.

Dedra must have had a particular set of PJ's in mind as she went straight to them. They were lime green with sparkles on the front of the long-sleeved shirt. They agreed on the size with Dedra and placed the $12.95 outfit in the shopping basket Andrea was carrying.

Andrea said, "I have to get some stickers for school." The kids all loved the stickers Andrea placed on their 'good job' papers. "Will you help me pick them out?"

Dedra smiled and nodded her head.

"Okay you lead the way." Dedra did, moving off in front of them toward the school supply area. Bea and Andrea walked along chatting but kept Dedra in their sight.

When they reached the school supply area Dedra was waiting. She was holding a set of stickers in her hands. "Miss B," the kids often called Andrea Miss B, "I like these stickers."

"We have a few more things to do Dedra before we head to check-out. I want to buy you a new book and Mrs. Johnson needs some things. You'll have to help me pick one out for you." Again, Dedra smiled and nodded. Soon they'd accomplished that mission and after Bea finished shopping they were in the check-out line. Bea and Andrea decided Dedra should pay for the PJ's separate from the other purchases. Being ever teachers, they wanted her to have the experience and the chance to talk with the check-out clerk herself.

Dedra's turn came and she proudly offered the money to the clerk. "Those are nice pajamas honey," she said.

"I picked them out myself. I need new ones," Dedra declared proudly.

"Well those will do fine won't they now?"

Dedra nodded, with her chin almost touching her chest. She then proudly held out her hand and accepted the change. It was an awkward moment and Dedra wasn't quite sure what to do with the extra money.

"You keep the change Dedra," Bea said. "We're going to the grocery store after lunch. Maybe you'll see something there you'd like, if you want to go with us when we shop."

Dedra smiled and declared, "I like the grocery store!"

Both Bea and Andrea took this as a yes in response to Bea's invitation.

The local diner was filling up for lunch on this brisk Saturday morning. But Bea, Andrea and Dedra were soon seated at a booth. Looking at the well worn menus, they each decided on what they wanted for lunch. Andrea, sitting next to Dedra helped her with the menu. Dedra, choose a hot dog and fries.

While they were waiting, Bea asked Dedra what her favorite thing was at school.

Dedra smiled and said softly, "I don't know." It was a shy girl's response as she was feeling a bit overwhelmed by all this attention from two teachers.

Andrea said, "Mrs. Johnson what was your favorite thing when you were a little girl going to school?"

"Hmm, let me see. I guess I liked music class the best. I always like to sing. What about you Miss B?"

"I always liked quiet reading time, but I liked gym a lot 'cause I always liked to run."

"Me too," Dedra exclaimed.

The three talked on about things and soon lunch arrived. They were all surprisingly hungry and ate for several minutes without much talking.

Once finished, and the check paid, they were off to the grocery store. As always this was as much a social experience as a shopping one. Bea chatted with her friends and Dedra and Andrea were largely along for the ride. They laughed with each other as Bea talked and talked. With some of the money Dedra had left she decided to buy some chocolate chips. She made sure her mom would have one too when she got home.

When they arrived back at Dedra's home she jumped from the car and ran into the house with her PJ bag. She couldn't wait to tell her mom about what she bought. Bea and Andrea quietly high fived each other, believing the day's experience was as good an outcome as they could have hoped for.

Andrea hoped she could build on it at school on Monday. She was already thinking about journal time and what she'd say about this. She was also thinking about how the other children would feel and how she would need to do something special for them. In this moment though she was happy a little girl had such a special day, but then again so had her teacher.

CHAPTER 36

MOVING FORWARD

It was Monday of Thanksgiving week. Mary Jane Thomas asked Ann to put her on Dr. Handler's calendar as she had some items she wanted to discuss. John looked forward to the upcoming holiday and some time to see his children. But he had three days of work ahead of him, with Mary Jane Thomas first up on his calendar.

This morning, John really did not know what was on her agenda. But it was not like her to schedule a meeting or to dally in much casual conversation. As she came into his office, John was sitting in one of the comfortable chairs in front of his desk. When working with his staff he often liked to sit face-to-face rather than across the desk from them.

Mary Jane sat down and quickly got to the point. "John, I attended one of School #3's subcommittee meetings on elementary program change. I want your okay to disband the group before they go any further."

"Mary Jane, you'd better tell me what your concerns are about the subcommittee. Disbanding them so soon after they've started seems to me a serious step to take."

"John, they are talking about preschool programs not K-5 program improvement. Dorothy also spoke to me about the construction of a new building and if program changes could influence the planning. It was a brief question, but Dorothy never asks one without a lot more going on in her head. I think they will develop something which will put us in a corner and we won't be able to support it. I want to nip it in the bud."

"Mary Jane, did you talk with Dorothy about your concerns?"

"Yes. She was defending the ideas being discussed and when I said I was going to ask you to disband the group she said she would accept whatever you decided."

"You told her you wanted to shut down the group?"

Mary Jane shifted in her chair, sensing John was probing her thinking more deeply than she'd expected. "We need a uniform curriculum, and district-wide response. Her group won't be team players. They are going off on their own tangent John and I can't support their thinking." She'd put it on the table directly. John had to support her or choose to support Dorothy, something she was confident he wouldn't do.

"This is a big decision and there will be reaction to it no matter what I do. You've put me between a rock and a hard place with your absolutes. It would have been better if you'd shared your observations with me after attending the meeting without taking a position. I am not sure what to do now, Mary Jane."

"You can't be serious John. Her group will sell us down the river and go off on their own!"

"I told you and everyone else I want out-of-the-box thinking. Now you want me to shut down a group exploring something different? What message does it send? No, Mary Jane, if you came here thinking I'd say shut them down, you are mistaken. I need to call Dorothy and get her take on things before I make any decision. But you could have handled this better. I'll get back to you with a decision when I have thought it through."

Mary Jane left John's office angry he did not simply support her. Previous superintendents did whatever she recommended, but this guy was a wrecking ball swinging through the district. She did not respect him or his approach since he was too willing to break step with tradition on how things got done. She was certain he'd fail in his change plan. She decided to make sure those close to her knew how she felt about his leadership.

John called Dorothy Washington shortly after Mary Jane left his office. When Ma'am answered, John asked her to summarize how things went at the last subcommittee meeting.

"John, Mary Jane was tough to deal with. She challenged the group on even thinking about pre-school options. Reverend James took her on. When she could not persuade the group to drop our 'out-of-the-box' brainstorming she pouted. She crossed her arms and sat there. The next morning she called me and told me she was going to recommend our committee be stopped in its tracks. I imagine she's shared most of this with you at this point."

"Dorothy, she came in this morning and told me I needed to shut your group down before you went much further. Remember our previous conversation about avoiding a showdown with her?"

"I do John. She invited herself to our last meeting. She argued with the group. I tried not to mix it up with her as I did not want the folks to see two administrators fighting in an open meeting. I really don't know what else I could have done. She came in with the bit in her teeth and she could not be slowed down."

"Okay, tell me about where you think your group is headed. It's obvious Mary Jane thinks you are going south when everyone else wants to go north."

"John, I am not sure where we are headed yet. We have open-ended conversations about the developmental needs of young children. We talk about the poverty cycle and how deeply it affects our kids and we talk about how difficult it is to connect with the parents, grandparents and others involved in raising these youngsters. We are confirming what we know, but somehow I still think it's important to do before we start seeking any solutions."

"Dorothy, Mary Jane believes you are going down the wrong path. She is fearful you are going to propose things we can't afford or we will not be able to replicate."

"I know she has those fears John. I had a difficult conversation with her the about them. I can't get my head around the notions new materials and smaller class sizes will solve the problems we are facing. Our society is different. Solutions which worked fifty years ago aren't the ones to solve our problems now. I wish I knew the answer, but I have some strong beliefs about what will no longer work."

"Dorothy, I am not sure what to do at this point. I totally understand what you are trying to do; it is in line with what I encouraged. But the formal group she chairs isn't going in that direction. If I continue to empower your subcommittee over her objections it's going to be a tough pill for Mary Jane to swallow."

Dorothy shared the important points and had been honest with her superintendent. She knew he was between a rock and a hard place on this one. "John, can I send something over to you to read and ask you to attend our next meeting before making any final determination? If you decide to disband the subcommittee you will have my public support for your decision."

"Dorothy, I appreciate the position you are taking on this. When is your next meeting?"

Ma'am prepared an email for Dr. Handler with the journal entries from Andrea's class. She had saved them and decided this was the right moment to use them. She had her secretary, Janet, scan them along with Andrea's cover letter. Ma'am thought about what to add as her message and decided to say,

John,

Andrea Bauer is a fourth grade teacher at School #3. She is in her first year of teaching. You may recall Andrea was also the teacher who was victimized in the parking lot at our school.

While there is nothing surprising in the journal entries, they often remind me our students struggle daily with neglect, violence and the overall ravages of poverty. It is this constant 'life condition' that causes me to want our team to think outside-the-box on how to make lasting improvements to increase the chances the children we serve will be successful learners.

Dorothy

CHAPTER 37

THE BOILER

It was finally Wednesday afternoon and Thanksgiving was upon him. "John you'd better rest up over the break because next week's calendar is a real busy one. Monday you have the Quality School Committee. You also have a Board meeting prep discussion with Shantell and a working lunch with Tom Wheaton to begin budget planning for next year. Tuesday night you've got the Board meeting. Wednesday's the Community School Violence Committee and you have a prep meeting with the mayor. On Wednesday you also have a meeting with the school architects on project planning. Thursday you will be attending the School #3 planning meeting at 4:00. Before the meeting you wanted to talk with Zack James about his chairing a new anti-bullying strategy committee. Basketball season gets underway on Friday; you have several games you could choose to attend. There's lots on the agenda, so don't say I didn't warn you."

"Thanks for the warning Ann. You are right. There will be a lot on the agenda when we get back. You better rest up too!"

Both laughed and enjoyed the light moment. From experience they knew the holidays were a busy season and after the first of the year the budget process would kick into high gear. This year the finances looked to be particularly tough, especially with the poor financial conditions prevailing locally, state-wide and across the country. Ann did not envy John for the hard choices awaiting him.

The Thanksgiving break was one everyone looked forward to. So when the district's buildings and grounds director, Bud Peck called, John suspected something serious must be brewing. When he picked up the phone he heard Bud's deep voice on the line. Bud was a big guy who always smelled of cigars, although nobody saw him smoking during work hours or in any district vehicle. Bud had a great sense of humor and was well liked by his staff. He was not afraid of hard work and many times could be found working alongside his crew. "Hi Doc, the main boiler at Jefferson High decided to cook itself. Must a thought it was a turkey! Anyhow, we are running on the alternate boiler over there. That boiler is older than my grandmother and I don't know how long it will keep working. The main boiler is nearly 50 years old. We've kept that old honey running with lots of spare parts, but we don't have any way to fix it this time." Both knew Jefferson was one of the schools the architect study indicated should be torn down as it was deemed beyond repair.

"Bud, what's your bottom line on this?"

"I have no confidence the old spare boiler will keep running. It could go at any time. We have to replace the main boiler as fast as possible. But it's not going to happen for several months. First, we'll need the architects and engineers to work on specs for this one as a fast-track item. We can't get any quotes until we have their documents. I have no idea how quickly they can get them. Once we have a good quote we can move forward. Since it's an emergency repair, I think we can avoid the usual bidding laws. Once a contract is awarded, we can order the new boiler. It will have to be manufactured and delivered. Hard to guess how long that will take. Beyond all the technical stuff, the damn boiler room is old and there's lots of asbestos in there around the pipes. It all has to be removed. We can't remove it if school is running. So it would likely get done over the December break. Then we can start the actual replacement. Assuming the boiler is manufactured and delivered on time, we can install it in February."

"Bud any idea what this is going to cost?"

"Doc it's a wild guess at this point but there's lots of asbestos. That alone is going to cost us. We're going to have to remove the old boiler and custom fit a new one to all the old controls. Man, I think we should expect the final cost to be close half a million dollars by the time we're done."

John quietly said, "Shit."

"I hear ya Doc, this is a big deal and there's no easy fix for it."

"Ah, what a nice Thanksgiving turkey you have served us Bud."

Laughing Bud said, "Well I'm sorry this turkey is so overcooked boss."

"Have you broken this news to Tom Wheaton yet?"

"Yes, I called him first."

"I'll walk down to his office; we'll have to see what we can do on finding the money. The cost will more than blow out our regular maintenance budget. In the meantime you guys better start getting Sara Vaughn and her team up to speed writing the specs."

John decided to call the Jefferson principal, Neil Batten to get his take on things. Neil was a wiry guy in his forties. He was a good manager and attended to the details well. He was not the strongest instructional leader on the team, but his management skills were what the doctor ordered in this situation. John learned Neil had been to the boiler room and talked with Bud and his team when they were lighting the back-up boiler.

"Dr. Handler, so far so good! We're calling the old boiler 'Jenny' and we hope she keeps us warm for the next several months. Jenny hasn't been run in several years and we're all watching to make sure she doesn't leak. We are going to ask as little as possible of her. We've decided to run the building cooler than we'd like. I am already hearing the groaning. I suspect Carl will be hearing from the unions soon on it. We'd also like the ok to shut down a lot of after school activities if we can locate them elsewhere. Over the vacation period we plan to really drop the settings back. This place will be an icebox. But, we think the less we ask of Jenny the better."

"Neil, those sound like good steps. I'd like to have a list of the activities we might have to relocate. There may be some hard kick back and we all need to be on the same page if we shut things down. Speaking of that, what are the temperatures you're running at?"

"Bud wanted me to run things at sixty degrees. I told him I felt that was too cold. We compromised and decided on sixty five degrees as the target. This place is old so it means some rooms will be in the seventies while others are likely to be much cooler than 65."

"Okay Neil, let's run the boiler at in-session temps for a day over the break so we can see what the range is. Can you have your custodial staff check room readings and record them. We will have to pay them overtime for coming in; however, knowing we are going to have complaints I'd like some accurate figures to reference. You also will need to call Jerry Croton and begin contingency planning on what we do if Jenny decides to quit." John wanted Jerry involved in the planning. As the Assistant Superintendent for High School Programs he'd have to sweat the details of any plan and coordinate things with the other two principals.

After the conversations, John briefed Ann on what was happening. She knew this was really bad news and everyone in the know would be on pins and needles every day, dreading the call that said the back-up boiler was down.

John decided to wait until he had more information before sending an email out to his Board on the problem. He wanted better data and a chance to talk with Tom Wheaton about how they'd fund the expense of a new boiler.

He asked Ann to see if Jerry Croton, Tom Wheaton and Carl Gardner could meet with him briefly before they left for the holiday. It would be the first of several conversations regarding the new problem. In the meantime, he headed downstairs to Tom's office for a one-on-one regarding his views about where they'd get the money to pay for any boiler replacement.

CHAPTER 38

THANKSGIVING

Andrea, Jason and her mom and dad were coming to Bea's for Thanksgiving dinner. Bea wanted to have a celebration in her home and she and Jasmin had been busy throughout the week making preparations. Andrea's mom was bringing dessert and Andrea was bringing appetizers. Jason's family lived in San Francisco, and they were celebrating there with his older brother and family.

Andrea's parents had not been to Bea's home before and they were looking forward to the visit. Jason liked Bea and knew he was welcome as Andrea's boyfriend. He was actually more nervous about being with Andrea's parents, especially her dad, who was very protective of his daughter, especially since the assault.

Andrea and Jason were getting back into a rhythm together. They'd reestablished routines and both were looking forward to the time away from work Thanksgiving afforded. They arrived early as she and Bea discussed, to give them a chance to talk and get things settled before her parents joined them. The Thanksgiving weather was cool with a rain snow mix falling. The sky was a deep gray which promised to remain for several days.

As they approached Bea's front door, Jasmin was there to welcome them. This was Jason's first opportunity to meet Jasmin. He was struck by her lively eyes and great smile. He immediately felt welcome and comfortable meeting her. Andrea gave her a big hug. After Skyping several times over the past month they were forming a friendship where conversations picked up naturally.

The house smelled wonderful. As usual Bea's fireplace was on; however, she was busy in the kitchen when they arrived and yelled out, "Jason, you find your way here, I need a man sized hug!" Andrea was pleased, but quietly reminded Jason to be careful of her shoulder. Jason nodded, as he immediately responded to Bea's command.

Meanwhile, Andrea and Jasmin started talking. "My mom looks terrific, I was so surprised by how much better she looked than when I was here before. I could see some improvement when we Skyped, but seeing her in person, it's such a relief. I can't thank you enough for helping her out."

"Remember Jasmin, this whole thing started when she saved me! I love your mom. She's been a fabulous mentor too."

"Mom's told me all about you and your teaching. It sounds like you've taught my mom a thing or two. I mean she plans to Skype once a week with me. Her computer skills are so much better since you've taught her a few things."

Jasmin and Andrea were so busy talking they forgot Jason was in Bea's clutches. She was already putting him to work in the kitchen. While the Macy's parade was on the TV in the kitchen, they peeled potatoes and Bea started her friendly interrogation of Jason.

"How you doin' with my girl Andrea? I told her you two gotta make time for each other."

Andrea told Jason how quick to the point Bea could be. He was finding out how true her warning was.

"Well that girl of yours is gonna be a great teacher. Don't tell her I said so, but we all know she's got the gift. She not only knows what to teach, but she can listen to kids and make each one feel special. Not everybody can do it let me tell you. It must be something in the room 'cause Riley had it too."

Jason smiled at Bea as he continued to peel the potatoes. He wasn't sure how to respond and figured if he listened Bea would continue; he was right.

"I'm tellin' you this cause you got to realize good teachin' takes time. I tell Andrea to take some time off and make time for you and her. You have to understand when you start teachin' kids, they become important and you can't stop thinkin' about what you need to do for 'em."

It was at this point Andrea and Jasmin realized Bea had been alone with Jason for some time in the kitchen. They decided he might need to be rescued.

"Mom, you are working this nice man too hard here in the kitchen. What are you filling his ears with?"

"That's between this handsome man and me. You mind your own business sweet child." Bea said this smiling and chuckling as she knew what the girls were doing. "You come to save this man from me. He don't need savin' from you two, right Jason?"

"I'm fine here. We're just talking and I'm getting an education on potato peeling." Jason winked at Andrea as he said this, letting her know things were fine. They heard the doorbell ring, Andrea's folks had arrived.

Andrea's mom and dad had not met Jasmin before and they too were captured by her energy and bright disposition. Before long the conversation was on Duke's basketball fortunes for the coming season. They were always good, but Jasmin assured Craig Bauer this year the national championship was almost guaranteed.

Andrea and Jasmin gave Craig and Diane a full tour of the house. They were impressed with all Bea did with the place. They paid special attention to Andrea's temporary room and quickly understood the growing friendship between Jasmin and Andrea. Out of a horrible moment some good things had come to pass.

The Thanksgiving turkey needed carving and Craig was given the honor. It was a beauty. Along with the rest of the meal, nobody was leaving the table hungry. Once they were seated, Bea asked Jasmin to say grace. Everyone joined hands and Jasmin prayed, *"Dear Lord, we ask you to bless us and the food we've prepared. We give thanks for the well-being of my mom and Andrea. We also give thanks for the friendship and care we share together and pray the lives of all around this table grow in joy and peace. We also pray my brother Ford stays safe in that submarine of his under the Atlantic. We ask this in your name. Amen."*

The conversation over their feast was a lively one. Craig asked Bea when she planned to return to work. "As soon as they'll let me, but he doctors are sayin' not before the first of the year. I have my physical therapy three times a week and they are not sure yet about a second surgery on my shoulder. They are thinkin' maybe I won't need it if my mobility continues to improve. It's sure hard waitin'."

Without a TV in the living room and the one in the kitchen shut off, the conversation continued as everyone pitched in and shared the clean-up load. For Andrea it was one of her most memorable and enjoyable Thanksgivings. She knew the same was true for her family and Jason as well.

On their way back to the apartment, Jason and Andrea debriefed on all the conversations. Andrea was particularly interested in Bea's grilling of Jason. He shared what Bea said about her teaching abilities; Andrea felt a deep sense of pride as he did.

CHAPTER 39

AUDIT TROUBLE

How quickly the holiday flew by. Despite the boiler problem at Jefferson High, John enjoyed the time away and the chance to be with his children. But Monday had a way of always coming around too fast and there he was, back in the saddle. Ann reviewed the Friday mail bringing one particular piece along with coffee. They always tried to start Monday mornings reviewing the week and discussing things in general. It was a helpful and important half-hour making the week run smoother for both of them.

"John, we have a notice from the State Education Department. It says an educational audit is forthcoming due to the district's numerous failing schools, poor test scores, poor graduation rates and high levels of reported violence."

John took the letter from Ann and read it. He noted the auditors would be coming in January. The letter advised they needed a dedicated work space, access to copy machines, fax equipment, phones and the district's computer system. The letter also listed on two pages a large number of documents and reports to be ready for viewing upon their arrival.

"This is going to add a ton of clerical work and administrative time to prepare the reports and data needed. In addition, they want to interview principals and staff at the schools listed; this is going to be real fun Ann."

The list included several elementary schools, Hudson Middle School and all three high schools. Past experiences with quality audits indicated it was likely the State Ed team would be on site for at least six weeks.

The final report summarizing their audit would be released to the public within 60 days after they finished the on-site visits. John knew this was going to be a big deal, but at this point all he could do was add it to the stack of items on a long 'to-do' list.

"I warned you this was going to be a busy week," Ann stated. She was upset they now had the State Ed request. 'How much could any team cope with while at the same time try to make things better for the students they were hired to serve?'

Once Ann and John finished their meeting, Shantell was next in the queue. "Well I hope you had a nice Thanksgiving John," Shantell began. "It looks like we have a packed agenda tomorrow night. We have received nearly 30 emails or letters opposed to renaming School #3. I think there's a real groundswell of opposition developing."

"Shantell, did you notice every one of those people writing or emailing us no longer lives in the catchment area of School #3? They are fondly recalling the past, and while I don't mean to minimize it there isn't a groundswell of opposition from the students, staff or people who now live in the School #3 community."

While this observation gave Shantell a moment's pause, she wasn't going to give up easily. "You know John, those people have a point. Some of the letters were well written saying a school's history and name, even if it is a number, are long remembered. I don't know what we should do, beyond waiting another meeting or two to see how strong the feelings are around this."

"My counsel is to move forward and rename the school. We can do much to dignify its past but the future is calling and having a role model like Rosa Parks will be very helpful. This was something we all agreed was a good idea. You know it has strong staff support. So if you turn away from this you'd better be prepared for a possible groundswell of opposition." John kept thinking to himself she'd let the genie out of the lamp. Unfortunately, it was his job to figure out how to get him back inside.

"We'll have to see what the Board wants to do John. I am not sure we are prepared to go ahead with renaming the school at this time. I also was copied on the letter from the State Education Department. Do we have to make any announcement of the audit?"

"They will likely send out a press release on it, so I think it's wise we say something first. I have Janey Eisen working on a statement for you to read tomorrow."

"Okay. Now remember when we had our meeting on roles? You were going to get some contract language drafted penalizing you if you left before your contract ended. Have you got a draft ready?"

"Not yet Shantell, I've been wrapped up with so many other things I have not had a chance to give it any thought."

"John you did promise we'd have it by now. I think you should keep your promises don't you?"

"Shantell, I do, but I had to prioritize my time. The events at Hudson have taken a great deal of it lately. We now have a whole new agenda on addressing bullying behaviors. I have also been working on the anti-violence initiative with the mayor's team, just to name a few. There are only so many hours in the day; I felt this could keep for a bit longer. I'm not going anywhere."

"John, I am going to keep reminding you until you keep your promise. We need to get your contract amended to address this issue."

"My only promise right now Shantell is not to forget it, but we have a great deal to do at the moment."

Shantell realized she'd pushed John as far as she was going to today on this. She wasn't satisfied with his answer, feeling he was dodging his promise. She'd revisit this with the Board members to see how hard she should push John.

Their meeting lasted about ninety minutes. John and Shantell reviewed each item on the agenda. They talked about the personnel actions, budget data and the report on transportation department needs which was mostly an update on bus purchases and spiraling fuel costs. No action was required on the report.

After spending time making calls and preparing for the Quality Schools committee meeting, John was ready to meet with Tom Wheaton. Ann ordered sandwiches for them as they were meeting in John's office to begin their conversation on the following school year's budget. Developing a budget took months of work. The process began in earnest right after Thanksgiving and concluded in May when a final budget was approved by the Board and submitted to the City Council.

Tom was an experienced Chief Financial Officer. As the district's CFO he had sweeping authority to oversee the budget development, investment and expenditure processes. It was a big job; John was grateful Tom was so skilled at his work.

As they sat down the first thing they had to do was agree on a data collection timeline. Usually various schools and departments were asked to prepare their budget requests including supplies, equipment and needed repairs. The principals and department heads were asked to complete requests before the December recess. John and Tom initially confirmed they would follow the same procedure this time around.

The real work would begin after the first of the year as they prioritized requests and began looking seriously at both projected revenues and expenses for the coming school year. Tom had already started those projections. He was concerned about what was taking shape.

"John, I hate to say this, but I think we are going to have a hard time putting together a balanced budget. I've run some preliminary numbers and they scare the hell out of me. We have our health insurance figures for next year. Premiums are going up on average about twelve percent. Our pension costs will rise from over eight percent of our gross payroll to eleven percent. We also have firm contracts in place. The teachers are booked for a four point one percent raise next year. Putting those numbers together on a roll-over budget, we're up more than twenty five million dollars next year. Our revenues from the state are projected to drop by at least ten percent. That's over fifteen million. Adding repairs and other needs I think our first run budget, not doing anything new, is going to mean a nearly forty-five million buck increase on the local tax base. There's no way anybody can afford that. We're in real trouble, John. No way around it."

"Tom it's going to be a struggle. We are going to have to look at serious reductions across-the-board. Maybe asking people to fill out those requests is something we should reconsider. I am not sure we will be able to do much with them anyhow. If we ask for them, we'll only create work and frustration out in the field."

"Let me think on it John. You may be right. It would send a real signal business as usual is over." For over an hour they reviewed budget projections and costs. No spots jumped out where cuts would be easy to make.

"Tom, switching gears, what's your take on the boiler situation at Jefferson?"

"Oh boy, there's a lose-lose if there ever was one. We get to spend a ton of money on an a school we plan to tear down or play craps with an aging boiler likely to quit on us at any moment. I believe we have to replace it John. I have asked the architects to choose a boiler we could reuse at another site. But I am not certain, knowing the state's finances, they will give us the usual aid offset to help pay for a new boiler. I think we may have to fund more of this ourselves. It will have to come from our overall reserve account and it will mean we won't have much to spare if anything else comes up."

"I don't think we have a choice other than to replace the damn thing! How long before we have specs, a firm estimate and a timeline on it?"

"At this point, I think we'll have it by late December. Once we have it we can then move to get quotes and see how fast we can get things done. I alerted good asbestos contractors we are going to have work over the December break. I am getting quotes on this so we can have a contractor in place. It is going to be a quote based on time and materials as we don't have the scope of the work clearly defined."

They talked about a number of other issues including Tom's candidacy for a position in another district out of the region, much closer to his wife's family. John was surprised to learn this, but as Tom pointed out, it was early in the process and he wasn't sure how things would go. Nonetheless, he felt John needed to know he was an active applicant. Turning back to the budget they agreed Tom would update the district office leadership team on his initial projections at their next meeting. It was going to be a grim update, no doubt about it.

CHAPTER 40

FINDING NEW WAYS

The week after Thanksgiving had been a busy one for Ma'am. She'd attended the Board meeting on Tuesday night. A lengthy conversation about changing School #3's name took place. The teacher's union president, Cliff Greer spoke in favor of the name change. He cited the strong staff support for the overall concept and the particular selection of the name Rosa Parks Elementary School for School #3. It was obvious to Ma'am her staff communicated their feelings on this issue to their union president. She was pleased they did and thankful Sue Jones had taken a positive stand on it as their building representative.

Two former graduates of School #3, now in their sixties, also spoke to the Board about the change. While they acknowledged the proposed name was one to be proud of, they described the long tradition of the city referring to its elementary schools by number. They pointed out they could follow events and news about their former elementary school whenever it was referenced by its number. They noted many former students would no longer have a connection if the name changed.

When it came to the vote, nobody was sure how it would go. In the end, by a vote of 3-2 with Shantell Williams and Sara Fieldstone opposed, the name change was approved, to take effect on February first and Ma'am and the staff were encouraged to plan a rededication ceremony.

What was becoming apparent to those in attendance was the growing rift between the Board members and their willingness to support the superintendent's actions. The experienced players had seen this many times before, but they were more discouraged than usual by it, as most of the team supported John's efforts for change. Few at the meeting noticed the smile crossing Mary Jane Thomas' face as she watched both Ma'am and John Handler hold their breaths when the vote was taken.

Ma'am read the newspaper the day after the Board meeting. It was one for the School #3 scrapbook. The story about the name change was the lead article in the local section. There were quotes from different people. Sara Fieldstone stated the process was too rushed and she hoped other schools working on name changes would slow down so they could seek more public input. Others commented favorably on the change. At the school, the staff and students were excited about the name change. Ma'am was already thinking about asking a team to begin planning the rededication ceremony. There'd be a lot of work to do, but she knew a great deal of enthusiasm was present.

The week's events pressed on. It was hard to believe it was already Thursday and Dr. Handler would be attending the meeting today of the ad hoc Committee on Elementary Program Planning. The agenda for the meeting had two major items. The first was to discuss ways to reach out more successfully to the community served by School #3 and the next was to begin an initial discussion on school size. It promised to be a lively conversation as Ma'am knew members had strong opinions on both topics.

Ma'am alerted committee members Dr. Handler was coming. She did not tell them they were on the edge of being disbanded, but the group was smart enough to realize a visit from the superintendent was important especially following the stormy session with Dr. Thomas.

When the meeting started, Dr. Handler spoke briefly. "I am pleased to be here. I came to listen to what you are discussing. It is a very important topic for me and I want to learn all I can. So, I ask you to do your best to ignore me, my agenda is one centered on listening more than participating in the session."

People around the table smiled and appreciated his agenda. It was certainly different than what they'd experienced during the last visit by an administrator from downtown.

The first topic was reaching out to the community. Reverend James spoke on this item. "I think we have to find a way to reduce the fear people have. Many of my church goers speak about how they are afraid to talk with people at school. School was often not a good experience for them and you all are holed up in this big building many don't think of in a positive way."

Tom Coleman, the city fire captain spoke next. "Ya know Reverend James has a point. People do fear the school too often. I'd hear it from folks as we did home checks and people who stopped by to talk on the sidewalk out front of the fire hall. People rarely came inside the fire hall to talk, but when our garage doors were open during the summer folks would stop by and talk things up for a while. I think openness is a key. We gotta figure out a way to open the school's garage doors."

Sue Jones spoke up saying, "But at the same time we have to lock the front door so we have safety inside. When the doors were open we had purses robbed and some real unsavory characters walking inside for no purpose. Bea, you were shot on school grounds. How do we become more open and respect the need for the safety of the staff and children? I wonder if we can do both in this neighborhood."

Bea acknowledged the contradiction, "It is hard to respect both at the same time. But most people here are good folks. If they saw the school more connected to the neighborhood maybe we'd overcome some of the problems because we'd know more about 'em and how to deal with 'em. Fear is a big blocker to communication all 'round."

Ma'am skillfully guided the conversation; prompting and probing points of view. No decisions were made on this topic, but for over a half an hour people shared opinions. Ma'am summarized key points: overcoming fear and finding ways for the school to become a greater part of the neighborhood.

They moved on to the second agenda item, school size. It was Mryna Gaylord's turn to jump in with both feet. "I think we need to have small class sizes, I mean twelve or less in the early primary grades. If we don't do a great job teaching literacy and math concepts at a young age we lose the window and we end up needing lots of support. Kids falling behind almost never catch up. We have to front load the program with lots of literacy experiences and that takes small classes."

Reverend James listened to Mryna's views on this and appreciated her perspective. But he had a point to make, "You know we have small class sizes in Sunday school. I think we have good success in building a young child's understanding of Jesus. We have lots of volunteers and none of them are teachers. Do we have to achieve these small class ratios only by using certified teachers? It seems to me many of the literacy experiences you talk about could be done by caring adults who are guided by a good teacher's plans and suggestions."

Sue Jones jumped in. "They may understand Jesus as a young child, but not as they grow into teenagers."

John paid close attention, noticing the edge in the room due to Sue's hostile comment. 'How would Ma'am behave as the facilitator?'

Ma'am did interject. "Sue has a point; I think she's saying even if a child gets a good start, sustaining it is a challenge. How would we build on a good start if we were able to achieve it with most of the children?"

Bea was the first to offer an answer. "We can't push 'em all down the same pipe! We gotta see each child as special and we can't define what they can and can't do usin' only those damn tests. Some kids do it with their hands, others can sing, and we know some kids are born leaders. We gotta find better ways to build on those talents. I get the literacy part. We can't ignore it, but we gotta use literacy to a bigger purpose than just a good test score otherwise we're gonna lose way too many of 'em to the streets like we do now."

Sue Jones added, "I see many kids come into my gym who have real physical talent. They love being there, but most of those same kids, too often boys, are way behind in reading and math. I agree with the need to get them off to a better start. If we did, their physical talents could be a springboard for college scholarships and success. We have to think about how we get our kids off to a strong start. I think Myrna has a point."

Ma'am prodded, "Okay, how does all of this class size conversation tie into the question of overall school size?"

Myrna picked up again, "I think the overall size has to be small. We can't have four or five hundred kids under the roof and expect we're going to know all the children. The mobility in our community makes it even more difficult to stay on top of kids' names and their families. I think a school should be no larger than two hundred kids."

"Wow, that's a different number," Bea said. I support it, but we don't have enough schools. It's a whole new way to look at things. I'll bet it'd cost a pretty penny too."

Betty Jackson, who was a parent and school aid at School #3, spoke up for the first time. "We have to think different on all of this. Before we worry about money, I'd like to at least consider what's best in our minds, then see if we can make it work; not shut things down before we look at it from all sides."

"I didn't mean to shut things down by my comments. We gotta understand we have to propose something in the end we can really make work. You're right to call me on it. I did speak too soon on the money."

It was clear, after further conversation, almost everyone supported the idea of a smaller school size. Two hundred to two hundred fifty students was a number most settled on.

It was time to summarize the meeting. Ma'am noted, "It seems like we have a lot of barriers to break down. We've got fear, we have communication issues, and we have to think about how to dramatically improve early literacy. We also have a whole different notion about how big a school should be. These are things for us to think about."

When the meeting was finished, John stayed behind to talk with Ma'am. As they sat in her office he asked her, "Okay you've got a lot of strong points of view coming out. How do you see it moving forward?"

"John, I think we are going to have to develop something outside-the-box. Going in a different direction will be hard for the union to accept and Sue Jones will be forced to take a strong position on their behalf. I don't know where the other teachers on the committee will go either. We also need to think about a whole different physical structure. I thought Tom Coleman made a powerful comment about the fire department and open garage doors. We have to figure out how to create a less imposing structure. If we move forward I want the committee to work with the architects. I suspect what we're doing will give you a real headache John. It's not going to end up, if it moves forward, as a business as usual with new materials proposal."

"You have a real dedicated group and you're doing a nice job facilitating them. Your meeting, along with the kids' journal entries, gives me a great deal to think about. You were right about the journal entries by the way. They are not so much surprising as they are a stark reminder of the difficult lives of our students. At this point you keep going unless you hear anything different from me. I also want you and Myrna to stay on Mary Jane Thomas' main committee. But don't rile things up there please!"

"We won't John. I appreciate the corner you are in. Like I said, I will support whatever you decide. What a close call this week on the name change here. How are you feeling about it?"

John wanted to be careful on his answer. While he was disappointed with the Board's vote and the message it was sending, he didn't want his growing rift with Shantell and Sara to be the subject of any further conversation by something he said. "Well, we got it through, the first one is always the hardest. Hopefully the Board will find it easier to move forward on the next one, but we'll have to see."

Overall, Dorothy felt it was a successful meeting. She was pleased she had at least a temporary okay to proceed.

CHAPTER 41

WHAT DO WE DO?

It was Thursday night and Andrea was headed to Bea's after work. Since the School #3 Elementary Program Committee was meeting until 5:30, Andrea stayed at school until Bea's meeting was done. While some mentoring certainly continued, the two women now used their Thursday dinner night to talk about the children and catch up on the news. They looked forward to their time together.

Bea had a recipe working in the crock pot and the house smelled great. After spending her time with Bea, Andrea learned a number of good crock pot recipes so she and Jason frequently came home to an apartment with terrific smells.

It wasn't long before they had a beer in hand and were sitting by the fireplace. While Andrea sometimes preferred wine, it was a tradition to drink a Bud by the fireplace with Bea. Tonight was no exception.

When they were settled Andrea started, "We teamed again this week on James Tharp. His tantrums are becoming more frequent and because he's growing, he is becoming harder to control. I am thinking, a new placement for him may make sense. I'd like to make a home visit, but his mom does not return calls and she doesn't respond to my notes. But then who knows if they make it home. From school records it appears mom does not work. There's no dad in the home and he has three siblings, all older and each by a different father. James lives in an apartment over on Clyde Street."

"Oh my, what a real mean part of the city! You live in an apartment on Clyde Street there's nothing good about it. You can't do a home visit there by yourself girl. I am not even sure if I'd do one. Mom doesn't have a job and with the kids and all, I wonder if social services has been involved with the family. My bet is they have. Did anyone say they'd check that out?"

Andrea replied, "No. James' older brother is at the middle school. They were going to see what's happening with him. The oldest sister has dropped out of school. She'd be in the tenth grade this year. She just turned sixteen."

"Let me talk with Ma'am. Maybe she'll let me do some home work on James and his family. We can bet conditions at home are real bad. I'm not sayin' his tantrums are only because of that, but I'll bet you it's a part of it. Does he have any rat bites?"

"He's talked about rats in journal time. I have seen some nasty sores which look like rat bites. His clothes are rarely clean and he can wear the same thing for days in a row. But then that's true for a number of my kids."

"Andrea, his life is the worst kinda' poverty. I know you know this, but you gotta recognize, this boy has nothin' goin' for him on Clyde Street. Let's see what we can do for him. Like I said, I got some time."

"Don't go making any home visits by yourself. Promise me Bea you won't get impulsive on this."

"I promise, but we can do some diggin' and see what turns up. Then we'll decide what we need to do."

"Now, how did your committee meeting go?"

"We had a good talk about how to make the school more connected to the neighborhood. Ideas, no final decisions though. We also talked about school and class size. We all think we've got to get a better start on literacy. Dr. Handler was there too, but he didn't say much, he listened. After Dr. Thomas's visit at the last meetin' we were glad he listened."

"The earlier start on literacy is on the mark Bea. Most of the kids have not had the kind of language experiences they need before they come to school. Myrna is right about the preschool part of this. Small class sizes are also key in the early grades. We've talked a lot about this

Bea, but I don't know how we can afford to do it. Even I see how tight money is."

"We can't do it with the current way we do things. We've gotta have a new approach."

"What do you mean?"

"Andrea, we don't think we can do it with teachers and be able to afford it. We think we should use people from the neighborhood to work with the children and use a few teachers overall to plan what happens, choose the materials and work with the kids in different ways."

Andrea was surprised by this thinking, as close as she and Bea were, this was a real revelation. Bea for her part was trusting in their relationship and decided it was time to test the idea and see what somebody else thought about it.

"Wow Bea, you two are thinking about a whole different structure. Is it because of the money?"

"No, we are tryin' to figure out ways to break the disconnection between the folks in the neighborhood and the school. Reverend James sees it too. We gotta make better connections. Getting more people involved will help. It also may help change minds and give people some chance for work. It would put money back in a neighborhood that doesn't have much."

"You'll have the teachers association up in arms. They are going to have to protect the current model. If you go this way it means layoffs of teachers and a whole different structure. I don't know how I feel about this Bea."

"I wasn't sure I'd tell ya about it. I also don't know what we're gonna do, so I'm sharin' this right now just with you. If we move it forward as a proposal, then the union will have its chance to respond. I am trustin' our friendship to ask ya to think, react and listen and not get others involved until Ma'am does in the committee."

Andrea realized the process would reveal itself and she didn't have to say anything at this point to others. But she responded, "Bea the different model and the layoffs are gonna be a big mountain to climb, you know that right?"

"Yeah, but Ma'am talked to Carl Gardner testin' out a thought. Ya know each year we have about ten percent of the elementary staff leave.

They retire, get pregnant, get another job, or they relocate somewhere. Ma'am said Carl calls it the 'attrition rate'. We think we can make the change without too many layoffs. We'd use the attrition rate to go in a new direction. But some people still would get hurt no matter how we do it."

This was new information causing Andrea to think about it less defensively. She was still trying to digest what Bea was sharing. It was a great deal different from what she expected the committee to do.

Bea knew for her part she'd only shared a piece of what she and Dorothy had in mind. More needed to be shared, but Andrea had to digest what she'd just put out there.

"Andrea, enough about the committee, tell me more about how your kids are doin'."

"Dedra is having a good week. She is talking more and she's not sitting alone in silence at lunch, small steps in the right direction. Antonia Juarez is starting to use some English sentences. We still haven't done the testing, but that won't matter now because her family is on the move again. We've learned tomorrow will be her last day with us. Bea, how can we help children who come and go from school with such regularity, all we're doing is providing free day care, but no real education?"

"I know, I know, we just get started with a child and off they go! Along with all the stuff we try to do, we have the problem of children not havin' any real home where they live. They are stoppin' by school."

"I have no idea where she's headed and when she'll be back in school. I think she's a bright little girl, and with some time and work she could make real progress. But that's lost now. It's sad Bea. On a more positive note, Michael Makin is doing great. He is reading way beyond grade level. He's exceptional as a student, but his older brother has a strong influence on him. He's in the MA street gang and Michael can't stop talking about him. I am worried he'll succumb to the street life and his future will be lost."

"James is around and he told you to take care of his brother. Maybe, when the time is right, you can turn the tables and talk with him about what he's gotta do to help his brother keep movin' in school and on to a better life. Now, how's my class doin'?"

"From what I see they are doing okay. You have stayed away, which I know is tough, but you might want to consider a holiday season visit. It won't be long and maybe your doctor will let you go back to work."

"I saw him this week. I didn't tell ya cause I wanted it to be a surprise. But he says I am makin' good progress and he thinks I can go back to work right after the New Year."

"Oh Bea, that's wonderful! I am looking forward to having you back across the hall." Andrea's emotion on this was evident as she could feel the warm tears of happiness dropping down her flushed cheeks.

"Hey, let's have some dinner girl. Too much joy isn't good for us. Speakin' of joy, you gotta tell me what's goin' on with that cute man of yours."

CHAPTER 42

IT JUST KEEPS COMING

John was reflecting on the week gone by. It was another Monday on his calendar. The drive to work this morning was especially dreary. The cold weather had set in, with a winter mix smashing huge slush drops on his windshield. He hoped it wasn't foreshadowing the week ahead.

During this morning's drive to work he thought about where things stood. On the positive side, he was happy about the progress the Quality School Committee was making. They had come a long way since fall. With Christmas only a few weeks away they developed the Framework for Quality. The framework had four cornerstones: Student Success, Learning Environment, Educational Program and School Culture. John recalled the active conversations that took place regarding each cornerstone and the twenty-three aspect categories the committee defined within them. In the months ahead he wanted the committee to take the final development step, to identify the depth of quality for each aspect from high to low. He was sure this would be a rewarding and challenging task. John was proud of the work and felt the group had gelled. The development of the quality cornerstones would serve as the foundation for the long-term change effort.

He then turned his thoughts to facilities development. Since the first meeting with the architects, a district office team had been working to address the scope and pacing of the project. He was concerned not only about costs but also because a discussion was taking place absent a deep connection to an instructional vision for the 21st century. Schools over the past 100 years had been tied to a vision connected to the industrial revolution with its factories and assembly lines. Schools ran on bell schedules and had long factory-like corridors of classrooms that did not promote interaction, teamwork or collaboration. He was worried the district would get wonderful new buildings steeped in an outmoded conception of what work and life were like in the current century. At this juncture, the only committee thinking about a different conception of school construction was the ad hoc one chaired by Dorothy. The traditional views of school were powerful and the three program committees (elementary, middle and high school) were each too zeroed in on current versus long-term needs. It was becoming apparent they lacked a capacity to develop a future-focused vision. He was disappointed by this and was trying to think of ways to break the mold controlling the thinking of the groups.

On the flip side he thought about the good conversation he'd had last week with Hudson Middle School's principal, Zack James. They talked at length about the bullying study and the intervention committee John wanted him to chair. Zack wanted it to be a student only group. Zack said he'd facilitate the students and help them with agendas and any resources. He wanted John's okay to have the structure be something different. John supported the thinking and gave Zack the thumbs up to proceed with a student study team to address bullying behaviors and how to stop them from happening.

As he pulled into work he knew he'd be meeting with the district office leadership group right after his Monday half-hour overview conversation with Ann. The agenda for the meeting with the team was three-fold: facilities planning, budget development and preparation for the state education department audit. They were going to have a busy morning with those three topics and John was anxious to get to them.

Walking into work, his cell phone rang. It was the Transportation Manager, Tom Foley. Tom was all business as he had bad news to share. "Dr. Handler, we've had a serious bus accident this morning. A driver of a pick-up truck ran a red light. One of our Lincoln High School buses t-boned the truck on the driver's side. The driver of the truck bounced hard off the bus and spun into another car head-on. The driver of the truck was pronounced dead at the scene and the driver of the car was pretty banged up. The twenty-two kids on the bus at the time were shaken up by what took place. Three kids went to the hospital with what appear to be minor injuries. The other kids have been taken to Lincoln and are being attended to there."

"Okay Tom. How about our driver? What do we know about him or her?"

"Physically, he is in good shape. Sam's been with us for several years. The preliminary investigation indicates the accident was not his fault. They will do the usual drug and alcohol screens, but I would be amazed if anything showed. He's a good man and a respected driver with a great record. He is upset by the whole thing. He had a clear view of what happened. The guy driving the truck wasn't wearing a seatbelt and went partially through the windshield. Not much more I can tell you at this point, but I'll keep you posted on it when I learn more."

John took a deep breath. Bus accidents didn't happen frequently, but since they were a common enough occurrence people generally knew what to do. John was always thankful buses were built like tanks. Fortunately more often than not, students weren't seriously injured when an accident happened.

John headed into the elevator shaking off the cold rain accumulating on his coat. As he did so he realized the morning's ugly weather claimed a life and placed a bus full of students in the middle of the tragedy. Once upstairs he called Lincoln principal Ted Vassen's office. John wanted a quick update on the students involved and Ted's take on things. When he called, Ted was in the nurse's office so his secretary promised to have him call John as soon as he came back.

John told Ann about the accident at the onset of their meeting. He dictated a short email to the Board and asked Ann to alert Janey Eisen so she'd be able to prepare a press statement. After sorting out the rest of the week's tasks with Ann, John got ready for his leadership team meeting. Once all the players arrived and shared their weekend news they sat down and got to work.

The three assistant superintendents, Tom Wheaton, Bud Peck and the architects had been discussing the facilities project. Jerry Croton spoke on behalf of the group. "John we've looked at this and think we should break it down into three stages. The first stage is what we've labeled 'Necessary Repairs.' This includes things across all levels in need of the most immediate repair. It's largely plumbing, heating and electric issues along with some roof repairs that can't wait. We think these should be developed first and put out to bid. The rough estimate for Stage One repairs is about four hundred million dollars. Once we've got Stage One underway we can move on to Stage Two. This includes major building renovations and the construction of new schools. We've identified three schools which are in absolute need of replacement. They are Jefferson and Schools #3 and #7. We think the other two, Schools #8 and #11 could be closed or possibly renovated. The total cost for Stage Two is roughly three hundred fifty million dollars depending on the design and build strategies. Finally, there's Stage Three. These are necessary long-term repairs. We see this stage being addressed in five to seven years. It includes roofs and mechanical repairs not yet at a 'must do' point, but they will be by then. There's also some preventive maintenance that should be done. We think this stage has a working estimate, using today's figures of about two hundred million dollars. If there's any good news in the numbers we are under the one billion dollar figure, although barely. We believe going in stages gives us the chance to manage what really is a massive undertaking. It also gives us time to plan for the construction of the new schools and acquire any needed land for them."

John took a deep breath, "I like the idea of stages. But the numbers are still too big for us to swallow. What would happen if we really downplayed Stage 3 at this point and talked about a two-stage plan?"

Tom Wheaton entered the conversation, "John, it would pull a big number down and help in minimizing the immediate complexity of the challenge we face. But the down side is it postpones a real need. If we ignore the Stage Three items altogether we'll be back with a mess on our hands when everybody thinks we've addressed the problem."

John knew he was right. But he had to prioritize the possible and not overreach their capacity for getting things done. "The political part of this equation has to be balanced by answering how much can we lift at this point in time and still obtain the needed support. Whatever we do, two stages or three, we have to get the number down. Remember the meeting with the mayor's team? To get support from city hall we've got a lot of cutting to do. Even at two stages, the numbers are too big."

After back and forth comments among the team, John decided some direction was needed, "I appreciate the work so far. For now I want to think of Stage 3 as a parking lot. They are future items to attend to, but we won't address them any further at this point. On Stages One and Two, I like the concept and what we are trying to do. But we are going to have to decrease the cost of each stage by at least twenty percent. Let's see if we can take a further look at ways to cost engineer this thing."

Tom Wheaton spoke again for the group, "John it's an unrealistic target which will force us to push things needing to be done off to a Stage Three parking lot list. While dropping Stage Three from view is a good political strategy, we will regret doing it if people think we're finished after Stage Two."

While John respected Tom's advice, he felt he had to set some boundaries in place, "Let's move forward over the next six weeks with a two stage strategy in mind. We can see how things come together and then revisit it with more information and thought on the table. For now the challenge is to see if we can get the overall costs down to under six hundred million dollars. Now let's talk about the next easy thing on our agenda, the budget for the coming year."

Tom Wheaton took the next fifteen minutes to summarize how the increase in costs, combined with the expected cut in state aid, was going to wreak havoc on things. Conversation moving forward was going to be about painful cuts and program reductions.

Carl Gardner, who had not said much during the construction part of the agenda, entered the conversation. "John, there's little doubt we are going to have a large layoff of staff. It will impact not only teachers, but aides, secretaries, custodians, mechanics and administration. I'd like to work with the group here to get started on projections. How big a number is what we'll need to settle on so we can get to work on it."

John knew this was the real question and he'd thought all weekend about his answer, "I want us to prepare two different estimates. The first would be a no tax increase budget cutting $45 million. The second assumes we are willing to propose under a four percent tax increase. If we go that route, it means we'd have to cut about $29 million. I don't see city council buying anymore than a four percent tax increase for residents and businesses. Does anybody around this table see it differently?"

Nobody did, so John continued, "We will also do all we can to lobby the state for aid, but the dire straits they are in means it is going to be a fruitless effort. Tom and I talked about cancelling the call for budget requests that usually go out to the principals. What do you think?"

The team supported the idea of not asking for input on additions to the budget. It seemed like a wasted effort and would send a conflicting message. However, they did discuss how they could get input from the field on items to cut. John asked Carl to lead the effort to identify the scope of layoffs. He wanted to have a preliminary plan developed by the middle of January, now only five weeks away. "Let's go with a working assumption we will cut all non-personnel related budgets by 18%. The balance of the reduction would have to come from staff layoffs or wage and benefit changes if the unions agree."

"John, do you want me to open any doors with the unions on the idea?" Carl asked.

"Let's assume they won't easily agree to any changes. With last hired first fired requirements the unions will likely give up the new-borns before they'll cut salaries, pension or health benefits. Since you and Tom will be brainstorming on ways to get suggestions for possible cuts. I think you could open the door on that with Cliff and the other union presidents."

As if the team didn't have enough on their plate they had to discuss the upcoming state audit. However, Ann came in to tell John Ted Vassen was on the phone.

"Morning Ted, what's the news on the kids involved in the accident?"

"John, I know you have the leadership team there. If you want to put me on the speaker phone it will save me a couple of calls. "We have examined all the kids and talked with 14 of 22 parents. The team here thinks each youngster is physically ok to stay in school. We have a few kids who were really upset by the accident and the death and serious injury to the other drivers. We have the counseling staff talking with them as we speak. We'll keep a close eye on all the kids involved and we plan to reach every parent we can by the end of the day."

"Ted be sure the nurse documents the condition of each youngster. We can expect there will be lawsuits to follow and we'll need good documentation."

"We know the drill. My secretary is in the health office right now to assist. We'll have copies sent to you for the district's records on this accident."

Jerry Croton asked, "Tom, what can you tell us about the kids taken to the hospital?"

"Jerry, I have one of my VP's there. She tells me the kids are all under observation. Two had some stitches. But it seems everything is in the minor injury category for our kids, which is great news."

John interjected, "Do we know anything about the driver of the car who was taken from the scene with serious injuries?"

"We know she is in surgery John, but not much else at this point. It was a tough scene and the kids who have shared things about it were certainly upset by it."

"Ted, do you need any other support from our end?"

"John, I'll give Jerry a call if we do, but I think we are in okay shape on this one."

John turned their attention back to the upcoming state audit once the update was finished and everyone was refocused,

"I wasn't here during the last audit six years ago. I understand it was a time intensive process."

Joanne Walters sighed, "It was an awful experience. At the middle school level the school visits were disruptive. Two of the five auditors didn't have education degrees; they were testing experts. The other three did have degrees in teaching, but only two had been in the classroom in the last five years, none at the middle school level. Yet there they were, telling us what we had to do to improve our test scores. It was hard to take I'll tell you."

Jerry echoed the same sentiment. He knew similar criticisms had been leveled by districts; hopefully the team coming this time would have better training and a deeper knowledge of how schools operate. Nonetheless, nobody was looking forward to the audit and the possible outcomes. In extreme cases, it might require staff to be dismissed for consistent failure to meet state standards. The State Education Department also had the right to take control of a failing district if the Commissioner of Education judged the situation to be dire.

"They are going to be with us in the middle of a budget crisis. There will be lots of angst to go around. All we can do is put our best foot forward and hope they finish as quickly as possible with their review. I want you all to cooperate. We'll use the conference room down the hall as their work space. Please be sure to tell Ann about any data you are asked to provide. We want to keep a running list in one central place."

The team broke from the meeting before lunch. They had a great deal in front of them and John was worried about the work load this group had to take on. As they left he asked Mary Jane to stay behind for a moment.

Once they were alone John got right to the point. "I attended last week's meeting of the ad hoc group at School #3. To be frank, I was impressed with their discussion. I am not going to disband the group."

Mary Jane was on her feet, "I can't believe you are supporting them! How can you do this? You aren't backing me; I've never worked for a superintendent who didn't back his leadership staff."

John felt the pressure building in him and knew he was going to relieve it by expressing his thoughts forcefully, "This superintendent backs his team when they deserve to be backed. Right now your narrow-minded ideas and condescending manner is far from an asset. You and I are not in agreement on this. I'd encourage you to rethink your positions if you want my support in the future."

Mary Jane stared at John with an incredulous look. She'd never experienced this kind of criticism and was at a loss on how to react. Her emotions got the best of her and she exploded, "You are thinking about changing things here in ways which will never work! I can't believe you don't see it." She left before John could say another word. Ann saw the tears and red face as Mary Jane rushed by.

Once Mary Jane was out of range, Ann came in. "Many people would applaud what you did. She's needed tough feedback for years John. I know how hard it was to deliver it, but it was time somebody did."

"Thanks Ann. What I need is a quiet lunch."

"You have 90 minutes open on your calendar. Remember the weather outside is still cold and wet so put your boots on John." Ann smiled as she said this and John appreciated her support and caring humor.

Leaving the office, John knew Mary Jane had the ear of Board member Sara Fieldstone. They went to lunch together on a regular basis and he was sure she would do whatever she could to undercut his standing with the Board and thwart his agenda for change.

CHAPTER 43

POVERTY'S CHILDREN

Andrea thought about how quickly the days were moving towards the New Year. She noticed as the daylight hours grew shorter and the temps colder, too many of her children, as well as those attending School #3 across all the grades, were poorly dressed for the conditions. Warm coats, mittens, boots and scarves were often absent on children.

Andrea talked with other staff members about this. They all agreed it was a problem growing worse with each passing year. Many staff members brought in family hand-me-downs and some even purchased items for a few of their most needy students. Poverty was a ruthless predator. It was having its way with the children at School #3 as the weather turned and temperatures fell below freezing.

Andrea spoke with her mom and they decided Trimbell High School's service club could take on another project; the collection of winter clothing items for the children. Andrea needed to get an okay from Ma'am before she and her mom put things in motion. Andrea was headed to the office before school started, hoping to catch Ma'am to get approval.

As she entered the busy main office Andrea noticed Ma'am's door was open. Janet knew she wanted to see her and gave a nod to go on in. Andrea was now comfortable talking with her principal and she looked forward to seeking her advice and help with this important project.

Ma'am looked up and smiled as Andrea was standing at her office door. "Come on in, I bet you're planning something and you want to spring it on me don't you?"

"I've been thinking."

Ma'am interrupted laughing, "Oh no, not again dear!"

"Yup, so many kids here don't have good winter clothes. I talked with my mom and she thinks the Trimbell High School service club would take on a clothing drive for us. I'd be willing to help coordinate and sort things. Colleen said she'd help too if you think it's okay."

"It's more than okay; I think it's a great idea! Too many of our kids don't have what they need. I'll bet Bea will help. We can designate a day for sorting and welcome volunteers to help us when things arrive. I am assuming your mom thinks the kids at the high school will be successful. From what I've seen on the book drive, I would bet they will be."

"She wants me to go to the service club this week after school and tell them about our needs. It's a perfect Christmas project for them."

"You go for it! Tell your mom thanks for thinking of us."

Andrea skipped from the office. Ma'am enjoyed Andrea's energy and enthusiasm. How much her thoughts about this teacher changed over the past three months. Andrea was a real find; she was making a difference at School #3 already. She owed Carl an apology for questioning her hiring and placement at School #3.

When Andrea returned to her classroom, she noticed the frost on the windows. The old windows were single panes of glass with no storm windows to protect them from the cold. Unless you scraped the frost from a window you could not see out of the room. It was a strange feeling to be in a space where light came through the glass, but its frosted state prevented anyone from seeing what was happening outdoors. Andrea had a snow scraper in her room; from time-to-time she'd go to a window pane and scrape off the frost to see what was going on in the street below. The windows were drafty and she moved desks as far away as she could to help the kids stay warm. Towels sat on each window sill, helping to stop the draft and to collect the moisture running off the frosty glass.

As Andrea reflected on the needs of her children, she decided to re-read the cumulative record for each child in her class. Doing so, with a more experienced perspective, she started to note the ages of the mothers of her students. The oldest current age of the moms of eleven of the twenty-seven children in her classroom was twenty-six or less. It was hard to comprehend such a large number of mothers were teenagers when they gave birth to the child now sitting in Andrea's class. How she missed this was surprising, but the realization brought on a deep sadness. Several of the children in her class had mothers who were only fourteen or fifteen years old when they gave birth. She also realized the grandmothers taking care of several of the children in her class were only in their late thirties themselves. It also added perspective on why so many great-grandmothers were key caregivers. The cycle of poverty was generational and ongoing. How many of the children in Andrea's class would become mothers and fathers themselves in five or six years? Andrea thought about Bruce Springsteen's song, 'Glory Days'. These kids too often never experienced those days; they simply passed them by.

At the end of the school day Andrea was thinking not only about the ages of the mothers of her students, but also the journal entries this morning. Three of her students lived on Del-Mar Avenue. In its time it must have been a beautiful city street with big old houses. A tree-lined median divided the avenue making it especially attractive. But, like many areas past their prime, the big homes had been converted into apartments. The neglect and harsh realities of time scarred this once beautiful area. This morning the kids talked about the drive-by shooting on Del-Mar last night. Two gang members were shot and an innocent victim in her early twenties had been gunned down in the crossfire. The kids talked about the crime scene and knew what happened.

Andrea was used to hearing these stories. At first the life on the streets surrounding School #3 shocked her. Now the daily realities of what took place were ones she hated, but understood as the norm for her class. As she re-read the journal entries Andrea felt light-headed as her emotions overtook her. How can we overcome so much? In the next breath she knew right after the first of the year the state literacy test would be given and she had to prepare her children knowing most would fail. Nonetheless, her reading training helped her recognize the good growth found in her classroom. Sadly, it wasn't nearly enough to meet the state's standards for fourth grade literacy. As she was thinking about all of this, Colleen walked in to see if Ma'am said okay to the service club's clothing drive.

"Ma'am gave it the okay, so I will talk to my mom tonight. There are only three weeks before Christmas so they're going to have to work fast. Hopefully we can get all of the clothes here before Christmas and pass them out before the break. Ma'am said she'd help get more volunteers. I think we should encourage all of the staff to donate anything they may have."

"I think so too. We know it will make a real difference for the kids. I hope the service club at your mom's high school can really go to town on this. A lot of our kids need winter clothes."

"I am speaking to the club on Thursday. Do you want to come with me?"

"That'd be great! Plus, I get to meet your mom too; I am not going to pass up that opportunity."

Later when Andrea arrived home she shared the day's events with Jason while they were preparing dinner, "I talked with Ma'am this morning about the winter clothing project with the service club at Trimbell High School. She was excited about the idea and said we could go for it. I called my mom and told her it was approved by Ma'am. Colleen and I are going to speak to the service club kids this Thursday. I hope they can make it work this close to Christmas."

"Andrea you know your mom and the spirit her kids have for things like this. I think you are going to get a lot of clothing donations. It's great you are helping out. Have you called Bea yet to tell her what's going on?"

"Not yet, I'll call her after supper. So tell me about your day."

"We have a new regional manager. She was announced today. It's got everybody buzzing. Because she was working for another company she's got no history with us. We've all been trying to use our networks to see what we can learn. So far, it seems positive. We'll see what changes are in store for us. When they bring in somebody from outside most of us think it's because they want to make changes. We'll have to wait and see how things work out I guess."

During dinner Andrea shared her discovery that the moms of a number of children in her classroom were now only in their mid-twenties.

"Jason, I thought a lot about it today. I see how it could happen to one or two who might get pregnant. I can remember Sue Jenkins getting pregnant and how we all felt so bad for her. She made the hard choice to give the baby up for adoption. But she was the only one in my high school class I remember being pregnant at fifteen. I'm thinking about how it plays out when it's so common at the high school level for girls to be pregnant. I think about the girls in my class and wonder what they will be experiencing at fifteen. Will a lot of them be pregnant then? There are so many needs; I guess I never realized how different life can be from what we experienced growing up."

"Before you started working in the city, I didn't really see it either. We live in a different world Andrea. Yet these kids and all they experience are only a few miles away from where we are sitting. It's not in a third-world country somewhere far away from here. I worry about you every day working in that environment, but I understand how important it is to try to do more. I don't get why our country isn't seeing the problem and doing something about it."

When dinner was finished Jason said, "Let me clean up. You've got to call Bea and share with her the clothing drive plans. I think you should talk with her about the age of the mom's of your kids. I wonder what she'll say about it."

CHAPTER 44

OPENING THE
GARAGE DOOR

M a'am was sitting in her office waiting for Sara Vaughn to arrive. John gave the okay for the architects to talk with Ma'am and her committee. Ma'am scheduled some one-on-one time with Sara to see if she was receptive to new ideas before she was introduced to the whole committee.

As she turned her heavy chair to look out the small office window, Ma'am wiped the frost away and noticed the 'Right Now' flag blowing in the breeze. It was funny how the flag was hitting her this morning. Most days she saw it but didn't reflect on it much. Today it seemed to be speaking directly to her. She felt a real sense of urgency. It was surprising after all her years of work it was at this moment she felt the strongest sense of what she needed to do. Her life experiences and training were shaping a new vision for how to educate impoverished children. At her age she wasn't expecting it, but there it was consuming her thoughts day and night.

Ma'am's husband Jessie was used to her work life. The demands on a school principal's time were much more than people in the outside world realized. The constant calendar of night meetings was an ongoing part of the job. While a crisis would consume time, it was the mundane day-to-day things which controlled their days and nights. He recalled the years of 5:00AM calls from sick teachers and the morning calls his wife had to make to find substitutes. While their three girls were growing up, it was

Jessie who made sure they were ready for school when his wife was on the phone trying to be sure classrooms were covered.

Lately Jessie had been telling her she was often not present even though they were in the same room. She tried to share what was happening and the vision taking shape. Jessie supported her at every step through their marriage and told her he was proud of her. He encouraged her to do all she could to listen to the inner voice speaking to her about what needed to be done.

All those thoughts were spinning through her mind in a moment's time while looking at a flag waving on a pole. It was amazing how much ground could be covered in self-reflection sometimes lasting only a minute or two.

Five minutes later Sara Vaughn was sitting in Ma'am's office. Ma'am exclaimed, "I'll get right to the point, I don't want to talk with you about building a nice new school. I want to work with you on reinventing the design. I want someone who won't be uncomfortable exploring a whole different way to do things."

Sara thought, 'I have heard similar versions of this before.' Most of the time she accommodated them with illustrations of new technology access and more windows and light, so she was startled when Ma'am said, "I want a school with a front porch."

Ma'am noticed Sara's face was scrunched in a puzzled shape. Her lips were twisted and her eyes were wide open. Ma'am chuckled when she saw it, "I'm not crazy and I'm not kidding!" She spent ten minutes telling Sara how people were afraid of a school's physical structure and the conversation Tom Coleman shared about how people stopped to talk at the fire hall when the garage doors were open.

"Okay, what else are you thinking?" Sara asked.

"The school needs to accommodate children from birth through age seven. I want space for cribs and small beds for little children to take naps. The classrooms need to be smaller, not bigger. I want them to feel more like living rooms, windows with drapes, comfortable floors to sit on more tables than desks. Each room won't need to hold more than a dozen children. The total school enrollment won't be more than 250. There should be a kitchen so we can make simple meals and sandwiches. I don't want a cafeteria! We need a room where the kids can come to play and share things. We can talk about a simple office area and a few other special spaces. From the outside I want this to look like a big house not a building. That's important."

John told Sara Ma'am would surprise her with what she wanted to see in a school design. After many years in the business she was not often surprised. But here she was sitting with a 62 year-old women who rocked her world. Her mind was spinning.

"Mrs. Washington, I need to give some thought to what you've shared. Dr. Handler said to provide you up to 150 hours of billable time. I want to share your ideas with my team and get back to you. This is different from anything we've ever thought about."

"If we are going to work together on this we can stop the formalities. How about I call you Sara and you call me Dorothy."

"I hear they all call you Ma'am around here," Sara said with a smile.

"Yes they do, but I think Dorothy will do."

"Okay Dorothy, give me a week to do some initial planning and then let's talk again. I am not sure what to think right now."

Dorothy smiled, "You know sometimes I am not sure what to think about it either. But doing the same old dance in a new dress doesn't change things much, does it? We need to reach these families and kids in a new way. Having the right structure is one part of what we need to do to create the right conditions for learning."

John asked Sara to call him after she'd left her meeting with Dorothy. She was sitting in her deep blue BMW in the School #3 parking lot, with her heated seat coming up to temperature. "John you told me to expect something different, but this woman is well beyond different. She wants me to design a mansion, not a school! John, this is way off the charts! I mean she wants a front porch on the thing. What are we doing here? Are you sure you want me to spend time on this?"

John started laughing, Sara ranted for over a minute and he could not insert a syllable. "Sara, she is thinking along a whole new path. I don't know what we'll do in the end, but go with it for now. I said give her 150 hours of time. See where it leads."

"Oh boy John, I think it is going to lead us down a path to something I've never seen in school design."

"Sara, I supported your firm because you said your folks were creative and innovative. Are you telling me you aren't now?"

Sara sensed a touch of an edge in John's voice. He was in a business frame of mind and she needed to settle down. "John we are, and we'll run with this knowing you support it. I'll put fresh faces on it and see where it leads."

CHAPTER 45

TROUBLE COMES EARLY

On Wednesday morning, Ann came into John's office to tell him Albert Denton was on the phone from the State Education Department..

John rolled his eyes at Ann and picked up the phone.

"Dr. Handler, this is Albert Denton. I will be the team leader for the department's audit of your school district. I am calling to tell you with the long list of serious problems we see in your district we want to come earlier than planned. We have a lot to review and address in your district and it's going to take some time and effort on our part to outline the problems and means for improvement."

John felt his blood pressure rising but he responded with a question, "I'm sorry, but exactly what serious problems do you see?"

"You have a lot of failing schools, Dr. Handler. The scores at those schools have been bad year after year. The drop-out rate for your district is the worst in the state. There's not been any improvement; in fact it has only gotten worse over the last five years. You've been there less than two years I know, but many administrators have been in place at those failing schools for a long time and nothing has improved. It has to change."

"Tell me Mr. Denton, how will that happen? Have you got some magic potion you are bringing with you?"

"Dr. Handler, you're getting defensive. It happens a lot with you superintendents. We are trying to help, yet you always react the same way. Based on your results, even before we come out, there are going to be people who will have to move on and if we have to, the department will withhold aid until they do."

"Mr. Denton, your definition of 'help' is in a different dictionary than the rest of the world's."

John hung up the phone angrier than he had been in years. He knew big trouble hovered on the horizon, much worse than he'd anticipated. These folks were coming to town with a judgment already in place. All they were going to do was compile evidence for their decisions.

After the conversation concluded, John stepped out of his office. He looked quickly at Ann telling her to cancel whatever was on his calendar. He was in no mood to see anyone. He needed time to cool off and think.

Ann had never seen John so upset. He handled the most challenging situations with grace and thoughtfulness. She rarely saw him lose his temper..

When John got angry he usually found a constructive way to vent it. Today was no exception. He knew he needed to see something positive in a school setting and he headed for the closest school. In this case it was Lincoln High. After going through the security checkpoint he headed for a nearby classroom. Before he did, he called the main office to alert them he was in the building and dropping by classrooms. The first was an English class. John walked in and settled into a chair in the back of the room, the teacher, Mr. James, couldn't have looked more startled and surprised. John said, "Please ignore me, I want to spend some time visiting classrooms."

John visited at least six more classrooms before he dropped by the office to say hello to Ted Vassen and have some lunch in the faculty room. When he went in Ted's office he was greeted, "Whoa boy you've got this place buzzing. You visit a bunch a classrooms unannounced. Man everybody here is talking! I'm glad you gave me a head's up coming through the front door!"

"I had to get out of the office. I needed a reality check. You were the closest place. Hopefully it will calm down a bit after I leave." John was still thinking about the State Ed. call. He wondered, given Lincoln's poor results, if the state would be telling him Ted had to go. It made the bile rise in his mouth again.

Nonetheless, he and Ted had an enjoyable half hour conversation. Ted shared how pleased he was with the new school counselor, a "fireball" in his words. The kids loved her and they were really enjoying her sense of connection. The counselor was Hispanic and the kids appreciated her bilingual abilities. John was thinking as the last counselor hired, her stint at Lincoln may be short-lived since the budget hammer was about to fall.

But at this moment he relished being in the school. John missed his time as a teacher and principal. The kids had so much energy and each day was filled with life and action. Now his job was to open doors so others could do the instructional work. Lately, he knew he was going to have to close a lot of doors that should remain open. It was a task he dreaded when so much needed to be done, right now.

CHAPTER 46

GIRL'S NIGHT

Andrea and Colleen met with the Trimbell High School service club members. As expected, the kids were enthusiastic about the project and started brainstorming ideas on how to get the word out to their classmates and others. Since it was a Thursday night, Andrea was headed to Bea's for their weekly dinner and conversation. Andrea asked Colleen if she'd like to join in, she was certain Bea wouldn't mind.

Colleen had never been to Bea's home and it would be a new adventure for her. Andrea called ahead on the drive over so Bea was not surprised to see Colleen stepping in off the porch. As usual Bea had the fireplace going. Like Andrea's first visit, Colleen took in what she was seeing with some surprise and admiration. The living room was comfortable. Bea had the beers open. Colleen would have to go along with their traditions tonight.

"So girls, how did the meeting with the kids at Trimbell High go?"

Andrea spoke first, "It was a great meeting. The kids were really excited about the idea. They were already sending out an e-blast and text messages. I think they'll get a great response."

Colleen added, "The group was bigger than I thought it would be. There were more than forty kids. Andrea's mom told me they get a mention of the service on their transcript, but no grade or credit. They have to give one hundred hours of service before the transcript note is added. It doesn't hurt their college applications to have it."

"Whatever the motivation, if we can get some good winter clothes for the kids it will be a great thing. Have you girls started to plan the sortin' party yet?"

Andrea smiled, "Nope, we need your help."

"Good, because I've been doin' some plannin'. I think we could have a sortin' day' in the gym before the break. We could pass out the clothes durin' gym class, everybody should get somethin'. I can volunteer; it'll be good to see the kids before I come back for real right after the break."

Colleen spoke cheerfully, "It sounds like a good plan. Andrea smiled reminding Bea Ma'am wanted to pitch in too. Colleen added, "Maybe she could spend some time in the gym with you."

"Now there's an idea! I like your style girl. In fact I like it so much I think you should suggest it to Ma'am!"

Colleen wasn't sure if Bea was kidding or serious. Andrea knew she was serious. Colleen suggested it, she should propose it. Bea ever the pragmatist saw things that way. Besides, it would be good for Colleen to talk with Ma'am, maybe it would help build a stronger relationship between them. Bea knew Ma'am liked Colleen and respected her teaching. It was also clear for unknown reasons Colleen was a bit afraid of her principal.

During dinner Colleen shared some of the things going on in her third grade classroom. She was concerned about the turnover since school started. Five students entered and four children left. "How do we get ahead with these kids when they keep passing through? They bounce from one place to another. I looked at the record. I have two students who have re-enrolled at School #3 twice since kindergarten. From kindergarten through now they have attended three different schools and enrolled or re-enrolled a total of five times. But in my class this year you'd hardly notice because out of my twenty-four students only three are reading at or above grade level. I have two students who cannot read at all! How does this happen?"

"I know what you are saying, I looked at my records and eleven out of the twenty-seven children in my class have a mother whose current age is twenty-six or less. I have another six mothers who were either eighteen or nineteen when their fourth grade child was born. My God, I was sharing this with Jason the other night. We were stunned. Neither of us could believe those numbers. It's awful to think about how disadvantaged they are right from the start."

Bea shook her head. "You girls think it's a revelation. It's not if you've lived it all your life. Too many girls think the only way they can hold onto a man is to have a child. They have it all wrong, but they don't learn until it's too late. Way too many men around here enjoy screwin' but they don't want to bring up a baby. Those who do care are in the same tough spot as the girls. They don't have any skills, no diploma and they try to make a livin' on the street 'cause it's all they know. It turns out bad way too many times. They end up in jail or dead before their children have a chance to grow up with a dad in their life. We know education is the key, but we ain't makin' much progress are we? But enough about that. I want to hear about your men."

"Jason's got a new regional manager and is concerned about what changes she has in mind. So we're not the only place worried about change. He is also helping on the winter clothes collection. He's told people at work about it, as well as some of his clients and believes he'll get a good response knowing how well people have reacted."

"I knew Jason would come 'round on things. He needs time, and you know what else ya both need?"

Andrea blushed, "Bea!"

Colleen couldn't resist, "What else does she need?"

"Ah you know, I'm not tellin'!"

They all laughed. Andrea through the laughter thought about Bea and wished for a man in her life. It was a subject, despite their closeness, she did not probe very much. She knew Bea was lonely, but she didn't seem to be interested in doing something to overcome it. Andrea and Jasmin talked about it and shared their concerns about Bea's lonely lifestyle.

"You aren't off the hook girl," Bea said while looking at Colleen. "Tell me about the man in your life."

Colleen smiled, "His name is Trace. He's a middle school teacher and he coaches track and soccer. We met in college and we've been together for seven years now."

Bea, never shy, raised an eyebrow and looked at Colleen. "You mean you've been together seven years and you aren't married. You gotta tell me how that works."

Andrea interrupted looking at Bea saying, "No she doesn't." While it was said kidding, Bea caught Andrea's look and understood this must be a sensitive topic and she was skating out on thin ice.

Colleen sidestepped the question, "We'll get married at some point; he's too busy with sports right now."

With the conversation drawing to an awkward close, and the dinner dishes waiting, the women began clean-up chores. Andrea shared Sue Jones was talking in the faculty room about how interested the union was in the ad hoc study committee. "She told us you guys are talking about small class sizes. They are in strong support of it." From their earlier talk, Andrea knew Sue did not know of the deeper plan to use non-certified teachers. She was giving Bea some important information about the misconception clearly forming.

"I think that's a real need," Colleen chimed in. I can't possibly help all the kids who have learning gaps. Even with Rita, it's still impossible to meet all the learning needs I see in my classroom."

This was an opening for Bea. "How does Rita help you?"

"She's a great help. I have her working one-on-one with Jerome Johnson. But in addition to working with JJ she helps other kids too. She's great with the kids. One-on-one she's made a real difference with several children I otherwise couldn't get to during the day."

"That's good to hear. The one-on-one help and support is what so many of the children need."

Time flew by and before they knew it, it was nearly 9:00. They said goodbyes and Andrea and Colleen walked out to their cars together. When they were outside, Colleen thanked Andrea for stopping Bea's probes on her relationship with Trace. "I don't know what to do Andrea. We've been together for a long time and yet he can't commit. I want to have children and settle down. All he talks about is coaching and sports."

Colleen's frustration was showing as tears formed. They couldn't carry on the conversation long in the cold. So Andrea gave Colleen a strong hug. "We can talk after school about it sometime soon if you want."

Colleen smiled at her friend. "We'll see," she said as she stood by the open door of her car.

CHAPTER 47

A LOAD TO BEAR

Lincoln High's principal, Ted Vassen was talking with his boss, Jerry Croton, about the superintendent's visit to Lincoln. "Boy, he shook things up here, Jerry. He dropped into six classrooms and had lunch in the faculty room. They didn't know what to think of it."

"Ted, John's under a lot of stress. When he gets that way he loves going back to the classroom. It's refreshing to have a leader who remembers where the action is. I'll bet he scared the crap out of some of your folks. Have the union reps seen you yet?"

"Yup, they wanted to know if the visits were formal observations. They were upset he came in unannounced. The reps didn't like it."

"They complain when we aren't visible. Then when we are it's a problem as well."

"Jerry, I know. John said he'd write each of the teachers a note. More questions from the union will follow."

"Yeah, they'll ask if a copy will be placed in their personnel files. They'll also say if he has any critical observations or questions it must be an off-the-record communication. The poor guy can't even pick up a pen and write a simple thank-you note without a production. Ann called asking me to talk with John and see how he's doing. I guess a State Ed. audit call ticked him off. Ann said he's headed back to the office so I sent him a text asking him to stop by. If he does, I'll remind him to be careful on the notes Ted. Anything else going on I should have a head's up on?"

"Jerry, my reps also complained about your Secondary Program Committee. They don't want a review of current graduation requirements. They see it as a threat, no doubt about it. They're happy with the current expectations."

"I got a lot of push back at the last meeting Ted. They were upset about my suggestion to rethink the science sequence. One in five of our kids take physics. We have to find new courses and sequences in science if we are going to increase the number of kids finishing more than a two unit science requirement. The science department is fine with more courses, but only as electives, not as an alternative combination to satisfy sequence requirements. We aren't getting kids to take enough science. They are resisting any change which might help."

"I understand Jerry, but you have to consider going slow if you want to make any progress in the committee."

"Thanks for the heads up, Ted. I am sure the boss will feel good about it!"

They both laughed, knowing how hard John was pushing for change right now.

A few minutes after Jerry concluded his call with Ted, John was sitting in his office.

"What's up Jerry? You asked me to stop by."

"Ted called; I heard you visited some classes over at Lincoln. He's already had the union reps stop by to talk with him. Did you misbehave over there?" As Jerry asked this his eyebrows raised in an attempt at humoring his up-tight boss.

"Jerry, I didn't misbehave, I was visiting some classrooms and trying to blow off some steam after a call from State Ed."

Jerry shifted in his chair, and his voice took on a different tone, "Uh oh, you want to tell me about that?"

"Jerry this guy Albert Denton calls me to say he's the leader of the team. He says they want to come early because they have a lot to do here. He tells me we have some of the poorest performing schools in the state. He told me some heads need to roll here. I think they plan to recommend to the Commissioner several of the principals be let go."

"John they can do it. We have to take the threat seriously. It could spell real trouble for us on many fronts."

"Don't you think I know that Jerry!" The air went out of John as he said it.

Silence dominated for a few moments while both men pondered what was on the horizon.

John then spoke, "But we have a more immediate problem. Bud Peck called me to say the old back-up boiler at Jefferson has sprung a leak in one of its tubes. They have to shut it down ASAP to do some stop-gap repairs. They think they can close off the leaking tube and keep the old boiler running but they need to close school at Jefferson for the next two days while they attempt the repairs. Neil is up to speed on all this as he and Bud talked before I got the call. I think we have to give the okay to close Jefferson down for the repairs. Do you see it any different?"

"No, looks like we've got no choice. John, are you asking the staff to report anywhere?"

"We know they can't report to Jefferson since there won't be any heat. It will be hard to get any training together on the fly so right now we are not planning on asking them to report. Do you have any other ideas?"

"It would be great if we could get the department chairs and school counselors together. We have to finalize the course of study booklet for the coming year so they can begin course registration with the kids. It's a great opportunity to do that."

"Jerry, with everybody else out the union may take the position anyone we call in should have extra pay."

"I know we might have to pay them extra, but we could really take advantage of the time and get ahead of the curve on the course registration process. Their work would also be a help for both Lincoln and Roosevelt."

"Okay Jerry, talk with Tom Wheaton to see if we have funds we can tap, and alert Carl Gardner. If they are both supportive then why don't you take one day for it; I assume you'll bring them here."

"Yeah, we can use the large meeting room downstairs if it's open. If not, I'll find a place. Now back to your visit at Lincoln John. Remember to be damn careful with your notes to the staff. The union will be all over you if you say anything critical. You don't need the work and neither does Carl."

John took a deep breath. He knew Jerry was looking out for him. He sensed how tightly he was grabbing the arms of the chair. His knuckles were white and his forearms were flexed. "I will," he said. "Seems like we both have lots to do. I'll check in later or you can send me an email to let me know if the Jefferson crew is coming in to work. I want to drop by and raise a ruckus if they do."

"Okay, as long as it's a good ruckus and you don't write them any notes! We should talk more about Albert Denton and his visit John. Let me make some calls and see what I can learn about this guy."

"Okay, see what the grapevine tells you. I'm going to do the same with my counterparts. We'll have a leadership meeting on it soon."

"Yeah, I hear Mary Jane will be looking forward to it."

John turned to speak but before he could say anything, Jerry smiled and said, "No secrets around here John."

As John headed back to his office he thought about the boatload of issues confronting him and his team. Earlier, he had a call on his cell phone he did not answer. When he checked the voice mail, he learned it was from a headhunter named Joe Moreland who left a message about a great job opportunity in a well-off suburban district. He said John was on the district's short list of highly desirable candidates.

CHAPTER 48

WHAT'S NEXT

It was hard to believe Christmas was less than two weeks away. Ma'am had several major things pending. The first was a request from the State Education Department auditors. They were planning a lengthy visit right after the holiday. In preparation for it they asked for a number of items to be compiled. First on the list was the most recent written observation report for every teacher, as well as a copy of the previous annual evaluation. They asked for copies of all violent behavior referrals since last year's state report. Ma'am knew this was going to be problematic given all the bus behavior reports filed in the fall before the driver's contract was settled. Next, they wanted a listing, by grade, of every child who had been continuously enrolled at School #3 for more than 18 calendar months as these were the children they'd hold the school accountable for on any state measure of their academic growth. Finally, they requested a copy of every special education youngster's most recent Individual Education Plan, which everyone referenced as IEP's. The compilation of these items would take days. Janet was swamped with office work and now this. Ma'am wondered if the auditors had any idea what it would take to accomplish their request, not to mention it was hitting the school on the eve of Christmas.

Ma'am contacted downtown to advise them of the state's requests, seeking counsel on what to do. Mary Jane Thomas told Ma'am they were auditing schools having a consistent pattern of failure on state tests. She reminded Ma'am her school was at the top of the list of failing elementary schools. Unbeknownst to Ma'am and others, Mary Jane strongly encouraged Albert Denton to visit School #3. She'd told him its principal and staff did not place a high enough value on state testing.

Despite the upcoming state audit, Ma'am had been working with the Rededication Committee on the plans for School #3's renaming as Rosa Parks Elementary School. She'd also talked with Andrea and Colleen learning the Trimbell High School Service Club did a tremendous job collecting enough clothing items to fill a big U-Haul truck. They had their work cut out for them sorting and sifting through the donations. In addition to these tasks, there was the upcoming holiday assembly, numerous phone calls to return, a lengthy in-box of emails plus three bus referrals Ma'am had to follow up on before the end of the day.

This morning she was also meeting with Sara Vaughn and another architect for an update on the preliminary plans for a new school. She was looking forward to the meeting as Sara advised they had a first sketch to share to see if they were even close to what Ma'am had in mind.

Since their last conversation, Sara had given the project a great deal of thought. She was beginning to see the power inherent in the idea of a school building whose street appeal was different. It was far from anything they'd done. She'd talked a few times on the phone with Dorothy who asked her to work inside a maximum budget of six million dollars for the overall construction of the school.

When Sara arrived she had another experienced architect with her, Sean Peters. He'd been working with Sara on the project and was excited to try something unlike the modern schools they had been designing and winning awards for over the past decade.

"We've been talking about your ideas and trying to come up with a concept. It is challenging to do this on a tight budget and also remembering we must meet state codes for fire suppression, handicapped access and hallway widths, to name just a few."

Dorothy didn't know much about codes and state building requirements for schools, "I hadn't thought about that part of the task. It must be more of a challenge than I'd considered."

"We have a sketch we want to show you. It is a preliminary attempt to go down a different road. We've given the structure the look of a large home." They opened the portfolio Sean was carrying and set a sketch in front of Dorothy.

Looking at it, she knew they were serious about trying something different. She gave them lots of feedback. "I like the concept. It sure doesn't look like a school! But I want a lot bigger porch. Could we do something across the front and down one side?"

As they talked about ideas and changes, Sean took notes and probed Dorothy on why she wanted particular features. He explained why some things were important or needed for code compliance. Dorothy shared her suggestions so they could incorporate them in a future rendering.

Their conversation went on for nearly an hour. Dorothy was excited to be working with Sara and Sean. They were taking the concepts to heart and starting to conceptualize them in a working plan. She looked forward to meeting with them again in a few weeks as they modified and revised the plan. Dorothy felt it was nearly time for the whole committee to react to what they were preparing. If they liked it, they'd be taking a path less chosen, for sure!

CHAPTER 49

THE VOLUNTEERS

Andrea and Colleen were thrilled by what the service club students accomplished. They were overwhelmed by the amount of clothing needing to be sized and sorted. She talked with Jason about the hours of work needed for the project. It was over dinner he surprised her. "I've been talking about the project with the people at the office. My office manager agreed we could help. We can give you a dozen people for a day. She said the company supports community service projects and was certain this one would get an okay. We could come in on Friday and, if needed, I have some people who said they'd volunteer on Saturday to finish up. But I think we can do this in a day if you guys give us basic directions."

Andrea was thrilled, "Jason, wow that is terrific! We could use the help. I can't believe you did this! What a great surprise."

"We're gonna need somebody to direct us so I called Bea. She said she'd do it so no substitutes would be needed for you or Colleen."

Andrea looked at Jason with moist eyes, "You really went the extra mile on this one. You and Bea kept a secret too. Wait until I talk to that woman!"

"Yup we did. Jasmin gets home this week, so she'd be sure to have her come along; I think we've got plenty of helping hands. Think about how you want us to get things organized for distribution. Your mom told me you may have more hats and mittens than you need so think about what to do with any excess clothing."

After dinner Andrea spent time on the phone with Bea and Colleen. She also Skyped with Jasmin, catching up and sharing some holiday plans. Andrea wanted Jasmin and Bea to come to the apartment on New Year's Eve for dinner. Jasmin thought it was a great idea.

Andrea went to sleep tired but excited. The idea of sharing warm clothes with children who really needed them was coming together. She thought it might be the most satisfying Christmas ever. However, the teacher in Andrea was also worried about the upcoming state literacy test. Like all the staff she'd heard the state auditors were coming. They'd be there when the tests were given adding further stress.

When sorting day came, lots of people were on hand to pitch in. Ma'am was excited so many volunteers came to help out. She thanked everyone, making sure coffee and Danish were on hand. Bea had labels for everything. The team of volunteers assembled the items by class for teachers to pick-up.

Jasmin knew what her mom planned and floated around the room giving directions and encouragement. Jason noticed Jasmin's energy and easy manner with people. She was an attractive young woman and he wasn't the only guy in the room who noticed. Two younger office mates were already asking Jason what he knew about her and if she had a steady boyfriend. Jasmin was the big hit of the day for these guys.

At lunch time Andrea dropped by to see how things were going. Andrea noticed Jasmin, giving her a warm hug. "It's so great to see you! Thanks for helping out."

"I wouldn't have missed it. With mom here, no doubt I was going to be working."

Jasmin and Andrea talked for a bit and agreed to catch up over lunch on Saturday. Andrea noticed the guys eyeing Jasmin. "Looks like you've got your choice on a date over the break if you want it. I can tell you the blond guy is a wolf. Jason says he talks in the office about his conquests. The other guy is cuter anyhow, and he's real nice. No steady girl right now."

Jasmin giggled and replied, "I haven't had this much attention from men in a while. I should volunteer at clothing drives more often!"

Andrea laughed knowing Jasmin was kidding. Later, when she arrived at the cafeteria, she learned James Tharp threw quite a tantrum.

The aides were upset. Ma'am had to wrestle him out of the room. It had been a tough time for everyone, especially for Ma'am as it was the third discipline incident of the day. Holiday's always seemed to bring more problems to the surface and this year was no exception.

Andrea's kids were upset. James was a difficult child, but he was part of their class. It was going to be a different afternoon than what she'd planned. She'd have to spend a little extra time settling them down before they took the practice test on literacy.

When she got home both Andrea and Jason were tired. Throughout the day staff members stopped by while they sorted clothes in the gym. Jason was impressed Sue Jones had given up the gym for the day. She did some basic physical education exercises in the classrooms. "It must have been a hard day for Sue," he said.

"Sue can be great on things. We all think at times she can be too much of a pit bull on the contract, but she really cares about the school and has no trouble pitching in when it's needed. You got to meet a lot of the staff. What did you think?"

"I liked most of them. But, I did think Barbara Lovell was cold!"

"What did she do?"

"She came into the gym and never said a word to us. No thank you, nothing. She spoke to Bea for a few minutes and left. She certainly didn't interact with anybody."

"I am surprised. Barbara is usually friendly. I'll have to ask Bea if she said anything. By the way, Jasmin and I made a lunch date for tomorrow so you're on your own."

"That's fine by me. I've got some catching up to do on emails, given the volunteer time today."

"Jason, I can't thank you enough for all the help. How about you pick a place for dinner and chose a movie for us to see tomorrow night. It will be my treat."

CHAPTER 50

FIRE!

The holidays always seem to pass by faster than they arrive. Andrea and Jason had a splendid Christmas. The New Year's Eve dinner party with Bea and Jasmin was a good time. Jasmin accepted a date with Tony Blevin, the cute nice guy at Jason's office and Colleen and Trace were also with them to ring in the New Year.

Now School #3 was back in session in a new calendar year. Albert Denton and two other auditors arrived on the third day back as the children were entering school. They requested work space so Ma'am had no choice but to give up the school's only conference room. Shortly after the auditors arrived, Mary Jane Thomas checked in to make sure they had the information they needed. She said little to Ma'am or the office staff as she went about her schmoozing of the auditors.

Ma'am checked on the three person team camped down the hall. She learned Albert Denton never taught an elementary class nor had he ever given the state literacy test to a classroom of children. His two colleagues were both teachers. One was an elementary teacher who had excellent training but little practical experience, having worked only three years in a suburban school before going back to graduate school to obtain her doctorate. Her name was Dr. Linda Grinold. She now worked as a consultant to the State Education Department and taught at the college level in the state capital. The third team member was Samuel Baxter, a retired middle school principal. He had lots of practical experience, but had been retired for two years, having never taught or worked in an urban setting. The team was all business, spending the first day reading materials they had requested.

On the second day of their visit they asked to meet with Ma'am once the school day was underway. Ma'am walked down to the conference room not knowing what to expect. In fact, she was about to step into an inquisition without any counsel or guidance on what to say or do. Albert Denton started the questions. "Mrs. Washington we've been reading your annual evaluations. You hardly mention student growth or progress in your reports. Can you tell us why?"

Ma'am took a deep breath, she knew this was going to be a stress filled conversation. "Mr. Denton, the union contract does not allow me to do any annual evaluations before May 1st. So practically speaking I have only six weeks to complete the annual evaluations and follow-up conferences with my entire staff. As you know, the state usually does not complete its norming and score compilations on the tests until July, so I don't have the official scores for reference when I'm doing the annual evaluations. At the start of each year we set goals for student success. I discuss the children's progress towards those goals each month in our grade level meetings with the teachers. I know my staff and I know my kids. My evaluations focus on each teacher's work ethic, student/parent relationships and how well they have achieved the goals we've established."

Dr. Grinold interjected, "Mrs. Washington, I don't see where raising state test scores is ever a listed goal. Why is that?"

"Dr. Grinold, let's look at this year's goals. Last year we had more than 20% of our student enrollment enter or leave this school. One goal we all shared was how could we help so many children and families who seem to be in constant transition. We also have, for all practical purposes, a 100% poverty rate here. We had a school-wide goal this year to improve student nutrition and address basic needs. Too many of our children lack the simple necessities for a healthy life. If you visit the nurse's office during your time here you will see we often treat 8 to 10 children a day there for rat bites. Like I said, we focus on instructional goals every month in our grade level meetings. I believe those direct conversations and my teachers consistent efforts to informally assess student progress keep us focused on literacy and math skills."

Sam Baxter was sympathetic to her workload. But lacking an understanding of the breadth of the issues and union constraints in an urban district pressed the points made by the other two auditors. "Mrs. Washington, I took a look at this week's faculty agenda. It was posted in the faculty room and I read it when I went to get coffee. You have a number of committee reports on the agenda. The first is the Rededication Committee's update, then a follow-up report on the clothing drive and a report on the work of the Elementary Program Committees. Dr. Thomas said you are running your own program group, even though a district committee is underway. However, state tests are next week and there's no mention of it on the agenda."

"Mr. Baxter, I have 45 minutes once per month for a general faculty meeting. The union contract is crystal clear on the number of meetings I can schedule and the length of time they can run. I try to focus the agenda for the general meeting on items that inform the staff and keep them abreast of the work of key committees. We do the instructional work in the monthly grade level meetings. You have not looked at my calendar, but if you did, you'd see I am meeting with each grade level before school this week or next to make sure they are prepared for the tests they have to administer."

Albert Denton closed this first meeting. "I am sure we'll have a lot more questions for you and the staff as we move along in the audit. Do you have any questions for us at this time?"

"I do have one. Can you give me a schedule of activities or the length of time you will be in the building?"

"Mrs. Washington, we will take as long as we feel necessary to understand the needs of your school. Right now I am sure you know this is the poorest performing elementary school in the district. Quite honestly, it is one of the poorest performing elementary schools in the state. We'll take whatever time we need to develop our findings and recommendations for improvement." Dorothy was summarily dismissed with no clear understanding of what would happen next.

She did learn one thing from the exchange. Mary Jane Thomas told the team about her ad hoc committee. From the tone of their remarks Dr. Thomas had made sure they understood her distain for the effort.

She knew she could not turn to Dr. Thomas for advice or help on the audit.

When she reached John later that morning she shared the inquisition experience. He was not surprised by what she told him. "Dorothy, I will send some help your way. I want Kelly Slocum to answer any training questions. I will ask her to drop by with School # 3's teacher training logs. All of your staff have been trained by her crew in state standards and effective strategies so let's be sure they know it. I will also ask the pupil service staff to stop over since they are reading the children's IEP's. Have you talked with your counterparts on this?"

"John we've been buzzing about it on the phone. We decided no email since they might read them at some point. We are troubled about this John."

"I know. I would encourage you to contact your state leadership association to see if they have any advice for you as well. I am doing that with the State Superintendent's Council. I think they are taking a run at us. We all have to think carefully about what we say and do."

Dorothy couldn't hold back, "Well John then you better tell Dr. Thomas to stay in her office because I think she's feeding them information."

John's anger with Mary Jane was palpable, but to act on it would be a mistake. All he could do was make sure the rest of the staff did what they could to help out. "I understand what you are saying, but we'll do what we can to help you put your best foot forward there."

"I know you will John. My colleagues and I will keep you posted on whatever we learn. Hopefully these folks will get this done and be on their way. My staff have the jitters with them around."

"Hey, changing the subject, you sure have Sara Vaughn excited. She says you have some interesting ideas on a new neighborhood school concept. She's also excited about a construction approach that could save us some money. She wouldn't share any sketches with me yet. She wants to get a second generation drawing completed before she does. I think, from the sounds of it, you may be on to something."

"Thanks, they brought me a preliminary drawing, but we've got lots of work to do. We talked for about an hour. She brought along another guy, Sean Peters, who I think is doing some of the heavy lifting behind the scenes. I am hopeful we can put something together. The staffing attached to it has to be different. That may be what causes the biggest stink. One step at a time I keep telling myself. I am anxious to see how the committee reacts when we show them a basic concept."

Over the years Dorothy made a number of innovative suggestions to address the growing needs of her school. Few were ever endorsed by the hide-bound culture that preceded John Handler's arrival. It was the first time in Dorothy's long career where she could think openly about how to encourage her staff to plan outside of what was previously a tightly closed box. However, the old box was still closely guarded by Mary Jane Thomas. Dorothy could not lose sight of that, nor could John.

After her conversation with the superintendent, Dorothy turned her attention back to the tasks at hand. It was almost the end of the second quarter and report card writing would begin soon. State and district literacy testing was taking place next week so she had grade level meetings scheduled to provide final directions and support. She reviewed her script several times knowing the auditors would likely attend each of these meetings. She also had James Tharp's most recent cafeteria meltdown to address. Dorothy was thinking an alternative placement for James was warranted since his uncontrollable outbursts were becoming more difficult to handle. At the same time, she did not want to give up on him. She knew Andrea felt the same way. Nonetheless, they'd have to team on him soon and make bottom line decisions on what to do.

After John hung up the phone with Dorothy, he sighed feeling the heavy weight of leadership. He'd had the update from Bud Peck on the Jefferson boiler situation. Bud explained, "Doc it is like an old Chevy truck that's been through more winters than we can count. The fenders are rotted out with rust and it seems the motor burns as much oil as gasoline, but the damn truck keeps runnin'. Our boiler is like that old Chevy, she's not given up, but for the life of me I can't tell you why she hasn't quit!"

John knew the new boiler had been ordered. If things went according to plan, they'd be able to install it over February break when school was shut down. The asbestos removal over the Christmas break had been accomplished and they were now waiting for the new valves and equipment to arrive. In the meantime John could only hope the old unit would keep on going.

After lunch he was meeting with Cliff Greer to talk about the budget. Cliff heard rumors of the impending cuts and wanted to hear from John where things stood. For his part, John was not sure yet as Carl Gardner and the team were still pulling the plan together. However, John knew the layoffs were going to be large and it would be a difficult conversation with Cliff about what was on the horizon.

No sooner had he started his next call when Ann came in and interrupted him, handing him a note, 'Fire at School #3.'

"Dorothy Washington called and told me the school is filled with smoke. Apparently someone started a fire in the boys' bathroom. The fire department is there and it seems the fire had a chance to do some real damage. The department has not yet declared the fire is out. Dorothy has called for buses but the staff and kids are still out in the freezing rain as we speak. It sounds to me like they are in rough shape."

"Nuts! If the children and staff have been out in this weather they must be soaked and freezing by now."

It was a long ten minute drive to School #3. The street in front of the school looked like a Vegas casino with flashing lights of every color. Once he was identified, the police let him drive through to a closer point. John's feet carried him swiftly over the slippery sidewalk to where the staff and children were shivering and soaked to the bone. Every car in the parking lot was being used as a shelter. Dorothy was talking with a fireman who was shaking his head as she asked him if it was safe to relocate children to the gym or cafeteria.

John stood back letting Dorothy do her job. He decided to call the bus garage to see if any buses were on the way yet. The dispatcher who answered said, "We've been waiting for drivers to come in. We put out the call but only a few are here now Dr. Handler."

"Why aren't their fannies in a seat and driving this way! We have children standing in the cold. Damn it, anybody who has a license to drive a bus should be in one right now and headed this way. Get mechanics driving; I mean anybody qualified needs to be behind the wheel of a bus!"

John walked over to where Dorothy stood with the fire lieutenant. "We can't let you in the gym, the school is old and there's wood framing in many parts of it. The bathroom fire is a nasty little one. Even though we think we have it out, we have to be sure the school is safe before we let you in. The halls are filled with smoke and it's going to take some time to get it out once we are sure we have no working fire in the walls or ceiling we can't see. I know it's bad out here and shelter is needed now. But if we put people back in there it will be worse than out here if something else happens."

Dorothy noticed John at her side. She turned, "All the kids and staff are out and accounted for, everyone is safe, but you can see what shape we are in!"

"Dorothy, buses are on the way".

She nodded, "John, I talked with the police and they are establishing a safe loading area around the corner on Warsaw. Since there's no chance to get back into even the gym we'll start walking the kids down to the corner. Our back up plan is to relocate everyone to School #17. I've told them to expect more than four hundred guests. We will begin moving the youngest kids up the street. I don't want to overwhelm things on Warsaw. Can you help me by going up there? I need to stay here until everyone has left."

John quickly agreed, "I'll let the police and fire folks know we're on the move while you tell the staff what we are doing."

As the line of small rain soaked shivering children moved along the sidewalk towards Warsaw Street, the scene was heart wrenching. On the sidewalk with the children John said to the police sergeant escorting them, "Can you ask the Red Cross for some help? We are going to need to get these children and staff warm. They are soaked to the bone."

"Mrs. Washington asked us the same thing. We are already on it. The fire department has blankets and they are making a run to School #17 as we speak." No sooner had these words been spoken when John was confronted by a panicked parent who was running towards the school.

"My baby, is my baby all right?" Her eyes had the intensity of lasers even though her body was trembling with terror.

"All the children are safe. We are moving them to School #17 to get them out of this weather."

This mother barely seemed to hear John's answer as she looked for her child and called, "James, James!" In the distance she heard a cry, "Ma ma!" She and her child embraced on the mud soaked grass near the curb. It was a scene captured by the newspaper's photographer. It would be the lead picture on the front page of the paper the next day under the headline, 'Chaos at School #3.'

As the group moved along to the corner John saw more frightened parents running towards him. It was impossible to prevent them from seeking their children. As each saw their child or continued down the road in a panicked search, it was hard to keep the children and staff moving. John was grateful the audit team members were pitching in. They were soaked like everyone else and he could see their concern for the children. However, he couldn't help but have a brief second of satisfaction they were soaked and completely dependent on his direction and support. It would be the only time he'd have much influence over them.

Back outside the school, Andrea and Bea stood huddled with their children. After what seemed like hours the fourth and fifth grades were finally asked to head down to the corner where buses awaited. As they trudged down the sidewalk they looked like a group of refugees. Stepping into the warm buses was a moment everyone would remember. Once inside, the fear and discomfort they tried to ignore rolled across them all like a tidal wave over an unsuspecting shore. Children were sobbing in their seats and their soaked clothing became noticeably uncomfortable.

With all the fourth and fifth grade children safely on the buses Dorothy was able to walk down the sidewalk confident everyone escaped without serious injury. As she walked her body shuddered unexpectedly. She knew more awaited her at School #17; this rough day still had some energy.

Al Dixson was the principal at School #17, a giant with a booming voice. Dix, as his friends called him, stood in the middle of the gym at School #17 giving orders and offering suggestions like General Patton commanding the troops. Dorothy was exhausted and welcomed Dix's command of the situation in the gym.

It was a triage area. EMT's were checking children and staff as they entered. Exposure to the elements was the main concern. But children with other health issues received special attention as well. By the time the whole school passed through the doors the EMT's sent three children to the hospital for observation. Two were in kindergarten and the third child was in second grade.

John watched his two principals confer and make decisions. He too was exhausted, but felt tremendous pride in this moment as he watched so many people selflessly dedicated to the welfare of the children. Keeping track of the students and reuniting them with parents soon became a necessary task. The police department was of great assistance, assuring parents arriving at School#17, the children were safe and no serious injuries had been reported. Believing them was difficult seeing the line-up of emergency vehicles in front of the school. Parents were directed to the school cafeteria and asked to wait there while things were settled with the children.

CHAPTER 51

SEEKING NORMALCY

Andrea drove home reflecting on the grueling day. It was hard not to think of the children and all they had been through. Michael Malkin wanted to run across the street to the warmth of his home and Andrea said no. Then his big brother James walked over a little while later to retrieve Michael from the miserable weather and Andrea didn't know what to do, but James stood in her face saying, "I'm takin' him home!" When this happened, several children also said they wanted to walk home. Before Andrea could say anything she was surprised to hear James Tharp say, "Shush, teacher take care of us now!"

The stoic ones stood silently and did whatever was asked without a complaint. Andrea smiled remembering Dedra noticed how wet her teacher was and laughed saying, "Your hair looks real funny."

Bea, Andrea and their fourth grade teaching partner Pam Kilborn worked together when they got to School #17. Parents who came to pick up their children often escorted them out the door with the blankets still tightly wrapped around their child's body. The fire department's inventory of blankets would be reduced as most of them would not be returned. They would be welcome additions to homes with few to spare.

Andrea craved a warm shower and once home she headed there leaving clothes strewn along her path. It was a half hour before the cold truly left her body. Jason hadn't heard anything about the fire and was surprised to see Andrea sitting on the couch in her bathrobe drinking tea. "Are you sick?"

Andrea let the emotions of the day free. She settled on the couch with her head on Jason's shoulder. Jason was shocked to learn what happened, quickly realizing the severity of the day. As he lived with Andrea through the school year he learned how (all) consuming the job of teaching was. He'd gained a deeper understanding of the level of responsibility and deep affection Andrea felt for the children in her care. She was exhausted, but relieved the children were safe and nobody was seriously hurt.

The next morning the staff were instructed to return to School #17, not sure exactly what to expect. They assembled in the school's cafeteria and quickly settled in, awaiting Ma'am's update.

Ma'am began, "I want to thank you all for everything you did to keep the children safe. I am pleased to tell you all of the children came through yesterday's ordeal without a scratch or injury. Jeremiah Thompson and Sadia Jones, our two kindergarten children who went to the hospital for observation are fine. Our second grade student, Jerome Fellows, had a significant bout of asthma and spent the night at General Hospital. I called his mom and she tells me he is doing much better. He will likely be home before lunch today."

With this news the entire staff clapped.

Ma'am continued, "I'd like to thank Al Dixson and his staff for these fine accommodations and all of their support."

Once the laughter and warm applause died down, Dix spoke for a moment in his deep baritone voice, "I too want to praise all of you. We faced an unexpected event with the potential to become a tragedy. Yet here we are this morning, laughing and drinking coffee knowing everything turned out okay. I am proud of my staff and all of you. We hope you enjoy our hospitality this morning."

John stood in the back of the room unnoticed until Ma'am introduced him. The staff gave him warm applause as he walked toward the microphone. "Thank you, what a great pair of words they are. I can accept your applause and in the same moment turn it around as a compliment to you for all your efforts. I wanted to stop by this morning to say how proud I am of you. I know the images on the front page of this morning's paper are filled with emotion and drama, but the true story is one of concern for the safety of every child at School #3. Your efforts, along with the wonderful support of our fire, police and emergency personnel made us an unbeatable team. So I will close with those two simple words, thank you."

Ma'am jumped back in, "Okay, all the good stuff having been said, let me update you on where things stand. We know the fire was set, so we have arson on our hands. The police department will be interviewing many of us over the course of the morning to see what information we may recall. We also have cleaning and repairs underway as we speak. We will be closed tomorrow. I've been told we will be able to open after that. The biggest issue will be the loss of the main boys' bathroom on the first floor for several weeks. We still have state and district tests scheduled for next week; we have to get the children back on track for them. We will be allowed back in the building tomorrow although Fred and his crew, along with some district folks, will still be cleaning and getting us ready to resume school. When you see him, be sure to thank him; he's already put in long hours getting the mess on the first floor cleaned up. Now, what questions can I answer?"

The staff had numerous questions and the discussion went back and forth on them for the next half-hour. It was a relief to hear they could get back in the building in the morning. The group left everything behind and welcomed a day to sort things out and prepare for the children's return. They also needed some time to discuss the logistics of using an upstairs bathroom. For the younger children this would take a little direction and review. The kindergarten rooms had their own bathrooms so it would not pose an issue for the youngest in the school.

Andrea wondered how her kids were doing. Many of the parents and grandparents worked during the day and did not have child care arrangements for their children, assuming they'd be in school. Andrea knew a number of her students would be on their own. "Bea, do you think the kids will be okay with nobody to care for them at home?"

"Andrea, stop and think about it girl. These kids have to take care of themselves lots of times, they'll be fine. But you know that, why are you so worried?"

"I don't know, I will be glad when they are all back in my room. I need to know they are okay. I have an uneasy feeling I can't explain."

"Girl, sometimes worrin' about things can grow uneasy feelin's. Just 'cause you have 'em doesn't make it real."

"I know you are right, I do worry more than I should sometimes. I guess seeing all the children so cold outdoors is a memory I can't shake. I'll be relieved when I see all my kids come up those creaky old stairs."

CHAPTER 52

A DOOR CLOSES

It was hard to believe the first semester of the school year was drawing to a close. With all the hope for the year and its theme, 'Right Now,' John decided a mid-year meeting of the leadership team was needed. He'd asked all the building principals and district office administrators to meet with him. In addition to updates from the various committee chairs, he also had things to share on the Quality School description. The agenda for the afternoon would be the coming school year's budget and the myriad of issues it would place on the leadership table.

As people entered the main conference room the words 'Right Now' were projected on the screen. As usual, the team was enjoying their coffee. Clusters gathered throughout the room. Dorothy was with a group of elementary principals. Dix was discussing the fire and how pleased he was things turned out okay. Teresa Simpson, the principal at School #5, said to Dorothy, "I hear they identified the child who started the fire. Third grade, were you surprised?"

"Not much surprises me anymore, but this was a child none of us would have suspected. But he quickly confessed when he was confronted. We have no doubt he's our little firebug. We're trying to sort out his future. I am not sure what we'll do."

"Don't send him to my school!" Dix roared.

"Ah Dix, you are just the guy to handle him. Big tough man like you can surely make that little one behave." Teresa was having fun kidding Dix this morning knowing he could take it as well as dish it out.

The banter continued for ten minutes past the starting time. John enjoyed walking around and talking with people. He was proud of his team and felt they needed the extra minutes to socialize before beginning a difficult agenda. As much as he would have liked to let things continue longer, it was time to start. He picked up his lovelier microphone, clipped it to his tie and turned on the battery pack. His 'Good-morning,' was a call for everyone to settle.

Mary Jane Thomas was the first to speak, "The Elementary Program Committee has met a dozen times from the start of the school year. We've made excellent progress. We've discussed the need for a new reading program and updated materials. This will be one of the key recommendations in our report. The other major issue is class size, especially in the early primary grades. We feel strongly it needs to be reduced to, at the most, 15 students per class in grades K-2."

It was Dix who raised the first questions, "Have you discussed staff training? Will we as principals have any voice in what reading program is selected?" He added with a touch of sarcasm.

"We project the cost of a new reading program adoption and the related training to be over two million. Our textbook budget will have to be used over a three-year period to cover the cost, so we won't do a district-wide one-year roll-out. The committee is looking at the various programs available. They have whittled it down to three to pilot next year in some settings."

Teresa Simpson jumped in, "Are you saying the texts we'll pilot next year are being chosen by the committee? So the elementary principals don't have a voice in the process? How will the pilot schools be chosen?"

Mary Jane was uncomfortable with the rebuke. She stated with her own edge, "You will have a major voice in the final selection. Bottom-line, if we move forward with this recommendation, I will choose the pilot schools."

As this back-and-forth took place John took careful notes. He supported the need for new materials, and knew the high cost of them would have to be phased in. It was evident the principals were feeling out of the loop. In fairness to Mary Jane, leading twenty-three principals, each with their own fiefdom, was no simple task.

Next up was Joanne Walters, the Middle Level Assistant Superintendent. Her committee's work was well known amongst the three principals. They had much easier access to Joanne, given the size of the group. "Our team has been working on a number of key issues. Overall school size is one of them. Most on the team believe each of our schools is too big. With twelve hundred 11 to 14 year olds under one roof a lot can happen, not all of it is good by the way." Joanne's style was engaging. The group laughed as she spoke about hormones and the high activity rate of early adolescents. "We don't think it is realistic to build another middle school. So, our conversations are around how we can create smaller settings within our three middle schools. We've shared lots of perspectives and had some spirited conversations. How they'll gel is an open question now."

Gail Butterworth, an elementary school principal asked, "Are there any guiding themes as you discuss this?"

Joanne smiled, "Yes, we've hooked onto the Gates Foundation's new 3R's. We like the *Rigor, Relevance* and *Relationship* linkage. We want anything we recommend to respect and build upon those three traits. But our perspectives on how to apply them are divergent and the challenge will be for us to develop some manageable recommendations over the next few months. Quite honestly, it is going to be tough to do."

John knew Joanne was an excellent facilitator and she earned the respect of administrators and teachers alike. Nonetheless, many different forces (practical and political) played out in this committee and she had her hands full trying to gain consensus. John feared the committee's ultimate recommendations might end up being window dressing with lots of good rhetoric, but not much substantive change.

Jerry Croton was the next to speak, "Our group has been bogged down in sequences and graduation requirements. The teachers on the team want a new attendance policy much tougher than what's in place now. We have not made much headway on the drop-out problem either. It's tough sledding and the resistance to change is significant. They are all good people, who work hard, but they operate in silos: math, science, English, social studies, you name the discipline, each in their own silo. Trying to get any cohesive change is like herding cats. To try and break the current place we are in, John and I have talked about funding some benchmarking visits to blue ribbon schools. I am hoping this may be the incentive we need, because not much is happening."

John knew Jerry had been unable to get a serious conversation going on what a 21st Century high school needed to be. Each department was possessive of their content and sequence of delivery. They also held a strong view the administration was there primarily to deal with student discipline. The interactions on an instructional level often happened in the departments. Whole school conversations were difficult to initiate, let alone sustain. Thinking of alternatives like, evening school, virtual classes, and different sequences, were not easy conversations. Jerry knew John was discouraged with the group's progress and overall resistance to substantive change.

As the program summary wrapped up, John asked if anyone had further questions or comments. School #19 principal Carol Crane made a political move she and Mary Jane previously planned. "Dr. Handler, can you update us on the work of the ad-hoc Elementary Program Committee Dorothy Washington is leading?" Many in the room were unaware of Dorothy's team and were caught by surprise. They also had been in the game long enough to recognize when a hard inside fastball was being thrown over the plate.

"I can. Dorothy is working with a small group in her school's community to explore ways of addressing the needs of children who come from the highest poverty area of our city. You know each other's test scores, so you know School #3 is the poorest performing elementary school in our district, something the state auditors have been pointing out to us throughout their visit here by the way."

Carol Crane pressed the point nonetheless. "Dr. Handler, does it mean any of us could form our own ad-hoc groups? I thought we had three committees and we were trying to unify our program efforts. This seems to run counter to that approach."

"I told Dorothy my support was conditional and any recommendations forthcoming from her ad hoc group would be considered, but not necessarily supported, by me. We have all heard this morning how difficult it is to move forward with change. Ford can design and build a new car quicker than we can implement a new program. You all have an invitation to make a proposal for change which would improve the right conditions for learning at your school. That proposal may or may not get my support, but I am not going to close the door on innovation before I even hear the idea!"

John knew this serve and volley was far from the last of it. The risk in forming an ad hoc group was it could undercut the work of a larger committee. He knew a number of principals would wonder why he'd given Dorothy a green-light none of them had. He'd opened the door for something different and nobody said it wasn't going to get messy when the winds of change started blowing. "Let's take a stretch for a few minutes. Then I want to update you on several other items and get your advice on the school name change process before we break for lunch."

Jerry Croton followed him out the door of the conference room and spoke in a quiet corner of the main foyer, "John I am glad you took a stretch. I think you said what you needed to; given the larger agenda she was serving."

"Jerry, she did have a point. I let the horse out of the barn when I gave Dorothy my support to look at things on her own. It's hard to be both loose and tight on the reins at the same time. I'm not sure how this whole thing will play out, especially when I am flying so often by the seat of my pants. Let's see how people feel about innovation and change when we discuss the upcoming budget after lunch."

The second half of the morning began with John updating the group on the Quality School Committee's efforts. He distributed a draft document and broke the group into small teams. John asked each team to develop three questions or comments and boil the three down to one they would share with the whole group. The three would be written on a sheet to be returned to him. Overall, the group was impressed by the draft. It was apparent progress was being made. John got good feedback as well.

Moving on, John asked Zack James to share the status of his work with students on strategies to reduce bullying, "I'm excited by the kids' efforts. We've talked a lot about cyber bullying and I've had my eyes opened. What I am most excited about is they want to develop a seminar on the impact of cyber bullying and teach it to their peers and the staff. I think we have the makings of something which could be positive."

While the group respected Zack's relationships with students, they wondered if he could take a big idea and form it into a real program.

John then turned to the last topic of the morning, "Okay, I need your advice and counsel. We've all seen Dorothy and the School #3 staff put through the ringer on renaming her school. Nobody else has stepped forward, so what's up?"

Dix was comfortable speaking on behalf of the principals. "John, we are bogged down in the public feedback loop. Most of the feedback we get from the larger community is negative. Inside the school there's good support and we see lots of great suggestions for school names. But with the negative feedback, and the mixed Board support for the change, we're all reluctant to move on with a specific recommendation. You and Dorothy really took some shots from Board members. With their divided vote, we're not sure we'll all get approved. I can also tell you it's a lot more work than we expected, including the follow up rededication planning that has to take place."

John listened carefully as other principals reinforced Dix's message. It was clear the principals wanted to support the renaming project, but they were overloaded with agendas and daily workloads. With a divided Board they'd found a reason to step back. John didn't blame them; he'd probably do the same thing if he were in their shoes. "I am second guessing myself on this one. But we are in it and I can't have only one building renamed. Let's see if we can get some positive momentum going on this. Let me know if any of you are ready, I need at least two or three volunteers to help me see if this process can move forward more easily with our Board and community." John knew he had not addressed their workload concerns on this effort. The workload was more time-consuming than he'd originally thought. He had under estimated it and his plea did not include an answer to this issue. He was uncertain about this initiative and whether or not it could be sustained. The team broke for lunch and would reconvene in the afternoon to discuss the upcoming budget development process and status of the facility project.

CHAPTER 53

NOW IT BEGINS

John took his lunch break in his office between the morning and afternoon sessions. Ann saw him walk in and followed asking, "How did it go this morning?"

"It was the easier session Ann. Things went about as expected. I got some push back for giving Dorothy Washington the okay for her ad hoc subcommittee on elementary program development. I can't say I was surprised. Zack did a nice job updating the group on his student bullying committee. I think he's on the right track with the kids. As I walked back here for lunch, I was thinking about the renaming of schools process. I am second guessing whether or not it was a good idea. The principals don't believe the Board will support them. They know it's a lot of work with little gain, especially with all the other tasks they must address. It's interesting how what seemed like a good idea in September can feel very different four months later."

"John, you have to stay the course. If they see you backing off now, they'll wonder if they can trust your staying power on tough decisions."

"That's one view Ann. Another is that I am smart enough to change course and recognize the cost/benefit on the idea isn't there. That's good leadership too."

"John, you have a hard message to deliver on the budget. Give the naming process some time; be patient a while longer on it."

"Thanks Ann, is there anything I need to address on the break?"

"Nothing that won't keep, but Shantell wants to see you after the meeting if you have time."

"Did she say what she wanted?"

"No, she often doesn't tell me. But I know she and Sara went to lunch with Mary Jane the other day, so the pump may have been primed with one of her agenda topics."

"Thanks for the heads up Ann. I see a winter storm is brewing, I may have to postpone meeting with her to another day."

John sat in his office feeling uncomfortable; a sense of misgiving was overwhelming his thoughts. The leadership team had dutifully reported their efforts to improve things in the district. Despite everyone's hard work, he held little hope what they were doing would truly improve student learning. He wondered, 'Why was there such disconnect between schooling and learning? Why did so many students fail despite the significant and ongoing efforts of their teachers?'

As he went through this mental wrestling match, John noticed the wind and ice pellets striking the roof. It sounded like a thousand birds pecking above his head. He knew what the storm was serving up would shorten the afternoon session as principals thought about returning to their schools. John also knew the storm would soon command his attention. After school sessions and sports would likely need to be cancelled. The transportation office had already called alerting him of the possible need for a decision.

As John entered the room for the afternoon meeting he noticed the clusters of people buzzing. He immediately sensed the anxiety the weather was creating. He knew he had little time to join one of the many different groups around the room. Instead, he headed for the front asking people as he went to take a seat. Once they were seated, John began, "I know you are concerned about the weather. It has turned for the worse and we will have to attend to it soon. So I will keep my remarks short and we'll head off. You know when I was sitting in your chairs I was always asked to help brainstorm ideas for cuts when a budget was in need of reduction. I am not going to ask that of you. I feel it only divides a team and builds resentment. Instead, I want to briefly share with you where things stand.

Over the past several months we have been examining the condition of our schools. The architects' reports have been comprehensive. Most of our schools are old and in need of significant repair. I have been surprised by the scope of this. Especially, when the first pass cost estimates were in the billion dollar range. I kept saying to myself, 'How could this be? It can't be right.' But as I listened to the reports I knew we had serious problems. Years of neglect, combined with patch work repair, have left us with a huge gap. I talked with our mayor about this and we realize we both face the same problem. The city sewer and water systems are in poor condition and we all know the shape our roads our in." The chuckle in the room at this gave John a brief moment to collect his thoughts. "Given the state's finances, we know help in the near term on these challenges will be hard to come by. At the same time, how can we raise taxes on our local property owners when their burden is already a large one? I truly believe, without any exaggeration, we are at a crisis point. Our needs are great and our resources are extremely limited. Frankly, that's why I gave Dorothy permission to think outside of the box on elementary program changes and school structure. We cannot afford to simply polish what is quickly becoming a rotten apple." A disquieting shift in peoples' posture was readily apparent. "We have to look at our problems through new eyes."

Carl looked directly at Mary Jane Thomas as John was saying this. He was proud of John for being candid with the team and his expectation to think in a different manner about the problems. Mary Jane was seething. She felt personally attacked by John's comments. She thought he was exaggerating the problems and using them to serve his personal agenda for radical change. She had to stop this guy. She was determined to do it before disaster struck.

"I looked at the storm outside and thought about its connection to the budget storm we need to tackle. In the face of a winter storm we usually hunker down and dig out after it passes. It is the mental set we could bring to this fiscal crisis. We just need to hunker down and ride it out. I believe that is the wrong attitude. We need to seize this crisis as an opportunity for real, substantive change. I know how hard we are all working to meet the needs of our students. However, the data speaks loudly; our efforts, and use of resources, are not bringing anywhere near enough success. I am beginning to believe the physical structures and even the basic delivery models which have shaped instruction for the past century will not serve us well in this one. We cannot simply hunker down and ride this one out. I challenge us all, including myself, to rethink what we do, how we do it, where we do it, when we do it and, ultimately even who should do it. It is all on the table for consideration. I realize this is a disconcerting message; one that may raise your anxiety as it certainly does mine. In the weeks ahead I will be putting new ideas before you, the community and our Board of Education for discussion and action. While I will be seeking your counsel, business as usual is not an option. Hunkering down will not be the strategy we pursue. In fact, there are some budget decisions I plan to make in the coming weeks. We can't postpone all the tough actions until July first when we start the next budget year.

John asked Tom Wheaton to summarize the preliminary budget figures with the team. When he finished the group sat stunned by the enormity of the financial hole confronting them. John concluded, "I wish we had more time to talk about all of this today, but old man winter is singing a different song."

CHAPTER 54

TURNING POINT

With a winter storm blasting, the buses taking the children home from School #3 ran forty minutes late. Once everyone was dismissed, Dorothy sat in her office with a cup of coffee getting the chill of the bus loop out of her bones. Bea entered the main office after dismissal.

"Okay, start talkin'. You don't usually hang around when a storm is ragin'."

Dorothy took a deep breath, poured Bea a cup of coffee and for ten minutes shared the gist of the downtown meeting.

"Wow, you have the public okay from the big guy, but Mary Jane is gonna try to take you out any way she can. This is an opportunity we may never see again. We've got to give it our best shot no matter the odds."

"I think so too; but how do we proceed from here? Is it time we put all the cards on the table, Bea?"

"You are gonna piss a lot of people off with your ideas. You know with Mary Jane's take on things she'll use anger to her advantage. I think you need to go to the Super and tell him what you are really thinkin'. You need his help. If he doesn't like the idea you got no cover and a lot of new enemies."

"Yeah that's certainly true. It will take a lot of guts for him to get behind all of what we're thinking. How do you think the committee will respond if I do have John's support?"

"The union is gonna want to nip it in the bud. They won't like the way you are thinkin' about things. The new model will cut some teachers out of the picture. They can't go along with it. Other folks will give it serious thought, but there's no tellin' how things will go. But it is the next step in the process if we are goin' to develop an alternative proposal for the Board to hear. If the committee doesn't support it, I don't see it gettin' on a Board agenda for consideration. You know even if it does get there, it's not likely it will get their support. Look at the trouble we had renamin' this school. I don't think they can hold the rope on this one; if they let go you will be fallin' into a sea filled with hungry sharks."

"Bea, I am 62 years old. I can retire if it doesn't work out. But you, that's a whole other matter. If you support me on this, you too will be an outcast."

"You let me worry about it. This girl can take care of herself."

"Aren't you the tough one! I know you can, but you know what I'm saying. Once we go forward, the road ahead will lead us both in a direction where we won't be able to ever go back to the place we started."

"So let's get started and see if we can change things. As our vision statement says, 'Create the right conditions for learning' for these children who need something much better than what we've got now."

"Let's talk about what we need to do. Assuming John's okay with it, we have to decide what's next. I want to go back to the architects and press them on the plan and layout. We need to know if the place we have in mind is feasible and what it will cost to construct. Next, we can't drop this on the committee one night. We've got to talk to them off line and see if they are receptive to the overall ideas."

"Dorothy, I can help. I can talk to fireman Tom. I think he'll see the way we are thinkin' and come on board. Then I can talk with Betty Jackson. She's in the neighborhood and she'll see it our way for sure. I think you gotta go to Myrna and see where she stands. It will be tough for her to go against the union, but I think she will. Reverend James you can convince. There are no teachers in his congregation and the union won't budge him off a good idea. Sue Jones and Linda Morgano are gonna oppose this; no question they will take the union position, they've got to. I wouldn't say much to 'em beforehand 'cause it will give the union more time to shoot it down before we get it on the table."

"I believe you and I can split the contacts like you've said. We'll need to spend some time to make sure we are saying the same thing and prepared with the same answers to questions. I will follow John's advice on how to deal with Mary Jane because she's going to pull out all the stops to prevent this. John is going to have his hands full if he gives us the go ahead. He's also got huge budget problems and the Board doesn't know when or how to make a tough call in support of their leader. No doubt about it, the storm raging outside isn't close to the political one we are about to put in motion."

Realizing the storm had piled on another few inches they needed to leave. "Dorothy, why don't you give your husband a call and tell him you are gonna spend the night with me. Even your four wheel drive Lexus is gonna have trouble getting all the way home now."

"I'll do that; it'll give us some more time to talk about how we are going to do this thing."

SECOND SEMESTER

"No Turning Back"

…Yet knowing how way leads on to way,
I doubted if I should ever come back…

Robert Frost

CHAPTER 55

TRAVELIN' MAN

Nearly a month passed since the fire at School #3. Throughout January, the winter winds howled against Andrea's classroom windows. Old man winter seemed to delight in hurling freezing rain and snow against the school's tired walls. Despite his best efforts at making them all uncomfortable, a sense of warmth that had nothing to do with the temperature inside or out was present. A comfortable emotional temperature filled Andrea's classroom. Her strengths as a teacher truly blossomed as she gained some experience and perspective. While the struggles and daily issues remained, a deep sense of trust and care flowed through her room. Andrea knew with certainty this was her life's work and this place was special. Clearly the needs of her children challenged her in ways that drew the best from her.

Driving home at the end of the day, in the teeth of a fierce winter storm, took more than hour, a drive usually accomplished in less than half the time. She wondered if the life of her city could ever return to its glory days. The winter storm howling through was one of the reasons she was growing more pessimistic.

Andrea knew a different kind of storm would begin brewing later in the week. Staff members would be correcting state tests, getting their first indications on how the children did. While her class tried their best, she knew it was far from good enough. 'Why, after working so hard, did so many children fail?' She didn't understand it. As a first year teacher, her enthusiasm for the work made it doubly hard for her to accept.

Turning her attention back to the winter storm, Andrea had only a minute to talk with Bea after school. Bea told her to get home and she'd call her later to be sure she was okay. Bea said she was going to talk with Ma'am to make sure she was okay before leaving herself.

They all saw how Ma'am stood watch over the school's children as they boarded buses to go home. She was her stoic self, but everyone knew she had been in the cold for over an hour and the frozen ice particles on her hair and coat collar reminded them when it came to hard work and doing the job, Ma'am was one who did not shirk on her responsibilities.

With so many different feelings and thoughts flowing on the drive home, Andrea was surprised to see Jason already there when she opened the door, "Wow, you are home early today. Did they let you out of the office because of the storm?"

"Not really, I have something important to share with you. I've been offered a promotion. It's an assistant manager's job in a great spot. It would mean not only more money, but also the promise of promotions down the line."

Andrea, shaking off her winter coat, was now standing in their small apartment's kitchen turning on the gas stove to make a cup of tea, "What do you mean about a great spot?"

"It is in the Montgomery, Alabama office. It means a transfer Andrea. I have to let them know my answer by the end of this week."

Andrea had many different emotions all fighting for supremacy. She wasn't sure until she spoke which one would win, "When would you have to leave if you said yes?"

"They want me there by the first of March so we'd have to get packing and find a new place to live."

Then anger burst forth from Andrea like a volcano erupting. "Jason, I am not leaving my kids! I am not going anywhere. I love my job and I don't want to leave."

It was Jason's turn. "Andrea, this promotion means a salary increase almost equal to what you make now. The company will pay for the move and the placement office will help you find a new teaching job there. Given how fast the area is growing, and with your training they say you will be able to find a teaching job real fast."

"This conversation isn't about money! You are not hearing me Jason, I'm not leaving my kids."

"Then I guess they are more important than our life together. I really want this job and I am sick of the weather here. We can make a better life for ourselves. Please don't dismiss it flat out like this."

"Why doesn't my job count? Why is this only about you and your work! I said it and it's final, I am not leaving my kids." Andrea, took her tea and with sobs forming in her throat she headed for the bedroom door. Jason heard it slam behind her.

CHAPTER 56

BEGINNING AGAIN

"Well here we are, two women sittin' at the supper table talkin' about how to change things for the better and we're havin' to plan like its gonna be a war ...'cause it will be!"

Dorothy laughed, but she knew Bea was right. "Well it's cold outside and the wind is roarin' tonight. Maybe that's a sign Bea, because once we get things moving there will be a lot of howling from people we work with, even inside the school. Changing what is to what can be is a trip down a different road which many would rather not take."

"Yeah let's talk about it some. Where do you see the new school sittin' in the neighborhood?"

"You've seen those empty lots over on Warren Street, I think it's the place for it. It's in the middle of this neighborhood. The way I look at it the school should be a place for about 200 or so children. We can't let it get too big Bea. If it gets big it is not going to be tightly connected to folks. The school cannot look like a school. That's the last thing we need."

"Dorothy, you still want a front porch don't you?"

"More than ever Bea. I know it sounds crazy, but we need to be able to sit out there and be a part of things happening in the neighborhood."

"You aren't gettin' me out there on a day like today lady. So if you get your porch then I get my fireplace! But seriously, Dorothy, there will be many who say it's not safe for the children to be out there. The drive by gangs, bums … you know what will be said."

"I know it sounds silly Bea, but normal things like a porch and a fireplace help us build relationships not only with the children, but folks in the neighborhood. If we are going to be successful we have to be connected to people. They have to see the school as a safe and inviting place. They have to feel comfortable coming to talk and help teach their children. It's more than poverty we're fighting. It's a cultural disconnect the current physical structure of schools promotes. We have to fight this war on all fronts and it begins by reinventing the place we call school. And those critics, they don't seem overly concerned about turning the children loose to those same streets all summer long. So I'll risk it with the children on the front porch!"

"While you've been spendin' a lot of thinkin' time on the building, and how it helps us connect to the neighborhood, I've been thinkin' about what Myrna was sayin' …you know, gettin' the kids early. By the time they come to us in kindergarten at age five Dorothy it's way too late. I know we got programs like Head Start. But we have to get 'em all much younger, if folks will send 'em, 'cause we can't mandate it."

"You're right, and when I say room for about two hundred or so children, I am counting kids as young as babies in the number. We need a school going from birth through age seven. If we can get them from the start and carry them through second grade we have a real chance to turn the literacy piece around. But we can't afford to do it by staffing the school with just teachers. This is the conversation we need to continue so let's talk sitting by your fireplace."

Bea's cell phone had an old fashioned ring tone and it was clanging. When she picked up her phone she saw it was Andrea. She no sooner answered when Andrea's emotions blew through the phone like a geyser spewing powerful blasts of steam and heat. Her emotions ran nonstop on the phone for nearly five minutes before Bea could say anything more than a brief 'yup' or 'I see.' Then it finally was her turn as Andrea's voice trailed and settled.

"Girl, there are so many things I need to say to you. You be quiet while I talk. I know you love teachin'. Most people who don't teach don't understand how attached we get to the children. They become like family. Some children, they will climb in and park in your heart forever. I know you will always carry Dedra with you. You love that little girl and you will think of her and what's happenin' in her life for the rest of yours. That's the way it is. It's different than makin' or fixin'a thing. Teachin' is all about connectin' and carin'. So your Jason seems to be askin' you to step away and ya can't do it. But come this June you will step away 'cause those children you love will move on. Maybe you can't leave and shouldn't leave now, but in June you could follow him to Montgomery. I know you think you should stay here 'cause of what these children need and 'cause this city is your home. But I can tell ya, poverty and its offspring are alive and kickin' in Montgomery. It's a sad thing, but poverty has more homes than the richest soul on this earth. You can do good work there too."

"Bea, you are telling me to move! I can't leave School #3. It's where I want to work."

"Girl, you know the budget is bad and layoffs are comin'. You know you stand real low on the seniority list. Do you think, School #3 job is just waitin' for you? It isn't how it's gonna work child. That's the hard part, you're too young to realize right now. Teachin' is a job and the real world can jump up and take it away. I don't want us to lose out on you, but the fact is that's likely gonna happen. You need to be a teacher. The place to do your teachin' isn't as important as the doin' of it. That's what I'm sayin'. If you love that man, and he loves you, and that's what I see, then you gotta make a life for yourself. You think on it child and then we'll talk some more."

After a few more exchanges, Bea hung up. Ma'am could not help but overhear the conversation. "I didn't know you were such a good counselor! Andrea is a lucky woman to have met you. You talked about Dedra always being in her heart, I know Andrea's got a special place in yours."

"Well let's sit by my fireplace and start talkin' again about what we gonna do to help the children learn. The rules mean Andrea and lots of good young teachers could lose their jobs with the changes we're talkin' about here. That's the hardest part in startin' a revolution, the casualties are certain to happen. So our planning better be real smart."

CHAPTER 57

PUSH OR PULL

J erry walked up the dingy back stairs at district office to the tower. He was meeting with Carl to talk about the plans for the upcoming budget. John asked the two of them to discuss his proposals while he was at the state capital.

Jerry walked into Carl's office catching his breath, "Well you certainly should take the back stairs more often if one flight does you in!"

"You are the guy who is overweight, me it's the damn cigarettes. Between us, with all the crap we're facing, either you or I should have a coronary sometime soon."

"Shut up; we have enough other problems right now! So Jerry, what do you think of the big guy's ideas for cutting the high school part of the budget?"

"Closing Jefferson was a surprise. He reminded me in the old days, when enrollments were growing faster than schools could be built in the suburbs, they went on split sessions. He is proposing an early and late day start. He's thinking some kids may actually like starting their school day at 11:00AM and finishing at 5:00PM. He may have a point."

"I can see it from that perspective, but the unions are going to have a field day with us. I can hear them now."

"I know they'll want extra comp for the late hours and they will lay out a string of reasons why it's a bad idea. But rest assured they'll give up their first born before the old guard will take a pay cut or pay freeze to prevent it."

"Not sure I blame them Jerry. The old guard is close to retirement and any decrease hurts them for years on their pensions. But, you are right give backs are hard to come by and they are always only temporary in nature. The boss isn't into temporary, he's looking for real long-term reform. He actually likes alternate hours for students. In this day and age, I think it's probably well worth considering."

"Carl, he is also thinking every senior next year must take at least one course online. While this will reduce the pressure inside the two remaining high schools, I am not sure how we get the logistics settled between now and next September. Again, we have to get the unions on board. Can you do it given this kind of scope?"

"Jerry, I don't think so. The online stuff will play into another agenda of fears. The leadership will see it as an erosion of the traditional classroom. With the looming layoffs, they will connect the dots and see this as a financial savings agenda, not an instructional improvement one. They will not want the camel to get his nose in the tent. It will be a battle for sure."

"So from a bargaining standpoint we have to tell him there will be hell to pay?"

"No doubt about it."

"On the logistics side, I have to say I am not sure we can pull off the number of online courses he's proposing and get the teachers and tech set in six months time."

"So Jerry what we're saying to him is go back and do things as best you can and cut elsewhere?"

"Carl, we both know it isn't the answer. I think the spilt session idea makes sense. Closing Jefferson will save a lot of money. It also sets the stage for some different thinking about school hours. I think we should counsel him to go ahead on it."

"Jerry, you know I am thinking about John's leadership style more and more. I think for years we have expected superintendents to push us forward. It's the way this culture works just push a bit along the edges. Get more out of the same. But this guy's pulling things in a whole new direction. The system doesn't know how to respond to a leader who pulls rather than pushes. Mary Jane sure isn't responsive to it. The unions won't be and I wonder how it will work out in the end. We need guys with vision and a willingness to pull us along. But the system will work overtime to get rid of him. I think if education is going to succeed, given its current large scale failure and spiraling costs, we are going to have to be pulled, kicking and screaming if need be, into a whole new millennium. I think we are going to have to protect and support him. I for one think we have an innovative guy who might be pulling in the right direction."

"Wow, aren't you jumping into the deep end of the pool. Sometimes John can be a ready, fire, aim kinda leader. I do see his innovative ideas and I want to follow them. But you know Carl, we may all be out of a job if he goes off on a tangent."

"Damn it Jerry, he confides in you more than anybody. He respects your advice and seeks it on most things before he does shoot. You and I both know Mary Jane is trying to cut him off at the knees. She's no leader. Her style is to push the old agenda harder. That isn't going to work; the failures we are experiencing won't yield to more edge pushing. It's time to follow somebody who is willing to pursue a different agenda. Maybe we'll fail, but I think we are destined to if we keep doing the same old stuff, riding the same old horses up the same hills we have for years. "Pull or push Jerry. That's the leadership choice we have. It's all the difference in the world which style we support right now."

CHAPTER 58

THE CONVERSATION

John was traveling to the state capital to meet with the Commissioner of Education. The two-hour session was scheduled by the Commissioner to discuss the audit. Stepping into the Commissioner's office, John noticed the usual trappings of power. A state flag stood on a gilded stand in one corner with a host of pictures of important governmental officials nearby. A huge oriental carpet covered part of the oak-pegged floor. Office furniture was covered with chocolate brown leather and the view down the mall to the Capitol Building was impressive.

Commissioner Appleton rose from his desk when John entered, "Good morning John, have a seat, I'll be right with you. There's coffee on the table, help yourself."

"Thank you Commissioner, I will have a cup, can I pour you one?"

"Yes, and John it's Jim, we've both been in this business too long to throw around titles."

John poured coffee and settled into one of the comfortable leather chairs. He suspected this might be the only comfortable moment he'd experience today.

"John, let me get to the point," Jim stated as he picked up his coffee and sat in a chair across from him. I have a draft of the audit team's report. I wanted to discuss it with you before it is finalized. The report recommends the Department take over the district in light of its long history of failing schools. It also recommends the firing of most of the district office team, with the exception of Mary Jane Thomas and letting go seven principals upon the state's takeover."

John knew he wasn't asked to meet with the Commissioner because the report had good news to share, but he was stunned by the recommendations he was hearing. He took a few sips of coffee and let the silence hang in the air for a moment. John then set his coffee cup down and reached into his pocket. From his key ring he peeled off the master key to district office, "You'll need one of these if you accept the report's recommendations." John gently placed a district master key on the coffee table between them. "When I came to the district a little over a year and a half ago I knew the Board was going to be hard to handle. The five of them have chewed up superintendents and spit them out on a regular basis. On top of that the test scores were dismal. Jim, I am not sure why I took the job. Many of my colleagues thought I was crazy to do it. However, I have learned a great deal since I arrived. The staff is hard working and the roots of failure have a lot more to do with poverty and history than with who is in charge at the top. Maybe the staffers here need a real dose of reality to gain the perspective they need on the problems we are facing. Can you tell me if Dorothy Washington is one of the principals to be fired? "

The Commissioner looked at the report, thumbing through several pages. "Yes John, she is. The report notes she was well organized for the fire which took place at the school. The team said if she brought the same level of leadership and organization to improving the scores at her school, they suspected the students would be doing much better."

"Jim, there isn't a more glaring example of a mistake than that. Dorothy Washington is probably one of my most innovative leaders. She doesn't see improving test scores as the purpose of schooling, but she believes if we organize schooling in a different way, good scores will be a by-product of the effort. If you don't implement the report's recommendations, I plan to give her a free hand to innovate. We need a whole different approach to schooling and I too believe test scores are not the end purpose for what we do, but we should get good results if we have the courage to realign what we do and how we do it."

"That's all well and good John, but the fact is your Board does not work as a team. We both know you are resource poor. I've tried to get more aid for you but it is not going to happen this year. You are going to have to make dramatic cuts, so how do you innovate without the resources?"

"The key is sitting there. You can pick it up and give it to your staff. I am sure they must have the answers." John knew he was letting anger get in front of logic and he quickly added, "But I see this as the opportunity to innovate. I don't know if I can pull it off but I'd like to try with the people I have. They know the system and they are for the most part a hardworking group."

"Does that include Dr. Thomas?"

"Why do you ask?"

"My team has a great deal of confidence in her assessments of your staff and her clear focus on improving results. I hear in the background you two are not in agreement. If I give you more time and amend this report's recommendations, my staff will want someone they have confidence in keeping a place on your leadership team."

"I cannot easily fire her with her seniority and tenure status as it is. But she is not an innovator. I am not going to have her get in the way of what I feel needs to be done. So she will be on the team but much more isolated and marginalized than she has been, that's for sure. I also need to end her sideways conversations both here and with my Board."

"John you've given me things to think about. I'll keep this key and let you know in a bit whether my staff is going to use it or not."

John did not want a sword falling at some unknown time hanging over him. He either had the support of the Commissioner or not, "I appreciate the rock and hard place you are between, but I can't work wondering if or when you and the team might decide to stroll in and take over. I cannot promise quick results, but I can promise you a serious effort to find new ways to educate children who are victims of poverty. If you keep the key, I will resign and tell my Board your staff will be in charge. I believe you will be a colossal failure, but then it will be your political problem, not mine."

It was the Commissioner's turn to sit back. His grapevine suggested John could be manipulated and the threat of a take-over would bring him in line. Now it was clear this was far from the case. This man was not going to be pushed into line as his staff had suggested.

"John, suppose you talk to me about what it is you really want to do if I don't pick up the key."

For the next hour John laid out his ideas. He shared Dorothy's plan for a different kind of elementary school, both in physical structure as well as how it would likely be staffed. He talked about a twelve month school year with alternative hours for high school students. He shared his ideas for community service that would be required of every high school student and how he felt technology should be used. It became a thoughtful and easy back and forth between the two which ultimately brought them back to the key.

"John, you don't lack for ideas! I am not sure you will be able to get them off the ground, but I will give you the key back on the condition you keep me informed of your progress on a regular basis. You also can't fire Mary Jane. That's a bone I have to throw to my staff. But how you deploy her 'many skills' is entirely up to you. I want to see if your ideas can make a difference, so don't you go jumping ship on me and leaving my team with a bigger mess than the one you have now."

John picked up the key, "I will keep you informed; however, I have two conditions as well, it's you I talk to, I don't want my reports going to some staff member who then translates them for you." John then shared his second condition. The two men shook hands and agreed to move forward step by step. Neither knew how things would turn out, but new strategies were needed in the losing war against poverty and school failure.

CHAPTER 59

SPEAKING FRANKLY

After returning from the Capital, John asked for a workshop meeting with the Board. Shantell was in rare form, "John I am glad you want the meeting, I do too! I hear rumors you and Dorothy Washington are planning some new program and we want to know why we haven't been informed."

John knew this was Mary Jane's backstabbing effort to kill any chance for a new idea to take root. He was more than fed up with her behavior. This wasn't the time to mix it up with Shantell; he had more important fish to fry. "We can certainly talk about it, but there's nothing firm yet. Dorothy has some good ideas worth further thought. I've asked her to take the time to develop them. I can update you all on the initial ideas she has in mind. By the way, I have encouraged all the principals to try new things to improve student success, so you may hear more rumors in the coming months. But the reason I want the meeting is to discuss the seriousness of our budget picture and to update you on my conversation with Commissioner Appleton regarding the results of the Department's audit."

They agreed to meet the following Tuesday night. It would be a working session including pizza for dinner.

Before he knew it the time flew by and John was meeting with his Board. He asked Tom Wheaton to join him for the first part of the meeting. He wanted Tom to summarize the dire financial straits they were entering. They found themselves in this awful place not only because of the state's fiscal crisis and the reduction in aid support likely to follow, but because the costs associated with pensions and employee benefits were climbing so rapidly it was becoming almost impossible to pay for them. Between finances and results John believed the overall model for public education had run its course and could no longer be sustained. He wanted to set course in a totally new direction; this crisis might provide the rare opportunity to do that.

Tom did an excellent job summarizing the problems and how important it was to take steps to cut expenses even in the current year. Board members had questions answered by Tom and John over dinner. Everyone knew business as usual ended with the last bite of their pizza.

After dinner John met alone with his Board. He was well aware what he was about to share would cause a great deal of unrest. He'd planned as carefully as he could for this moment. "Now that you have a grasp of the budget challenge, here's what I think we need to do to address it. Some of the steps will require your approval, others I can take on my own. Let's start with the ones I am going to ask you to consider. At our next regular meeting I will recommend the closing of three elementary schools as well as Jefferson High School. The closings would take effect at the end of this school year. On their own, the closings won't take care of our money problems, but they will certainly be an important and necessary part of putting our financial house in order."

As John spoke those words, you could hear a pin drop. Don Karst broke the silence, "Which elementary schools will you be recommending and why did you choose them?" John answered his question explaining consistent school failure was part of the rationale as well as the overall condition of the buildings. To Shantell's surprise, School #3 was one of the schools John recommended be closed.

Sara Fieldstone was upset about the closing of Jefferson High. She started the questions by asking how the other two schools could hold so many students. John answered these and many other Board questions. As the initial conversation died down, John said, "We will have several months ahead for public hearings and comment. But out of the gate I want to bring the harsh reality of where things stand to light. I also plan to make some staffing changes which will not require your approval. Those I plan to do right away." Every Board member was attentive as John told them what he planned to do.

Don Karst interjected, "John you are going to layoff district office staff and reorganize your administration as a first step. I see the logic, but wow what you have in mind takes the wind out of my sails I'll tell you!"

"Promoting Carl more than takes the wind out of my sails!" Sara replied. I don't agree with it John! You know my reasons and you are ignoring my concerns."

Shantell's arms were crossed and her face was drawn tight, her eyes flaming as she spoke. "You've overstepped your bounds with this staffing plan. How can you make Carl a Deputy Superintendent and pass over Tom Wheaton? Never mind you are doing this without our approval!"

"My contract gives me the right to organize the district office staff as I see fit. It does not require your approval unless a pay raise is attached. There won't be, given the budget problems we face. As for Tom Wheaton, he has accepted a position in a great suburban district in New York State. He wants to be close to his wife's family and the money is much better. He'll be leaving us in six weeks. That's why I passed him over."

The conversation was as hot as a summer day in the Sahara. The next half-hour was the toughest John ever experienced with his Board. Sara Fieldstone's temper was nearly out of control. "This heavy handed approach, ignoring our views, is too much for me to stomach. John maybe you need to move on from here.

As if he were sitting in the calm eye of this hurricane of temper, John simply said, "Before you decide on a course of action let me share with you my meeting with Commissioner Appleton. The State Education Department has concluded we are a consistently failing district. I've made copies of a letter from the Commissioner confirming this. His letter also indicates if I resign at your request, and I accept that request, you will be hiring the fourth superintendent in less than four years time. As a result, he would conclude the Board's leadership is also dysfunctional. It would be the final straw in his mind and would lead to the Department's takeover of the district and the disbanding of the Board." This letter was the second condition John asked of the Commissioner as he knew with the bold steps he was planning he would need some cover. He had anticipated some on his Board would not support any of the changes he had in mind. He also knew the real changes he was planning hadn't been laid on the table yet. The district office reorganization raising such a ruckus tonight was only stage setting.

"My God, he can't do this!" Sara shouted out to no one in particular.

"Yes he can, and he has made it plain to us he will." It was Terrell Whitner who spoke now in his room filling baritone voice, "We are in a heck of a mess here John. To tell you the truth I am not sure what to think of it. But standing still isn't going to fix it!"

John then passed around a second document. "You asked me for a commitment a while back. This document, signed by me, confirms if I resign from my position due to the acceptance of another superintendency, I will be obligated to pay this district a 10% penalty up until the last twelve months of my contract. The penalty will be calculated taking ten percent of my remaining gross salary. I will not leave this district in the lurch. We are in for one hell of a ride. I know some of you don't agree with the things I am about to do, but I will see them through and I will be accountable. However, I can't work here with a no confidence vote from my Board. You all need to decide tonight how you want to proceed. If you don't have confidence in my leadership, as some of you have clearly expressed, then I will resign. I'll give you some time to talk. When you are ready let me know and I'll come back here."

It was ninety minutes later when John got the call to walk back. He was not sure which way the Board would go, but he had no choice but to call the hand. Even John was surprised by what he saw when he came in the room. It was Terrell who spoke. Shantell and Sara were no longer present.

"John by a three-two vote you have our support. You can guess the two no votes. John, we have also made a leadership change on the Board. I will now serve as its President. Knowing Shantell's opinions, we felt it was in our best interest as a Board to make a change. It was approved by a three two vote. It is going to be a real challenge to proceed. I am sure we are going to have our moments, but the three of us think you are the person for the job and we will support you. Shantell and Sara are not willing to, so I am afraid we will be a badly divided group moving on from tonight. We can only hope tempers and feelings will settle, but it isn't going to happen any time soon!"

Terrell signed the contract amendment John gave the Board. Handing it to him he sighed, "I hope you don't ever have to pay us this penalty. The three of us are counting on you to see things through."

And so his journey into uncharted waters began. John could only hope what he was planning to do would lead them to a secure harbor at some point in the future. In the meantime the seas were going to be unforgiving and the winds of change would blow cold and hard.

CHAPTER 60

MOVING ON

A week of stony silence passed between Andrea and Jason since he first told her about his promotion. Jason decided to accept it and would be moving in six weeks. Andrea was still confused about the whole thing. The longer the silence progressed between them the greater the emotional canyon they had to bridge.

Andrea was headed to Bea's house for their Thursday night session. While they still shared classroom ideas and stories about the children, this was only one part of what they talked about. They also had a regular Thursday night Skype session with Jasmin. 'The girls' talk-athon,' Jasmin called it.

As Andrea entered Bea's house she could smell the wonder of Bea's crockpot. That too remained a Thursday tradition. Tonight a stew had been simmering throughout a cold and wet day. Bea hit the switch on her fireplace and they settled in with their beer and let the talk begin.

"Andrea, I think it's simple to argue, you ever notice how easy sometimes anger can come to the surface?"

"Oh no, where you going with this Bea?"

"No I am serious child, I see how anger wins all the time and when it gets big we see it turn into violence way too many times. It's simple to let that emotion rule, especially around this part of town."

"Yeah, I know what you mean. It is something I've seen way too many times. Michael Makin was telling me today his brother got punched by a kid on their porch last night. Apparently, they were arguing over a sweatshirt. Michael described his brother as bleeding badly. He had to go to emergency to get some stitches. He told us his brother is so mad he and some of his friends are going to do some real hurtin' to the kid. I was worried about what he said and passed it along to Ma'am. I'm not sure there's much we can do, but it is a good example of what you are talking about."

"You know there's lots of different kinds of anger. Anger has lots of family. One of his cousins is silent anger; that can really hurt too. Yup, anger has lots of relatives."

"So you have something you're trying to say I'm missing so far?"

"Well, I see some anger in you. It's the quiet kind. I think it is doing some serious work on you and Jason. You seem too proud to overcome it and talk to each other. It's a different kind of violence …it's breaking you apart. So why don't we talk about it a bit?"

"I don't have much to talk about. He's leaving in a little over a month because he's finished here and moving on, leaving me behind as well."

"Oh really, he said he didn't want you to come with him?"

"Bea, we've been down this road. You know I will not leave my class That's final and even you know better than to talk me out of it!"

"So you are blockin' me from sayin' my piece here with you, sayin' I can't talk you out of it. I am not tryin' to talk you into or out of anything. I'm noticin' you and Jason aren't even explorin' your options. Why?"

Andrea sat quietly by the fireplace, not quite sure of herself or what to say to Bea. "Like I've said, I am committed to my kids, I can't leave them now. I also don't have a ring Bea!" Andrea's face was almost tied in a knot as she spoke.

"I know ya can't follow a man like a puppy dog. You are right, it's a man's responsibility to propose to the woman he loves and Jason hasn't done it, though I think he loves you. I can't give ya the words to speak to him. You have to find those. But too many times anger and hurt lead to silence which kills all chances for important talk. You have to figure out how to tell him what's important. Then he has to decide what to do."

"It's the first time I spoke out loud about getting a ring, Bea. I can't ask Jason to marry me. Like you, I'm old-fashioned enough to think that's his job. I need to stop the silence in our house, but once it's settled in like it has between us, it's hard to find the way to start talking again now." Changing the subject Andrea continued, "I do want to hear what you are fixing to share about your proposal. The buzz in the faculty room is you and Ma'am are cooking something up and Myrna's in on it too."

As they served dinner and sat at the kitchen counter Bea began to open up on the depth of their plan. She needed to see how Andrea would react. It would help her grasp what questions others may have as they moved their ideas into the light of day..

Bea began by summarizing the school floor plan and its openness to the street. She also told Andrea they were thinking about serving a more defined neighborhood with the school open from birth through the second grade. It would be an Early Literacy Center. Then Bea really peeled the onion. "Andrea, there's much more we're thinkin' about. We want the school to be open year round. We can't give the children back to the streets for ten weeks every summer. You know what a good teacher violence is. These children see too much of it already without bein' helpless in a bad neighborhood day after day all summer long. We also think the people workin' in the school have to come mostly from the neighborhood."

Andrea stirred for the first time when she heard this. "Bea most people in the neighborhood have, at best, a high school diploma. Are you suggesting they serve as teachers?"

Bea took a deep breath, "Andrea, they can't be teachers like you and me, but they can do lots for the children people outside the neighborhood can't. They can tell stories, they can read to the children and they can relate better than most teachers to what is happenin' in the lives of the children. We think we need three regular teachers who will help plan and teach the children along with neighborhood aides workin' in the school. One teacher would work with kids from birth through age three. The second would take children from age four to age six and the third would take the responsibility for the children from age six to seven. We also want a full time social worker and a full-time nurse as part of the school's staff. If the model works, there'd be no full time principal. However, we'd want someone to administer at least three of these type schools. They can do the mandated stuff and all the reportin'. We don't see any place for special education staff 'cause we want no labels on these young children. As for custodians and lunch staff, we don't see much need for 'em as we'll do it with the aides workin' in the school. Heavy cleanin' can happen a couple times a month and could be from the district, or we could employ some young adults from the neighborhood to do it."

"Bea you are moving down a whole different road. In one way I'm excited, because I think smaller is better. I also see the cultural disconnect we all have with the neighborhood. I watch you with the folks in the supermarket. You talk and carry on in a way much different than most of us realize happens. I also know church plays a big part in the neighborhood, but you haven't talked much about that. Now on the other side, it means lots of people currently working, people like me, secretaries, Fred and lots of others are going to be out of a job if what you propose ends up being a model for change. That's a battle I think you lose. The unions are going to blow-up over this, and I can't blame them. Is this why you are encouraging me to move on with Jason?"

An unexpected edge surfaced in Andrea's last question. Bea could feel the tension; it was something she rarely felt with Andrea.

Bea took another deep breath, "Andrea, there's some more I need to share. We've always agreed what's said here stays here. That hasn't changed, right?"

"Bea, our private talks will never change. I may get angry, I may disagree with you on things, but I treasure what we have here. I will never betray it or you!"

Bea saw tears in Andrea's eyes and she hugged her. "Okay girl, at the faculty meeting this week Ma'am is going to announce School#3 will be closing at the end of the year. Superintendent Handler is closing a number of schools to meet the budget challenge and we're one of 'em. So your attachment to the school, and mine too, is about to end 'cause the city hasn't got enough money. Ma'am is also gonna say we're keepin' our old name and not changin' 'cause she doesn't want the school to close with the name Rosa Parks. We be savin' the name if we get a go on our idea."

"Oh my God Bea! How could he do this? The children will be thrown into new places. It can't be happening this way. We have to fight it, not for our sake but for the children."

"Andrea the flood gate is openin' and the river of change is flowin' over us. We can't stop the closin' anymore than Dr. Handler can. The way we do school with its cost can't work much longer. It is time things changed. The train must get movin' down the track. If it doesn't the flood is gonna wash it away. You also gotta realize School #3 is a failin' school. Our test scores are real bad and we got no support from Dr. Thomas or the State Ed. folks. They'll be glad we're closin'. No girl, you can't stop the closin' train, it's rollin' out of the station."

"I can't believe you are giving up so easily! You and Ma'am have spent your lives serving the children at School #3, now you are going to walk away!"

"Andrea, we aren't walking away. The stuff I've been talkin' to you about; well Ma'am and Dr. Handler been talkin' a lot and he supports what we are thinkin'. He is settin' the stage for a whole new way of doin' things and the first step is to shut us down. It closes one door, but a whole other one may be about to open which is much better for the children. I gotta get on the train and do all I can even if it means most people in the system aren't gonna like it or me much."

"Bea, moving on has taken on a whole new meaning. It sounds like I am going to lose my job and the school I love will be closed. At the same time Jason is leaving me too. I, I, I don't know what to say. I'm feeling numb right now."

"I am sorry Andrea to put all this out on the table. But I told Ma'am we were too close not to have this talk tonight. Honey, things are chan-gin', and it feels like it's too much for ya right now, but your life is in front of you. You gotta make it for yourself."

It was difficult for Andrea to comprehend all that Bea had shared. Her reflection was interrupted as the computer chimed, letting them both know Jasmin was ready to for their Thursday night talk.

CHAPTER 61

A TOUGH DAY

What a cluster of meetings John asked Ann to schedule after his workshop session with the Board. He was tired, but felt the need to meet with his staff right away, before Shantell and Sara started spreading their own information on his plans. One meeting was with Jerry Croton to discuss reorganizing his position. "Jerry, I am going to make a series of personnel changes with some of them taking place immediately. Tonight at the Board meeting I will be announcing a district office team reorganization." Jerry shifted uneasily in his seat. In fact he could feel beads of sweat forming on his forehead. "Jerry, with your support, I want to give you a new title and new authority. I'd like you to serve as Deputy Superintendent for Instruction. You will play an important role in our major reform agenda. All the instructional side will report to you, including Mary Jane Thomas. I cannot give you a raise at this point, but down the road I will do all I can."

"Holy shit John! What else are you going to do?"

John smiled, "I am going to promote Carl to Deputy Superintendent for Administration. I've shared this with him already and he has accepted. Tom Wheaton will be leaving to take a new job in upstate New York. His successor will report to Carl and so will all of the other non-instructional parts of the organization. He isn't getting a raise either. On the tough side, I will be meeting with Joanne Walters to say her position is being eliminated effective immediately. She is the first victim of our budget problems. She will get one month's severance plus earned vacation, but in these times I know it will be a real blow. I am also changing Mary Jane to Director level status. She'll have responsibility for only the K-8 curriculum and staff development programs. She will have no line authority starting tomorrow."

"John, I don't know what to say here. This is all hitting me so fast. Joanne gone, Mary Jane demoted! You are really changing things. I am not sure what to think."

"Jerry, I am going to make other serious changes and we are going to propose new ways of doing things. Like I said at the administrative meeting last week, these are tough times and we are not going to do business as usual. I need your support and will need someone the field trusts. You and Carl have earned my respect and confidence. I want you to take this on, but I will understand if you don't, that's your choice. I am making these changes as a first step and frankly, they're not negotiable."

"John, this is happening so fast and without any warning. That's not been your style. It's caught me off guard. I need some time to think it over. But you said I don't have any time to think. You are changing my title and I have to accept it or move on? That's what I think I heard; right?"

"That's what you heard. But you also should have heard I respect and trust your counsel. I want you in the role Jerry. It won't be easy from here. But if you want to take on a change agenda with me then sign on."

"Thanks for the trust John, but I need a little time to think on the long-term answer. You can sure count on me in the short-term. Do what you have to. "

"I am meeting with Joanne in a few minutes and then Mary Jane. Please keep what we said here confidential until the Board meeting tonight."

Jerry noticed Joanne was waiting in the outer office. He could not meet her eyes as he passed by her on the way back to his office.

John had given a great deal of thought about the upcoming meeting with Mary Jane Thomas. He knew she was sabotaging him with his Board and her behind the scenes conversations with the State Education Department auditors nearly led to the dismissal of a lot of good people. He was not about to forgive or forget her disloyalty. How to deal with it was the question. He'd made up his mind on what he was going to do.

The Elementary Study Committee's Preliminary Report was presented to him a few days before and it served as the backdrop for this meeting. Dr. Thomas, as always was punctual and was surprised to see Joanne Walters leaving the office in obvious distress. Shortly after seeing this Mary Jane was invited into the superintendent's office. John looked up, "Come in and have a seat, I will be with you in a moment."

John finished signing some documents and, after giving them to Ann, sat down in a comfortable chair facing Mary Jane. "I read the committee's preliminary report on the recommended improvements to the elementary program."

Mary Jane interrupted, expecting his lack of support. "Dr. Handler, it is a comprehensive set of recommendations and I believe it will put us on a path to success. I also believe the State Education Department will support it."

'Let the games begin,' John thought. "Mary Jane I think the report has sound recommendations on materials and training which have my support. However, the class size recommendations are not in the cards, especially with the major budget problems we face. "

"Dr. Handler, I am disappointed, as I am sure the committee will be, to learn you cannot support reducing class size. I think we could cut in other areas to make it a reality."

"Dr. Thomas, how would you find several million dollars in cuts to cover the added expense?"

"For starters, I would cut inter-scholastic athletics. We spend way too much money on sports when we are failing to meet the basic literacy needs of our children. I'd also make cuts in transportation and custodial services. There's way too much overtime in both areas. You could fund this Dr. Handler. I'm surprised you won't support the most important aspect of the report."

I believe in smaller class sizes, but we can't keep throwing more teachers at the problem. It hasn't yielded consistent improvements in other urban settings. I think we have to reexamine, from the bottom up, our strategies and models for providing literacy instruction. Your report is simply more of the same. While we may need new resources and more training, it is far from the innovative change I was expecting."

"Dr. Handler, you want to change a system in ways I cannot comprehend. In fact, I think you like to shake things up for something to do! Your approaches will do much more harm than good in my opinion."

John now became stiff and formal. His voice had the firmness of granite as he spoke. "Dr. Thomas, your slanted comments to the State Education Department Audit Team were disloyal to me and the administrators on our team. You also go behind my back to share your ideas with Board members. It's apparent to me and others you simply choose to go your own way on things without regard for this office or what I believe needs to take place. I do not respect you or your methods. Your report has my lukewarm support because that's what it deserves. You, on-the-other-hand, no longer have my support. I will not go on pretending what you are doing is okay, or by ignoring it outright as I have for months. So let me tell you how things are going to proceed from here.

First, all communications from your office to the State Education Department, including emails and phone calls are to be authorized by me. I will consider it insubordination if you do not follow this directive. Next, you will keep your salary but you will no longer have direct authority over the elementary principals. I am reorganizing the district staff and will be announcing at the Board meeting tonight the immediate layoff of Joanne Walters as the most junior ASI. I will be promoting Jerry Croton to Deputy Superintendent. That will take effect immediately. You will report to him on a daily basis for program issues in grades K-8. I am rewriting your job description and it will be given to you shortly. Your newly stated duties and Director title will not be negotiable with me."

"You have no right to do this! The Board will not allow it either."

"Dr. Thomas they have no choice. My contract gives me the right to organize the district office staff as I see fit. If I were adding positions or giving anyone a pay increase they'd need to approve it. You also need to know I will be announcing the closing of three elementary schools at the end of the school year. I will also be announcing the closing of Jefferson High. These are necessary steps to balance our budget. The decisions are painful and there will be more tough ones to come. I will put up with you at this point, but I'd strongly encourage you to polish your resume and start looking for work elsewhere. As long as I am superintendent here you will be marginalized."

Mary Jane could take no more. She stood up and yelled, "I'll see you fired before this is through!"

"Dr. Thomas, your efforts to accomplish that are not new news to me."

Next on his list of people to meet with was Cliff Greer. He wanted the union to know what he was recommending. But before his meeting with Cliff he gave Ann the go ahead to send his confidential email out to the principals explaining the reorganization of the district office leadership team. He knew it would send shock waves through the system, but there was no easy way to communicate the information personally to all who needed to learn of it. He scheduled a leadership meeting later in the week to answer questions and clarify where things stood. He'd spoken personally with each principal whose school was recommended to be closed. Each principal would have a faculty meeting after school today informing their staff of what John was going to recommend. He did not want people learning of it for the first time on the 11 o'clock news.

John's meeting with Cliff went as well as he could expect. Cliff was pleased with the administrative reorganization and encouraged John to make even more layoffs in the administrative ranks. "Dr. Handler, I cannot support closing the schools. Your plan will seriously compromise the quality of instruction and the overcrowding at the two remaining high schools will make them unsafe for the kids and staff. I know the budget issues are serious, but you are over-reacting in my opinion."

"Cliff, would you be willing to open negotiations on a pay reduction for teachers to prevent this from happening?"

"John, teachers are not going to carry this fiscal mess on their backs. It's through poor administration and waste we've gotten into this corner. We're not going to bail out things until we see a lot more cuts in administration. You could save a lot downtown with more reductions than you have proposed. Let me see those, then maybe we could talk. I am not going to put hard won benefits and pay for my people on the chopping block."

It was the stalemate John expected. He and Cliff would have many more meetings in the weeks to come. Some of what Cliff was saying was posturing for future meetings as both men knew the crisis was real and staff layoffs and reorganization were going to take place. The substance of future conversations would be around the scope of those reductions and any changes in overall working conditions taking place because of them.

By noon, John completed his first round of meetings and he was ready for lunch with the mayor. He was tired, but had many miles yet to go before the public Board meeting later. Throughout his day of meetings he had told no one, other than the mayor, of the Board leadership change. That was the Board's business and he and Terrell planned to discuss how it would be publically announced before the meeting.

It was a grueling day, one from which there was no turning back.

CHAPTER 62

BAD NEWS

The teacher's contract only allowed one faculty meeting per month; so Ma'am called a special 'voluntary' meeting to discuss the preliminary state test results and the audit report findings stating School #3 was officially identified as a 'Failing School.' It was a tough blow for everyone to hear their school had that official label.

"I know how hard you all work with the children. I also know poverty is a cruel and tough adversary and we've done battle with him day-after-day. Normally, we'd be asked to put a plan together to respond to this but there's more bad news to share with you today." Staff members shifted uneasily in their seats. Ma'am was not one for drama, and if she said there's more bad news coming, they knew she wasn't kidding. However, few were prepared for her next words.

"At tonight's Board of Education meeting Dr. Handler will be announcing his recommendation to close School #3 at the end of this school year. We are victims of bad test scores, a terrible budget situation and the poor physical condition of this building. Three strikes you are out in baseball and with these three strikes against us I told Dr. Handler I understood why he was recommending our school be closed."

Several teachers at School #3 had spent more than 20 years within its walls dedicating themselves and their teaching careers to the children the school served. They had no simple way to digest the information, let alone accept it. To be deemed a failure and to be closed after all they had done, or strived to do, was more than a number of them could take. Anger, sadness, and disbelief were waves rolling over them.

It was fifth grade teacher Tom Dowling who broke the silence. "Ma'am I know you have to tow the party line on closing School #3, but we don't! I for one can't let this closing happen without a fight. These children need us. Nobody knows them better. If this school closes they will be lost in other schools. This is their home!" Many of the staff members clapped as he finished speaking.

Sue Jones was next to speak, "Ma'am, you have been a part of this school for as long as any of us can remember. It is unlike you to walk away from this without a fight. Where do you stand on this?"

"Look, the architects have said this school is in need of such extensive repair it cannot be refurbished economically. At our administrative meetings we've been getting an earful on the budget for next year. I can tell you the hole we are in is a deep one. The cuts to balance the budget are beyond anything I have seen. He has to close schools, there's no way around it. I can tell you we are not the only school closings to be announced to staff today. Elementary schools #8 and #11 are being recommended too, as well as Jefferson High School." Ma'am could see the stunned looks across every face in the room as she spoke.

Sue Jones was still standing while Ma'am answered her question. She spoke again, "This can't be happening! We can't be closing three elementary buildings and a high school. Where will we put all the children?"

Ma'am decided to let this sit as a rhetorical question. Ma'am learned over the years not to feel a burden to answer every question raised in a staff meeting.

Sue sat down, with a hand hovering over her mouth, finding it nearly impossible to comprehend what had been shared. Others in the room had the same reaction.

After letting the silence linger, Ma'am spoke, "This is tough news to share. We all need time to digest it. I can tell you the budget shortfall is nearly 45 million dollars. Even with these four school closings, we will not have closed the gap. The financial support for education at the state level has dried up. The economy has dealt us a crushing blow. Also, the cost of our benefits, mine too, are going through the roof. I would not want to be in Dr. Handler's shoes for all the tea in China. But many of us, including a lot of children are going to be victims of this collapse. So if you plan to ask the Board to keep us open, because…" Ma'am's voice cracked "…we have a history with and love for these children; it isn't going to cut it. Business as usual in education is quickly coming to an end in our district."

Many of the younger teachers lingered after the meeting. They knew the budget conversation and school closings would affect them and their jobs. Colleen looked at the group, "We're finished after this year! Trace works at the middle school. He's likely out of a job too. I feel sad about this school closing, but what are we going to do?" Colleen was reduced to tears as she said this.

Andrea said, "My boyfriend got a transfer to Montgomery, Alabama. He wants me to leave here now and go with him. I know I am out of a job the end of this year, but I can't leave my kids like that."

"The hell you can't! The district is going to let you all go without a second thought." Sue Jones was chiming in. Her words and timing were hardly helpful.

"I don't suppose you and the senior staff are willing to take a pay cut to save some us are you?" Colleen said.

Sue didn't expect this bitter and sharp response. She ducked her head and backed off.

"Didn't think so," Colleen quipped, not letting Sue retreat quietly.

Ma'am saw this and the beginning stages of the disintegration of her team. The months until June were going to be filled with angst and emotion. The challenge to keep everyone focused on the children was going to be a formidable one.

After the meeting Bea found Ma'am in her office, staring out the window, "You doin' ok?"

"What do you think? I am sick about all of this and the hurt it is going to cause. I was thinking before about how excited I am to be able to think outside of the box. After seeing the hurt on my teacher's faces, I am second guessing myself!"

"I'd be disappointed if you weren't hurtin', these are tough times and nobody expectin' 'em to be this bad. But we've talked a lot about what these children need and it isn't what we been doin'. We both know we are not gettin' it done no matter all the hard work. It's time to go back and rethink the whole thing Dorothy, despite the hurt it puts on people. Our responsibility is to the children first."

"I know Bea, but my heart is aching today. We gotta keep that perspective in front of us too."

"Okay, you have your pity party today; then let's get on with what we got to do."

"Are you forgetting Andrea is one of the victims in all of this?"

"No I am not, but she's young and she will survive. We can't own all the pain and we can't assume only bad things will happen 'cause of this change. In her case this may push her to follow Jason and make a life with him. Right now, if we stay open with no layoffs, she'd keep teachin' here and lose out on a better life with a man who loves her."

"You sure of that?"

"No, I'm sayin' there may be a silver linin' in change for some folks. It's just gonna take some time for them to see it."

CHAPTER 63

A MEMORABLE
BOARD MEETING

John met with Terrell before the meeting. Once they were alone in John's office Terrell opened up, "John there's no calming Shantell and Sara down. Both have refused to talk with me. I hear through others they are planning to boycott tonight's meeting as a form of protest. They also plan to hold a news conference out front before the meeting."

"Terrell, my advice is to let them have their moment without much comment. They'll be at the next Board meeting, you can count on it. Can you three hold together? You personally are going to feel the most pressure."

"I hope we'll be better once we get a meeting or two under our belts. Like you said, in the meantime we are going to have to keep our composure and not take the bait. Emily is the one who concerns me the most. She sits on the fence a lot. She doesn't like conflict and the season we're coming into is filled with it. She's the one Shantell and Sara will work on to see things their way. The teacher's union will start working on her too. Then we'll see if she has any backbone."

Shantell began the press conference by reading a statement, "Sara Fieldstone and I have been outvoted by the new Board majority. The majority wants to have its way by blindly supporting Dr. Handler and his reforms. We are opposed to his ideas and believe the district will be poorly served if they are enacted. As a protest we will not be attending tonight's Board meeting. In the future we will do our best to speak out and protect the children and community from his radical approaches to solving this district's problems."

While they hoped for more on camera time, Terrell was bringing the meeting to order inside the Board room and the press was eager to get whatever he said on tape. Sara and Shantell were left standing as the reporters rushed to get the other side of the story.

Terrell also had prepared a written statement and opened the meeting with it, "As you can see the Board of Education has made a leadership change. It is clear we are divided on how to proceed. However, I have accepted the President's role reluctantly and hope we can become a unified group for creating the right conditions for learning. Dr. Handler, would you set the stage for the major items on our agenda tonight?"

John was front and center. He spent the next ten minutes outlining the district's preliminary budget estimates. It was a bleak summary, aired for the first time in public. He then presented the State Education Department's audit report. "You will see within the pages of this report we have a number of consistently failing schools. They are identified by years of poor state test results and at the high school level, by unacceptable absenteeism and the highest overall drop-out rates in the state. On top of this, the report also notes the high levels of student misbehavior and suspensions. As a result, we have been placed on 'Performance Probation'. We have a three-year window to dramatically improve our results or the State Education Department will take over the operations of the district."

People in the audience were stunned by the obvious change in Board leadership, followed by the budget crisis summary and now the State Education Department's formal declaration of 'Performance Probation.'

John knew the stage was set as best he could for what he needed to say, "Knowing these things, I have recommended a series of changes with more to come in the days and months ahead. I do not believe tinkering at the margins will get the job done. Knowing we have a huge decline in financial support we have to suspend the traditional ways of addressing academic shortcomings by simply adding more staff. That cannot happen."

John went on to outline the reorganization of the district office team. Many of the people in the room heard the rumors all day long as the shake-up was occurring downtown, but now it was confirmed.

Along with the middle school assistant superintendent position, John also cut three other administrative positions in the special education area along with Kelly Slocum and two other trainers in the staff development office. Staying with cuts downtown, John announced the elimination of eight clerical positions. It was what he shared next which captured everyone's attention.

"I also am recommending the closing of three elementary schools at the end of the year. My rationale is three-fold. First, all have been identified as failing schools by the State Education Department. Next, all three have been identified by the architects as beyond cost effective repair and restoration. Third, we must reduce costs due to our looming fiscal crisis. In addition to the elementary school closings, I am recommending the closing of Jefferson High School at the end of this school year. It too is a school beyond cost effective repair, making it the best candidate for closing."

John went on to say the resulting actions would lead to the layoff of more than two hundred teachers. While this seemed extreme to many, it reduced the forty-five million dollar shortfall by a little over ten million dollars. Other layoffs and the reduction in operational costs due to the buildings being shut down would save another eight million.

"The fiscal reality is a compelling reason in its own right to make these changes. But even before this decline in resources, we have earned a failing grade as a school district. Business as usual in any form is no longer acceptable. We must reinvent the way we educate children. The reasons for doing so are compelling and obvious. I believe the 20th Century model of educational delivery will no longer stand as a viable and successful way to educate children in this new century."

The gauntlets were thrown down. John was going to try and take the district in a different direction. It was going to be one heck of a ride from here. Nobody understood it better than Mary Jane Thomas who thought if she waited patiently on the sidelines she could come riding in like the Lone Ranger on a white horse to save the day.

CHAPTER 64

PARTING WAYS

ndrea and Jason continued their silence on the issues mattering most. Having lived together as long as they had, they intuitively knew what the other was often thinking. However, for some reason deep feelings remained unspoken. Jason was asked by his new office manager if he could come to work about two weeks earlier than first planned. He agreed. He was anxious to get started knowing Andrea was going to stay behind no matter when he left.

This would be their last night together as the movers were coming in the morning to take Jason's things and he would be driving south after they left. Andrea would be teaching since it was a Thursday when all of this would transpire. Because the apartment had a lease through August, the company paid the remaining portion of the rent. Andrea decided to take her time deciding whether to renew it or make other decisions on where she would be living. She was certain she'd be without a teaching job. Absent solid work and Jason's portion of the rent, she was pretty sure a move was in her future.

They decided to spend the last night together having dinner in the apartment. Neither was sure how it would go. Jason arrived home at 7:30 after the office staff threw a small good-bye party for him. Even though Andrea knew this was taking place and encouraged Jason to let it happen, she was annoyed he came home later than she expected.

"How was the party? Must have been ok because I thought we'd agreed to have dinner here at 7."

"I'm sorry, it was tough to leave. Everyone had something to say and by the time we all stopped talking, well I lost track of time."

"That's okay, I kept myself busy with school work. Since we are having pasta we can put the water on whenever you are ready. There's some red wine on the table. It's our last bottle. Would you open it and pour yourself another and me one too?"

Jason could hear the irritation in Andrea's voice. He knew on this last night he stayed too long at the party. But he spent a great deal of time with the people at the office and he was going to miss them. As they sipped wine, Andrea turned to the stove and put the water on and checked the sauce. Over her shoulder she said to Jason, "Have you got everything set for your move tomorrow?" It was an awkward statement. She, like Jason, didn't know what to say either.

"I've got to put some last things in the car after the movers leave and I should be on the road before lunch time. The weather doesn't look too bad, some light snow flurries here but by Friday I'll be in much warmer weather. Andrea, you know you could still come with me."

"Jason we've been down this road. I cannot leave my kids. It isn't fair to them."

"Lots of staff do it. Teachers get pregnant and leave during the year. The kids survive."

"I know, but it doesn't feel right to me. This job is too important to leave unfinished."

"Well you know at the end of the year your job is finished. Then what will you do? It took you a long time to find a teaching job and with the economic conditions up here, I don't think you'll find another any time soon. I think you'd have a much better chance in Alabama."

"Jason, that may be true, but I've got to do this my way. I can't follow my boyfriend wherever his work leads. I have to make a life for myself."

"Andrea, for the next several years it's likely not going to include teaching as a career choice. I don't understand why you are insisting on staying here in this frozen economic wasteland when there are much better chances for you to teach in the south."

"Jason we've been over this ground so many times since your transfer was set. Let's not go over it again on our last night together in this place."

"Okay, what do you want to talk about?"

"Bea told me today Jasmin was accepted at Georgetown. She's going to work on a Master's degree in public policy. Bea is so proud of her."

For the next hour over dinner the two talked about everything but what was important. Their relationship was off limits and they were at a standoff on what to say or do about it.

After a very restless night Andrea got up for work. Jason was packing his final items for the car as she did. The moment arrived. She was ready to go and he was standing next to her by the door.

"Looks like this is good-bye. I will call you when I get to Montgomery and text you tonight when I get off the road."

Andrea, with tears streaming, gave Jason a quick hug, a kiss on the cheek and left for work.

CHAPTER 65

THURSDAY NIGHT

Bea called Andrea on her cell phone before school started. "Hi girl, I got some appointments today. I won't be in school, but we're on for tonight as usual."

"Are you okay?"

"Oh yeah, I have some doctors and stuff to do that can't wait." Bea was half right on what she was saying. She now knew Andrea was headed to work and she had a stop to make. "I'll see ya tonight after school. We've got a lot to talk about. You have as good a day as you can. I know Jason's headin' south."

Once off the phone Bea headed straight for Andrea's apartment. She wanted to have a serious talk with Jason before he left. She caught him in the driveway talking to the movers. "Jason you and I gotta talk!" Bea was saying this as she left her big Crown Vic at the curb. Her voice was booming and he could not mistake her demand for attention.

"What's the matter with you, leavin' our beautiful girl behind? I thought you had more sense!"

"Bea" he started to say.

"Don't you Bea me! You just listen." Bea had her finger out stretched and was now less than a foot from Jason's face. "Andrea is the best woman you're ever gonna know! She loves you and you are too proud to know what you gotta do."

"Bea I don't know what you are saying."

"What I am sayin' is you get down on your knees and propose to Andrea. That's what I am sayin'. She isn't gonna chase her boyfriend all over this country, but if you two are married she is gonna do what she needs to support her man. You both been dancing to different music and it's time you fixed it if you love her the way I think you do."

"Bea, I am not sure you are right about this."

"What do you mean, you are not sure? I know the sun comes up every morning and I am just as sure that girl loves you. Are you gonna let her slip away, outta your life forever? She's comin' to my house tonight for supper. I'm invitin' you to join us, but only if you bring a ring with you."

Bea had spoken her piece. It was the real reason she'd taken the day off from work. Both Andrea and Jason played the silence game with each other for way too long and she felt she needed to speak her mind before he left town. She'd accomplished that; now things were in God's hands. "What will be will be," she grumbled to herself as she slid behind the wheel of her big Ford.

Andrea came by Bea's at about 4:30. It was their usual starting time. Bea had some beer and pretzels ready and they were sitting by the fireplace talking. Andrea said Michael Malkin's brother James was arrested for assault. It seems the sweatshirt argument was unresolved and James felt the need to get into a fight on a street corner. The whole incident was witnessed by the police and he was quickly arrested. Andrea felt this was a good thing and perhaps Michael would gain a new perspective.

"I'm not sure you can count on it," Bea said. "The boy worships the ground his brother walks on. It's gonna take more than an arrest to make him see things different."

"I guess you are right. He's such a bright boy. I hate to see him grabbed by the street. It's a shame to see him so connected to the bad things his brother models."

Changing the subject Bea asked, "How are you and Colleen holdin' up?

"It's hard for me to think I won't be teaching here next year and may not be teaching at all. I know it's what I want to do as my career. But I only have one year in; while it's hard, I can't say it's totally unexpected. But Colleen's got a lot more time invested. She's in shock Bea. It hurts to see someone like her and Trace being affected they way they are. I don't know what I'd do if I were in her shoes."

"It is a bad time for all of us in teachin'. Things have to change and it's gonna come down hard and fast on us now."

Andrea's phone chimed. She opened it and her eyes darted across the open phone screen, "It's Jason texting to tell me he had a safe trip today and he's in Nashville for the night."

"Really, you and your man are now separated by a lot of miles. What are you thinkin'?"

"Bea I don't know what to think. There's a lot we didn't say to each other. You were right about silence and how it can hurt a relationship. Neither of us has been able to speak our minds to each other."

"Girl, you got to patient with things, an answer will come. I don't know what it is, but it will come."

CHAPTER 66

AIRING IT OUT

Following last week's Board meeting a buzz filled many conversations. People were clearly taking sides on the closing issues and the Board split. Even Ma'am was surprised by Mary Jane's demotion. The administrative union's leadership had taken a formal position in opposition to the closings and reductions. In fact, every union president said publicly they were opposed to the cuts. It was a difficult backdrop to the subcommittee meeting scheduled to begin at School #3 in a few minutes.

During the past week Ma'am or Bea talked with most of the subcommittee members about their ideas. Myrna was supportive of the ideas but knew if she took a public stand she would alienate herself from most of her colleagues. This was especially true now since teacher layoffs were a conversation in the faculty room every day. Ma'am appreciated Myrna's position. It was the same head versus heart battle she was facing herself.

Sitting in her office reflecting on all of it, Ma'am realized how tough the change process was becoming. Lives were affected and how could she be sure what she was proposing would be any better. She had no clear evidence it was. Many knowledgeable people would certainly strongly disagree with the ideas she was going to put out there.

As she was sitting with her reflections, Myrna lightly tapped on her door frame. "Got a minute?" she asked.

"Sure, I was thinking about the proposal; Myrna I am second guessing the ideas. But you didn't come by to hear your principal carry on. What's on your mind?"

"I've been thinking a lot about all of this too. Honestly, on a purely personal level I can't support it. Too many people's professional lives will be affected, especially if it really takes off as a model. But then I keep thinking about the children I have in my classroom. Dorothy, they have so little advantage in life. We must try something different. Not because of the scores, but in a much larger sense, I think we are a failing school. Not because we don't care or don't try, but because our structure doesn't fit. The other day I happened to pull an old college sorority tee-shirt off my shelf. I have a lot of good memories wearing the tee-shirt. I pulled it over my head and that's as far as it went. I was a different sized woman back then. This School is like my old tee-shirt, I love it, but it doesn't fit anymore. I will support you tonight and down the road. I won't like doing it because I sure love this place, but it doesn't work anymore." Myrna turned her face away and slowly left the doorway behind.

It's strange how ideas ebb and flow. Much like a football game, momentum and timing play such a significant role. Myra's remarks couldn't have been better timed. Dorothy pulled a Kleenex from the box on her desk and blew her nose as she rose to do what she felt was right.

The committee members were all there when Dorothy entered. "Let's get started," she said with a smile. "I know we could spend the night talking about what to do about the closing of our school. But, I want to share with you some things I have been working on and get your reactions and advice."

Knowing the power of her presence, Ma'am used it and moved forward. "The closing of our school could be a real opportunity to propose something new. Over the past several months we've talked a great deal about the things which truly affect our kids. Myrna said we need to get them started with us at a much younger age. We all agreed."

"Except Dr. Thomas," fireman Tom added humorously.

"Okay, almost all of us agreed. We also talked about your idea of being more open Tom and how we could create something more inviting to the folks around here. We also talked about smaller class size and the fit of technology in a new approach. Did I leave any big concerns out of the summary?"

"You forgot to mention the security concerns for staff working in this neighborhood," Sue Jones added. "I think knowing what happened this year with Andrea and Bea, the thefts we've experienced, all the little and big things which have happened, we can't ignore them or sweep it under the rug. Safety is a real issue."

"You are right Sue. It needs to be added as a significant concern. Is there anything else we should include on our list?"

Reverend James added, "Test scores. We've been identified here as a failing school. It doesn't seem like the state is gonna forget. Whatever we do we have to remind ourselves how important those scores are."

Bea smiled, "I hate to be the one to bring this up, but knowing how tight money is, we gotta be smart about how we go spendin' it." Everyone nodded affirmation of this last item.

With the summary finished, Dorothy felt the best place to start the ball rolling was with the second generation conceptual floor plan and front elevation she had of the new Rosa Parks Primary School. "I have been working with the school architects on a concept for a new primary school. It has been shaped by our committee conversations and my thoughts on what a 21st primary school should be." Dorothy unrolled the plans and the group gathered around them. For several minutes people looked at them. Making small comments and pointing things out as they looked at what was unfolded in front of them. Tom spoke up as things settled down after the first look. "It doesn't look like a school. It looks like a big house. That's real different. It's going to take me some time to digest the look. It is not at all what I expected."

"Me either," said Reverend James. "But, I think I see what you are after. Folks are sure going to look at it different. Maybe it will knock down a few of the barriers we've been talking about, you know, how uninviting a school can look to people."

Sue Jones piped in, "Where's the gym? I don't see a gym anywhere."

"No, you don't. You don't see a library, art room, music room, cafeteria or auditorium either. What I learned from the architects is how square footage costs money. I also learned about state aid formulas and how we can maximize our aid and minimize the cost on the local taxpayer."

"How are you going to provide a space for these classes?"

"If this model moves forward, we'd provide those services to young children in their rooms or in the single great room depending on how things sort out. Sue in this model there'd be no physical education teacher, music teacher, art teacher or librarian. Right now the average teacher salary in our district is over fifty thousand dollars. When we add pension, social security and health insurance premium payments the overall cost of an average teacher exceeds seventy thousand. We can't afford those expenses if we are going to run the school longer hours, provide birth through age seven support and keep the school open in the summer. Those new ideas are all part of this model, but we have to do it with the resources we have or less. What's proposed here is a social/literacy services model. It is different than what we think of when we think of a primary school approach in a more traditional sense."

"Dorothy, what other staffing changes do you have in mind?" Sue asked with an incredulous tone in her voice.

"There'd be no special education services through age 7. If we get the adult/student ratios right, I think we can hold off on IEP's for the first years of schooling. That will save us more than $100,000 in special services staffing we can use to hire additional classroom support. The instructional model is to have three master teachers with lots of adult aide support from people living in the neighborhood. We'd also use work/study students from the high school who are looking at human services careers."

Linda Morgano spoke up, "Ma'am I see what you are doing, but this is such a major change. It's also going to lead to lots of teacher layoffs and restructuring of services if it were adopted on more than a pilot basis. I don't know what to think at this point, the whole concept takes my breath away."

Reverend James commented, "I see there's no library. I am surprised since the focus is on early literacy. "

"This is one of the toughest things. But if we use technology, lots of tablet computers and regular computers then we can bring more to the children. The thought is to use books, classroom libraries in fact, but technology would take a lead role."

"There's a lot for us to think about here. But I think what is on the table meets the needs we've been talkin' about these past several months. We gotta' go down a different road." Bea said this calmly but with the full force of her personality. Everyone in the room knew where she stood.

"You got it right, we've got a lot to think about," Sue Jones added. The layoffs, lack of the arts and no physical education are more than a game changer; it's bad thinking from my point of view. I can't agree with it no matter how you tweak it."

"Whoa, let me make it clear we are not dropping the arts or physical education. This is a conversation about who delivers those parts of the program. I am sorry but we can no longer support paying nearly $70,000 per teacher for basic movement, art and music services. I wish we could afford it, but when you face the choices and priorities we do, I think we have to go in a much different direction. On this we'll have to agree to disagree."

The conversation over the model and school plans went on for another hour. It concluded with no agreement, but with all saying they needed to think and reflect, Dorothy was pleased. The model was now out in the open and in-depth conversations and reactions would take place in the weeks ahead.

What was out there for everyone to see was a birth to age seven literacy center concept. The importance of neighborhood connections would be elevated to an essential level. Knowing the children's cultural connections and environment were believed to be critical elements for literacy development.

CHAPTER 67

OVER THE FALLS

John and Cliff had monthly meetings to discuss, 'Issues of mutual concern'. But Cliff asked for this meeting before their next regular one was scheduled. In light of all that happened, he felt a need to talk with the superintendent about the state of things and his ideas for reform.

Once they were settled in John's office, he began. "John, I know the budget situation is bad. Anybody can see you are between a rock and a hard place on things. But wow, what are you thinking, are you going off the deep end with reforms using the budget as an excuse for a personal agenda?"

"Do you really believe that Cliff?"

"I am not sure what to think ; that's why I am here. My Executive Committee is upset with the closings and all the rumors they are hearing. Is this only the beginning of the changes you have in mind?"

"What rumors are you hearing Cliff?"

"Well, Sue Jones called me really upset about the School #3 ad hoc committee and what Dorothy Washington's layin' on the line. Holy cow John, she can't be serious!"

"I'm not sure what Sue Jones told you. I can tell you I've talked a great deal with Dorothy Washington and she has my full support for making some major changes in the way we do business at the primary school level."

Cliff started to interject and John retorted, "Let me finish. I think you'd agree we need to get the children in school before age 5. Too many kids from impoverished homes start too late and their language development is way behind. I also think you'd support a model where teachers have a more powerful and professional role in setting the instructional agenda at a school. The model is different and it prioritizes literacy over other parts of the program. It also uses a staffing model which involves people from the neighborhood."

"John, to pull off what she's talking about, a lot of current teachers are going to lose their jobs, especially if you propose to do what she's thinking district-wide."

"Cliff, you and I have been over a lot of this ground already. You know what an average teacher costs, salary and benefits. You also know administrator salaries are steep. The current model cannot sustain itself. Did Sue Jones tell you Dorothy is proposing one principal for every three primary schools? I'll bet she didn't share we can build at least three of them for the cost of one K-5 elementary building."

"John, she's going to violate state and federal guidelines for special education. How do you propose dealing with them?"

"We aren't violating those guidelines if children aren't referred for services. Don't get me wrong, I understand the concerns you are raising, but if we get adult/student ratios low enough I think we can provide the support the kids need."

"Alright there's a rumor going around you want all seniors to take at least one course online. My teachers are saying it doesn't have to be one offered by the district. Tell me it's not true!"

"Cliff, it is true. In this day and age our kids have to be tech savvy and quite frankly it helps solve a space problem with the closing of Jefferson. No, it doesn't have to be offered exclusively by us. Jerry Croton is talking with the community college to see if they would be willing to offer some courses for dual credit. We'd pay a bulk tuition much less than what we'd have to pay to offer courses online at the class sizes in the contract. Are you willing to discuss online staff ratios and loads different from what we have in the contract now?"

"John, that's subcontracting unit work, you know you can't do it without bargaining it first. My people are not going to let it happen lying down and neither will I."

"I am not sure you are right about the subcontracting piece, we are working with another governmental body and offering the kids dual credit. Why aren't you willing to look at these options? I think you know they are the right things to do, but we're so locked up in the past ways of doing things we can't look at new possibilities."

"Not when teachers are losing jobs we can't! John your proposals may have merit, but you will be laying off teachers if you have your way. Like I said, that isn't going to happen without a fight."

"Cliff, at the risk of asking, what would you do if you were in my shoes?"

"I'm not, and I don't want to be an administrator."

"Cut the crap Cliff, you lead a large union, you are the lead administrator of it and you know the budget problems and failing results are real issues. Come on, what would you do?"

"I'd start by laying off high paid administrators John."

"A classic union response which may play well outside these doors; but let's look at what you are saying. The average administrative salary is ninety-six thousand and with benefits, let's call it an even one hundred twenty-five thousand per person. We have about sixty-eight administrators in this district. Suppose I lay them all off tomorrow and it's just the two of us sitting here. We'd save about nine million. No small sum, but added to the eighteen million in the cuts I've proposed we've now got about twenty-seven million cut towards a forty-five million hole. Without even talking about whether we'd survive with everyone cut from the administrative team, what are you going to do now to get the rest of the forty-five million?"

"John, stop playing this argumentative game!"

"Cliff, I am not playing, I'd really like to know what you'd do. I don't see how the model we've got in place can sustain itself. If we don't start thinking outside of the box, using technology and new strategies somebody else will do it for us. I don't expect you to agree with all I am doing or will be proposing. But sitting on the sidelines with a blanket no and cut administrators is pure bullshit. The real issue is can we get past it and do something for the children we serve?"

"John you serve the children. My job as union president is to serve the interests of my members."

"Serving their interests is going to require real leadership and vision. I am open to the union's suggestions and ideas, but if you are going to bark like a cranky dog, don't expect much sympathy or openness from me. We can't afford to keep doing what we've been doing and think something better will happen, because it hasn't and it won't!"

"I came wanting you to lay things on the line. You sure have. It seems like most of the rumors we are hearing have an element or more of truth to them. John, my Executive Committee is angry and I don't see them supporting the reforms you have proposed or the ones I can only begin to imagine you are thinking. In the end, you'll be gone from this job and my members will have to clean up your mess. We will outlast you and your ideas. You are jousting with windmills. I hope you come to your senses real soon."

"Cliff, I have never been more clear-headed about what I have to do. You may be right about me being out of a job, but I am trying to make things better. I will be open to good ideas and good intentions, but if opposition is all you offer then it is ultimately the children who will suffer."

CHAPTER 68

WHAT'S NEXT

John was meeting with his two deputies. The agenda was simple and open-ended. How could they fundamentally change the way the school district went about its mission (student learning) while operating in a highly unionized and regulated environment? The challenge was formidable. As they sat in the comfortable chairs in John's office, he asked them to share their ideas about what a great education for 21st century students should look like. It was a no holds barred conversation.

Carl was the first to respond, "I think we have to have kids who know how to access information and use it creatively. I mean we used to fill our kids with what we thought they needed to know. Now most of that stuff and a lot more they can *Google* on their smart phones if they need it. It's really different, John. It's a whole new way to access and use knowledge. Yet in our high schools we ban the use of cell phones and the new tablet computers. We don't even have Wi-Fi in any of our buildings!"

"I get what you are saying Carl, but if we let kids walk around with those things they would not tune in to their classes. Our high school folks would have a discipline nightmare on their hands."

"Jerry, I didn't say it was going to be easy if we let kids go forward with the stuff they use all the time outside of school, but John's asking us to take the gloves off. Hell, you carry a smart phone and you use it all the time. Shouldn't our kids be able to?"

"Carl, they'd cheat on tests and be texting their boyfriends and girl-friends all day."

"No they wouldn't. If the curriculum kept up with the technology it would be a different ball game. We have to use this stuff, use it innovatively and change the way we do education."

"Is school still a place or is it evolving to be a concept?" John thought about this himself as he asked it. "So much of today's work is no longer bound to a specific place. Do kids have to be placed in large buildings with bells going off every 42 minutes as they move through long hallways on a learning assembly line, or could learning be distributed? Guys, what if we weren't bound by our current buildings and structures. How would we do it if it was a clean sheet?"

For a moment Jerry rocked back in his chair then exhaled, "John, I wouldn't build high schools as we know them. Certainly not for juniors and seniors, I'd approach their learning experiences differently."

"Keep talking Jerry, we're listening."

"Well, I would place kids in real-world settings. I'd want them out in the community doing things, applying what they'd learned. Working, taking on community service, you name it. It would be time to apply all those concepts we supposedly taught them. We don't give our kids enough hands-on, minds-on relevant experiences. I'd also use the technology to connect them. We'd need outside help, but with some real IT expertise available we could create a virtual network and plug our kids in. We'd walk the talk and reduce our overhead at the same time. I'd deploy teachers as strategic mentors and guides. Hell, I'd eliminate report card grades as we know them for seniors at least. I'd want the kids to take on a much larger role of self-evaluation. We'd have to write new exit standards and redefine course sequences. It would be entirely different from what we have now."

"Guys, the other day the mayor and I were talking about the city's bid to get Subaru to locate a new assembly plant here. You can imagine the competition. What if we offered to place a few hundred seniors every year in their factory at no cost other than they must spend the previous semester before the placement in seminars and training we co-design with them. I wonder if anything like it would be attractive in a bid."

Both Carl and Jerry looked at John, "Oh boy, we are thinking on another planet," Carl chimed in.

"I know, but how could we take what we are talking about, real-world experiences and totally different kinds of practical training in team-work, technology and basic engineering concepts and give the kids authentic perspectives? I bet the kids wouldn't be texting to each other with those cell phones in their pockets due to boredom!"

Jerry was quiet for a minute then asked a new question, "What about middle level kids John? Early adolescents at the middle school level, I mean how do we see things for them?"

"You asked the question Jerry, how would you answer it?"

"I think it's about relationships and interpersonal skills. We also need to build rock solid math and communication skills at that level. It's a tough age. Bullying behaviors, all sorts of stuff comes out of the woodwork. That's why focusing on relationships is so important; we need to be much closer to the kids. We have to really know them."

"It is a tough age; I think we need to create a lot more team interactions and personal connections with the kids. I am not sure how we accomplish it," Carl interjected as he rubbed his tired forehead.

"I want us to twist and turn these ideas in our heads. I also want to decide on a set of clear goals to initiate fundamental change. I am not putting this out as some strategic planning exercise led by consultants. If we do, the process will be filled with busy work and take us in fifty different directions while nothing at the most important level, student learning, really changes. I want us to do it here, and then put in motion the steps over the next three years to set it in place. No joking, I mean we reinvent what we are doing. More than fifty percent of our kids are failing and dropping out. Those who stay with us are not really prepared to compete in this world we are all living in. Hell, more than half our grads don't finish a college degree! Guys let's try to do it different, not for difference sake, but because the world is flat and our kids are on a whole new playing field. If we're lucky we may get some of the ideas to take hold."

"John, you aren't really seriously considering this are you? I mean it's a great conversation, but you can't escape the current reality of how school is done and create your own world. It can't happen in this setting!

Maybe a private school somewhere, but on Main Street we'll be taken out quicker than you can say our names."

"Jerry that may be so, but I am talking big here and the problems we will face with a radical change agenda will be huge. But what's the alternative? If you see one then I'd like to hear it."

"John, I don't have a good alternative. But what we are talking about today is way off the charts."

"I know, and maybe I am working on a pipe-dream. I am asking you guys to come along with me on what may well be the Titanic. But the right conditions for learning don't exist in our district today. We have a stewardship responsibility to do everything we can to create them. We are knocking on a different learning door. Let's see if we can get it to open. Wouldn't it be great if we could? We know it would be better. You said it Jerry; you wouldn't build the factory school we have now if you had a clean sheet. Let's act like we do have an opportunity. I need you with me on this. We will also need to enlist many others in the effort in the days ahead. There will be casualties, it could and may well include us, but right now all the casualties are kids. That can't continue."

CHAPTER 69

OFF WITH THEIR HEADS!

The three women met on Saturday morning at Sara Fieldstone's home. They did not want to risk being seen meeting at a local restaurant. Shantell Williams and Mary Jane Thomas arrived at almost the same moment. Once the coffee and Danish were set out on Sara's kitchen table the talk became serious.

It was Shantell who spoke first, "I am not sure where things stand inside the district; Mary Jane what are you hearing?"

Mary Jane shifted in her chair. She knew she no longer supported her superintendent, and here she was working openly with these women rather than behind the scene to secure his ouster. It was new territory for her and she wasn't quite sure how to navigate it. But both women had been good friends and long-term lunch partners so she figured she'd jump in the deep end of the pool and see where things went. "He's been meeting regularly with Jerry and Carl. The rumors are flying about what they are planning. Nobody really knows for sure, except it is clear they are developing something big given the time they are spending. I also spoke with Cliff Greer. He tells me the teachers' union Executive Board is meeting and they are not pleased with what Dr. Handler has in mind. Apparently, Dr. Handler and Cliff had a real pointed exchange of views. Cliff wouldn't share the substance, but it is clear he didn't think much of the conversation."

"Shantell, did you talk with Emily about where she stands on all of this? Those other two are clearly behind Dr. Handler, there's no moving them, but Emily she's the one to work on."

"Sara, I didn't do it yet. I wanted to talk here this morning before making any contact with her. I know she voted with the men, but I think she'll be uncomfortable with the changes coming forward, especially if they involve layoffs."

Mary Jane noted, "Since she is a teacher, I wonder if the first contact on things should come through the union. Her district's president could do a reach out on things and start applying some pressure on where her loyalties should lie."

"What a great idea. I'll call Cliff and invite him to lunch. He used to meet with me four or five times a year when I was president. Knowing what's going on now, I'll bet he'd be happy to talk about what we might be able to do together."

"We could do a lot more if Emily joined us!" Sara said this while she was pouring everyone a second cup of coffee.

Shantell turned back to Mary Jane once the steaming coffee had settled in her cup, "Mary Jane where does the State Education Department stand on all of this? Will they really come in and take us over like Dr. Handler says?"

"I talked to my contacts there, even though Dr. Handler has directed me not to. They assured me they would not break confidence and talk with Dr. Handler about our conversations. They see him as a real rebel and they think the Commissioner will too in the end. So I think we can get by the Department, as long as we have a sound plan for improving the scores. There's no doubt they trust me."

"Well you are a key player in all of this. I hear you've been encouraged to apply outside the district. Can you tell Sara and me where things stand?"

"I am putting my resume together, I have to. But my heart is here. I am going to put the word out to the headhunters and there are a few districts where I may apply for an opening. But I'm only looking for a superintendent's job; I am not going to be a second tier player anymore."

"You know we'd support you as Dr. Handler's successor if we can get the house in order. But we have to get him out first."

Sara added, "Mary Jane, I think you'd be a great leader and we need you here. But, I understand why you are looking since Dr. Handler has treated you so badly. We all thought he'd be a great leader. It looks like we were wrong on that score!"

"Ladies, we've got work to do to make things happen. I will call Cliff and see if I can get him to lunch this week. We can talk later. Let's see where the support and lack of it sits inside the district. We will need to keep our conversations tight and careful. I suggest we don't use district email addresses to share things. Let's start using our personal emails from this point forward."

The first meeting of the loyal opposition came to a close. They had their first agenda set. Now they had to make it a reality. They were confident they could if they played their cards right and Emily came to her senses after a little push from her district's teachers' union.

CHAPTER 70

IT'S STILL ABOUT THE CHILDREN

Andrea didn't make a habit of stopping by the faculty room for a cup of coffee before the children arrived, but this morning she needed one. The faculty room had its usual group of morning players. When they saw Andrea come in they motioned her to join them.

Cheryl Shepard, a second grade teacher smiled, "Good morning Andrea. How are you doing with your guy off to Montgomery?"

"I am doing alright. He's been busy getting settled and he wants me to come down over spring break. It will be nice to get away from all this cold weather."

"We were listening to Linda fill us in on the program committee's last meeting. Did Bea share much with you?"

"Only a little," Andrea felt like she was walking into a conversation with lots of sharp edges.

"There's a lot more they are discussing. We can't believe what we are hearing. Teachers being replaced by neighborhood people who don't have any training beyond a high school diploma. What are they thinking?"

Linda wanting to be fair added, "They are still putting teachers into lead roles. They also are talking about having kids start much younger and going year round. Those aren't bad ideas."

Cheryl Forst, a fifth grade teacher sitting at the table, ripped into Linda, her face beat red as she spoke. "How can you say anything positive! So many people around here are already losing their jobs. They're closing this school at the end of the year. Poor Andrea and Colleen aren't the only ones who will lose their jobs because of thinking like this. You better wise up quick and tell the committee the whole thing is bad thinking. Isn't that right Andrea?"

Now she was squarely on the spot. She wasn't sure what she felt, but she did not want to get caught up in this maelstrom! "I want to hear more details. I know I need a job so it's my main focus right now."

Cheryl looked at her, "Well this idea sure isn't going to help you find one. You know Bea is a strong advocate for this change. She's your mentor and she's betraying you and all of us!"

Andrea could feel her emotions rise. While she was upset people were attacking Bea, she did not want to get drawn in. "Like I said, I need a job at this point. We all need to think before we leap to conclusions about people." Before anymore could be said, Andrea quickly headed for the faculty room door.

Once outside Andrea stopped for a moment to collect herself. She warned Bea things would get ugly when the plan was out in the open. It was evident her prediction was accurate. The next several months were going to be difficult. People were upset and angry; those emotions always need a focal point and they had one in Bea.

As Andrea prepared for her kids, writing a riddle on the old slate chalkboard, Bea stuck her head in to say good morning. Bea knew Andrea well and sensed she was upset. "What's up with you this morning? I can see trouble in that face of yours."

"I stopped by the faculty room for some coffee. There's lots of angry talk in there about the committee's possible plan. Bea, I am not sure how I feel about all of this, but I can tell you there are a lot of our colleagues who've already made up their minds on it."

"I know what you sayin' I'm gettin' the cold shoulder from a lot of folks. It is gonna be a real fight to get this idea off the ground. I know we've gotta get ready for the kids. It isn't Thursday either, but we're both by ourselves, why not come over tonight and we can talk about it then."

"That'd be great. I don't like sitting alone in my empty apartment every night."

The school day zoomed by and before long Andrea found herself holding a beer by the fireplace in Bea's living room. "Andrea let me tell you what I think about this. Hear me out on it 'cause I need to say a number of things and try to connect them so they make sense altogether. First thing, is you gotta accept poverty like we got here is a generation after generation thing. Folks know only hard times. It's never been easy for 'em. So we have to do somethin' which breaks the cycle. We gotta get children young and we gotta keep them with us as much as we can. You see summer on these streets with these families is so different than what you experienced. So we can't waste any time gettin' started with poverty's kids."

"Bea I agree with you. I think everyone on the staff does. That's not the problem."

"The problem is there's never been money to do what's right for these children. There isn't gonna be in these times. So we gotta do a lot with a little money. We can't do it payin' a teacher's salary. Dr. Handler was right too when he said people gotta live here to really know what to do with these kids. There aren't many who plan on livin' on these streets and raisin' their kids here. I don't blame them, but if you don't live 'round here, you don't know what these kids are really doin' and livin' with. You gotta be a part of it to know. That's why usin' folks from here is so important; what they don't have in education they make up in knowin' the kids and these streets. They can talk to 'em different. At the same time we're givin' folks here a job and a chance to have a better life. It's not only the kids we're savin' it's the neighborhood we're tryin' to raise up."

"Bea, are you saying people with no training can replace a teacher? These same people you are talking about often don't like us or see how important education is. Now you are putting them with the children and expecting them to make a go of it. I don't see how it's possible, honestly, I don't."

"It's a reach. We'll have to do some trainin' and coachin' for sure. But if we have some good teachers plannin' and helpin' them I think there's a chance we can do okay. Remember, we're talkin' about young children. We aren't teachin' algebra. We're talkin' about basic literacy and buildin' basic skills. There's a trade-off, but we can hire at least two aides to cover the whole year for less than one teacher. It's a reality which has to be a part of the plan. It's both money and location that's important. Balancing the two with the right level of professional support is what we gotta figure out. Anybody in the faculty room talk to you about the plans for the school buildin'?"

"No, they are so upset by the lack of teachers in the plan nothing else was talked about. At least while I was there anyhow."

"The place we do this has to be different too. We gotta use technology every chance we can, lots of sounds, pictures and graphics. We can also use it for trainin' folks and takin' lots of virtual field trips. The place must be inviting and part of the neighborhood. Ma'am's got a real grip on it. Andrea it's all about the children, not you and me. I know jobs are gonna be lost, but we've been losin' kids over and over and that's gotta change!"

"Bea I know much of what you are saying makes sense. But you can't under estimate how upset people are about this. Our school seems like it's going to explode at any moment. I can feel the anger every day I walk in now. I am not comfortable anymore. Don't you see the same thing?"

"I do, and I am not sure how things will turn out in the end. I keep remindin' myself it isn't about us."

CHAPTER 71

TAKING STOCK

John was sitting in his office reflecting on the lengthy planning meetings with Jerry and Carl over the past two weeks. Their conversations were taking shape into a three-year plan for changing the district's structure. John believed in the ideas. He felt they were on the right track. However, he was not certain they'd ever get off the ground. The tone in the district had changed and everyone was on edge knowing the budget gap was still looming and more cuts were likely on the horizon. He finished writing an overall summary and was waiting for Carl and Jerry to join him so they could review the main points.

Carl came in first, carrying sub sandwiches he'd picked up around the corner. The smell of salad dressing and oil quickly filled the air. John hadn't realized how hungry he was until then, "Thought we'd need nourishment since we're planning a revolution."

John smiled, "You know you aren't even half wrong on either count. I look at the bullet points in this summary and I think we are taking a huge leap of faith here. I am not sure we can pull it off Carl."

"John, you know what Bill Cosby once said? He said, *'I don't know the key to success, but the key to failure is trying to please everybody.'* John, you know this is going to upset the apple cart, no doubt about it, but doing the same thing with less is only going to make matters worse, not better. You have to try something different."

Jerry walked in, "Man it smells like a deli in here! I don't know what else we're gonna do, but those sandwiches sure make me hungry!"

"Sit down and join us. We were ruminating about the plan and Carl here tells me Bill Cosby likes it."

Jerry gave Carl a quizzical look, "When did you run it by Bill Cosby?"

"Nah, just kidding; John is worried about the backlash we're going to get. I reminded him you can't please everybody."

"I'm no expert, but I think Cosby pleased a lot of folks given the ratings for his show. In fact, pleasing people was how his show stayed on the air."

"Guys, I have been looking at the outline of actions we are contemplating. While we can't please everyone, we can't go forward alone. We have to get some folks on board with this; helping both publicly and quietly. Let's look over the outline again and then talk about how we might get support for it. First, if Dorothy Washington can pull it off, we are anticipating starting two new pilot literacy schools like she's outlined. They would both serve the current School #3 attendance area. We'd link them to Dix's school which would serve grades 3-5 in a more traditional pattern. Have I got that right?"

Jerry looked up, "You do. There's lots of detail but the headline is new Early Literacy Centers. It will give us a chance to see if the new model holds promise as the kids move on from the two small centers. I really hope Dorothy can get the committee support for it."

"Dorothy usually gets what she wants doesn't she?" They all laughed at this knowing it was often the case. "Next is the middle level piece. The grade 6-8 stretch is a tough one. We've got more work to do here. I know we will be stressing relationships and communication skills. I also know we will place the kids in smaller team groupings. It's a start, but we need more clarity on instructional objectives. Jerry, you need to talk to the three principals and see what suggestions they have. Sue will be especially good on the curriculum piece. Bob on the teaming and scheduling ideas and of course, Zack on all the interpersonal and bullying stuff. Let's see if we can pin down the details better on this part."

"John, let me take a run at describing the high school part of this. We will close Jefferson as a budget cutting strategy at the end of this year. We will do the double sessions and some online course stuff next fall. It's the following two years when we really plan to step things up."

"You have the gist of it, now, how about the next two years?"

"I was coming to that. We will close Roosevelt High to juniors the second year and then juniors and seniors the third. We will start remodeling old storefronts and small abandoned business properties in key locations. These will become satellite schools and mentoring spots for the seniors as they begin their real-world work. We'll use Lincoln High for the more traditional junior and senior classes. We have a huge ramp-up task for needed technology, remodeling and developing connections for the placement of our kids. That's gonna take a serious staffing commitment and we are short on funds. Not sure how we pull that one off!"

"Yeah, that's another real soft spot we have to work on before this draft hits the streets. Carl, we also need to have a union strategy on this."

"I've been giving it a great deal of thought. I have an idea I want to run by you guys. I've been looking at our attrition rate. We've averaged almost 9% a year in the teaching staff. What if we didn't hire replacements when people left; instead we used our attrition rate as a means to shrink staff in years two and three? I know the staff leaving will not all be in the areas we want, but if we could get more flexibility in assigning the remaining teachers, we might be able to make a go of it. I am thinking as we moved forward we could consider offering the union a no layoff provision in return for real flexibility in assigning staff."

"Now there's an out-of-the-box idea! Cliff might go for it if we sweetened the pot with a good retirement incentive. At least it would open a dialogue without all the other shouting we are likely to get. If we could pull something off with the union that would be big. I think you should work on some draft proposals, and then let's talk more about it next week."

"Now on the political side do you have any thoughts or ideas guys?" John was worried and wondered what his two deputies were thinking. "Carl it looks like you've got something to say."

He moved to the edge of his chair as he spoke, "Mary Jane is working behind our backs. My secretary told me she's been talking to the State Education Department. She was on the phone twice this week with them for over an hour. Did you give any okay I don't know about?"

"No, I didn't. It doesn't surprise me she's working against us. She's upset with her standing and knows she has no chance to convince me otherwise. But I am surprised she's calling the Department."

"Carl, pull the phone billing records. I'd like to have proof she has been insubordinate. I'm not sure what to do yet, but let's line things up."

"John, Cliff Greer was seen at lunch with Shantell the other day. It is obvious she is aligning herself with their agenda."

John sat back pondering this information. "In the end, they have to put pressure on Emily. She is the swing vote they need to get. Using the union to reach her is my guess on what's happening. Shantell's no fool. She has to figure out a way to convince Emily to change her support."

"John, can Emily hold up under this pressure?" Jerry wondered aloud.

"I am not sure. She is the wild card in all of this. If we can reduce the pressure by resolving things with the teachers' union we would be on much better ground. Carl, we really need to think about what kind of a deal we could make with Cliff. He knows the district's probation won't help him or his teachers. We've got to get creative and see if we can meet the union off-the-record somewhere away from here."

"Guys I will get to work on some proposals. But my staff and I are really jammed up with the budget cuts and all the layoff notices and meetings. It is going to take me some time, even if I do it after hours."

"Ok, Carl. I understand the pressure you are under. We all have a great deal on our plate even without planning a revolution. Let's meet next week and see where things stand. In the meantime, this conversation remains behind closed doors. If you need to prepare something, you can give it to Ann. I'd rather any documents that are put together be done solely in my office. Let's not put your secretaries in the middle of it yet."

It was nearly 3:00 when they finished. John wanted to call the mayor. The Subaru bid was on his mind. 'Could they really put something together that would be helpful to the bid and the education of a number of high school students?' He'd see.

CHAPTER 72

MOM AND ME

Andrea was pleased to see the weather breaking towards spring. She hoped the better weather would improve the mood of the staff. Sue Jones was often angry. She and Ma'am had gone toe-to-toe at the last two faculty meetings. With School #3 closing it seemed like all the rules for decorum changed for the worst. Coupled with the committee's vote to propose a new Early Literacy Center, Ma'am, Bea and Myrna felt unwelcome in their own school. The staff was giving them, by agreement, the silent treatment. There were no pleasant exchanges, with business only conversations the rule. Andrea found it hard to comply and nearly hid in her room as a result.

Even the children noticed the change. One of her students, Laticia, an especially sensitive girl, asked her during their journal times why the teachers were always so mad. Andrea told them everyone was sad School #3 would be closing and that's why the teachers were upset. "Well I saw Miss Sheehan cryin' in her car yesterday before school." It was Michael Malkin who announced this. Andrea had little doubt he was telling the truth.

Andrea was having dinner at her parents' house tonight. She did this more frequently since Jason left town. She was looking forward to talking with her mom. It was hard to know what to do or say. At school she never thought she'd have to walk on eggshells with the children, but now even they were caught up in the drama.

As she left school for the eastern suburbs, Andrea was relieved to feel the familiarity of the streets where she grew up. She wondered what it would be like to be a teacher down the road at John Kennedy. Things would sure be different there.

A half-hour later, Andrea stood in the kitchen with her mom making a salad. Tonight, the conversation's center was around what was happening at Andrea's school.

"It's tense there isn't it?"

"Yup, every day mom there's some new incident; there's no civility left. I hate it! I can't believe people can behave this way towards each other. I don't know what to do or say. You are either with the committee proposal or against it. I have tried every way I know how to stay out of it. Bea is unhappy with me. She feels I should support her out of friendship I guess, if nothing else. She's always been so patient with me. Now she's only focused on the Early Literacy Center proposal. It's hard to talk with her. I feel so alone."

"Andrea, I wish I could tell you it will get better, but I don't think it will. The cuts are hurting people and when you take a person's livelihood away, you know how painful that is."

"I know mom, but the whole district is off balance. The union talk is constantly focused on the Board and Dr. Handler. Then in our school it's got a personal layer with the silent treatment on Ma'am. There isn't much talk about the children and their needs. It's their school that is closing and nothing is being done about it. We should be doing something for them but it's not going to happen when the atmosphere is so toxic."

"Maybe it's a good thing you will be leaving at the end of the year. You've had your taste of working in a city district. I'm not saying teaching is easier in a suburban school, but I can tell you there's different stress than what you are experiencing."

"Mom, maybe I am a dreamer but I still believe poor children need all we can give them. I feel called to teach in a setting as Bea says, 'Where poverty rules'. I am not interested in teaching at Kennedy, even though I wonder what it would be like to have the resources to teach and work with kids where opportunity serves up so much more."

"Maybe you need a different perspective Andrea. You may be called, as you say, to teach disadvantaged children, but you are first called to teach. If you can't do it in the city, then I think you have to keep every option open, at least in the short-term."

"I feel like I'd be running away if I did. I get what you are saying, but I don't want to compromise. However, fate is sure dealing a tough hand. If the change plans happen in the city there won't be a job opportunity, beyond subbing, for a long time."

"Andrea making a living and what to live for are two different things. Your dad and I always taught you to go after your dreams. I believe you will find the answer. But the toxic environment at School #3 has put a lot of people on their knees and shattered their dreams. It's a bad combination. Figuring out an answer for others isn't your job. You have to figure out a way to pursue your dreams dear. You know your dad and I will always support you."

"I know mom, but so many of the kids I teach don't have support. I think that's why I have to figure out how to give back to them. I can't be a parent, but I can be their teacher."

"Okay, I also need to ask you, what's happening with you and Jason? How is my girl's heart holding up?"

Andrea turned to her mom, her face red and eyes swelling, "Mom I am so lonely! I don't know what to do."

"Let it go, just let it go honey."

"I'm sorry mom, you don't need to see all of this."

"No apology Andrea, I am your mom and this is the best place for you to let it go. You have a lot on your plate right now and you need to let it out and not stuff it down. So don't apologize. I am glad you are letting go and talking to me."

"Mom, it's so hard. I don't want to confuse my loneliness with love. But I don't think I am. I love him mom, and I am not sure what to do about it."

"You mean following him to Montgomery?"

"Yes, I need to know it's more than a relationship that maybe someday will lead to something. If he loves me like he says, why doesn't he propose?"

"I can't answer that and neither can you. But withholding your love as a condition for marriage isn't the answer. You have to follow your heart and if you trust his, then things will work out the way they should. I can't tell you what to do, I can only see how unhappy you are now. Is this the way you want to live your life?"

"No mom, it isn't."

"You are a strong woman Andrea. Your dad and I are so proud of you. You know you can always count on us no matter what happens or where you go. Our love is unconditional."

"I know mom. I love you and dad so much."

"Unconditional love isn't just for parents and their children, your dad and I share it too."

Andrea reflected on the meaning of her mother's statement and said, "Thanks mom."

"You know the same thing is true at school. You love those children you are teaching. Maybe you should stay sitting on the fence with all that's happening. But then again, maybe you should follow your heart and say what you feel when things are said. Maybe you should remind people the school is closing and something special needs to be done for the children, especially if nobody is talking about it."

CHAPTER 73

THE IDES OF MARCH

Carl and Cliff Greer were meeting to discuss the status of things from a labor relations perspective. Carl wanted to propose an off-the-record negotiations process to see if they could get things on track for the scope of change John, Jerry and he had been discussing.

"Man Carl, things are more tense than I have ever seen them! Dr. Handler's proposal to close three elementary schools and Jefferson has put the whole place on edge. My members are screaming for us to do something to stop this."

"Cliff, you know the budget bind we are in and you know there's no money at the state level to bail us out of a real jam. These are extremely tough times. I don't know what else we can do but pull back."

"Carl on top of the closings, my people are hearing a lot about the secret meetings here in the tower. We hear things Carl, and what we hear isn't helping us relax or feel good about where we're headed."

"Cliff, we have been brainstorming how we can restructure in the long-term to create the right conditions for learning. You know the state has placed us on probation. Hell, we are considered to be one of the poorest performing school districts in the country at this point. Doing the same thing isn't going to cut it. We have to rethink how we do things. So we want to talk off-the-record with you about it."

"Carl, I am not talking to you off-the-record. I am not at all sure we even want to talk on-the-record! You guys are only one Board member short of getting tossed and even if you keep the three together, and I don't think you can, they are never going to support some pipe-dream. You've been in the tower too long. Carl you guys are going to be looking for jobs yourself. No union president is going to support you. You're all alone up here. The Board will realize that before long. Then they'll dump you and your ideas."

"Are you saying the union wants to fumble along and miss an opportunity to do something which might make a real difference for kids?"

"Look, you can't lay down any conditions at this point, but I will. If we meet it has to be fully on-the-record. We also want to know all about your long-term plan before we negotiate anything. I am not coming to negotiate something and then be duped by a plan seeing the light of day only after we've bargained. It's not happening. Carl, even with that I am not sure I can get my Executive Board to agree to meet. There's a growing consensus we should wait you guys out. In a short time you'll all get your walking papers and we can sort things out with a Board and administration that has a much better grip on reality."

"What are you saying to me, Cliff? We have worked together for a long time."

"Carl, we both know Emily is the swing vote on the Board for all of this. Do you really think she is going to hold up under pressure? I know you are smarter than that, or at least I thought you were. Carl, there are a number of your administrators already working against you. All the unions are lining up against you. In fact we are all meeting later this week. You guys have been so busy in the tower you've forgotten to look out the window, let alone go over the moat and talk with the people outside this place. We are all feeling left out. You've got some top down plan you want to spring on us. Well, you guys are not going to change anything except your own jobs. Carl, I am telling you for your own good, wise up. Open your eyes man! The house of cards you are building is going to feel a real cold March wind gust."

"Cliff, I sure don't see it that way, but I appreciate your candor. Let me share our conversation with John and get back to you. Can we at least agree this meeting was off-the-record?"

"I'll give you this one, but any future ones aren't going to be. Like I said Carl, wise up! I'm telling you for your own good."

After Cliff left Carl took a deep breath. He'd been warned things would not happen the way they were planning. Strong forces were lining up against them. Those forces were not insignificant, nor should they be discounted. They'd been captured in a moment by a dream, but in the harsh light of day would it stand the test? 'Could he? What about his family and their needs?' He was risking everything. He knew he had to walk over to John's office and reveal what had transpired. What would be his counsel to the superintendent?"

He didn't have more time to think or to take the walk to John's office; John came to him. "How did it go?"

"John it was not a good meeting. Cliff will not meet off-the-record. He wouldn't even guarantee the union leadership will meet with us on-the-record. For the next ten minutes Carl gave John the blow-by-blow exchange that took place. "John, I don't know what to say. Cliff was honest and open, but he's not receptive at this point to us. I really believe he will have a hard time bringing a group to the table for an on-the-record talk. He was serious about needing to know our plan first, it was a definite condition."

"I came across something on the Internet. It struck me and I printed it." John handed the piece to Carl.

It's real simple
It's real simple to put you down.
It's real simple to throw mud around
Oh yeah it's real real simple.

It's real simple
I can push someone out.
Oh yeah it's real simple.
Watch me do it no doubt.

You could do it too ...come on it's simple
Yeah it's so simple!
Change your stripes.
Don't take the blame.
It's simple, so simple.

   (R.Stein)

"John it is simple to oppose us and stomp on our ideas. I see why this piece resonated with you right now. But there's nothing simple about what we are thinking. Making it happen is such a long shot. I believe in what we're planning, but the pragmatist in me thinks more than a warning shot was fired across the bow. Maybe it's no coincidence we are at the Ides of March."

CHAPTER 74

SEEKING SUPPORT

John wondered, 'Can I marshal support for a different way to provide a public education to the city's children?' Sitting in the mayor's office seeking her support for what he was about to make public he stated, "Jane, you know the problems we are facing. It's a crisis in education and now our financial resources have been ripped to shreds. I cannot ask you or the residents of this city to continue to support a failing model. I also can't ask you to cover a budget deficit by raising taxes on residents by a figure well into double digits.

But, I need help. I need support for what I think needs to be done. I don't know where you may stand after I share it with you. I'd appreciate at least your advice and comments, and hopefully your public support."

"John, we hear quite a bit of chatter from your union leaders. They've tried to work us over, quietly so far, but with some serious pressure, to support a large increase in your budget. I've told them it won't happen. The days of deep taxpayer pockets to reach into are long gone. But you are asking a great deal of me and my administration if I take a public position of support for a plan that hasn't been road tested."

"I know, but hear me out and then you can tell me how you see things."

For the next hour John laid out his plan. The risks and key strategies were plainly on the table. Jane was stunned by its scope and the boldness of what he was considering. "John, I get the retrenchment part of the plan and the budget cuts to be made right now. You can count on me not to criticize you for them. But let's talk more about the other aspects of what you are thinking. Did I hear you say a 12 month school year for all your kids?"

"You did. You know many of the worst acts of violence take place in the warm summer months. Those same months our kids fall back in their studies and we lose way too many to the streets. Jane, the district will be alone in this proposal. None of my suburban counterparts are going to get on board with this. Our kids and many families will oppose it. But it's the backbone for everything else. I am going to have to speak frankly about the effects of poverty and violence. The gloves will be off. There's been no political will to do this anywhere in our country. But a 12 month school year is simply a must. I will need legislative help. I will need you saying how this could help the kids and our streets."

"John, you are asking a lot and listening to you it's only the opening salvo."

"Jane we cannot afford to staff our schools 12 months of the year using the current model. Hell, we're broke now, we can't add new costs. A whole new structure with more differentiated staff is needed."

"You mean a lot fewer teachers John. Call it what it is."

"I am proposing we go down a different road with staffing. If I compare it to the medical world, the teacher is like the well trained doctor. They call the shots, but we need more nurses and other technicians in the mix. The current structure is top heavy with doctors and the hospital can't function that way and provide high quality affordable care."

"I get the medical metaphor John, but nurses have a lot of training too. You've got a big gap if you drop from teachers to people from the neighborhood. That model won't work either."

"I know we are going to need people with two year degrees; people who have a demonstrated ability to learn with good technical or humanities backgrounds. They need to deliver a teacher's plans, their prescriptions for learning. There's a lot more to this Jane. We want to close another high school in three years as the new model and plan unfolds."

"What!"

"Here's the idea. I drive down our city streets; in fact I'm looking out your window at what we used to call 'Main Street.' It's full of abandoned buildings and store fronts. High schools are big buildings. Kids are too often unknown in them. It's the old 20th Century factory model. We need small technical centers, places where kids, we're thinking mainly seniors and some second semester juniors, take classes, do projects and collaborate as teams. These will be led by teachers, those folks with the advanced training. They'll be backed up by staff with varying levels of training and expertise, depending on the focus of each center. These same places can be educational 'hot spots' for adults and used in many different ways. Lots more thinking and planning has to take place. But think of school much more conceptually rather than as a single place. We also plan to use technology much more actively than we do now."

"John, I don't know how to think about what you said. What a totally different approach. Wow!"

"Jane, taking it further..."

"Further, you're already in the barrel going over Niagara Falls!"

"Then there's not much more to lose is there? But I want to talk with you about Subaru and how all of this could connect to the proposal your team is developing for them to consider."

Jane and John talked for another hour. When he left the mayor's office he knew she was going to give a great deal of thought to all he shared. That was all he could ask.

Before the day was over he drove to the capital for a meeting in the morning with the Education Commissioner. He needed to lay out the plan as it was taking shape, get his advice and hopefully continued support for what they were thinking. With so many state hurdles to overcome he would need to have the Commissioner squarely behind him. 'Was there a reasonable chance he could count on him to back the plays he was developing?'

The next morning John spent more than an hour updating the Commissioner on the plan. Commissioner Appleton quizzed John on many aspects of it. One thing for certain, he felt John's timeline was overly ambitious. He urged him to think over a six-year span rather than a than the three-year one John was outlining. However, in general John was pleased by the Commissioner's conceptual support. Both expressed their worries about whether or not John's slim board majority would hold when the rubber hit the road. This was no minor concern for either of them. Both men reflected on how much hinged on the type of Board you had, and their ability to grasp and support a different vision.

Commissioner Appleton had a breakfast meeting on his calendar the next day with the Governor. He asked John to hold over another day so they could discuss what John had in mind. The state teacher's union had been a strong backer of Governor Pickering and the Commissioner was not sure if the Governor would be able to throw the weight of his office behind John's ideas. But political support was clearly needed, and only one way to discover if it was there.

CHAPTER 75

POLITICS

John stayed over at the Commissioner's request. He was excited to have the opportunity to speak with the governor about his plan. However, he was not naïve about his chances. Governor Pickering was deeply beholding to the state's teachers' union. They worked hard to get him elected, making major contributions to his campaign war-chest. They also worked to secure the election of key legislators who would support the governor and the union's objectives. But the dreadful national economy, and high unemployment within the state's borders, placed the governor between a rock and a hard place. Education was a major part of the state's budget and it had to be reduced whether the union liked it or not. A strong public backlash to the pension costs and benefits afforded public employees was growing. The governor was a political creature and knew right now he had to get out front on those issues or his re-election in two years would not be easily accomplished.

The three met in a conference room not far from the Governor's office. The breakfast they were served was a modest one. Governor Pickering was on a tight schedule and 45 minutes was afforded for this meeting. "Governor Pickering, "I've brought with me today Dr. John Handler who is..."

The Governor held up his hand, "I know who he is. Dr. Handler, you've been raising some cane in your district. You also have poor test results there. I understand the Education Department has you on a very short leash. Do I have it right gentlemen?"

John looked the Governor in the eye. He held his gaze for a moment, then he said, "You sure do have it right, and if we continue to do the same things we've been doing it's only going to get worse."

"Now there's an optimistic opinion from a school leader."

"Governor Pickering, the single biggest challenge is the extent of poverty in my district. More than 85% of our students are on free or reduced lunch. In many of our schools it's well over 95%. Poverty is so pervasive it follows one generation to the next. Any reform effort has to begin by recognizing the real enemy."

"I can't say you are telling me anything new Dr. Handler."

"No Governor, but our strategies for overcoming it in the classroom are antiquated and unresponsive to it. Sure we have a unique charter school here or there, even once in a while a single public school seems to get in front of it, but overall our public school systems are a failure. They will continue to fail if we don't reinvent them wherever poverty is the prevailing common factor."

"You've made a strong indictment of public education Dr. Handler."

"I know. But it is the one major institution which has failed to change as the times have. We are living and competing in a different world Governor and we have failed to adapt. You know what Darwin has to say about that."

With a smile on his face and a chuckle in his voice the Governor replied, "Let's not get Darwin and education in the same sentence this morning."

John, laughing agreed. "Okay, but my point is we need to develop new structures."

"The Commissioner, knowing how quickly the time would pass said, "John, lay it out for Governor Pickering, big picture, ten minutes."

He did while Governor Pickering ate his breakfast nodding occasionally as John spoke.

"John your plan will lay off teachers. The state teachers union isn't going to take it lying down. They have a way of making their opinions felt."

"Governor, this year I am laying off staff because of the terrible economy and the fiscal condition we all find ourselves in." John wanted to be cautious here, not overly blaming the state for the layoffs, even though they were a major cause. "I would propose to the union, if they'll listen, a no layoff provision going forward as long as we gain needed flexibility on staff assignment. We can shrink the staff through attrition over the next six years. The state could help if a retirement system incentive were offered."

"You'll want a lot of flexibility given what you have described to me. Mr. Commissioner, where do you stand on all of this?"

"Governor Pickering, I agree with Dr. Handler, we must take a different course. I can't guarantee he's on the right path, but like him I feel if we stay on the current one we are destined to continue to fail."

"I can't say it's a real vote of confidence gentlemen. You are asking me to put my office behind something that may work, but sure as hell will be controversial as well as a big gamble. Not sure I am in the game for it."

"Governor Pickering, may I take five minutes to share my thoughts with you about the proposal to lure Subaru's new plant here." He now had the Governor's full attention. John told him about the state funding an educational center, how this could be tied to the model for a different junior and senior year of high school. He also shared how he would propose creating a different kind of 2 plus 2 program with the community college. He also shared his ideas on how this would link to the storefront training centers and the role technology could play in all of it.

When he was finished, he gave John a long quiet look. "Well you sure as hell don't lack for ideas! I must say it has been a stimulating breakfast. Let's see if you have any luck getting the unions on board with your plan, or if Subaru bites on your ideas. If either of those happen, then let's talk over a longer working lunch."

John was encouraged and challenged by the conversation. He was also thrilled by the Commissioner's support. "Thank you for your support and help in there. I hope we don't let you down."

"I know you'll give it a shot. I will do my best to protect your back. But remember, I have my own foes inside the Department and people do play out their agendas. Let's be sure to talk every week and see if we can make a go of things. Maybe you are in the right place at the right time to make things happen. Work on the Subaru idea. It has a lot of political traction. It could make an enormous difference in how things go with the Governor."

CHAPTER 76

'SECOND LOOK'

Andrea was concerned about her children and the upcoming school closing. After talking with her mom she decided she needed to do something. It was Monday morning and it seemed like as good a time as any to talk with Ma'am. Andrea walked into the main office knowing things were not the same. Even Janet chose sides and spoke to Ma'am only as the much as the job required. She also kept Sue Jones informed on what happened in the office. It was a quiet and unpleasant setting, nobody lingered much and few staff members talked with Ma'am. Into this morgue Andrea was now venturing. She smiled and said good morning to Janet asking to see Ma'am. "Go ahead, she's in there."

Andrea knocked lightly on the old oak door casing. Ma'am looked up, smiled and motioned for Andrea to come in. "Like always, I can tell you have something on your mind," Ma'am said with as much of a smile as she could muster these days.

"I do. I am worried we have not started any kind of planning for School #3's closing. I think we need to do some things to remember the school and help the children move on. I know things around here aren't the same, but we all have a responsibility to do something. I'm willing to try to get something started, if it's okay with you."

"It's more than okay. But you will be stepping into a lot of mud puddles when you do."

"I know things are tense and there will be people upset we are even talking like this, but the children are going to be the victims. This school with its history deserves a special send-off, especially if it's going to be torn down. I want to try."

Ma'am could see the level of conviction in Andrea's face. She had no doubt this young woman was going to do all she could to help plan something special. "I want you to keep me up to date on the planning Andrea. I will do all I can to help you. But getting started, I think you will be pretty much on your own."

"I understand and will keep you in the loop."

Before leaving Janet stopped her. "I want to help. You are right the children and school deserve this. No matter how mad I am about things we need to do this. Let me talk with Sue Jones on it and see how she sees things. If she agrees it will go a long way. If not, it will be very hard for many of the folks to go against their union on it."

"Thanks Janet. Somehow I knew I could count on your help. I'm glad you'll talk to Sue. I think you have a much better chance than I do of getting her to help."

"Sue loves this school. When she thinks about it, I believe she'll agree we need to do something special."

Leaving the office, it was the first time in more than a month Andrea's step was lighter going up the stairs to her room. She felt good she'd acted on her convictions. She decided there was more to do today. But first she had to prepare for the children as they'd be bounding up the stairs in little more than a half-hour.

Because most everyone stayed in their rooms, Andrea had time to prepare without interruption. It was five minutes before the bell when she stepped into Bea's room. Pam Kilborn, standing outside her door, noticed this and scowled at her as she went by. Bea was the teacher most despised now by her colleagues. Anyone talking with her was quickly dismissed by the rest of the staff. Even Andrea would pay a price for stepping into her room, despite the fact the staff knew how close they were.

"My goodness girl, what are you doin' in this room?"

"I came to share an idea with you." For the next couple of minutes Andrea laid out her thoughts.

"I think you are doin' a good thing. Not sure how it will go down, but a good thing. Now get outta here before people start thinkin' you conspirin' with the enemy."

As the morning turned into lunch time Andrea often found herself eating with the children. Today was no exception. The faculty room was now far from a pleasant respite from a morning's teaching. The talk was always the same and the mood was consistently depressing. Following lunch Andrea planned a new activity. The children had scored poorly on the state's document based questions test, really struggling to look at graphs, maps, cartoons or other items and use them to answer the questions. She gave them lots of practice both before and since the test, but they still had difficulty looking for details. Her idea would be fun and may help them become better at looking for clues and facts.

After lunch and 20 minutes out on the playground, Andrea's kids returned and settled. She quickly divided the class into seven four person teams. She scanned a page from *People* magazine called 'Second Look.' This was a page where two nearly identical pictures were placed side-by-side on the same page. Ten subtle differences between the two pictures existed and readers were encouraged to look for them. Andrea told the kids they'd have 15 minutes to look at the pictures projected and see if they could find the ten differences.

The children went to work, excited by the challenge. It was amazing to watch them discuss what they saw while a recorder in each group wrote down their answers. The first few differences in the photos were more obvious than others. After five minutes most groups were searching for the toughest ones. After 15 minutes, Andrea checked the group's listings. The best group had eight and the poorest had five. They summarized the results and then as a whole group circled each on the projected picture.

It was great to hear one of her shy students, Falto Perez, asking, "Can we do more of them?"

"I promise we will do this again soon." Andrea wished she could share this with her colleagues as she thought it could be a good way to help students become more discerning when looking at documents. She planned, after several more experiences with 'Second Look' pics, to return to documents and ask the teams to do the questions. She hoped this strategy would help kids both enjoy the challenge afforded by the questions and not be so intimidated by documents too often seeming foreign to them.

Of course, the second part of the struggle kids had with these state test questions was their poor reading skills. This was a totally different issue. Here Andrea's training in reading instruction convinced her the children needed more language development experiences. So many of her children had a limited vocabulary and they lacked sound decoding strategies. When they could decode a word they had little ability to gain meaning from its context in a sentence. While she did not agree with all of the ad hoc committee's proposals, she did agree starting the children at a younger age and extending their school year were both important steps that could make a significant difference. But she was concerned the proposal was seriously flawed in that it did not include enough trained educators to deliver early life instruction to poverty's children.

CHAPTER 77

BETWEEN A ROCK
AND A HARD PLACE

Board member Emily Garza had a conversation with her district's union president. He was open about the needs of teachers and her important role in protecting their jobs. Emily felt uneasy after the conversation. A few days later she got a call from Shantell asking to meet with her for coffee at a local Starbucks following work. After the two conversations Emily was now talking with Don Karst. They were at Don's house on Saturday morning as she expressed her misgivings.

"Don, I don't know if we are doing the right thing. We have a lot of upset people. Shantell told me all the union presidents are meeting and the teachers are pressing for a no confidence vote in Dr. Handler's leadership. She told me even the administrator's union is discussing it."

"Emily, I am hearing the same buzz. But what are the options here? Suppose, for the sake of a conversation, we joined with Shantell and Sara and fired Dr. Handler. It doesn't change the financial crisis we are in. It won't change the test scores and we will likely be excused from office by the State Education Department. We have the warning remember from the Commissioner."

"Shantell says it's a load of crap. She says Dr. Thomas has talked with people at the Department and nothing will happen. I am not sure what to think Don. I'm not sleeping, the stress of all of this is getting to me."

"Emily, being a board member is a thankless and pressure-filled job."

"So what are you going to do?"

"Right now I am going to stay the course. I believe Dr. Handler is making the calls he has to under the circumstances. However, I don't know what his long-term plans are yet. I think we have to be sure of his plan before we support it. That's where I am holding my card, long-term. But in the short-term we have to cut staff and programs, there's no choice since our aid and revenues have dried up."

"I wish I had your confidence; I am not sure what I will do."

"Emily," Don's voice cracked as he said her name, "you have to hold on, you can't jump ship now! The district is depending on us to help get through this crisis."

"Shantell and Sara think Dr. Thomas is the right person for the job. She has strong connections to State Ed. She won't cut as many teachers and she'll work to get the scores up. They feel she's the one to move us forward and a change in leadership needs to be done soon."

Don could see Emily was vacillating.. After she left, he immediately picked up the phone. "Terrell we've got trouble!" For the next ten minutes he summarized the conversation with Emily.

After they talked for nearly an hour, Terrell agreed to contact John and tell him what was happening. John was not surprised by Terrell's call and his fears Emily could change sides. As a result, John asked Terrell to schedule a full work session with the Board as soon as possible after the upcoming spring break.

"What are you going to do?" Terrell asked.

"Terrell, I am not sure, but I will not go down without swinging. I am going to have to put things on the line sooner than I planned. I want to lay out the full strategy for change and improvement. At least then we can see where everyone stands. This is not going to be easy, considering all the loose ends in the process at this point."

John decided he had to take a big risk. He called Cliff Greer and asked if he could meet with him.

"Is it your turn to have an off-the-record conversation with me now, Dr. Handler?"

"Cliff, it can be on-the-record or not, your call. I don't want to meet here in my office though. There's too many who will say something to others if we're seen meeting."

"How about meeting here in my office? Come in tonight about seven. There's not much scheduled here since spring break is only a couple of days away."

"Great, I'll be by in a few hours. Just hear me out and I'll listen to you as well. Then let's see if we have enough common ground to continue talking either one-on-one or with others."

"Okay, but like you said, it's my call if it's on-the-record. "

"Yes, it is."

CHAPTER 78

THE FIRST
CONVERSATION

John arrived at the union office building before seven. It was in a three story office complex off Main Street. The union occupied all of the first floor. Cliff was waiting for him in the lobby. He greeted John warmly. "Welcome to my world Dr. Handler."

John smiled, "Glad you let me in!"

They walked down a short corridor lined with certificates for one award or another. A large framed poster was displayed in the lobby encouraging teachers to build their power by donating to the political action fund. It was a clear reminder to John of the tremendous sway the state teachers union had in the capital.

In a moment John was entering Cliff's office. It was spacious, but not ostentatious or extravagantly decorated. Three comfortable chairs were placed in front of Cliff's mahogany conference style desk. On the credenza behind his desk Cliff had pictures of his three boys and his wife and parents. It was a comfortable space, busy and well-organized.

Cliff offered John a cup of coffee which he readily accepted. "Well here we are, you must have something important on your mind to come and sit with me in this office." Cliff was enjoying the moment and he had a teasing lilt in his voice helping John relax.

"I need to convince you what I am proposing as a new plan makes sense and is worthy of your support. It is a real change from the way we are doing business now. But in the long-term I believe it can make a big difference not only for kids but for the teachers who work with them."

"John, I am willing to listen, but I got to tell you up front it will be a tough sell, not just to me but to my members. The layoffs on the deck are hurting a lot of people and there's little support for anything you might propose. I've got real pressure from my members and other union leaders to take a no confidence vote in your leadership. Most around here, including almost a majority of your board, want you out. So why should we help you?"

"You shouldn't help me. You need to make a clear-headed judgment on whether or not what we are planning is in the best interest of teachers. But I must tell you, you are going to have to look through a long-term lens. In the short-term there's nothing we can do about the upcoming budget year and the necessary layoffs. Unless that powerful lobby of yours can bring more state aid to the table, there's no way we can prevent a serious retrenchment from happening. It's hell on all of us. We are all victims of this fiscal crisis and I see no answers on the horizon to improve the aid picture. In fact if it continues, I don't know how we survive. I am the scapegoat, no matter who sits in my chair layoffs, big ones, are inevitable next year."

"Dr. Thomas certainly takes a different view. She tells me she'd reduce sports, change the mileage on transportation so kids had to walk further, she'd reduce the cleaning staff and cut administration before she'd make any classroom cuts. She also said she'd never close Jefferson and what you have proposed is draconian. She claims it's an excuse for your plans to radically change things. I know you two don't get along, but she's putting out something which plays much better with my members than your current cuts. She also has the support of two board members, that's been made clear to me. I'm sharing this with you John, not to break confidences but to point out what's lined up against anything you may share and the tough place it puts me in. It will be very difficult for this union to support any changes you might propose when we know the status quo has such strong support."

"Cliff business history is filled with examples where holding onto the status quo looks good and then the company is only a shadow of what it once was. Look at Kodak, they thought the business was film not imaging, they hung on and now they're simply not a player anymore and thousands who worked for the company now find themselves out of a job. What makes you think education is any different from Kodak?"

"John, we could debate the issue of the need for change in education forever. I understand your rationale, but let's talk about the details. I want to know what you have in mind and I will tell you candidly what I think and where my members will stand on it."

"Cliff, I think we are failing the children we are charged to educate. The data, tests and measures currently used along with the dropout rates in our district are a clear testament to that. If we think the solution is we do more of the same thing, I believe we'll continue to fail no matter how much money we throw at it."

"John, you are saying if we place more teachers in classrooms, dramatically lower class sizes it won't make a difference? I think there are many who would take issue with you."

"Cliff, if we could add the number of teachers it would take, you know in our city alone that would add tens of millions of dollars to our budget. That's a reality I don't see on any horizon. There's no political will for that, and there's no way to pay for it unless this country dramatically reprioritized its spending. It's not going to happen. So we can tinker at the margins and continue to fail way too many of the children. The reality I see is one you need to at least consider being viable."

"In this office, just the two of us, it may be the reality. But it is one we are trying hard to change. You are asking me to concede defeat and take a different turn in the road. Not sure any union is going to do that yet John, least of all this one."

"Cliff, let me assume your most basic agenda is to save the jobs of your current members. Suppose we talk about a different layoff concept connected to whatever else I am going to propose we do. "I'm listening."

"Okay, this year I don't believe we can ask the community to accept more than a 4% property tax increase. For the sake of this conversation, I am going to ask you to support the number publicly. In turn I will work with the leaders of every union, as a team, to develop the necessary proposals to meet that target; including whatever pressure you all can bring to increase our aid and reduce the layoffs. But Cliff, you own the number with me and you participate actively and publicly in whatever is needed to get there; period end of conversation. Next, I will agree to a contractually binding statement giving the union the right to veto any layoff of teaching staff greater than 2% in any budget year for the next four budget cycles beyond next year's. In turn, I want the flexibility to assign staff for their six and a half hour work day any consecutive hours between 6:00 AM and 9:00PM Monday through Saturday. We can talk about the details, but there are the broad strokes."

"Damn it John, what the hell are you thinking? I want to know what you are planning to do!"

"Cliff, I am willing to go into all the details. In fact, I'd like to have Carl and Jerry with me after the break to do that with any team you want to bring. But before I do, I have to know, given what you've heard, you are willing to discuss it in good faith. Otherwise there's no sense in our meeting."

"John I can't make an assurance here tonight. But I will share it with my Executive Board."

"So Cliff, when they ask you your opinion on what to do will you say reject it and push for the status quo or will you support serious consideration of something different?"

"John, I am not going to tell you right now where I stand. I need time to think on this. What you said is not what I was expecting and I thought we'd have a conversation that went nowhere. I can say you are making me reflect, that's more than I thought would happen. But changing work hours, the work week and allowing more assignment flexibility, you are shooting for the stars. You have to realize it is not going to get much support from my members or me."

CHAPTER 79

DIXIE

The long drive gave Andrea time to clear her head and let go of all the tension and mixed emotions she was feeling about School #3. She was surprised by the sense of relief growing with each passing mile and realized how much she was looking forward to spring break.

Jason lived in a loft apartment inside the city limits. As Andrea entered Montgomery she found herself looking at it with a critical eye thinking, 'Could I live here?' It was a place steeped in history. The Civil War and the civil rights movement 100 years later were in the grain of the place. The flowers and southern charm of the area were apparent as she drove along tree lined streets. The magnolias were blooming and the scent of spring was wafting through car windows opened wide for the first time in several months. The city's aura was unmistakably different from anything she'd experienced up north.

She had texted Jason when she stopped on the outskirts of Montgomery to get gas and stretch. He knew roughly how far away she was and he was standing on the sidewalk when Andrea arrived. When she saw him, her heart skipped more than a beat. She missed him terribly and found her hands sweating on the steering wheel as she guided her Civic into a nearby parking spot. Jason was beside her car door before she turned the car off.

Across the street an older woman stood with a grey poodle resting at her feet. The woman had on a pair of khaki slacks and a loose fitting pale blue top. Her grey hair seemed to almost match that of her dog's. She had an inquisitive eye and a clear view of Jason and Andrea across the street. She watched as Andrea popped out of her car and fell into Jason's waiting embrace. She could see these two young people were powerfully connected as their embrace moved from a long hug to a passionate kiss. Even her grey poodle seemed to take notice as the two lovers held each other in their arms. The woman gently tugged the leash, "Come on little guy, the show is over for us. Just starting for them I think," she said under her breath.

Jason gathered Andrea's things and the two moved quickly over the sidewalk to Jason's second floor apartment. When Andrea stepped inside her eyes were filled with interesting shapes and smells. The building was an old civil war era warehouse. The heavy ceiling beams were roughly hewn and added great character. The wide planked floors had experienced a rich history she could only begin to imagine. "I love it Jason!" This place is a wow." She walked to one of the nearby double hung windows. It was new, but designed to blend with the building. Through the clean glass she looked over the street and could see the old brick sidewalk. There she noticed an older woman walking her dog. She wondered for a second who she was and what brought her to this time and place. The charm of it all was capturing her.

After turning around she saw Jason place her suitcase in the bedroom. He thought she might be hungry and she could see he set out the makings for some sandwiches. "Give me the full tour; I want to see everything before we eat."

Jason led her through the first of two bedrooms. He converted the smaller one into an office. A makeshift desk had two concrete block sides and spanning them was a heavy piece of old glass. The office chair was simulated black cane. It looked expensive and comfortable. Jason noticed her eye falling on it, "I spend a lot of time in here talking with clients on the phone and doing paperwork. I needed a good chair."

Continuing to examine the room she noticed the outside wall was constructed of old red brick with a double window sitting off center. Jason put imitation wood blinds over the windows. "That needs some work Jason." On the floor was a sisal rug. The other walls were painted beige. Jason had no pictures hanging on any of them, nor did he have any book cases, just a four drawer metal file cabinet undercutting the ambiance of the room. "So far you get a C- for decorating and an A+ for the place. What else do you have in store for me to see?"

Jason showed her the bathroom. It had a big glass enclosed shower, but no bathtub. The sink was mounted on what appeared to be an old table. The floor tile was a rough slate. Above the sink was a large wall mirror with a three bulb chrome fixture. Three ceiling lights made the room bright. "The bathroom is workable, but no tub and no linen closet makes it a bit less than I would have liked. But you can't get everything you want I guess."

"It works, but I agree it is just adequate. Knowing how the rest of the place looks I am surprised they didn't do more with it."

Andrea noticed a second door off the bathroom which she assumed led to the bedroom. She opened the door and took a deep breath, "Oh my God Jason this is fabulous!" The door led to a large room with two French doors that opened to a wrought iron balcony looking out onto the street below. Two of the walls were made of the old brick and the ceiling had rough beams, like those in the living room. It was a dramatic space Andrea instantly called her favorite room in the apartment. "We have to spend time in this room" she said with a wink and sparkle in her eye. "But, I have to admit I am famished and need to eat first."

She playfully bounced from the room and headed back to the kitchen. It had a long single row of cabinets with stainless steel appliances. The counters were rich brown granite. An attractive island separated the kitchen from a nearby nook with a small wood table and four chairs. The island had an overhang and two backless wood stools were parked beneath it. At the island they shared their first meal together in Alabama.

After lunch Andrea looked at Jason, "I think I'd like to take another look at the bedroom." Jason laughed, took her hand and they walked back to the room where they spent the next hour reconnecting. Lying in bed with her head on Jason's shoulder, Andrea recognized there was something more important in her life than teaching.

Over the next two days they walked and visited places throughout the city. They had lunch in *The Alley*, walked along the Alabama River and visited Dr. Martin Luther King's Dexter Avenue Baptist Church. History was readily evident along many of Montgomery's streets, especially as the former Capital of the Confederacy. "Jason the city is beautiful. It's so different from home."

"I want to take you out to dinner tonight at the Olive Room. It is a great restaurant here in the River Region. I made reservations at 7:30 so we can walk there."

The rest of the day flew by and before long they were walking down Montgomery Street to the restaurant. Andrea loved the décor and the quiet nook where they sat. Once they had their drinks Jason looked at Andrea. As he did she felt goose bumps rising. He looked across at her, "Andrea, I love you and want to make a life together." He gently moved a ring box across the table.

Andrea opened it and saw a sparkling diamond engagement ring that took her breath away. Jason was watching intently and when she looked up he smiled and said, "Please marry me. You will make me the luckiest guy on earth."

"Oh Jason, we will both be the luckiest people. I love you and will marry you." The evening seemed to fly by. The meal was wonderful and the staff knew what was taking place. The service was fabulous and the night would be one they'd remember for a lifetime.

It was a glorious evening as they walked hand-in-hand back to the loft. "Andrea it is a beautiful area and the opportunities here are terrific. I thought we could look at some schools. My office has set up a visit to one for us. I am not sure what we'll see, but there's politics and poverty here too just like back home."

"It will be great to see some of the schools here. I wonder how different things are. Bea says poverty knows no boundaries so I suspect many things are the same for children no matter where they live."

CHAPTER 80

HARD NEWS

When Andrea arrived home she had a large pile of mail awaiting her. In the pile was an official looking envelope from the city school district. When she opened it she found her formal layoff letter. Her hands trembled as she read the words telling her she'd no longer have a job at the close of the school year. While holding it she wondered how many of her colleagues received the same letter. She'd soon learn nearly 300 had.

Letter in hand, she sat in her chair reflecting on all that transpired to this point in her first year as a teacher. The children came to mind and she went through a mental checklist thinking about each of them, knowing they would always be a part of her memory. She also thought of Bea. She knew this wonderful woman had been and still was her mentor. How lucky she was to have her guidance. She knew that her teaching skills were growing due, in part, to Bea's advice. She was sad many teachers new to the classroom did not have the good fortune to have a person like Bea to help them.

As she sat, her mind drifted back to her students. Her favorite, though she tried not to show it at school, was Dedra. Since the first adventurous trip to Wal-Mart she and Dedra had taken several other trips to different places around the city. Next week they were going to hear the philharmonic. Dedra was excited by this latest opportunity to be with her teacher. Over several months Andrea and others had been able to help this little girl find her way back after having seen her brother die on the cold pavement.

Then there was James Tharp. The special education committee process labeled him 'Emotionally Disturbed'. His classroom outbursts were difficult to handle and Andrea was at a loss on what to do when he became aggressive. Both she and Bea had run out of ideas. This little boy was lost in her fourth grade classroom. His needs were so great it seemed hard to fathom how any setting could address them. Andrea sighed, as she knew his future was bleak and his violent actions would soon be played out on streets eager to absorb and even cultivate them.

Michael Malkin was another youngster her mental checklist paused upon. He was incredibly bright and despite his terrible surroundings Michael was an able student. But what would become of him? She challenged him in her classroom and Michael responded enthusiastically. But the streets and an older brother also taught him different life lessons. She wondered, 'Would Michael become a bright gang leader or would he go on to college and make a much different life for himself?' No way of knowing the road he'd choose at this point.

For the next hour Andrea sat in her living room chair reflecting on her life as a teacher. That life was never far away from her daily consciousness, but now with school about to start up again after the break she had to put lesson preparation back on the front burner. She knew she was on the home stretch to June with much to do between now and then.

Before she knew it, it was Monday morning and school was back in session. Andrea stopped by the school office on the way to her classroom. Janet McGee motioned to her when she came in, "I want to give you a head's up. One of your students moved over the break and we got a call first thing this morning to tell us she won't be attending School #3 anymore."

Andrea looked at Janet wondering who it was. Janet looked at her knowing the news would be a blow. "It's Dedra," she said. "Her mom said they are moving to Detroit to be with her brother. They are leaving later today."

The layoff notice had been expected and she coped with that bad news. But this was a body blow she didn't see coming. She sat on the student bench and felt the tears coming, knowing she could not stop them.

Ma'am came out from her office after Janet told her what was happening. She gently guided Andrea to a seat and closed her office door. "Andrea, losing a student you've given your all to is rough. This is a new experience for you and the pain and sense of loss you are feeling are hard for many to understand, especially those who don't work with children every day. But you've made a difference for that little girl. Don't you ever forget it."

Andrea looked at Ma'am and smiled through her tears. "Thank you . I guess I wasn't prepared for how kids and their lives come and go. Nobody taught us this in our college courses. The depth of feeling we get, and the attachment we have to these children. Then it ends. I don't want to ever harden my heart to it, but there's another part of me which wants to so I can protect myself from the pain I am feeling right now."

"You feel the pain. Don't ever harden your heart to it. When we give all we have to children and don't leave anything left behind, then we know we've done our best for them. I know you have to get ready for the day, but why don't you drop by Bea's room before you start. She'll be there for you if you need a break and so will I."

"Thank you. I may need to take you up on it. Knowing Dedra won't be running up those stairs this morning or any other day hurts." Andrea got up and headed to her mailbox before going upstairs to her classroom. Along with the usual mail, she saw a notice from Sue Jones calling a union meeting after school. She wondered what the agenda was. "Well no time to think about it now. The kids will be here in less than 30 minutes," she said to herself as she left the main office.

Andrea was still wiping her eyes as she walked down the hall to the stairs. Fred noticed her, "I'm sorry Miss Bauer, it ain't right you got a lay-off notice over vacation."

Andrea forced a smile and while not breaking stride said, "Thanks Fred. I know lots of people must have gotten them besides me. It is a sad time." She realized the union meeting's agenda was likely focused on this topic and the district's proposed budget.

Before she knew it she was at the top of the stairs and noticed Bea was standing nearby. "Been waitin' for you girl. First, I gotta give you a hug and see the ring your man gave ya. Does he know how lucky he is?" For the first time this morning Andrea laughed. She gave Bea a huge hug and held out her hand. "Bless me look at the thing on your finger! Your man spent some serious money on that ring honey. You two together, well it makes my day."

Andrea then stepped back. Looking at Bea she wondered if she knew about Dedra. "I can read those eyes of yours girl. Our sweet Dedra isn't comin' to school this mornin'. I know how upsettin' it is for you. But life here at School #3 has to go on and you got a whole lot of children comin' this mornin' who love their Miss B. You keep that in mind and we'll talk at lunch."

It was only a few short minutes later when the sound of excited feet and voices filled the stairwell. Children were coming enthusiastically up the stairs. Andrea found herself welcoming the sound and looking forward to seeing them. Life truly did go on and she knew she'd draw strength from the children. For a brief moment, she thought to herself what a wonderful privilege it was to be a teacher. This thought melted into the moment as the first child of the day, Alvin Park gave her a warm hug.

CHAPTER 81

SEEKING NORMALCY

'How quickly Monday's work day passed.' Andrea thought as she headed to the after school union meeting. During her morning literacy conversation she listened attentively to the children as they talked about what they did over spring break. Only one child took a vacation trip. The others all shared family events and time spent with friends. While no longer a surprise, Andrea was reminded their impoverished circumstances afforded few opportunities to see and do new things over a school break.

Andrea was jarred from her thoughts by the dower atmosphere present in the school library where the union meeting was about to start. Sue Jones stepped to the center and asked everyone to take a seat. "Will the people in this room who got a layoff letter over vacation raise your hands?" Along with Andrea, Colleen and sixth grade teacher Amy Fontaine complied with her request.

"It is awful to think anyone here is getting let go, but the bastards downtown sent out letters over spring break besides! We all must let them know how we feel about things. The budget being proposed raises class size, closes schools and does nothing but hurt children. We must take a stand against this. Last night all the union reps got a call from a member of the Executive Board. My call was from Cliff Greer. The union is opening a Facebook page with all kinds of information about what is happening and how damaging it is to our schools. We want you to 'Like' this and get as many other people to do it as possible. We are going to use this and other means to let our Board and administration know how people feel about these proposals. I want to ask our three colleagues to tell us about their letters and their thoughts about it."

Colleen stood and spoke first. "I can't begin to tell you how shocked I was to get a letter from downtown over vacation telling me my job was finished. There was no indication we'd receive it then and no support for me from my colleagues since we were all away. I..." Colleen's voice trailed and she sat back down not able to hold back her emotions any further.

Amy stood next. "I agree with everything Colleen said. I am so angry. I cannot begin to tell you the depth of my feelings. Those people downtown are heartless!"

Andrea felt all eyes turn to her as she was expected to say something. She hesitated a moment then knew she had to stand and speak. "I was one of the last people hired before school started, so I knew my job here was finished as soon as they said layoffs were coming. But I was surprised to get my layoff letter over spring break. I am going to miss teaching in the city with you." Andrea had much more running through her mind as she sat. But she judged it wasn't the time to talk about the kids and closing of School #3.

Sue picked up where the three women left off. "We all have to speak up. This is a time when we need to be one voice united for the children and their future. We can't let the administration get away with this. Dr. Handler and his staff are ruining education in this district."

Tom Dowling rose to his feet. As one of the few males in the building his perspective and seniority were respected. "I have listened to all of what Sue and others have said. I agree the budget is harmful to children and we need to do all we can to oppose it. I will do my part. But, we have shunned Ma'am, Bea and Myrna long enough. I think it is inevitable School #3 will close. I hate the thought of it, but I think it is a reality. We've talked about the children and their needs. Right now they need us to be working together in their best interests. There will be a lot to do between now and when this school closes in June. So let's focus our efforts on getting a better budget and not fighting with ourselves over a new pre-school and early childhood plan the Board hasn't even considered yet."

Sue Jones could barely contain herself. "Tom I can't believe what you said! We need to be tougher than ever on them. They are a part of the reason these women will lose their jobs and you want us to ignore it. No way!"

Andrea stood to speak. "Bea saved my life. I will not be silent. Ma'am was the first person I saw at the hospital. She also comforted me when I was trying to make a decision to return to teaching at School #3. She was there for me. While the plan being proposed may lead to big changes and layoffs down the line, it is not the reason any of us got our notices. I agree with Tom, the children need and deserve better from us. We are the adults in this setting and we need to behave much better."

Her fourth grade teammate Pam Kilborn rose from her seat. "Andrea you have reason to be beholding to those women, I don't. I totally agree with Sue. We need to continue to let them know their thinking is unacceptable. I for one don't ever plan to talk with them unless the situation compels it."

The room held its breath as Myrna spoke from the back of the library. No one saw her quietly enter and sit. "I realize many of you no longer wish to speak to me. I can see how angry you are with the new plan for teaching early primary grade and pre-school children. But, I bet everyone in this room was asked at some point in the hiring process why they wanted to teach at this level. I am also pretty confident most of us answered, 'Because we love young children.' We certainly didn't sign on knowing we'd become wealthy. I don't know if the new ideas are better than what we have. Time will be the judge if they are put in motion. But, I support the plan because of my answer to that interview question. I love young learners and want to do the best I can for them even if it means making some unpleasant choices." Having said her piece Myrna calmly went out the door into the empty hallway.

Betty Folger, a third grade teacher spoke next, "I think she said if we love kids we'd go along with the plan. The fact we aren't agreeing with her must mean we don't love them! I support Sue and Pam. We must continue shunning these know-it-alls!"

Tom and Andrea looked at each wondering if any support existed in the room for their point of view. The answer came from an unexpected person. It was Amy Fontaine who chose to speak again.

"That heartless bastard, Carl Gardner, gets no respect from me. Dr Handler doesn't get much either for his gutless slash and burn budget proposal. I'm losing my livelihood. So are two other people in this room. The rest of you are going to be relocated, and the work will be taking place in a different school, but not only will you still get a paycheck, you are also scheduled to get a raise. How many of you are willing to forsake a raise so we can keep our jobs? Sue will you do that and how about you Pam?" Both women lowered their eyes but said nothing. "My union wants me to do all these actions to help restore the budget, but when push comes to shove people won't make a personal sacrifice to help. So tomorrow morning I start talking again to all my colleagues in this building. The children and I have a right to have the final few months of our time here at School #3 to be the best they can be. I hate the smallness and self-serving anger I see and I can no longer condone it." It was a moment. The silence in the room was deafening.

Art teacher Jane Emert broke the quiet. In her soft manner she spoke thoughtfully, "I see we have very different feelings about this whole thing. I am not sure what the right answer is. I am not going to judge anyone else as they decide what to do next. I think we all agree the proposed budget for next year is awful. We should do what our union is asking and oppose it and seek to get others involved in opposing it. I love this school and don't want to see it close. I think we all wish the same thing. So we can agree to continue our efforts to fight it. But the silent treatment issue needs time for people to sort out. I think we have to accept each person's decision on it and let things go forward. Otherwise, we are going to be badly divided and fighting ourselves, like we have been for the last half hour."

Others around the room nodded their heads. It was a messy compromise but Sue was smart enough to let it stand as the last word on things and adjourned the meeting.

CHAPTER 82

JUST THINKING

The three women were sitting together in the Ma'am's office after school on Tuesday. Myrna had deep circles under her eyes and her lack of sleep was evident. As she began to speak her voice trembled, "I am upset by all the turmoil here Dorothy. Even though I think we are doing the right thing, it has certainly unsettled things in ways I guess I didn't see coming."

"I know Myrna, I know. We've been given the cold shoulder. But things seem to be thawing a little bit since the break."

Bea leaned forward speaking, "Well I for one don't think there's much we can be doin' to make 'em feel better about things. We gotta suck it up and keep movin' forward. But you been doin' lots of thinkin' on this, so say what's on your mind Myrna."

"There are the obvious reasons, layoffs and the plan. But there's more to it I suppose. Each school has its own culture; its own history as a place. When you work here you become a part of the culture. We eat together, share stories and truths about our families; we suffer through loss and celebrate the joy of new babies. All of it becomes a part of us. Doing this work together makes us a family. The closing of our school is loaded with grief and separation. It's something we haven't attended to yet."

Ma'am nodded, "I know what you are saying. Andrea came to me before the break asking for my okay to get the ball rolling on what we are going to do to acknowledge we are closing."

Myrna grinned, "Now there's one who has her head on straight, one good teacher too."

"Yup the girl's got the gift, for sure."

Dorothy took a deep breath. She then took a sip of coffee noticeably cooler than it was when she poured it 20 minutes ago. Both Bea and Myrna knew Dorothy had something forming in her mind and waited patiently for her to share her next thought. "Bea you said she's got the gift and we all nodded. What do you think the gift is?"

"The way Andrea relates to children. It's natural. I mean she has a way with 'em."

Myrna added, "I think it's more than the relationship with the kids. I think those with exceptional skills as teachers also love learning themselves. They really like what they teach. I also often see how comfortable they are in their own skin."

Dorothy paused, "Let's say that's really it. The gift we are talking about has no formula and there's no one way it's done. So what does all this have to do with our plan?" Pondering her own question, Dorothy went on with an answer for the women to consider. "The things we've been saying are the essence of the gift are not tied to any college or specific way of doing things. Does everyone have to have a Bachelor's degree in order to have them?"

Myrna smiled, "No, but that's the price of admission to running your own classroom Dorothy. At the same time, we can't underestimate the importance of college training. Good teaching requires good diagnostic skills and a sound knowledge of pedagogy. Those skills are earned with a lot of hard work at the college level."

Dorothy smiled, "Okay, there's an art and science part. Lots of folks say you need both of them to make a great teacher. So our plan has to include great teachers. We've never said they aren't important. But how many of them is the question we are trying to answer. Can we wrap around them folks who are good at the art of building relationships? That is so important when working with kids."

Dorothy returned the conversation to School #3 closing plans. "We need to get behind the planning effort. It may also help us bridge some of the anger and hurt we are coping with. Let's help Andrea and the others where we can."

CHAPTER 83

WHAT CAN WE DO?

On Thursday night Andrea and Bea were sitting with beers in her front room. After the rough union meeting, things changed a bit for the better. While cold shoulders and raw emotional edges were often in play, you could sense the struggle underway to find common ground. Bea and Andrea were reflecting on this.

"Well, you certainly called it when you said folks would not like the plan! It's been real tough on everyone. Our school family is fallin' apart and too many of us are stewin' in our own space when we need to be thinkin' about the children."

"Bea, we do have to get our heads around what needs to be done for our school. But you can't lead that. For once you are going to have to sit on the sidelines and let others take the reins. There are still a lot of hard feelings about the plan and you are in the middle of all of it."

"Oh, now who is tryin' to be the mentor here?"

"Bea, it's no joke. You can't make light of this! You know people are upset and they are not talking. But you don't hear all the things I do. People are feeling like their work has been devalued by what you are pro- posing. You are putting people in major roles with little or no training. That is not going down well even with me."

"What do you mean, even with you?"

"Bea, I get the importance of relationships and better connections to the neighborhood. I really like the proposed school's physical plan. But the changes come at the expense of teachers and their jobs. You must see that."

"We have to go down a different road Andrea. The current ways aren't workin'."

Andrea held up her hand, a gesture Bea scowled at. "I get all the reasons, but because you say them doesn't mean you are right with the solutions. In fact, many smart people think you are out of line and things won't get better. Bea, you didn't seek anyone's opinion on this. You ran your own race with a small group of mostly like minded people and then you've been moving forward with it on your own. Not many of us have ownership of the ideas or even had a chance to voice our opinions constructively. The only options open to us are to oppose it or accept it."

Bea sat back reflecting on Andrea's words. She understood they were heartfelt and not expressed with anger but concern. Perhaps for the first time, she needed to think deeply about what others were expressing and not disregard it as uninformed thinking. 'Maybe they didn't have it right.'

"You've given me some things to think on. Not sure what to do about it though 'cause the horse has left the barn. But let's do some thinkin', at least here, about the school closin' and what we should be doin'.

"I have been talking quietly with people. Tom Dowling thinks the fifth grade kids should play a major role since they are the oldest and have attended School #3 longer than any other kids."

"Hmm, we can't let the fifth grade children steal the show. Every grade, every child needs to do somethin', even if it is just movin' or singin' or readin', but they gotta do somethin'.

Andrea smiled, "I agree. Every grade has to play a part. Getting a planning committee together is going to take some arm twisting though. People are going to have to set aside some strong feelings and beliefs if we are going to get through this with the kids. Bea, I am going to have to take a more public position opposing the plan. I hope our closeness won't be hurt. Good friends can have different views. If I do that, I think people will let me take part in the planning. It will also position me to share ideas and suggestions from you and Myrna without getting you directly involved."

"Andrea, you are tryin' to tell me what I can and can't do here and you are new to the school. Me, I spent a long time here and I'm bein' shut out, even by you. Can't say I like it much."

"I know, but you have to trust me Bea. Do you trust me?"

Andrea expected the answer to be immediate, so when it wasn't she decided to sit. It was a bottom-line question needing an answer. If Bea needed to ponder an answer so be it.

"Andrea, it's not about trustin' you. It's about bein' shut out of the plannin' on one of the most important events ever at the school. It affects everyone!"

"But that's what you did with your committee! This time with all that's happened you do have to trust I will respect your ideas and share them. You have to give in on this Bea for the good of the children. The staff won't accept it any other way at this point."

"We gotta talk more on this over supper. This old girl is havin' real trouble sittin' in the back seat!"

"This way you're still in the car. Any other, you'll be looking for a ride!"

CHAPTER 84

WHAT IF?

When John left his meeting with Cliff he knew he had to meet with his Board and describe the full scope of what he was thinking. He had been heavy handed over the past several months. Despite the odds against it, he needed to see if he could get them behind the ideas. He called his Board president and asked Terrell to schedule a full-day workshop. They agreed it would be the Saturday after spring break. He had the week to get ready, not a lot of time but he knew what he had to do.

John spoke to the people he wanted to participate and knew they had a good understanding of their role. Each was willing to help and he was pleased with what they had in mind. What was unknown was whether or not, at the end of the day, it would further divide the Board or begin a reunification process. But no matter, it was his job to try and he realized the responsibility for the effort fell largely on his shoulders.

On Saturday, the weather was gloomy and overcast. The mood in the conference room was much the same. The body language of everyone underscored the depth of the challenge. Arms were crossed and the silence seemed deafening at times. The leadership team was there including Mary Jane which surprised her. But he remembered the old saying, 'Keep your friends close and your enemies even closer.' He hoped it was good advice. Dorothy was there as well as middle school principal, Zack James. The mayor, Jane Hueset would be joining them after lunch.

There'd be no PowerPoint presentations. John felt they'd lose an intimacy and directness if slides became the basis for conversation. Today he wanted people speaking to each other. Thus the room had a round table and everyone had a place to sit.

John looked forward to getting started. "I know many of us around the circle have different visions and beliefs about how we should get things done. In fact the tensions and intrigue have reached a high level. As superintendent, I have to accept responsibility for my part. In preparing for this meeting I asked myself what my most strongly held belief is about a school system's work. I realized, what we say in our vision statement goes to my core, and everyone's around this table." The body language, though still tense, changed subtly. "Over the years I've read many mission/vision statements and seen more than one strategic plan. They almost exclusively focus on the 'What' and 'How' questions, but rarely on the 'Why' one. They too often state a school's mission is to promote teaching excellence. But good teaching is simply a means to a higher end. I've seen countless committees formed by these plans. A great deal of effort is put forth to put a high shine on the status quo. Now, I am not condemning all these efforts, but as we share things this morning I want each of us to keep student learning in mind. Can we all agree on that?"

John paused. He knew if it was posed as a rhetorical question and if he moved on quickly, he would lose a moment for what he hoped would be the first consensus decision this group of players had made in a long time.

After what seemed like an eternity Terrell spoke, "John, I think we all agree this is our purpose. But, we have been flooded with emails and Facebook actions. It's been a tough week." Heads were nodding around the table. John wasn't sure which observation they were nodding in agreement to, but decided to press forward.

"All of us in this room know by whatever measures we want to use, state tests, discipline referrals, drop-out rates, you name it; we are failing. Not enough of our students are learning what they need to know and be able to do to be productive adults. It's not saying excellent teaching isn't going on. At times that is what makes our discussion challenging. Why is it we can do things well and yet have such terrible overall results? That question has been troubling me more than any other.

The other day I was talking with Cliff Greer. I used Kodak as an example. Here was this vibrant 20th century firm who understood its business to be centered on the medium of film, rather than on the fundamental goal of producing pictures regardless of the medium. In Kodak's case, film was more important than the image itself. They became so focused on improving film they failed to use other means to produce an image, despite inventing and holding some of digital imaging's most basic early patents. I believe schools have held onto a 20th century model for schooling. It's clearly failing, yet like Kodak we cling to the basic structures and keep trying to improve them rather than searching for a new 21st century way to create the right conditions for learning.

We know many of our youngest learners do not have the vocabulary, letter recognition and basic concepts to be sound readers and writers. Out of the gate many are way behind and may never catch up. With poverty's children we must start at a younger age if they are to have a better chance at being good literacy learners. I'd like Dorothy Washington to share some of her ad hoc committee's ideas to address this."

John noticed Mary Jane's scowl and closed body movements as the ball was handed to Dorothy. "You all know me as the principal of a state certified failing school. I am just sick about it. I see the children every day and know how hard they work. My teachers work hard too." With her voice cracking, Dorothy continued, "But no matter what we do it never seems to be enough!"

Quiet took over the room. Few had ever seen Dorothy express herself in such a vulnerable and open fashion.

"This past fall John asked me what I thought we needed to do. I asked, 'Do you really want to know!' Everyone knew this Dorothy and laughed. "You see School #3 has a long history of failure. Many of the folks in my school's neighborhood attended School #3 and often failed as learners, so the school doesn't always sit well with them. It's a place they send their children and they are failing too. They see it as a fortress filled with people who don't know anything about the neighborhood. The building and the staff aren't connected, despite lots of good intentions on people's parts.

I know John said our vision is to create the right conditions for learning. But if we go even deeper, I believe our purpose is to defeat poverty and a good education is a big step towards victory. But the learning journey for poverty's children now runs over perilous ground. That is why it must be changed if we are to triumph. Look, we know teachers are the backbone of every school. I don't want to change that. But they can't do all the work." She explained the use of people from the neighborhood. She talked at length about a twelve month school year and the need to provide support from birth to the end of second grade. "John, he's not a man to make this easy. He said we had to do this for the same dollars we are spending now for grades K-2. We haven't made that goal yet, but with the staff changes and different leadership plan, we can do it for a lot less than we thought."

She distributed copies of an architectural rendering of the new school with its front porch. John watched, pleased many in the circle were curious.

For over an hour Board members asked questions and shared their perspectives. They probed Dorothy's thinking and sought her advice. Overall, they'd spent nearly two hours on this part of the agenda. However, Mary Jane was silent throughout the conversation.

Before taking a break, John told everyone, "One of the reasons this is not a public meeting, but an executive session, is because what you have heard and will hear throughout the day will require teacher negotiations and bargaining with other employee groups. The plans themselves will be public, but we will have to develop a sound negotiating strategy. I want you to feel free to comment and ask questions on that part of the process as we go through these summaries today."

During the break John was sought out by Shantell Williams. "Dr. Handler I was interested in Mrs. Washington's ideas. She has certainly thought things through. Are you really thinking to do this district-wide? Why not let her start a charter school?"

John was relieved by her question. It was the first time in a while they were talking education rather than Board/superintendent relations. "Shantell, I thought a lot about the option. If we go the charter school route it is just another school working at the margin. What I want is inside the system reform. The pace we move to open early literacy centers is something we need to address. It will take time and we'd have to prioritize when and where we go next. We also have major union issues we will need to sort out."

"From what I am hearing it's a lot more than just a challenge Dr. Handler. Do you have any idea how many emails I got this week? Several hundred at least!"

John decided to bide his time a bit on her comment. "Shantell, let's go through the entire K-12 plan first. Right now my main focus is to share with you folks all the ideas and see if you can support them."

"That could be as big a challenge as facing the unions. I am certainly not convinced yet. The early primary literacy approach is a nice idea, but I need to see what else you have in mind."

After the break John summarized the next part of the plan. "Grades 3-5 would be located in existing elementary buildings. However, the children would be in vertical classrooms ranging over the three grades. This will let us focus more on meeting clear standards and minimize grade repeating, too prevalent now and known to lead to students dropping out of school at age 16." In education speak, he told them they'd be ungraded classrooms. A few questions about this aspect of the plan arose, but most were anxious to hear what middle school principal, Zack James, was going to say. He didn't waste any time jumping in.

"You know I've been working with early adolescent learners for some time now. When we get the kids they are often years behind in literacy needs. Combined with their raging hormones, we have our hands full!" Most everyone laughed as Zack emphasized the point in animated fashion. "I have been working on an idea over the past several months. I started thinking about it when working with the kids on bullying issues. We're not there yet with it but John wanted me to share my suggestions with you."

John piped in, "Zack is being modest on this. He has done a lot of thinking, and I really like his ideas for this age group."

Zack continued. "First, we need to consider the unique needs of 11 to 14 year olds. They have short attention spans and their self-identity is actively forming. The influence of their peers at this age is remarkably powerful. It is also the age where bullying behaviors are most prevalent. I believe we need to recognize 11 and 12 year old childrens' development is different than at age 13 and 14. I said to Dr. Handler we have the good fortune to have three middle schools. I would like them to each serve a single grade level. I also believe our sixth grade students need to be in self-contained classrooms and not departmentalized. If our middle schools are age focused we can develop specific programs to meet the needs of the learners we serve. This is just my gut, but I also feel we can minimize cross grade peer influence and reduce bullying behaviors."

Zack explained how the eighth grade would be transitional with more departmentalized experiences and a broader use of technology. Board members had nearly 45 minutes of questions and dialog with Zack. They liked him and listened carefully to his answers. They also wondered how things could be ungraded in the later elementary school years, then the reverse at the middle level. Both John and Zack explained the physical, social and emotional development needs were causing them to consider different approaches at different ages.

As Zack completed his presentation the Board was served lunch. Everyone took a short stretch and the room filled with informal conversation. After lunch the mayor joined them, an unprecedented event. The Board was interested in what her role would be regarding the conversation about high school education.

"I'd like to welcome Mayor Hueset to our meeting. The mayor and I have been discussing how the school district can help in the overall economic development of our city. Over the next 90 minutes we'll present our concepts. They will ultimately need your support if they are to move forward." John looked around the room. His Board members had had a long morning and he was hoping he'd made the right decision to have a major part of the afternoon focused on an entirely new secondary school direction. He had to put those doubts in his pocket and press on.

"Both the mayor and I have had separate conversations with our governor regarding what we will share with you. I met privately with Governor Pickering along with our Commissioner Appleton several weeks ago. He is interested in seeing whether or not we move forward with the concepts we outline." John knew he was name dropping but felt he needed to play some strong cards early in the conversation.

"I want to build on what your superintendent said. My conversations with Governor Pickering have been productive. He has a real interest in helping our community get back on its feet. The effort will require all of us to work together. The school district is a critical part of this community and you are directly connected to attracting and holding key industries. We are in the economic fight of our lives. We must develop creative solutions to long-standing problems."

John was thrilled by Jane's comments. Even Shantell Williams and Sara Fieldstone were listening carefully. He picked up where the mayor left off. "First, we must end our historically poor graduation rates. We can't do it by making the program easier. But we must make it more relevant and develop remarkably different settings where we can build meaningful relationships with our students. Large high schools are becoming teenage ghettos. They are a remnant of a 20th century education system built to support the industrial revolution. The evidence of their abject failure in this century could not be more compelling. I want you to keep in mind the students who do graduate this coming June in 2013 will be retiring in about 2060. What is it we should be teaching that will serve them past the middle of this century? Most of us in this room likely won't be alive at that point, but our graduates will be. Right now we are educating students for only a narrow definition of academic success, when the world in which they will live demands so much more. We have to find ways to tap the dynamic human capacities possessed by our students. We must cease educating and testing students solely for academic capacities. As a result, I am asking you to consider new ways to structure and organize our secondary schools. I am also asking you to accept that schools have a responsibility to nurture and unleash each learner's creative capacities.

Therefore, over the next six years I am proposing we close two of our high schools. We'd refurbish the remaining one and use it as a resource center and course offering site." Everyone in the room leaned forward. 'What the hell was this man thinking?' "In this city there are a number of abandoned buildings of various sizes. I would like this Board and a team from the community to identify ones we can refurbish. These would become 200 student grade 9 and 10 academies with a core team of teachers who would have responsibility for the program at each site. We would provide each center with a multi-faceted set of learning standards but allow them to decide the best way to meet the learning needs of their students. This would also include flexibility on school starting and ending times as well as the overall length of the school year. There's much to do to define this. But we would begin by recognizing the diversity of human intelligence realizing, for example, that some students need to move to think. We would need state funds to help us develop the program and waivers from regulations which constrain us. Commissioner Appleton has given me his conceptual support for this effort."

The mayor jumped back in, "From a city perspective, we will be refurbishing abandoned sites. They can, along with the neighborhood Early Literacy Centers, add vitality to neighborhoods that are currently in decline and decay. This is an urban renewal program in its own right. I believe we could ask the Governor to support it not only on educational terms, but also as part of an overall city revitalization plan. We think we could apply for federal grants on this basis."

It was John's turn to pick up the ball again, "At the grade 11 and 12 years we want to make things even smaller in size and more dispersed. We are proposing using old stores and, when needed, building new settings throughout the city. Many would be adjacent or near to key industries or cultural centers. If needed, the city would support us with condemnation procedures so we can locate in the right places. These sites would be linked directly to practical employment and real-world skill development across many different areas.

For example, we would have a center located next to our city's repertory theater. Students interested in pursuing drama, music or dance related careers would have a senior year that provided direct linkage to the arts. We also see these small sites as virtual centers for video conferencing and mentoring. Several would be connected to various parts of city government with students expected to help operate city services. As city workers retire, our students would step in to fill vacancies. They'd earn minimum wage and experience real-world applications of what they learned. This of course would need the support of the unions, not only in our system but over at city hall, a tall order for sure. Other sites would be linked to service and industry careers.

These sites would be run by the teaching staff serving them. Their hours would be different and could include nights and Saturdays. There would be extensive use of technology. Students would be required to take several virtual courses. I would also like to see us work in concert with our community college to develop dual credit offerings so students could get a jump start on college credit.

The mayor and I have also collaborated on an idea involving the city's proposal to attract Subaru to build a plant here. Mayor Hueset will outline that for you."

"Thanks Dr. Handler. We have been discussing over several months how we could make our offer to Subaru more attractive than some of those from our southern neighbors. One of the ways we can do it is to give them latitude to help design training programs coordinated by the school district in conjunction with the community college. We would, with the state's help, build a training center to industry specifications. It would be located at their factory site. We would provide a steady stream of interested students who would contribute, on a work-study basis, during their senior year of high school. The students would have to meet Subaru's educational standards and we'd agree to collaborate on the class-room versus factory floor experience. While a great deal remains to be developed on this, we need this Board's conceptual support for the idea. Many of the trainers would be employees of the company rather than traditionally certified teachers. We also need a union endorsement, as well as State Education Department waivers."

Once all the cards were on the table, Board members asked questions and joined in a back-and-forth dialog for nearly 90 minutes. John was pleased with the participation. However, he knew the day was drawing to a close and he had to summarize things. He wanted to do this solely with his Board. Before another short break everyone was thanked for their help and participation. Fifteen minutes later John sat alone with his Board.

"Folks you've had a long day. A lot was presented to you and I don't expect any action on your part right now. I am sorry you didn't hear these ideas before today, but I needed to define the broad strokes before we had this discussion. The agenda we need to tackle is filled with obsta-cles. Many of them could derail the process in their own right. The Governor, Education Commissioner and our mayor are all waiting on a clear signal from us. If we give it, I think we have a shot at gaining their needed practical and political support. I want you to take some time to digest this. I am hoping you will agree to meet in two weeks and then we can talk about where things stand and whether or not we move forward. While I need your initial okay on further planning and development, remember all things are created twice. The first is in the planning, the second in the doing. There will be plenty of opportunities along the way for you and many others to shape what we do. But your conceptual support for reengineering our educational delivery system is needed to get the ball rolling."

Shantell, though tired, had to comment. "Dr. Handler, you are asking us to take some bold and dramatic steps. I believe you are using this crisis to present a whole different way of doing business. We have many other options you haven't discussed. I still have serious reservations regarding your leadership. I leave today unimpressed by many of the ideas when we have so many more pressing issues that remain."

John expected Sara to comment in a similar vein, but she did not speak. Instead it was Emily Garza who said, "As a teacher I am stunned by what you have proposed. I am not sure what I think, but the unions will oppose you at every turn. I don't think it will work, even though I respect all the thought you've given it."

Heads nodded around the table and a weary group closed a significant Saturday session with a great deal to think about, including John.

CHAPTER 85

THE TALK STARTS

The following week John's phone and email exchanges were almost non-stop. Board members were clearly wrestling with the ideas presented at Saturday's meeting. They were also getting slammed with feedback on the budget development process and the closing of schools. It was difficult for everyone to keep the reform proposals separated from the current fiscal crisis and not see the reform concepts as a reaction to a lack of funds.

Along with Board calls John, Carl and Jerry were working to develop a clear-minded negotiations strategy. Cliff Greer called and said he and members of his Executive Board were willing to meet to pick up on the discussion John and he started before the break. Cliff was not overly optimistic things would go well, but John was heartened by the opportunity to discuss concepts with the group.

"How do we approach meeting with Cliff and his Executive Board? From what I have been hearing through the back channels, Cliff had his hands full even getting them to agree to a meeting. So things could fall apart quickly if we don't plan our part carefully."

"My idea of sending layoff notices out over spring-break sure went over like a lead balloon. I thought getting it done would be helpful and give people time before coming back to school. But Cliff gave me a real piece of his mind. So I don't think I should take the lead like I normally would. I think you and Jerry got this one. I will try to take notes and offer my advice privately to you guys."

"Cliff didn't speak to me, but I did hear from the principals. The buzz about the layoff letters was negative. So I think you are right on keeping a low profile this time. People see you as the grim reaper Carl. In the near term there's not much you can do to get over that hump."

"Okay, so we agree Carl won't be the chief spokesperson this time out. Since I spoke with Cliff one-on-one the last time, it is probably best I speak to his team. Knowing what we have on the list for them to consider it is probably best they feel like they can get the scoop directly from me. But Jerry, we are going to need you to backfill some key points of the plan if they have questions, since we won't be involving the principals in this process."

Jerry nodded. "John, should we have any Board members involved in the process?"

"You know I have gone several rounds with the same question. I've always felt contract negotiations were an executive function and the Board had no direct role in the process. The stakes are much higher now, but I still come down on the side of keeping them away from the bargaining table. I don't think it is their role. Besides they could easily be forced into an unexpected front chair if the union team starts bargaining directly with them."

For the next hour the team discussed their plans. The bargaining session was going to take place on Thursday. They agreed the seven Executive Board members of the union would be excused from their teaching duties, at District expense, so the negotiations could happen during working hours. "I have to say it ticks me off we have to pay to release their team. The union could easily reimburse us for the substitutes, but they are too damn cheap to do it!"

"Carl, I agree. But if we don't pay they won't show. It's not the fight I want to take on. But I understand the feeling."

After the group left, John was meeting with two of his Board members. Shantell Williams and Sara Fieldstone asked for some face-to-face time and John was anxious to hear what they had to say.

Shantell Williams was the first to arrive. John offered her coffee and was adding the flavored creamer she liked when Sara Fieldstone came into his office. Once everyone was settled in the comfortable leather chairs in front of his desk the conversation began.

"John, Sara and I have been bombarded with emails and even phone calls now. Everyone is angry about your proposed budget. We've told you we can't support it, and now the overwhelming proof of why we can't is as plain as day!"

"I agree with Shantell, the budget is a disaster John. Closing Jefferson is the biggest mistake in it. I am not surprised by how angry people are about it."

"I realize you've gotten a lot of email. My "in" box hasn't been empty. But outside of our employees, how many emails objecting to the proposal have we received?"

"I got plenty of feedback at Wal-Mart and from the kids John. Don't try to narrow this anger to the unions!" Sara nodded her agreement as Shantell spoke.

"Okay, but the unions are organizing the feedback. I learned this morning the *Star* is going to take an editorial position in support of the budget proposal. I also know it has city council's support. There are hard choices to be made here. Many have been forced on us by the fiscal crisis facing not only this community, but also our state. What is the tax increase you two would support?"

Shantell shifted in her seat and looked at Sara. "John of course we want a low tax rate, everyone does. These are hard times, but we have a responsibility to provide a quality education to the kids. That's what is most important here. I think if closing Jefferson wasn't in the mix, people would calm down and accept some belt tightening."

"Suppose for the sake of our conversation we didn't close Jefferson, it would take the tax increase to over five percent and the city council is looking at no less than a two percent increase related to their budget. That would mean a seven percent overall increase in taxes next year for city folks and businesses. How do you think it would go down with people?"

It was Sara's turn, "John you know that's too high. But what other cuts could we consider besides closing Jefferson?"

"I am meeting with Cliff and the teacher's union Executive Board to see if they are willing to help. The teachers are set to get a 4.1% raise next year. If they were willing to take a one percent cut Jefferson could stay open. But we suspect they'll be unwilling to consider a wage increase reduction. Are you hearing anything different?"

Shantell smiled, "No John I haven't, and you make a good point. The unions have to help, but they will want something in return for any give backs."

"You are right, they will want a lot and the price will likely be too high. Given the state of things they should be willing to do their part without seeking a whole series of give backs on other things. This is an opportunity for them to step up, but that's probably not how it will go down. They will carve us up like a Christmas turkey for proposing cuts or changes, but as for getting in the game and doing something different, it's not likely to happen. It is easier to blame the administration and blast any proposal. We are leading an entitlement culture and changing that is filled with conflict, as you are learning firsthand."

"John, besides union givebacks, is there anything else we should consider to get to an acceptable budget proposal for next year?" John could hear the earnestness in Shantell's question.

"We've been going over every line in the budget. We had a great proposal from Paychex which would save us some serious money on processing our payroll. But the work is currently done by members of our office professional union. The state collective bargaining laws require us to negotiate the impact of any decision to subcontract unit work. We cannot implement the change until we get an impact agreement. Do I have to tell you where the unit stands on the issue? The same holds true for subcontracting cleaning and custodial services. The unions won't budge on this as the loss of unit work is a significant issue for them."

Sara leaned forward in her chair, "John that's ridiculous!"

"Yup, we can lay off people and try to do more with less, but we cannot subcontract. Despite the fact we would save money and maintain or improve services. I am also considering eliminating all staff training."

Sara said, "That's a good idea in the short-term, at least it's better than laying off staff."

"I am glad you think so. If we do it, we'd also layoff everyone in the staff training office, including Mary Jane Thomas. How do you feel about that?"

Both Sara and Shantell squirmed in their chairs. "John, isn't there anything else she could do?"

"Sure but our goal is to find enough options to ultimately save Jefferson and keep our tax increase under 4%. The unions are all for cutting administration, I am sure we'd get their support." John decided to shift the conversation a bit and see where things stood with these two on reform ideas. "You know, in the longer run we need to reform the whole system. We have to reinvent ourselves and what we do."

Shantell smiled. "Ah you want to know what we are thinking of your plans for change. Well Sara and I have talked a lot. John, we like some of the ideas, but others seem way too radical."

It was John's turn to lean forward in his chair. "Can you give me an example of what concerns you?"

Sara piped in, "Sure can! If you follow through on your high school option what happens to school spirit and all of our sports teams. Juniors and seniors are not going to be spending a lot of time together in one place. That's not going to do much for student leadership and co-curricular activities. John, it's wrong thinking to curtail them!"

John considered this and knew it was a valid concern. "Good point Sara. It's something we clearly have to address. But how much school spirit exists for the more than sixty percent who drop out before they graduate? I don't want the co-curricular activities or sports to be dropped or not considered. But we can't be held hostage by them either."

"John," it was Shantell's turn to speak, "For many of the kids who stay in school, it's the sports that have kept them there. This is an important issue and it cannot be lost or minimized in any reform effort."

"I get your point, and don't disagree. You two could play a key role in making sure that doesn't get lost in the plan."

"John you are trying to co-opt us by offering participation. Not so fast! You are asking us to go down a road not traveled before. Why should we be the first ones down it?"

"Sara, because if we don't go down it, we will continue to fail, I am convinced of this. I know I am asking a great deal. But you both have been talking with me over the last hour about your concerns for the students. We may not be on the same page. But we do have a common aspiration for all our kids."

"John, I am not at all sure we can respond to the common aspirations you talk about by climbing out on the same limb with you. It's an awful lot to ask of us and the limb."

"Yes it is."

"Let's see how the budget process works out. We still have serious reservations about your leadership and whether you are the right person for this job. So it is difficult to talk more about reform and your ideas. "

CHAPTER 86

NO STEPS OVER
THE LINE

Andrea was discreet in her opposition to the early childhood center plan. But she did support the union and spoke out against the plan in the faculty room. This earned her enough points to be accepted on both sides for taking a leading role in the planning process for the closing of School #3.

The group was meeting for the second time, having agreed to meet once a week at the end of the school day for the foreseeable future. The team had seven teachers on it as well as the school's secretary, Janet McGee. They decided every classroom should be involved. The group also felt alumni of the school should have an open invitation to come and join in. Today they planned to calendar the activities.

Sue Jones spoke first once everyone was settled around the time-worn table in the lounge. "I think we should have activities scheduled over several days rather than a one day event."

"Sue, that's one way to go, but I think a full day of special events would be easier for us to handle." It was third grade teacher Betty Folger who offered this opinion. Over the next ten minutes different points of view on the topic were expressed. After some spirited conversation, it was decided to schedule the events on one day rather than spreading it out. Most of the teachers felt this would be easier on them and the children.

Next, they spent some time looking at the June calendar to find a day to hold the event. They still all struggled to call it a celebration. Janet McGee encouraged the group to schedule the "event" as it was being called on the day before the last day of school. Andrea thought this was a good idea. Some around the table wanted to have the event on the last day. Again, after considerable conversation, Janet's suggestion prevailed.

Moving on to actual happenings during the day, the group felt they should begin with a general school assembly. Andrea spoke for the first time on this. "I think we should invite the Jefferson High School Marching Band to perform for the kids. After all, as it stands right now their school will be closing too. I think all of our kids would enjoy the performance."

"Andrea, what a great idea! I can talk with the music teacher over there. I've known him for years." Andrea was pleased Sue Jones was so supportive of her suggestion. Her comments also led others to enthusiastically endorse the idea.

Time in this planning session was running short as 5:00 approached. Once more the issue of communication came up and Sue, the group's ex-officio chair, spoke up, "We have to tell Ma'am about our plans and make sure she is okay with them. Who gets the responsibility for that?"

Janet offered, "I am in the office all the time so I am the logical one to talk with her. Andrea, would you be willing to back me up on things?"

Andrea smiled, "Of course, if everyone else is comfortable with it."

Numerous heads around the table gave their non-verbal approval. All were relieved this delicate issue had been raised and resolved so quickly.

Since it was a Thursday afternoon, Andrea headed to Bea's for dinner. She knew Bea was still uncomfortable not being able to directly express her opinions on what was being planned. But after dinner last week, Bea conceded she'd 'try it' Andrea's way. Tonight it would get its first test when Andréa arrived to recap the initial plans.

"Okay girl, what did you all cook up without me?" Andrea had barely taken her coat off and settled with a beer in Bea's living room and already she was asked to summarize things. Andrea replied, "Well good afternoon to you too! How was your day with the kids?"

"Okay...okay," Bea was raising her hands, realizing her probe was a bit hasty. "I've had a good week with 'em. The new boy, Johnny Lopez, has been in four schools this year counting the move to my classroom. He's not readin' anywhere close to where he should be. He's a nice boy, shy and quiet though. His English is pretty good, but he's been in so many different places it is tough to get him to talk or get involved in things. I've been at this a long time but I still hurt when I see good kids strugglin' to make their way."

"I know, it's been the hardest lesson for me to learn. I want to scream out about how tough life is for the kids we teach. People in the neighborhood where I grew up have no idea how hard it is. They are so uninformed about real-life issues in this area. How is it we can spend so much on some things in this country and then so little on our real future?"

"Don't know the answer dear. But I do know nobody in Washington is really thinkin' about education enough. It's too easy to blame somebody else for the problem then to roll-up their sleeves and really do somethin'. But before we go down this road much more, I want to know what the closin' group you're servin' on is dreamin' up. That's much closer to home and somethin' I gotta make sure is goin' right."

Andrea smiled, "Don't you trust me on this?"

Bea gave a hearty laugh and said, "No!"

"We decided to have a one day event. We had lots of discussion about having different activities go on over several days. Sue Jones thought it would be a good way to go."

"And you, what did you think?"

"I agreed with Betty Folger, and so did the group. The one day event is better because it doesn't drag it out over a week. It took time for us to settle on the one day idea."

"Sue, she okay with it?"

"Yes, she accepted the group's decision. How do you see it?"

"Well not bein' there and hearin' the conversation, I guess I have to go along with the one day idea. I think that is probably the best way to go. Now what else happened since all you great minds were in one place?"

Andrea looked out of the top of her eyes, a mild admonishment while smiling. "We decided to hold the "event" as we're calling it, on the day before the last day of school. Again, we had lots of conversation. Tom thought it would be better on the last day. After we thought about it though, we felt the last day should go off like in the past. It also would give us time with the kids to say goodbye and do what we wanted to with them since the event day will be filled with other things."

"Now that was a real smart decision. Maybe you can do this without Bea bein' there!"

Andrea laughed. She told her about the plans to communicate with Ma'am and her idea to have the Jefferson marching band participate.

"I think those are good decisions too, I hope not too many of the band members have their last exams then. Did you think of that?"

"No we didn't. Hmm, maybe it won't work as an idea. We'll have to see I guess."

"When are you great minds meetin' again?"

"We are meeting every Thursday for the foreseeable future. So I can keep you up to date on things. I also can listen to your suggestions and share them at the next meeting. Do you have any in mind at this point?"

"Let me think over supper. I'm not lettin' you off the hook so easy girl!"

The fact she had to think on it was a great sign things were on the mark. Andrea knew if Bea had a different view she'd express it without hesitation.

"Okay, we are going to Skype with Jasmin tonight too, right?"

"That girl of mine doesn't like missin' a Thursday talk!"

After supper Jasmin was on line. Andrea smiled, "You look a bit tired. How is school going this week?"

"Andrea, it has been a tough week. I had a challenging paper due. So I needed to pull some all-nighters to finish. You remember those, right?"

"I do! In fact report cards for the kids are due soon and I'll be putting in some long hours getting those set."

"Okay, but how is that fiancée of yours? Have you set a date yet?"

"Things are going great. Jason had a good start in Montgomery. He's met a lot of new potential clients. He loves the office staff. He's coming up in two weeks for a few days and we'll discuss wedding plans then with my folks. Right now, it looks like we may get married sometime in late fall or over the Christmas holiday. It depends on if I can find a teaching job and mom's school calendar. We'll see. Once I know you'll have to let me know if the date works because you are going to be a part of the wedding party, if it's okay with you."

"That's more than okay. You set the date and don't worry I'll be there! Now how is my mom doing? Is she behaving herself?"

Bea was standing in the back of the room as the girls were talking, but this was her cue to get involved in the conversation. "Listen here Miss Smarty Pants! I do whatever needs doin'. Folks don't like it, well that's not my problem now is it?"

"Oh Andrea, she's been eating her Wheaties. Can you make my mom behave until I get home and take over the job?"

"I don't know, she's getting awful feisty and you know what she's like!"

"You two stop talkin' about me that way! I am doin' what I always do. Nothin' you say is gonna change me I can tell ya."

"Okay mom, but promise me you'll consider Andrea's advice before you jump into the deep end of the pool."

"No promises from this old girl! But I do listen to her when she makes sense."

Their conversation went on for another half-hour. All three relished their Thursday talks. Both Jasmin and Andrea knew Bea looked forward to it more than she'd admit. Both did their best to tease her whenever they could.

CHAPTER 87

JUST SAY NO

The negotiations session with Cliff and his Executive Board was about to begin. John agreed to meet at union headquarters. He believed the teacher team would feel more comfortable there and be less likely to walk out.

When John and the district team entered the conference room the talk amongst the teachers stopped immediately. Their faces were glum and the mood was tense. One of the teacher members was reading the morning newspaper. He did not fold it or acknowledge John's presence in the room. Nonetheless, John looked at the front page of the paper in front of Andrew Morgan's face. Looking at the headline he quipped, "Looks like the proposed convention center is on the rocks for now, another casualty of the state budget."

"Andrew dropped the paper down so his eyes could stare at John for a moment. "I suppose that's the district's excuse too, right?"

This was not the way John wanted to get the ball rolling so he turned to Cliff and asked if the coffee was hot. As they'd previously agreed, the district team brought the bagels and cream cheese.

"Yes it is, Dr. Handler. I see you brought some bagels. Let's take a minute to get something before we get to work."

John appreciated this effort by Cliff to sidestep, at least for the moment, Andrew's rude behavior.

Once everyone was set, Cliff started things moving. "Dr. Handler, you asked for this meeting and after a lot of conversation the team is willing to listen to what you have to say this morning. But we are upset over the layoffs." Then looking at Carl, he continued, "And the fact they were communicated in a heartless manner."

"I understand people are upset. But I ask you to park those feelings for a little time while I explain to you the problems we are facing."

It was Andrew who snarled, "The meter's running Dr. Handler, without much time on it!" The rest of the team nodded, although Cliff gave Andrew a look which reminded him who was the chair of the union's team.

John took off his watch and set it in front of him. "The meter has ten minutes on it. Let's see if I can use it to summarize the challenge." Over the next ten minutes John succinctly went through the numbers. He distributed a one page handout for everyone to follow. John practiced this part of the process and gave a good overall summary of the loss of revenue, current expenses and overall plight of the city budget and tax rate.

When he finished Cliff told John his team needed to take a 10 minute caucus to discuss privately what they heard.

Once the union team left the room and the door closed behind them, Jerry exploded. "That son-of-a-bitch Andrew, reading a newspaper and telling you the meter is running. Who in the hell does he think he is! You know he's a handful at high school faculty meetings. Reads stuff there too, and does paper corrections. I can't stand the jerk!"

Carl laughed, "Hey, see what I have to put up with. You haven't even seen what can happen in these sessions. I bet you their caucus will take more than ten minutes. They want us to sit here and be reminded they are calling the shots."

Carl was right. The caucus took nearly 40 minutes. All John and company could do was wait. When the team came back Cliff indicated they had no questions. An awkward silence hung in the air as it became evident the union team was not going to say anything. John had the burden of leading the conversation. He felt the anger rise within him, squelched it, and decided to put his proposals out there.

"I am speaking on-the-record. Feel free to share this information with your members and I will do the same."

Cliff looked at John, "And what does it mean, you are free to share it too?"

"I understood this was to be on-the-record. That meant you'd feel free to share it with your members. I have the same latitude to share it with my Board and the administrative team to the extent it is warranted." John also believed he could share his proposals with the teachers but he did not want to give the group an excuse to shut things down by arguing over communication boundaries. "This is no different than how it has been in every negotiation we've had."

"Okay, we'll agree this is an on-the-record conversation. If there are to be any off-the-record talks both teams have to agree. Correct?"

John nodded agreement and began before anything else could be said. "We have a three year contract which has one year left on it. What I am going to propose is an extension of the contract for an additional two years. Most of our community is suffering with job losses and no wage increases. I am asking you to consider a two percent wage increase next year instead of four percent. In each of the next two succeeding years, I am proposing a two percent raise. This is more than the majority of folks around here are going to get. In addition, I will agree not to close Jefferson High for the life of the agreement. The three elementary schools scheduled to close will continue on their path to closing at the end of this school year. Enrollment is declining and all three are failing to meet state standards. I will also agree to no more than 2% of the staff being subject to layoff during the two year extension period. However, I want the union to agree I have a free hand in staff assignments and placements. Transfers will no longer be blocked by seniority. I also want it to be clear any retirement, leave of absence or resignation does not have to be filled and will not be judged as part of the layoff cap. The district currently pays 95% of the health insurance premium for fulltime teachers. I am proposing in each of the last two years respectively, the district's premium payment will decrease by 2%. Finally, the district will offer teachers with 25 or more years of service, who are otherwise eligible to retire under the rules of the state pension system, a one-time $1,000 incentive for each year of district service to a maximum payment of $35,000 providing they submit written notice of their retirement on or before June 1st of this year."

"That's it?"

"Yes."

Cliff scowled, "Okay my team needs to discuss your long list of give-backs. Let's break for lunch. Why don't we agree to meet at 1:30?"

It was now 11:30 and John didn't see any point in arguing over the two hour break period, even though he felt it was excessive. "We'll see you here then," was all John said as the teams tensely went their separate ways. Once outside and headed for a nearby restaurant Carl looked at John and Jerry and said, "You know the proposal was dead on arrival."

"I think so too, John. I watched the team, they looked glum. Not sure what they expected, but it was evident they thought it would be something different."

"Well it's a place to start. Let's see what they come back with and if we can build on any counter they may present." Over lunch the three men talked about possible areas where they could maneuver and what was key to them. They also tried to predict what the teachers would do.

After two hours the teams were staring at each other across the long conference table in the union office. "John, we've talked about the proposal and quiet honestly we find it insulting! You are asking us to give back wages next year, cut health insurance and accept a pittance in wage increases. We deserve better from the district!"

Carl spoke for the first time. "Cliff, you've told us the offer is insulting. I strongly disagree with your characterization. What's on the table are wage increases when most working people are getting nothing more, taking a cut, or losing their jobs. No member of your unit is taking a cut. We are offering to increase their wages by six percent over three years. We also will be substantially reducing layoffs if Jefferson stays open. The retirement incentive is unprecedented and the district's premium payment for health insurance will still be over ninety percent when the contract expires. I think many working people would take that deal in a heartbeat."

It was Andrew who spoke for the union, "We don't have to sit and listen to you lecture us on what is a good deal. We can figure that out for ourselves! Your ability to transfer us whenever and wherever you want is never going to happen. So yes, your offer is insulting and unacceptable."

John looked at Cliff. "Do you have any proposal for us to consider?"

"No John we don't. Your offer is so bad we have chosen not to counter it in any way. You guys will have to bring us something much better than you have for us to even consider a counter."

John did not want the union to be able to say the district team walked out. So while he closed the door on the day he tried to keep a window open a touch, "We'll have to consider what has been said today and decide on next steps. Unless anyone else has more to say I suggest we adjourn for the day. Cliff, I will get back to you next week on where we stand."

Andrew picked up his newspaper again and started reading it. Jerry could not stand his behavior any longer. "Andrew, I have never seen such rude behavior from an adult when what's on the table is so serious. I find it insulting!"

Andrew lowered his paper slightly. "You're insulted Jerreee …it was said as a slur. Well think about how ridiculous your offer is and then maybe you'll understand how polite I am trying to be right now." Jerry was about to get out of his chair when he felt Carl's firm hand holding him back.

"Good day folks," was all John could muster as his team headed out the door.

When they got back to the central administration building downtown Jerry and Carl went directly to John's office. "What a waste of time!"

"Jerry, I'm not sure at this point. Carl why don't you follow up with Cliff tomorrow and see what he's thinking."

"Okay, I am not a bit surprised they didn't give us a counter proposal. Perhaps they want to paint us into a corner and they really don't want to get in the game. The union is going to stand pat and by doing so I think they believe they can get the Board to crumble."

John agreed, "They could be right on that. The budget proposals have the Board concerned, to say the least. They are between a rock and a hard place. Guys, I've got to write an email letting the members know our negotiations, at least at this point, have failed. I also suspect the union will be putting out a summary to its members which will cast us in a poor light; so much for making any headway today."

CHAPTER 88

ANOTHER DAY

Dorothy sat at her desk thinking about all the items on her 'to-do' list. For the last ten days she had been entirely focused on the future and ideas for a new way of educating young children. She was excited by the prospect, but not naïve about its chances for getting support from the Board and the teachers' union.

But today, the reality of being the School #3 principal was back in full force. She had a number of teacher observations to do throughout the week. One of the teachers on her observation list wasn't speaking to her. She talked to Jerry Croton, her new supervisor, since Mary Jane Thomas' work responsibilities changed. She was worried if she saw something during an observation she had a concern about, the teachers union would accuse her of revenge behavior.

Jerry's advice had not been helpful. He'd said, "Dorothy, if you see something affecting the safety and welfare of the students you cannot ignore it. But if you are offering some modest criticism of a professional practice, I'd say minimize your comments or ignore it. There's little to be gained with some of your staff who aren't receptive to your point of view."

Dorothy was not comfortable putting an effort into doing her job and then not giving advice she'd normally provide during the process. But this morning, as she faced the cold reality of stepping into Pam Kilborn's fourth grade classroom, she was beginning to second guess her convictions, wondering if she should heed Jerry's advice.

In addition to the observation load which was closing in on her, Dorothy was pressing the staff downtown to tell her what school(s) her children would be assigned to when School #3 closed in June. She needed to know this to help establish student transfer lists for the teachers. Every classroom teacher was going to have to label the student cumulative folders for relocation to their new school. She also needed to know what to do with all the supplies and materials in the school. Some of her colleagues had already put on their pirate costumes lobbying her for computers, texts, tables and many other items. If they weren't careful it could easily become a free-for-all raid on her school after it closed. She needed help and direction from downtown soon.

It was time for Dorothy to observe Pam Kilborn's language arts teaching. Dorothy had a fundamental respect for Pam's skills. But she also felt Pam needed to show more compassion and understanding. She was a good technical teacher, but not an especially warm-hearted one.

Dorothy visited Pam's classroom countless times over the years and always received some type of acknowledgement when she entered. Today there was no recognition of her presence. As was her practice, Dorothy took a moment to take in the classroom setting. The arrangement of things, displays of student work and any other items on the walls or around the room. As she looked, Dorothy was surprised by the lack of student work. The displays were largely commercial ones provided by various textbook vendors. The old slate chalkboard had the day's date on it and little else. Pam was seated at a kidney shaped table working with five children sitting along its outer perimeter. The other twenty-three children were busy at their seats doing pencil and paper tasks. The room was quiet and children were well-behaved.

Dorothy took about ten minutes to work the room. She spent time with different youngsters asking them what they were doing. Most of the children were familiar with the work, consisting of fill in the blank worksheets and a brief writing task. Pam was doing a story comprehension activity with the five children surrounding her at the table. Her teacher's manual was open and she was reading the comprehension questions developed by the publisher. While many teachers followed the manual, Pam was far from enthusiastic as she delivered the lesson to the four boys and one girl.

For the next half-hour Dorothy took good notes on what she observed. Two more groups came to the table during the time she was there. She noticed Pam left her table only once over the time she taught the three groups. Her classroom teaching certainly lacked passion, even for Pam. Dorothy felt Pam was making a deliberate effort to do only what was expected. As a result, Dorothy was clearly struggling as she left the room on what to say in the follow up conference after school. She hoped the other observation was much better than this.

Upon leaving the classroom she decided to walk through all the classrooms on the second floor. Her visits would be less than five minutes and would be completed in about 45 minutes, time she really didn't have, but she needed to see what was happening and talk with some of the children working at their seats or in a learning center within a classroom.

Forty minutes later, Dorothy was glad she had taken the time to do a walk-thru. Most of the third through fifth grade classrooms were buzzing with activity. Children were actively engaged in a multitude of activities. Many were hands-on tasks, coupled with deductive or predictive language arts assignments. There was a seasoned substitute, Ruth Jenkins, in Amy Fontaine's room. Amy had come down with a bad late season cold and finally conceded she needed to stay home. Ruth was doing a good job and Dorothy was pleased to see Amy left excellent plans. Despite feeling uncomfortable, Amy stayed late yesterday to make sure Ruth had everything she needed for a successful day as a substitute. Dorothy was proud of Amy's dedication and the extra effort she put forth when she needed to be home in bed recuperating.

Dorothy made another classroom visitation, this time to Brenda Hookings' kindergarten class. She thoroughly enjoyed the visit and the activities the children were engaged in. Brenda had some minor management issues Dorothy would review with her, but overall she had a much better feeling about Brenda's work than Pam's. Dorothy would conference with Brenda before school tomorrow morning. Right now she had to get focused on her follow-up conference with Pam.

Usually Dorothy sat in front of her desk in a chair beside the teacher she was meeting. She decided today would be no different, although sitting behind her desk was a tempting option since Pam's attitude was barely professional. It wasn't long before Janet was standing at her door. "Mrs. Washington, Pam Kilborn is here."

"Tell her to come in."

Pam was in the outer office talking with some staff members by the office mailboxes. She chatted with them for another five minutes before walking into Ma'am's office, as if she had not made her wait for more than a moment.

Swallowing the irritation balled up in her throat, Ma'am got up closed the office door and sat down across from Pam. She noticed Pam brought nothing with her; usually everyone brought a pad and pen to take notes during a post observation conference. Pam didn't say anything, sitting with arms folded and a plastic smile on her face.

"Pam, you know my practice is to encourage some self-reflection at the start of a post observation conference. How did you feel the lesson went today?"

Pam paused for a moment, saying, "Fine."

Dorothy felt like she was pulling teeth, but she needed to give it another try. "What do you think were the strong points of the lesson?"

"I thought it was all good."

Ma'am had had enough of Pam's attitude and decided to be candid about what she observed, despite the cautionary conversation with Jerry. "I was disappointed by your lesson. Your room displays were decorative but not instructionally linked. I was surprised because usually you have student work displayed and bulletin boards that are directly tied to what you are doing in the classroom. Did I misunderstand what I was seeing?"

Pam shifted uncomfortably in her seat and said, "I guess you saw what you saw."

Dorothy pressed on. "I also was disappointed by your lack of movement throughout the classroom. You did not spend time between groups talking with children and checking on their efforts. Your conversations with the children were brief and not reassuring. Quite frankly, I don't expect this from a pro like you and I am puzzled by it." Dorothy stopped. Looking at Pam she expected some type of a response.

None was forthcoming.

Dorothy took another five minutes, summarizing some of the good things she observed and advised her she would have a written summary of the observation to review and sign. Pam acknowledged this and simply left Ma'am's office, once it was apparent her principal had nothing further to share.

CHAPTER 89

MOUNTAIN CLIMBING

Carl reached out to Cliff and they agreed to meet for lunch. Cliff liked a diner on the west side of the city, a great old place with time worn traditions. The diner had a tin ceiling with the smell of fried food penetrating every pore of the cracked vinyl booths and the window treatments. The food was outstanding and many who's who from the area found their way to the place for a business lunch.

Cliff was waiting when Carl arrived. Both men were well known in the community. After several hellos and ordering their lunch the conversation turned to the situation.

"Cliff, where do we go from here? I can't believe you guys don't even want to discuss what we proposed."

"Why would we want to discuss all those give backs? You want us to be excited about what was on the table? Come on Carl, you've been around the block many times. You know what you proposed isn't acceptable."

"Cliff, the give back on salary would keep Jefferson open and reduce the number of layoffs. The retirement incentive was a generous one. It's something you have been wanting for several years. I don't get why you rejected the package out-of-hand. Especially since you could save unit member jobs with what was offered."

"Carl, I have more senior members than young ones. The give backs and small increases mean their pensions will be reduced. That will cost them thousands in retirement over the next twenty years. As for saving jobs, I am all for it, but not at the expense of our senior members."

"What are you saying? Greed trumps the right thing to do here!"

"Take a breath Carl. You know the senior members make the calls. My Executive Board is filled with teachers over 50. They aren't going to let me or anyone else hurt what they've worked their whole career to gain. They are not going to give in on health insurance and pay more of the premium in retirement. I can't move them on it and neither can you."

"You could have countered our offer in some manner. I don't get it."

"Carl, that's not going to happen. Your guy is on the ropes. We've talked about this already. I tried to warn you, but you haven't listened. We see John gone before the new school year starts. The Board will put in Mary Jane as the interim leader and we'll make a deal with her. It's going to happen. Carl, you and Jerry will be out on the street looking for work."

"But Jefferson will be closed, and the layoffs and other cuts will go forward no matter what happens to John over the summer."

"No it won't close Carl. How many times do I have to say this? We will have at least three Board votes to save it. You know we already have two and one of the others will crack. You are a smart man. You have to see it that way. We have no real reason to deal with John and we aren't going to. He's a nice guy, but this is business plain and simple."

The message had been delivered and Carl had to brief John. He thought about what Cliff shared and realized what he was saying would likely happen and he would be looking for a new job. Carl was shaken by the conversation much more than he expected. He was beginning to see Cliff was right and the union was playing its winning hand.

While Carl was meeting with Cliff, John had a visit with Sara Fieldstone. She'd called and asked if John could meet with her privately at her home. Over the past several months she always met John with Shantell at her side. He was surprised she asked to meet with him alone and in secret. He wondered what was on her mind.

Sara prepared some sandwiches and John found himself in her kitchen for only the second time since he came to the district. Her home was comfortable and cozy.

"I know this is unusual to meet this way John and before we go any further I need your promise this will remain a private meeting."

"Sara, I don't know what to think. This is unusual, but I can agree this meeting is off calendar, and depending on what we discuss, can remain that way."

Sitting across from John, Sara paused for a moment then began. "John, I am excited about what you have proposed to reform our schools. I would like to support you, but I have some things I need you to do if I am going to give you my support."

John was quietly stunned by this admission. He tried to keep an open posture and maintained, as best he could, a calm outward demeanor as he continued to let Sara talk.

"There are two things I want and you'll have my support. First, I want you to let Carl go at the end of this school year. I don't like him and the teachers hate him. Second, Jefferson has to stay open. Maybe, as we get into the reform effort things will be different, but right now Jefferson cannot be on the chopping block. You do those two things, you'll have my support on the budget and I will be very helpful to you on the reforms you have in mind."

"Suppose I don't do that; what happens then?" John was fishing and hoped Sara would reveal how things would play out.

Sara took the bait. "John, Cliff Greer is going to be meeting with Don Karst soon. He is going to tell him the teachers, with the city's local labor council's support, are going to start a boycott on his dry cleaning stores. They are going to label him as an anti-labor guy. John they will do what they can to ruin his business. Don's no dummy; he supports you, but he has a business to run and that kind of pressure will change his vote. You will be out and Mary Jane Thomas will be our interim superintendent. She may not get the long-term job, but she'll have the helm long enough to do what we want."

"If that's the case Sara, why are you making a proposal to me? You can get both things you want without my help."

"John this may surprise you, but I've been thinking a lot about what was shared at the workshop. I am starting to believe it could make a real difference. I want to support you, but I have needs too. You have to get on board with them. If you do, I think Shantell will come around.

Don Karst will resign from the Board because the union will carry out its threat. But you'll have at least three votes and we can discuss who fills the seat. It won't be easy John, but your agenda can move forward. I hold the keys you need."

John underestimated Sara, plain and simple. There he sat. He thought his question would reveal a strategy he could thwart. However, he knew what Sara told him could play out as she said. She wasn't revealing anything. She was telling John how things stood and leaving him to make a decision.

"Sara, I am not sure what to think at this point. You are asking me to sacrifice a good man because you don't like him."

"John, you know I am a Star Trek fan. There's a line that seems to fit right now. I don't know if I'm quoting it exactly but you'll get what I am saying, you have a choice to serve the needs of the many or the needs of the one. It's up to you John."

CHAPTER 90

A VISIT

Jason was flying in on business and Andrea was at the airport waiting for his plane. She was excited to see him as more than a month passed since they were together in Montgomery. The early May flowers were finally starting to bloom. It was hard to believe how quickly the calendar pages were turning.

She fell into his arms the moment he walked past the security exit. As they left the airport, holding hands, Jason talked about his work and plans for the apartment, "I've really settled in. Business has been good. I've made connections with several young professionals like us. A number of them are interested in buying insurance. I know I am going to exceed my first year transition salary guarantee. I think I may make $100,000 this year in earnings. But, tell me, what's been happening here?"

"Wow, where do I begin? I have been looking at the apartment and there are a few things I want to take to Montgomery. But next month I'll Craig's List some things and give away others. If we rent a small U-haul, we can drive my stuff down. But since you are making all that money, maybe we hire a mover and have things shipped. I want to be with you by July 1st."

Jason was thrilled, "Terrific! We can make that work."

"On the work side, we've planned most of the closing event. We're not calling it a celebration. I'm really going to miss the children. Overall, things are a little better, but the mood of the staff is tense and gloomy most of the time. I'm not going to miss that and it's making it much easier for me to leave."

"Have you heard anything from Montgomery on teaching in the city?"

"I have. I wanted to save the surprise for you. I had two phone interviews and then a Skype session with the principal. Ma'am gave me a terrific recommendation and talked to someone in district office about my teaching. They've offered me a reading teacher job at a new elementary school that will open next fall. I am going to take it of course! The salary is almost $6,000 less than I am making here, but I will be doing what I love and we'll be together in a beautiful city. I can't wait!"

Jason was sitting in the Civic's passenger seat as Andrea drove through busy Friday night traffic. Looking out the window, Jason was struck by the lack of new construction in contrast to Montgomery, where building activity was evident in many different areas. While it was a nice evening with temps in the high 50's, he also was glad he packed a warm sweatshirt. How different these two parts of the United States were. He felt sad to see the economic malaise had not lifted and so many in the area were struggling to get by having lost their once sound, blue collar manufacturing jobs.

Andrea pulled into her parking space at the apartment. Once through the door they embraced and discussed plans for the evening. Conversation continued while they boiled water for pasta and opened a bottle of red wine.

"Mom's all for a Christmas wedding; how do you feel about the timing?"

Jason smiled, "How about we just elope? It would be a whole lot easier."

"Jason, be serious! How do you feel about a Christmas wedding back here? We'll have to come home at Thanksgiving for planning and my final fitting on a bridal gown. We also have to decide on the wedding party. I want Bea as my maid of honor for sure."

"Okay, okay it sounds great, but we don't have to do all the planning tonight do we?" Jason said through his smile and bright eyes looking at Andrea.

"No we don't, but I wanted to be sure we were in agreement. By the way we are going to my folks for dinner tomorrow night. Otherwise we don't have any firm plans."

The weekend passed quickly. They had a glorious time and both were disappointed to see it come to an end.

"Andrea, I can't wait to see you over the Memorial Day weekend. It will be beautiful in Alabama. I got your ticket. You will have to fly through Atlanta on Friday night after school. I booked the return flight on Monday afternoon. You'll have to go through Charlotte on the way home. It was the best I could do on a busy holiday weekend. Besides, you insisted on flying back here on Monday and not taking a day off on Tuesday to travel."

"Jason, you know how I feel about my responsibility to the kids. I have to be in school when the holiday is over. Besides, you will be stuck with me full time in July. Then, watch out!"

They kissed goodbye, and Andrea watched Jason until he was through security and out of sight. She was relaxed and ready for the week ahead. It was a hectic time at school and she did not want to miss anything.

CHAPTER 91

HEART BROKEN

Andrea began her week at school, but was a bit surprised when her cell phone rang Tuesday night at 9:45. She knew from the caller ID it was Bea.

"Girl, I am gonna say this one right out, Ma'am had a heart attack tonight and it looks like they will be doing by-pass surgery tomorrow morning. I don't know much more. The woman don't show it much, but the pressure finally got to her. She's been tired and upset by all that has happened and now this!"

"Bea, I'll be right over! How are you?"

Bea did not answer for a moment. Andrea knew she was crying. This strong woman was also cracking. With Ma'am going down hard, Andrea was worried about Bea. "I'll be fine, don't you rush out now. We have to work in the morning."

"I know we do, but neither of us will sleep much tonight anyhow. I can be there in a half hour. Put the coffee on, I'm coming."

Andrea quickly packed a bag and headed out. Since it was late, traffic was light and she was at Bea's in no time. Andrea stepped through the door to see Bea shaken to the core. Tears rolled down her cheeks and she barely said a word as Andrea set her things down in the living room.

Andrea went to the kitchen seeing Bea had already put the coffee on. She poured them both a cup. 'This was going to be a sleepless night.' Heading back into the living room, Andrea handed Bea her coffee and sat quietly. She decided to wait and let Bea talk when she was ready.

After a few minutes Bea set her coffee down. "Dorothy's husband called me about 9:30. He said they were making dinner when Dorothy turned from the stove, looked at him and fell to the floor. He called 911. He said she'd stopped breathin' for a couple of seconds but then settled down. When they got to the hospital, the doctors said she'd had a bad heart attack and were takin' her to the cardio lab. An hour later they reported she had some major blockages. Things are set for surgery early in the mornin'."

Andrea held Bea's hand as she spoke, "Bea, she will be okay, I am sure of it. Ma'am is a strong woman and she's at a good hospital. This will be okay."

"Dorothy's been feelin' the pressure from all of this. You can't go into school day after day, have people behavin' like they are and not have somethin' like this happen. There's some folks gonna get a piece of this woman's mind! It's their fault this happened to that fine lady."

"Bea, you are Ma'am's best friend. I think tomorrow morning you need to go to the hospital and not school. There will be time to talk about things with everyone. You don't need to go into school and say things you'll regret later."

"I won't regret a damn word! I'm gonna start with Pam Kilborn. The bitch has been awful and sayin' hurtful things! She filed a grievance against Dorothy, said her observation was a poor one outta revenge. Ma'am was real upset. It was the final straw, I know it!"

"You need to take a breath and think about Ma'am. I don't want you having a heart attack next. You have a right to be upset, but it can wait until you see how Ma'am is doing." Andrea decided she could not tell Bea her anger was wrong. She could only hope to deflect it and help her think more reflectively later.

Bea slumped back in her chair. She was emotionally and physically exhausted. Andrea remembered how Bea looked when she was shot. Somehow, she looked more frail and vulnerable now. In the silence, Andrea began composing the email she would need to send to Jasmin before she tried to get some sleep.

Over the next hour, it was Bea who now needed support and understanding. In this moment Bea let her guard down and the words and feelings tumbled out. "We've been tryin' to do what's right for the children.

I don't expect everyone to agree with our ideas, but people have been so hurtful! Nobody's tryin' to make our ideas better. They are sayin' awful things and treatin' us bad. I'm tired Andrea. I am not sure I can go on with this if somethin' happens to Ma'am. She's been the heart an' soul of what we've been plannin'. Without her right now, well, I don't know what we can do."

Andrea listened. She did not try to fill the quiet spaces between Bea's thoughts. She thought about all they had been through this year. She looked across at Bea, knowing she was an exceptional friend. In her wildest dreams she never thought a mid-forties woman would assume such a meaningful place in her life. She knew she'd do all she could to help Bea through this time. Right now, in this moment, it was time to encourage her to get some sleep and prepare herself for the momentous day ahead.

Once Bea was in her room, Andrea went online and wrote an email to Jasmin. At first, she searched for what to say. But she quickly found her voice.

Jasmin, I am at your mom's tonight and plan to be here for the next few days. Dorothy Washington had a heart attack at supper time today. They did an emergency angioplasty and found three blocked arteries. She will have by-pass surgery in the morning. Your mom is coping, but is very upset by what has happened to her friend. I am doing my best to get her to take it easy. But you know what a challenge that can be! If anything further occurs I will call you, otherwise let's talk tomorrow night.

Once in bed Andrea tossed and turned. Sleep was an elusive companion. Her mind ran in many directions. 'What would happen next? Would Ma'am make it through the ordeal ahead? How would Bea do if she didn't? How would Bea behave in any event? What would the staff say and do when they learned what happened? How did they tell the children?' Andrea's mind was a like a creek rising to flood stage. The thoughts and questions flowed with quickening intensity.

CHAPTER 92

WATCHFUL WORRY

M a'am was the mortar that held together many different bricks at the school. Now nobody could tell what would happen. As Andrea stepped into the office she saw Carl Gardner talking to Janet and Sue Jones. She wondered what was being said, but knew they'd all be updated soon.

Just as Andrea was entering her classroom, she heard Janet's voice on the loud speaker. "Carl Gardner is here this morning and is asking everyone to come to the library for a quick voluntary meeting." Most heard through the grapevine about Ma'am's heart attack. Everyone was anxious; for the first time in many months they were concerned about something in common.

Carl stood waiting for people to arrive. Once Sue gave him a nod, he began, "I know most of you are aware Mrs. Washington had a serious heart attack last night. Three blockages of main arteries were discovered and she is undergoing surgery as we meet."

Andrea glanced around the room. Some faces showed concern while others quietly wiped away tears or whispered to those close by.

"It is okay to tell the children. Sue Jones and I talked briefly a few minutes ago and we'd suggest keeping your comments brief. 'She's ill and we hope she'll be better soon kind of message.' Mrs. Washington will be out of surgery mid-day and we hope to have a letter prepared to go home this afternoon with the kids. We know her recovery will be a lengthy one and she won't be back before the school year ends. Dr. Handler and I spoke this morning and as soon as we have determined how we will cover her absence, we'll let you know."

The message had been delivered and staff members spoke in small groups as Carl worked his way out of the library. Pam Kilborn was nearby and Andrea overheard her say to some of her cronies, "I sure hope she will be okay, but I for one am glad someone else will be running the place the rest of the year."

It took all of Andrea's strength not to say something. But, her eyes caught Pam's in a laser like glare. The tension at school had a back biting nature and Andrea was sick of it. She looked forward to climbing the stairs to her classroom and spending the day with the children.

* * * * *

The following afternoon the staff at School #3 learned two things. Ma'am's successful surgery was now seriously compromised by a post-op infection. The second was Dr. Joanne Walters would be filling in as principal for the remainder of the year. Most of the staff knew Joanne by reputation and were pleased she was coming to pinch-hit. Joanne was knowledgeable and judged to be steady and fair-minded, things everyone agreed the school needed right now.

Andrea wondered what the last six weeks of school would be like without Ma'am. While the current struggles had not waned; everyone was praying Ma'am would come through the health crisis.

Like many classrooms, Andrea's was busy writing 'Get Well' cards to their principal, simple, but wonderful, expressions of the children's wishes. Bea promised to take them to Ma'am. Bea had been absent for two days helping the family and staying close to her friend. She planned to return to work the next day having used her contractual two personal business days.

That night Andrea sat with Bea after she came home from the hospital. She was exhausted and frightened for her friend, "She looks terrible. She's got so many tubes runnin' into her. Makes no sense to me to see her sufferin' like that. I don't know if she's gonna live or die. Nobody else does either. But she's a strong one. That works in her favor for sure."

Andrea listened quietly until Bea asked how things were at school. Andrea tried her best to put a good spin on things, "Dr. Walker came in today. She talked to several people on their breaks and walked into every classroom. We were all asked to introduce Dr. Walker to the kids. She seems nice."

"Now tell me what they are really sayin'!"

"Bea everyone is really worried about Ma'am, even Pam. Of course, the feuding and bitter feelings haven't stopped. There's still a lot of faculty room talk about the budget and early literacy ideas. Not much changed there I'm afraid."

"Girl, it'd be naïve if to think Ma'am's heart attack would change any minds. It won't do that honey, no matter what happens."

"I know, but you have to promise me you won't go picking a fight with everyone who disagrees. We've got enough going on without Jasmin and me having to worry about you. The kids all need us right now." Andrea's voice broke and Bea gave her a huge, powerful hug.

"Nothin's gonna happen darlin'. Dorothy's a tough one! I'll tell ya it will be okay." Bea wished she half believed the words she was sharing with Andrea. Knowing what she had seen, she was not at all sure Ma'am would live through the weekend.

Bea was right. Ma'am was a real fighter. But the bacteria within her fought hard, each day taking its toll. It was Sunday when Bea and Andrea learned Ma'am's valiant effort to survive wasn't enough to overcome the infection ravaging her body.

CHAPTER 93

RECKONING WITH THE DEVIL

John wrestled with Sara's proposal. He knew he wasn't willing to sacrifice Carl for her vote. It was early Monday morning at the office when he asked Jerry and Carl to join him. He'd made his usual stop for bagels and Ann had the coffee on. The three men sat together in the comfortable chairs in front of John's desk.

John got the call from Dorothy's husband that she'd succumbed to a massive post-op infection. It was shocking news he could hardly fathom. Looking at Carl and Jerry he asked, "How could this happen to such a vibrant woman? We'll need to get a crisis team over to the school. There will be significant support needs to be addressed."

Jerry shook his head, "My God, she's gone. What a loss."

Carl sat with his grief. He respected Ma'am and found himself overwhelmed by her passing.

After several minutes Jerry spoke. "Your decision to bring in Joanne Walters was a good call. Her people skills and experience will be very helpful. She started last Friday and is glad to be working, even if it is under such a terrible circumstance."

"She is a talented educator Jerry. I will stop by later to see how things are going."

"That is a good idea. She told me there's lots of tension and a number of teachers are barely speaking to each other. It's all related to the early literacy concept and the different beliefs people have regarding it. But Dorothy's passing will add a whole different dimension to things there."

"Gentlemen, let's take a break to get the crisis intervention issues addressed and come back here in a half hour."

When the three returned, John began, "I met with Sara Fieldstone the other day. She told me she's willing to support the innovation strategies we presented at their Saturday meeting. But there is a price to be paid for her support." For the next ten minutes John shared the details with Jerry and Carl. He could see from the looks on their faces, they were shocked.

Carl asked, "What do you plan to do?"

"I've given it a lot of thought and I would appreciate your advice on it, as it looks like all of us could be out of work depending on how this plays out."

Both men nodded, anxious to hear what John had in mind.

"First, I plan to meet with Don Karst today for lunch. I want to give him a heads up on what Cliff will be telling him. I can't be certain how Don will react, but he's not a guy who responds well to threats. But his business, at least in the short-term, is gonna take a hit. No doubt about it."

"John, the union's threat of a boycott will piss him off. But if they unite on this his business will really suffer. The budget side of this thing and closing Jefferson has been rough on everyone. We've got lots of angry people out there who don't like that call."

"I know Carl. We may need to back track on that, but not because we're courting Sara's vote. I am not going to let you go to win her over. That's not happening on my watch. However short that may be!"

Carl sat back in his chair and let the moment sit. It was obvious he had something to say. He leaned forward, "You know in stuff like this, it's always sorting out who's to blame. Maybe you should let me go. That's what Sara really wants."

John gave Carl an incredulous look. "What are you saying?"

I got a call yesterday from Jane Hyatt. Her firm is looking to expand into public sector law and she asked if I'd like to come on board. The salary offer was terrific and the benefits package is good. I didn't know what to say. She knew I'd need to think about it and we agreed to talk further in a week or two. John, I don't know what the future holds here. I think the offer is one to consider, especially after what you've just told me. At the same time, I don't want to leave you guys in the lurch."

"Carl it isn't about leaving us in the lurch. You've more than paid your dues. You have to do what makes sense for you and your family. But no matter what I will not make it look like I let you go. Sara's deal is one with the devil and there's no way I want her to think I did this because of her political maneuvers."

"Carl, I feel the same way John does. You have to do what's right for you and your family. I totally understand the spot you're in. John maybe we all should say the hell with this. We could land on our feet somewhere else and the work would be much easier. I'm not lying when I say that I am giving the idea a lot of thought these days."

"I think it is wise for all of us to keep our eyes on opportunities elsewhere. This thing is a crap shoot and we'd be stupid not to be doing that. At the same time, I feel like we haven't lost the war yet. We have to adjust our battle plan, but I don't think we should simply accept defeat and leave without a fight. We have to come up with some other option on the Jefferson closing. It would calm things down a bit anyhow. Any ideas on how we could save the dollars we need to if we keep it open?"

"Boss, Jerry and I have been talking about that question. We do have some ideas but it won't be easy or painless."

For the next hour the trio talked and developed an alternative. When they were finished they felt it would be a sound option. Each had a role to play and the work on setting a new course was put in motion.

CHAPTER 94

SO MUCH GIVEN – SO MUCH LOST

Ma'am's funeral service was held on Thursday. While all the staff had paid their respects at calling hours, many wanted to attend the funeral service. John Handler made the difficult decision not to cancel classes at School #3 for the day so Ma'am's family agreed to hold the funeral service at 4:00 in the afternoon enabling students and staff to attend. Bea had been asked to speak at the funeral about Dorothy as an educator, friend and principal. Her husband Jessie and her three daughters decided the oldest daughter Johanna, who was now 39 with two children, would speak on behalf of the family.

Bea stood in church before the service began. Its empty pews were time worn. She reflected on the moments people sat to pray, sharing joys and losses with God. The church had a deep spiritual aura which was calming, but not at all pretentious. As 4:00 approached, the mourners began filling every pew. Those attending included not only Ma'am's large extended family, but many notables from the school system and the city, including the mayor. But the ones attending that Ma'am would most truly appreciate were a large gathering of former and current students from School #3. Bea was pleased so many came. They were the proof an educator's life is filled with unwritten victories.

Bea gave a great deal of thought during two sleepless nights composing what she wanted to say about this woman who had been her friend for more than 20 years. Before rising to speak, she paused, holding

Jasmin's hand. She had a commanding presence and planned to use each moment to honor Dorothy, who had done so much to help her along in life.

Bea let the silence in the church linger before she began to speak in her confident, room filling, voice. "We heard the good Reverend say this is a celebration and Dorothy has moved on to be with Jesus. Well, I believe that's true. But forgive me Lord if we take this time to feel the loss of a great woman and praise her to you. Besides her family, which I know is grievin', there are many here today who could share their personal story about how Ma'am cared for them in a time of need. Every once in a while a great woman like Dorothy Washington comes along, praise be to God. She earned our respect, so it wasn't surprisin' we often called her Ma'am. But I had the privilege of knowin' her much better than most in this church today. She knew I grew up in the School #3 neighborhood. When I got my teachin' license she asked me to come work at her school. Dr. Handler, sorry but we all knew it was her school ya know." Quiet laughter followed this statement.

"When I started teachin', I didn't know much. Some here likely say that's still the case." Laughter quickly filled the church for a moment and Bea let it quiet before continuing. "Dorothy Washington was this woman's mentor and she spent many hours helpin' me learn how teachin' is done. She told me more than once, someday it would be my turn to do it for someone. I am doin' my best to live up to that now." Several teachers present made the immediate connection to Andrea, who was sitting next to Jasmin.

"But the best part of Dorothy Washington was saved for her family and the children at School #3. She believed poverty was the enemy, and the battle to defeat him had to be fought in every classroom at School #3. Oh that women! How often I'd seen her cry when somethin' bad happened to a child who was attendin' or had attended School #3. Most folks didn't see that side of Dorothy. She was too proud to show it. But mind you, I saw it!" Bea paused for a moment, letting the statement sink in. She continued, "Most of you don't know it, but she visited any student who'd gone to School #3 and was in the city jail. She never missed a one. She told 'em she was there to help 'em get back on the right side of things if they wanted her help. She also told 'em what she thought of 'em and what they did to get locked up. She kept track of her kids. Children who attended School #3, then went on to college, got a note from Dorothy tellin' how proud she was of 'em. She considered each one a big victory in the war we're fightin' everyday. Some of you know she never missed a high school graduation where School #3 students were gettin' a diploma. She said she needed to be there on such a special day."

People were giving Bea their undivided attention. Her voice had a cadence and power building with each sentence. Her tribute was revealing and helped explain the depth of Ma'am's actions and commitment. Then Bea stepped from behind the podium and in voice filling the church to its rafters said, "Oh, but the woman didn't stop there. No sir! She'd been dreamin' for years how to help children grow up to be good citizens. She saw grandmas and great-grandmas tryin' to raise their children's children with no man to be found way too often, 'cause they skipped, are in jail or died on the street. These folks had so much taken from 'em and they were too often left to find a way through on their own. Dorothy Washington wanted to make things better for 'em. She gave everythin' she had to do that. Me, I think her heart was broken by the overwhelmin' battle she was fightin'."

Bea paused, she did not want her comments to be divisive, so she turned a different corner, just when the staff members present thought she'd be her hard-headed self.

"Now that she's gone, we gotta honor her by carryin' on the fight that defeats too many of our children. There are many ideas about how to do that for sure; but we gotta move forward together. It's what she'd want us to do. I hear her voice clear, sayin', 'You all get on with it! Don't waste time frettin' about me, but you sure better fret about my children and what they need!"

Bea stood silently with an unspoken prayer to God, 'Please get me through this for one more minute please.' Her eyes looking up to heaven she spoke in a voice booming like thunder, "I promise my friend here, in God's scared house, we won't let her down. We'll carry on. We will 'cause we love and respect your memory and, most important, 'cause you taught us not to give up on any child no matter what they do. Good-bye, sweet woman. Be with Jesus now and watch over us all."

As Bea returned to her pew, there were few dry eyes left in the packed church. Andrea was proud of her mentor and friend. Bea had spoken from her heart in a manner she hoped would heal and bind many together in Dorothy's lifelong quest.

The next morning Dorothy was laid to rest. Bea returned a few hours later to her friend's freshly covered grave. It was quiet in the cemetery. A beautiful May sun was riding the sky and white cotton-ball clouds drifted slowly by. Dorothy was buried close to large oak trees. When the sun set each evening, the trees broadcasted their shade on her grave like a blanket covering her for the night. Bea was pleased the family picked this spot for her friend's eternal rest.

In this private moment, Bea let her pain flow freely, like a river cascading over rocks. Her whole body trembled and her cries echoed their way to the heavens. It took time, not that it mattered, before Bea could pick herself up from the ground and move to a bench near Dorothy's grave. She knew about the stages of grief, but she didn't accept them. Bea believed it all mixed together and stayed with you, sometimes sharp like a knife, other times simple and reflective. In this moment her friend's passing was like a crater on the moon, a hole that would never be filled in her lifetime. Her grief would become an accepted part of her personal landscape, adding perspective and scars too.

CHAPTER 95

FIGHTING A BULLY

Despite contending with airport hassles and a tight layover in Atlanta, Andrea had a wonderful trip to Montgomery over Memorial Day weekend. She had to admit it was good to be away. Ma'am's death had been a shock and the emotions associated with it left everyone drained. Andrea was glad Jasmin would be home for a few weeks before heading to Georgetown to begin her work on a Masters' Degree.

Andrea was now face-to-face with being a teacher in June. The workload was heavy and with the school closing, many things demanded her attention. Dr. Walters was visible and supportive, giving Andrea advice when she seemed to need it most. Andrea really liked this thoughtful woman. She was sad she'd only have a short time to work with her. But then, she was learning people come and go in schools much more often than she initially thought. During the school year four teachers had left.

The children were tense and their behaviors showed it. Yesterday, Durrell Frazier and Daryl Owens got into a nasty fight in the lunch room. Some strong punches were thrown and Daryl kicked Durrell in the face while he was on the ground. The cafeteria monitors needed help separating the boys, with the custodian, Fred Welker, ultimately providing the needed strength to break things up.

When the fight started, Andrea's kids quickly chose sides, challenging each boy to settle things by yelling personal expletives and ideas on how each could hurt the other. Andrea was embarrassed and frustrated her class behaved this way. Both boys had been suspended for three days. With a night's sleep, she was ready to spend time with her kids talking about how their behaviors encouraged a greater amount of violence. She'd spent several hours re-reading the classroom journal. She chose excerpts the children had shared where violence hurt them or someone they loved. She wanted their own stories to promote a discussion and deeper reflection on how violent behaviors affected them.

It was Michael Malkin whose comments jarred Andrea. "Miss B. we gotta fight, or somebody will really put a hurt on you."

"But Michael, doesn't one fight make the person mad and want to put a bigger hurt back on you? Think about your brother James and how he got arrested for thinking that way."

"That's why you have to have friends help you."

"Michael, what are you saying?"

It was Jadira who joined in, "Miss B, he's sayin' you need to be in a gang. You need to have them help you."

"Doesn't that make things worse?"

"Miss B," it was Alvin Park speaking now. He was a cute boy who had a professorial tone. He was standing with his hands on his hips giving his teacher a lesson, "If you don't belong to a gang and do your part then you are alone."

"But what about yesterday's fight; it didn't need to happen."

Alvin continued his lesson with a more emphatic tone, "Oh yes it did. Durrell called Daryl a pussy and he lose face he doesn't take care of it."

"So punching and kicking is the way to act?"

Michael piped in, "So what you think he should do?"

"He should have told somebody Durrell was calling him a name."

Alvin jumped on her comment, "Then he really be a pussy!" which caused everyone to laugh.

Andrea responded sternly, "Alvin, I don't like that word. It makes me feel uncomfortable."

"Sorry Miss B. He had to take care of business. He can't be sittin' there lettin' Durrell name call him."

"You all cheered the boys on. I was ashamed of you. I lost face as a teacher because of how you behaved. Should I start punching and kicking you?"

The kids laughed at Andrea's comment. However, it was a reminder to Andrea the laws of the street prevailed; even though the kids understood others should not behave as they did.

After school Andrea headed to Bea's room. She was feeling down by the conversation she'd had with her class and wondered if any of her efforts had had an impact on the children's outlook. She was taking personal responsibility for the fight yesterday, feeling if she'd done a better job, it wouldn't have happened. Bea had to help set her straight.

"You listened to the children and they told you it was right to fight. You still can't believe they said that to ya?"

"Bea, I am sad they think it's okay to beat a kid up, to kick him in the face, to cheer it on. I thought talking about violence today would help them reflect. Instead I feel like I reinforced the behaviors. I'm not changing anything!"

"Ah, here we go with the pity party! Poor Andrea isn't makin' a difference! You talked with the kids about how you feel. They hear you better than you think but the street, like we've said, is a tough teacher and these kids aren't livin' in your world, honey."

"That doesn't excuse bad behavior Bea!"

"Nobody, especially me, is sayin' it does. But it makes it much harder for the kids to see it another way. Nobody got shot on your street growin' up. These kids know it can happen at any time. They're lookin' at the world through a different set of glasses than you. It makes it much harder for them to see things differently. But don't go blamin' yourself. We fight this thing one day at a time. Sometimes the street wins big, 'cause he's a strong bully."

CHAPTER 96

FINDING A DEAL

John met with Don Karst. They talked about the union's boycott plan. Don was worried about the impact it would have on his business. The bad economy had already taken a toll. If the boycott was forthcoming he was not sure his business would survive. He had five stores and over 60 employees who depended on him. He had to think about them and their needs. The guys were right. He was furious about the union's pending plan, but Sara was right, Don could not hold up under the pressure.

Knowing this John, Jerry and Carl discussed their next steps. "We need to keep Jefferson open for at least another budget cycle," Carl reported. "In order to do it we need a one percent concession in wage cuts from the teacher's union. If we can reduce them from the 4.1% raise under the current contract to 3.1% and make the other changes we discussed we can squeak by. But the union won't concede without other big concessions John."

"I understand, but let's fish it with Cliff and see what we can do. Give him a call and see if you can meet with him as soon as possible. The timeline for submitting a proposed budget to City Hall is closing in. We've got to get this thing done, one way or another. He knows that."

Cliff agreed to meet with Carl the next day. Carl explained their willingness to keep Jefferson open another year, if the union would agree to a wage concession. "Carl, why should we do that? The wage concession will go on forever and you are saying Jefferson will be open for one more year. It's not a good trade from where we sit."

"Okay Cliff, what would make it a good trade?"

"We liked the retirement incentive you proposed and we'd need a no layoff guarantee for teachers who have completed three years of service by this June."

"How long would that apply?"

"What do you mean, how long would it apply? It would carry forward as long as you take the one percent from my members. When you restore it we could talk about lifting the guarantee. But I need more than keeping Jefferson open if I am going to sell a wage cut to my members."

"So keeping a school open isn't enough?"

"You're only talking about a one year extension Carl. I can see where this is headed and so can you. Next year you will be closing Jefferson down and my members will be left holding the bag with a wage cut and more layoffs. I am not selling them out with that kind of deal. It's not going to happen, plain and simple."

"But if we give you a long-term no layoff guarantee and a retirement incentive, then you are saying a deal could be made?"

"No. My Exec Board would chew me up for that deal! I am not sure how it would go, but if you said Jefferson won't be closed for the life of the contract then maybe I could sell it."

"All that for a one percent wage cut when most in this community aren't getting anything and many are losing their jobs. What a generous guy you are Cliff!"

"Hey, you can take it or leave it, Carl. Like I said to you before, we know the Board can't take the heat and you guys are not in the driver's seat. You are going to have to make it worth our while to help you if you want me to try and sell anything to my members. You haven't got the juice on this. If you did, you wouldn't be talking to me now."

"Cliff, I am not sure what we'll do. I will talk with John and get back to you. But I've got to tell you if it was up to me, I'd tell you you're too greedy. You might like your chances with Mary Jane, but be careful what you wish for."

"My people don't see it that way. John is a reformer and it will cost my members jobs and rights we've bargained. We aren't gonna lay down and say 'sure' to that. You of all people downtown should know better!"

Carl met with John and filled him in on the conversation, "I think we can make a deal here but the cost is going to be high. Are you willing to go out on a limb on things? Can you sell a retirement incentive as well as a no lay-off guarantee for every tenured teacher? John, they are pushing too hard and I think we should be careful."

"Carl, we don't have a lot of room. If we don't get the teachers in the tent, we don't stand a chance of surviving beyond the summer. The reforms we are talking about are going to take at least three years of planning to get on track and underway. So let's look at things through a long-term lens. Tell him we can agree to Jefferson not closing for the next two years, but not three. We will not enroll a freshman class there next fall. Tell him we will agree to a no layoff clause only for the length of the contract and we'll also do the retirement incentive. Maybe enough senior teachers will take it over the next two years to make a difference. There are three on the Executive Board who could and they will take that to heart. In return we want a one percent wage reduction next year. We also want the union's participation on a K-12 reform committee we will set in place next school year. I don't want them blocking things out of the gate. We want their acceptance to at least participate in the study of things."

"John you know their involvement will not assure acceptance."

"I do, Carl, but we will at least have the opportunity to dance with them and see if we can influence their thinking. It is more than we have right now. Off-the-record, I also want you to tell Cliff that if the union announces the planned boycott of Don's business, the deal is immediately off the table. Be blunt about that and make sure he understands. We are not kidding. That is a flat non-negotiable item."

Carl smiled. He was happy to at least be able to deliver that message to Cliff. "I'm not sure they'll accept the deal but if they do you will have to move forward with at least one hand tied behind your back."

"It's better than where we stand now, Carl. So let's see if we can wrap this up."

* * * * *

Cliff rejected the deal, but finally countered. He proposed the current contract be extended by three years instead of the one year the district proposed. The raise in the third year would be equal to the cost of living. The union absolutely would not accept any reduction in health benefits. He also needed what he called a 'get back' of a half-percent wage increase in the third year over the COLA raise if he was going to be able to sell the deal to his members. John knew this extension would postpone any discussion on alternative work hours or staff assignment flexibility. Cliff was no fool; he was playing his hand out effectively for his members. But John knew he would have a deal that would secure; at least for the time being, a Board majority and Don's business would not be boycotted. He also knew he had a lot of work to do on the reform effort and the union was at least co opted into serving on the major reform committee he would set in place. He was pleased one hurdle, however high, had been leapt and a budget could be given to the city council.

He also planned to make some other changes. Since staff development efforts were drastically reduced he could eliminate Mary Jane's position. He knew the Board would support the cut by a 3-2 vote. Her disloyalty and the plotting had to cease. She was a cancer on his leadership team. Time would tell, but at least he felt he'd done what he could with the cards dealt to him.

Shortly after the deal was accepted by all the parties and City Hall endorsed his budget, John received a call from a well respected headhunter. "John, I am calling on behalf of a Board with a job offer you need to consider. It is a fabulous deal and they want you to join them. John was surprised by the call and the fact that a large city district out west wanted him to lead a wide-ranging reform effort. His salary would be sizably increased and he'd have a seven member board who at the start would be invested in his success. It was a dream job.

"John, a chance like this doesn't come around often. They recognize your skills and really want you on their team. I assure you, there won't be a better offer. You can make a deal that will set you up well for the rest of your career and beyond, plus you can bring on your own team to help. At least talk with them about it."

Shortly after hanging up the phone, the mayor called. "John, I am so excited! I just learned we are one of two cities still in the running for the new Subaru plant. They really like the training concept submitted but need a lot more detail. We will have to work hard over the summer to get things defined. With your help I think we've got a real shot at this! What a tremendous economic boon it would be for this region. The centerpiece of it could be the unique education collaboration we are developing. What an opportunity this is!"

Ann came into John's office after the light went out on his phone. Having worked closely together, she suspected what the gist of the headhunter's conversation was. "What are you going to do?"

"I don't know Ann, but would you clear my calendar for the next three days. I am taking a trip out west."

CHAPTER 97

PARTING WAYS

Today, Andrea found herself feeling many different things. It seemed empty without Ma'am. The closing event was a significant moment and her passing touched every aspect of it. The staff was parting, with the veterans being assigned to a number of different schools. Bea was headed to School # 17 where Dix was principal. She was pleased with the assignment, but Andrea could tell the loss of Dorothy had taken a heavy toll. Bea was struggling to carry on as she'd promised. Ma'am had been the spark and guardian angel for Bea. She was now vulnerable and uncertain where things would go.

Today was all about goodbyes and Andrea knew her last day with her class was a moment she would always remember. She knew Robert Frost had written 'Way leads on to way' and that was certainly evident now. She had a promising future and a new life waiting. At the same time, she'd learned so much by investing herself here. Saying goodbye was filled with a multitude of bittersweet emotions.

The children were excited about the school year ending and the freedom in the weeks ahead. But they loved their teacher too. Andrea had one last journal session. This morning she invited her mom and dad to come in. Her mom got the okay as all her exam corrections and end of year grades were done and her principal knew this was a special moment.

She sat with her class as her mom and dad came to the door. "There are two special people in my life I want all of you to meet, my mom and dad." The children were thrilled. Her parents told the children some stores about Andrea when she was a little girl their age. Andrea could see this was a memorable moment for her parents. Her mom was savoring the time she was spending in her daughter's classroom. She truly understood Andrea's deep connection to each child and was proud of her work.

After her parents left Andrea had one more surprise, a Blurb book for each child. Andrea chose journal entries from each youngster. She also included pictures of everyone she took throughout the year. A fifteen page memory book was handed to each child. Hugs and tears flowed between the children and their teacher. Andrea knew she would treasure this class for the rest of her life. Teaching demanded a lot but the returns were more than she could possibly have imagined eleven months ago.

At dismissal time Andrea walked her class to the main door one last time. She hugged her kids and wished each of them well, wondering if she'd ever see them again. What a personal investment she'd made in their lives over the past ten months. Now it was severed by the calendar and economics. The kids would move on and so would she. But her heart was captured and she'd always want to know how 'her kids' were doing in the years to come.

Andrea was heading south next week and she and Bea would have only one more Thursday night together. She'd miss this wonderful woman. Bea made all the difference. She had no idea how to thank her. Leaving Bea behind was like cutting an umbilical cord. Her teaching lifeline would be nearly eight hundred miles away.

That last Thursday night together they reflected on the year. "Girl, so much of you goes to the kids. Good teachers give a great deal to the job. Most folks have no idea what it takes. The kids climb into our heart and they don't ever leave. They are part of an extended family. You have to move on and so do they. But you never stop dreamin' about them. You hear their names, somethin' happens, it pulls you right back. But you go forward girl. You keep workin' with children. You will help them grow. Bea knows this for a fact."

Andrea hugged her one last time, knowing their time together would now be vastly different. She worried most about Bea and loneliness. She knew Bea would, in the end, carry on. She was a survivor.

As Andrea pulled out of Bea's driveway, Bea stood on the porch waving. Andrea wiped away her tears and headed down the road towards her new life, way truly leading on to way.

REFERENCES

- The reference to the Gates Foundation findings on effective schools including a new "Three R's" can be found at: http://www.gatesfoundation.org/speeches-commentary/Pages/bill-gates-sr-2006-bennett-college.aspx

  In his speech Bill Gates noted, "At the foundation, we've found that the most successful schools around the country—schools that get every student ready for college and work—all have three things in common. We call them the new 3 R's: rigor, relevance, and relationships."

- The three history questions John Handler poses to Mayor Jane Hueset were paraphrased examples drawn from New York State's United States History and Government Regents examinations.

- I have provided further links and suggestions related to this novel at: http://www.rickstein.net

www.ingramcontent.com/pod-product-compliance
Lightning Source LLC
Chambersburg PA
CBHW052026090426
42739CB00010B/1804